TRUE NORTH STRANGE & FREE

TRUE NORTH STRANGE & FREE

Reader's
Digest

TRUE NORTH STRANGE & FREE

An original book from Reader's Digest Canada
Written by Philomena Hurley-Rutherford

READER'S DIGEST TEAM

PROJECT EDITOR: Andrew Jones
SENIOR EDITOR: Pamela Johnson
PROJECT DESIGNER: Andrée Payette
ASSISTANT DESIGNER: Solange Laberge
COPY EDITOR: Gilles Humbert
DIGITAL SERVICES MANAGER: Ugo Morsani
PRODUCTION MANAGER: Holger Lorenzen
PRODUCTION COORDINATOR: Susan Wong
ADMINISTRATOR: Elizabeth Eastman

CONTRIBUTORS

PICTURE RESEARCH: Rachel Irwin
PICTURE RESEARCH ASSISTANT: Javier Olivera
IMAGE TREATMENT: Yves Lachance
COPY EDITOR: Judy Yelon
INDEXER: Patricia Buchanan

READER'S DIGEST BOOKS AND HOME ENTERTAINMENT

VICE PRESIDENT: Deirdre Gilbert
SENIOR STAFF EDITOR: Andrew Jones
ART DIRECTOR: John McGuffie

First published in Canada in 2002 by
The Reader's Digest Association (Canada) Ltd.
1125 Stanley Street, Montreal, Quebec H3B 5H5

For information on this and other Reader's Digest products
or to request a catalogue, please call our 24-hour
Customer Service hotline at 1-800-465-0780.

You can also visit us on the World Wide Web at
http://www.readersdigest.ca

NATIONAL LIBRARY OF CANADA CATALOGUING IN PUBLICATION DATA

True north strange & free : 1001 Canadian hard facts,
eccentricities, unusual stories & unsolved mysteries.

Includes index.
ISBN 0-88850-757-7

1. Canada—Miscellanea. I. Reader's Digest Association (Canada)
FC61.T78 2002   971'.002   C2002-903575-9
F1008.4.T78 2002

READER'S DIGEST and the Pegasus logo are registered
trademarks of The Reader's Digest Association, Inc.

Printed in Canada

03 04 05 / 5 4 3 2

On a September evening in 1964, a newly minted emigrant from Ireland drank in the immensity of Canada on a two-and-a-half-hour drive from Toronto northwest to Southampton, a small resort town on Lake Huron. The smells and sounds and emotions of that drive through a sultry purple twilight are still vivid.

That evening marked the beginning of my love affair with this country. My sense of Canada began to form while working as a reporter in southwestern Ontario. Through the stories I filed, I met a great many people from all walks of life—a microcosm of Canada's ethnic diversity, their stories a lesson in the optimism, decency, and strength of the Canadian people. All these experiences sparked a journey of learning about Canada's extraordinary character, its places, history, legends, Aboriginal peoples, dreamers, tycoons, writers, explorers, scientists, sports heroes, singers, songwriters, architects, and painters.

The offbeat has been a lifelong fascination of mine, so clippings and notes about absurd stories, unsolved mysteries, incongruous happenings, and eccentric Canadians were frequent additions to the story ideas folder that was part of my journalist's stock-in-trade. That folder was the embryo of *True North Strange and Free*. It continued to grow while I worked as a book editor in Montreal, collecting Canadiana—quirky anecdotes, out-of-the-way facts, local lore, and stories comic and tragic about momentous Canadian events. These pages are that folder brought to life, written with gratitude to my home and adopted land.

To Canada and Canadians with love,

Philomena Hurley-Rutherford

table of contents

A
vast land
filled with
wonders

OUR HOME AND NATIVE LAND

◆ Second to none

Canada encompasses 9,093,507 square kilometers, making it the world's second largest country after Russia. At its widest, it stretches 5,959 kilometers west to east, from the Yukon-Alaska boundary to Cape Spear, Nfld. From Cape Columbia on Ellesmere Island, Nunavut, to Middle Island in Lake Erie, Ont., Canada runs 4,634 kilometers from north to south. Its boundary with the United States extends for 8,891 kilometers, of which 2,343 kilometers mark the dividing line with Alaska.

Canada's mainland coastline—approximately 28,742 kilometers—is one of the longest of any country in the world. It is bounded by the Atlantic Ocean for about 9,833 kilometers, by the Arctic Ocean for 9,286 kilometers, and by the Pacific Ocean for about 2,543 kilometers. Another 5,077 kilometers of coastline lie on Hudson Bay. Coastal islands, many of them in the Arctic Ocean, add another 67,285 kilometers of coastline.

Coast to Coast: 5,959 kilometers

◆ Spans six time zones

When standard time, an invention of the Canadian Pacific Railway's chief engineer Sandford Fleming, went into effect worldwide on Jan. 1, 1885, Canada was divided into seven time zones—Newfoundland, Atlantic, Eastern, Central, Mountain, Pacific, and Yukon. There was a five-and-a-half-hour difference between the coasts. When the Yukon switched to Pacific Time in 1973, the zones were cut to six, resulting in a four-and-a-half-hour difference.

◆ Canada's highest peak ◆

Situated in the St. Elias Range in the Yukon Territory, 5,959-meter Mount Logan is Canada's highest peak and one of the most massive mountains in the world. Its three summits form one of the world's largest alpine massifs. First sighted in 1890, the mountain is named for W. E. Logan, founder of the Geological Survey of Canada. In 2000, the Canadian government decided to rename Mount Logan for the late prime minister Pierre Elliott Trudeau, but dropped the idea after public protest.

Canada extends across six time zones; the clock at Old St. Boniface City Hall in Winnipeg is on Central Time

◆ Forty-ninth parallel

The 49th parallel, the line of latitude separating Canada from the United States, runs 2,043 kilometers from Lake of the Woods between Minnesota and Manitoba to the Strait of Georgia on the West Coast. The famous line, demarcated in 1846, is the world's longest straight international boundary, and is marked by a 6-meter-wide path and 912 survey markers.

◆ A zone of its own

Newfoundland has a time zone that varies by the half hour rather than the standard of one hour. Standard time is based on 24 meridians, and each meridian is at the center of 24 time zones. Adjustments have been made to time zones for the convenience of its inhabitants. Newfoundland (but not Labrador) is located in the eastern half of its zone, exactly three and a half hours from Greenwich, hence the half-hour distinction. And residents are fond of their unique time zone. In 1963, the Newfoundland government attempted to bring the province into the Atlantic zone, but withdrew in the face of stiff public opposition.

a country of superlatives

◆ World's largest freshwater island

Part of the archipelago at the tip of Lake Huron, Manitoulin Island, at 2,766 square kilometers, is the largest freshwater island in the world. Manitoulin is a vacation haven for Ontarians, and boasts golf and tennis resorts, summer theater, cycling, fishing, and the popular annual powwow on the Wikwemikong Unceded Indian Reserve. Accommodations range from rustic pioneer cabins to luxury resorts, with nary a national or international motel or hotel in sight. From May to October, the MS *Chi-Cheemaun* (Ojibwa for "big canoe") makes daily trips across Lake Huron, between Tobermory on the Bruce Peninsula and South Baymouth on Manitoulin.

◆ The Great Divide

Every continent except for Antarctica has a continental divide, the height of land separating areas drained by rivers that flow to opposite sides of the continent. In Canada, the continental divide runs along the spine of the Rocky Mountains, and rivers flow to either the Pacific, Atlantic, or Arctic oceans.

◆ Canada's warmest lakes

With water temperatures in July averaging 23 to 24°C, Christina Lake, in Gladstone Provincial Park, is Canada's warmest tree-lined lake, although two other British Columbia lakes beg to differ: Wasa Lake (near Kimberley in the East Kootenays), and Osoyoos Lake. Whichever should have the honor, all three are immensely popular tourist destinations.

◆ Water, water everywhere

Fresh water covers more than 747,000 square kilometers, or some 7.6 percent of Canada's total area. Our five biggest lakes are Lake Superior (82,100 square kilometers), Lake Huron (59,600 square kilometers), Great Bear Lake (31,328 square kilometers), Great Slave Lake (28,568 square kilometers), and Lake Erie (25,700 square kilometers).

Canada's longest rivers are the Mackenzie (4,241 kilometers), followed by the Yukon (3,185 kilometers), the St. Lawrence (3,058 kilometers), the Nelson (2,575 kilometers), the Columbia (2,000 kilometers), and the South Saskatchewan (1,939 kilometers).

The largest falls in Canada by area are Virginia Falls, in the South Nahanni River, N.W.T., with a 1.6-hectare face. At 90 meters, Virginia Falls is twice as high as Niagara's Horseshoe Falls (which has the greatest waterfall by volume), but not nearly as high as 440-meter Della Falls in British Columbia, the highest falls in the country.

At 507,451 square kilometers, Baffin Island, Nunavut, is Canada's largest isle. Of the country's 12 largest islands, only two, Vancouver and Newfoundland, have any sizable populations. Like Baffin, the other nine are in the High Arctic.

Canada has 747,000 square kilometers of water

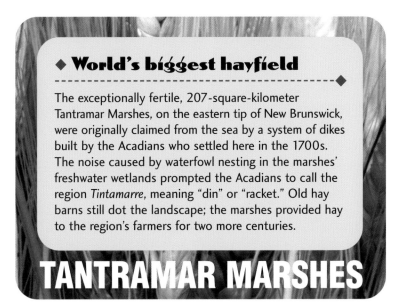

◆ World's biggest hayfield

The exceptionally fertile, 207-square-kilometer Tantramar Marshes, on the eastern tip of New Brunswick, were originally claimed from the sea by a system of dikes built by the Acadians who settled here in the 1700s. The noise caused by waterfowl nesting in the marshes' freshwater wetlands prompted the Acadians to call the region *Tintamarre*, meaning "din" or "racket." Old hay barns still dot the landscape; the marshes provided hay to the region's farmers for two more centuries.

TANTRAMAR MARSHES

◆ Yes, they once had bananas

Roadside stands awash in berries and fruits proliferate in Osoyoos, B.C., a town that calls itself Canada's fruit stand capital. Such produce is sold at the Fernandes market on the Crowsnest Highway east of town, where the offerings once included home-grown tree-ripened bananas. According to the Fernandes family, harvesting bananas in British Columbia generated more novelty than money; for now, Canada's lone banana plantation is closed down.

◆ A myriad of harvests

Agriculture is one of the oldest sectors of the Canadian economy and deeply rooted in history and culture. The first farming couple, Louis Hébert and his wife, Marie Rollet, planted vegetable crops and an orchard of Normandy apples in what is now Quebec City in 1613.

According to a 1667 census, there were 3,107 head of cattle in New France. Later the Hudson's Bay Company shipped cattle to western Canada, and escaping United Empire Loyalists in 1778–85 also brought their animal herds with them.

The earliest record of wheat cultivation is with the arrival of the Selkirk settlers in 1812. Thanks to the persistence of these Scottish immigrants, after several years of bad harvests their efforts were successful until the grasshopper plague of 1818.

The wheat commonly known as Red Fife or Scotch Fife, the variety that would eventually earn Canada a reputation as "the Grain Elevator of the British Empire," was first planted in 1842 by David Fife, the Ontario farmer after whom it was named.

Farm size varies from region to region. In the late 1980s, the average Canadian farm was about 230 hectares (570 acres).

Today, agriculture is one of the most dynamic and high-tech industries in the country. One can expect to find any of 100 or more exotic species of animal on Canadian farms. Reindeer are just one example, and one of the largest herds— about 14,000 head—can be found at Tuktoyaktuk in the Northwest Territories. Some 16,000 ostriches, about 60,000 emus, and even some of their South American cousins, rheas, are being raised on several farms, principally for their low-fat meat, but also as a source of leather and oil. More than 125,000 goats are being raised for milk and meat, some wild boar are being raised for food, and thousands of llamas in the West are used to guard sheep and as a source of wool. Some have even been put to work caddying golf bags. Aquaculture, the farming of aquatic species, is also gaining in popularity.

From corn to cattle, reindeer to ostriches— Canada's farms offer a myriad of harvests

a country of superlatives

Cacti typical of southern deserts thrive in unique Canadian microclimates

◆ Dunes of the North

Despite its reputation as the Great White North, Canada actually has a desert or two. These unusual microclimates can be found in British Columbia and Manitoba. Extending from Osoyoos to the Skaha lakes in B.C. lies a 15-kilometer-long "pocket desert," a continuation of the Sonoran Desert that extends from Mexico to the Okanagan Valley. While the Okanagan is kept lush and fertile through irrigation, the pocket desert gets long sunny days and less than 20 centimeters of rain annually, resulting in sparse vegetation, and desert plants and animals typical of those found at higher elevations of the Sonoran Desert—sagebrush, prickly pear and other cacti, rock rose, antelope bush, painted turtles, yellow-bellied marmots, pygmy horned toads, various lizards, and rare birds and bats.

The Manitoba Desert, also known as the Spirit Sands, is a 25-square-kilometer tract of sand dunes nestled in the Carberry Sand Hills, in Spruce Woods Provincial Heritage Park. Among its rarer denizens are painted turtles, hognosed snakes, plains spadefoot toads, and northern prairie skink, which are thought to have descended from of a species of horned lizards found from Minnesota to Texas.

As many as 600 species of moss and lichen thrive in Canada's polar desert, which encompasses parts of Quebec and the Northwest Territories, Nunavut, and the non-mountainous areas of the Arctic islands. Covered in snow from September to June, the area's average annual precipitation is only 200 millimeters, or one-tenth of that experienced in other parts of the country. Less than 13 millimeters of precipitation fell at Arctic Bay in 1949, giving the area Canada's all-time dry weather record.

◆ Vintages from the desert

The Osoyoos "desert oasis" lies at the base of the Okanagan. Its climate is not unlike that of central Mexico; hot in summer, while winter temperatures are cool and wet. The climate makes this area one of Canada's primary wine and fruit growing regions.

In fact, it has become one of North America's best-known wine producing regions. Vineyards here began as early as the 1800s, but gained international recognition only recently. British Columbia now boasts more than 40 wineries, with more than half of them located in the Okanagan.

Wine production spans three seasons: spring, fall and winter. During the winter season, the Okanagan produces its world-renowned icewine. The end of each season is celebrated with a public festival. The Fall Okanagan Wine Festival offers more than 100 fun things to see and do and is rated one of the top 100 events in North America.

◆ The earth's peripatetic pole

The northern tip of the earth's axis, the North Pole is the northernmost geographic point on earth. Here six months of the year are spent in complete darkness, followed by six months without a sunset. The North Pole lies in the Arctic Ocean, some 7,200 kilometers north of Ellesmere Island. From it, all directions are south.

All compasses may point north, but they actually point to the north magnetic pole, which is near, but not identical to the North Pole. The magnetic pole, which moves constantly, is currently near Bathurst Island, northwest of Resolute Bay. The north magnetic pole was discovered in 1831 by British explorer James Clark Ross. Because the north magnetic pole is in continuous motion, it is now hundreds of kilometers from the cairn Ross built marking its 1883 location, at Cape Adelaide on King William Island.

◆ The Barrens' fierce terrain

The treeless, rocky terrain that covers vast stretches of the Arctic is known as tundra or the "Barren Lands," or "The Barrens." This is an area of short summers and long bitter winters. Even in July, visitors are advised to be as prepared for snow and freezing temperatures as for swarms of mosquitoes and blackflies. Vegetation consists mostly of lichens, grasses, mosses, and low shrubs, although a few colorful flowers manage to bloom (*below left*). The term alpine tundra is sometimes used to describe the area above a mountain timberline.

Achillea

Kalmia

Cotton grass

Orange milkwort

◆ The big bog

Muskeg got its name from an Algonquin word for grassy bog, an apt description for the boggy, vegetation-supporting terrain that characterizes large areas of Canada's northern landscape. This peatland is extremely important for wildlife and consists of dead plants in various stages of decomposition, ranging from fairly intact sphagnum peat moss or sedge peat to highly decomposed muck or muskeg, and can cover extensive areas. While no surveys have been completed, experts believe Canada may have more muskeg (1,295,000 square kilometers) than any other country in the world.

◆ Librarians without borders

When the foundation that operates the Haskell Free Library and Opera House straddling the Quebec-Vermont border set about giving the 97-year-old building a million-dollar facelift in 1996, acquiring a million dollars was the easy part. Federal, provincial, and state government grants covered the bulk of the work for the building. Complying with various governmental acts and regulations, and the bylaws of Stanstead, Que., and Derby Line, Vt., was more daunting. All governments involved had to approve the work, which had to comply with Canadian and American building codes, as well as Quebec's language laws. Dueling American and Canadian architects were hired to draft plans. Americans were hired to work on the Vermont part of the building, where materials came from American suppliers. Repairs to the Stanstead section were done by Canadians using materials purchased in Canada. The renovated library reopened in 1999.

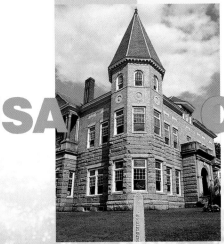

USA   CANADA

◆ Our lone cross-province city

Lloydminster's main north-south street is the 110th parallel, the provincial boundary line between Saskatchewan and Alberta. People on one side of the street, known as 50th Avenue, live in Alberta; their neighbors across the road, in Saskatchewan. After decades of red tape, in 1930 the two provincial communities merged into one. Lloydminster became a city in 1958, with one mayor and one city council to serve all citizens regardless of which province they live in. Even though most city schools are in the Alberta section, they are governed by the Saskatchewan School Act. However, educational costs are split equally between the two provinces. Each sector maintains its own city police force, provincial buildings, and provincial court systems.

◆ Canada's smallest jail

Two Ontario communities take credit for having the country's smallest jail. From 1899 to 1950, the 4.8- by 6-meter stone building that serves as Tweed's tourist information office was a three-cell jail that housed miscreants and homeless men. Creemore claims that its three-cell jail, measuring 4.5 by 6 meters and operational from 1892 into the 1940s, is not only Canada's but North America's smallest jail. Yet no one is making claims for the ghost town of Berens River, a one-time gold-mining boom town in northwestern Ontario. It kept troublemakers in a one-cell affair considerably smaller than either Tweed's or Creemore's cramped correctional facilities.

◆ World's oddest wind gauge

A Douglas DC-3 wind tee that served in the Second World War and as a bush plane in the Arctic is perhaps the world's oddest wind gauge. Mounted on a pedestal at Whitehorse Airport, the plane pivots on its pedestal in such a way that it always points into the wind. It takes a 5-knot wind to move the plane.

◆ Canada's tiniest bird in a park of rare wonders

Measuring between 7 and 10 centimeters in length, the calliope hummingbird (*Stellula calliope*), Canada's tiniest bird, is one of several exotic inhabitants of Haynes Point Provincial Park, near Osoyoos, B.C. One of British Columbia's most popular parks, Haynes Point is distinguished by a sandspit that stretches most of the way across Osoyoos Lake. The sandspit once served as a shortcut for horses being herded to and from the pioneer Haynes Ranch for which the park is named. Pygmy horned toads, painted turtles, and yellow-bellied marmots are just a few of the rare wild creatures that share the park with the tiny-throated calliope.

◆ Sufferin' succotash: What a pumpkin!

Giant pumpkins that tip the scales at over 360 kilograms regularly weigh in at the Windsor Pumpkin Festival held in Windsor, N.S. Every October, famous farmers like Howard Dill (*above*), four-time World Champion and developer of the Dill's Atlantic Giant Pumpkin™, compete for the biggest jack-o'-lantern.

◆ Victoria's blooming spring ritual

On a given day each February, when most Canadians are still mired in snow, residents of Victoria, B.C., enjoying balmy spring-like temperatures of between 11 and 15°C, hold a "flower count." This horticultural challenge involves homeowners from one end of the city to the other competing for the honor of being the gardener with the most blooms. Tallies are called in to local radio stations. In 1976, over 130 million blooms were counted. By 1996, with a growing population and more community participation, that figure rose to over 4 billion (4,220,401,563); a record to date. The most recent tally, 2002, was 3,923,384,760.

a country of superlatives

◆ Going cuckoo in Canada's highest city

Every hour on the hour in Kimberley, B.C., a jolly lifesize lederhosened figure, beer mug in hand, emerges from the upper story of a steam-driven cuckoo clock and yodels his greeting to the world. The figure is Happy Hans and the clock is the largest operating cuckoo clock in the world. Hans, cuckoo clocks, embroidered waistcoats, and lederhosen are only a few of the Bavarian touches in this city where stores have gingerbread trim and brightly painted shutters. Accordion music oompah-pahs in the town square—also known as the *platzl*. Kimberley, at an elevation of 1,113 meters, donned its Bavarian trappings to mark its status as Canada's highest city.

◆ All roads lead to Watson Lake

A collection of over 42,000 signposts from around the world can be found just outside of Watson Lake, Yukon. The Signpost Forest was started in 1942 when a homesick U.S. soldier working on the Alaska Highway erected a sign of Danville, Ill., his home town. Tourists have continued the tradition ever since, adding between 2,500 and 4,000 new signs every year.

Oldest, oddest, largest, biggest, highest...

◆ A phone booth where you can really make a trunk call

Salmo, B.C., began life as Salmon Riding, named for the salmon that flourished there before major dams interfered with their runs. Mining brought prosperity for decades, as did forestry in an area noted for huge cedars. Only a few isolated cedar stands remain. A telephone kiosk outside the SalCrest Motel in Salmo has been made from the stump of one of these ancient monsters. Carved into the 465-year-old trunk, it is said to be the oldest telephone kiosk in the world.

◆ World's largest Easter egg

Easter egg decoration, a Ukrainian folk art, is an exuberant blend of colors and geometric designs. Those skilled in the intricate craft call their miniature masterpieces *pysankas*, from the Ukrainian verb *pysaty*, to write. The folk art was one among several skills and traditions imported to Canada by Ukrainian immigrants, many of whom settled large sections of south-central Alberta.

Vegreville, the multicultural city they helped build, has constructed the world's largest pysanka, a mathematical, engineering, and architectural marvel that celebrates the city's diversity and harmony. The 2,270-kilogram giant, 5.5 meters wide and close to 8 meters long, towers 9.4 meters above ground on the city's outskirts.

A community project, it was completed in 1975 to mark the 100th anniversary of the RCMP in Alberta. Among its most prominent motifs are silver colored wolf's teeth to symbolize the protection provided to pioneer families by the Mounties. Bronze—the pysanka's most prominent color—gold, and silver six-vaned windmills signify good prairie earth and good harvests. Three-pointed stars (the Trinity) and a silver band (eternity) are reminders of the settlers' strong faith. Dedication messages are in English, French, German, and Ukrainian.

How to crack an egg, Ukrainian style: Vegreville's pysanka under construction.

◆ Oldest funeral monument

A burial mound near L'Anse Amour, Nfld., is the oldest known funeral monument in North America, marking the passing of a young Maritime Archaic boy who died over 7,500 years ago.

◆ **14 interconnected bodies of water**

Derived from a native word denoting "bright waters and happy land," the Kawartha Lakes region of south-central Ontario embraces 14 interconnected lakes that experienced a golden age of tourism in the 1800s. Steamboats fanned out from railway terminals, bringing vacationers to summer resorts. Regattas drew crowds in wide-brimmed hats and parasols, and canoeing was all the rage, courtesy of the locally manufactured "Peterborough Canoe."

Regattas were all the rage on the Kawartha Lakes in the late 1800s

◆ **Where *rivers* run backward**

The highest tides in the world occur in the Bay of Fundy, where the differences between low and high spring tides at Burntcoat Head, in Minas Basin near Wolfville, N.S., can be up to 16 meters. When a high tidal wave known as the Fundy tidal bore rushes up the Shubenacadie and Salmon rivers, both waterways actually run backward.

Near Annapolis Royal, N.S., a tiny portion of this massive tidal energy is converted into commercial electrical energy in the only tidal power plant in the Western Hemisphere at Granville Ferry, N.S. The peak output of the Annapolis Tidal Generating Station is 20 megawatts, about 1% of Nova Scotia's electrical power capacity. Other high-tide facts:

◆ Near mid-tide at Cape Split, some say they hear the "voice of the Moon" in the form of the roar emitted by turbulent tidal currents.

◆ Nova Scotia bends when the tide comes in. As 14 billion tonnes of sea water flow into Minas Basin twice daily, the Nova Scotia countryside actually tilts slightly under the immense load.

◆ **The island with a hole in the middle**

Donut Island is one of a group of 15 called "The Toronto Islands." Up to 1858 they could justifiably be called a "peninsula," until strong lake winds washed away the islands' connection to the mainland. The islands are home to unique neighborhoods, a bird sanctuary, yacht clubs, beaches, and more. Visitors often refer to them as "an urban Shangri-la," "a second Venice," or sometimes "the Coney Island of Canada."

HELL'S GATE

◆ **Fraser's narrowest point**

British Columbia's mighty Fraser River thunders through its narrowest point at Hell's Gate, a rocky gorge only 30 meters across by 180 meters deep. The difficulty of portaging around this canyon was recorded as far back as 1808 by explorer Simon Fraser, but its present nickname is considerably more recent, being associated with a 1914 rockslide that occurred as the CNR blasted its way west. The slide blocked much of the sockeye salmon run, adversely affecting the area's fishing industry for the next 30 years. Fishways, visible from a suspension bridge, were eventually constructed in 1944. Hell's Gate also has an Airtram that takes visitors across the gorge for a closeup look at the boiling cauldron below.

Niagara Falls at night. Inset: Intrepid ice climbers scaling Montmorency Falls in winter

◆ Higher than Niagara

At the junction of the Rivière Montmorency and the St. Lawrence River, 10 kilometers east of Quebec City, Montmorency Falls has captivated observers since the time of Champlain. With a drop of 84 meters, Montmorency is 30 meters higher than Niagara Falls. Each winter, spray from the cascade creates a 30-meter-high sugarloaf cone of ice. Careening down the cone was a popular pastime with 19th-century tobogganers.

◆ "Wonderful beyond comparison"

From the 1750s, Niagara's waterpower had been harnessed for mechanical use, but it took another 140 years to tame the mighty falls for electricity. Niagara Falls was lit early in 1896. Visiting one of the new powerhouses, inventor Nikola Tesla described it as "wonderful beyond comparison: those dynamos are the biggest in the world." Tesla believed that economical long-distance transmission of power from the falls was possible if the providers used the system of alternating current he had devised. The first successful long-distance transmission to Buffalo later that year proved him right.

the great white north

◆ Baffin harbors remnant of last ice age

One of the great ice sheets that enveloped Canada in the last ice age some 18,000 years ago originated on Baffin, Canada's largest island. The Penny Ice Cap, a holdout from the Ice Age, covers 5,100 square kilometers of Nunavut's Auyuittuq National Park. Three hundred meters thick in places, and reaching 2,100 meters in elevation, the ice cap provides an excellent record of past climates and has been the site of several major scientific studies into climatic change and global warming. Baffin Island is a nesting ground for millions of birds—thick-billed murres, kittiwakes, eiders, buntings, and redpolls—and walruses, ringed harp, bearded seals, and spiral-tusked narwhals also inhabit the offshore waters.

Ice climbing on the cliffs of the Penny Ice Cap, Baffin Island

EXPLORE CANADA'S ARCTIC
G3050
NORTHWEST TERRITORIES
MAR · 95

◆ Paw plates

The Northwest Territories is unique in Canada as having the only non-rectangular automotive license plate in North America—its blue and white license plates are in the shape of a polar bear. In 1969, the territorial government held a school competition to mark the Territories' centennial in 1970. Klaus Schoene of Sir John Franklin High School in Yellowknife came up with the winning ursine design.

Alert is closer to Moscow than to Toronto

◆ The world's most northerly address

Alert, a weather station and Canadian Forces base of 50 people on Ellesmere Island in the territory of Nunavut, is the world's most northerly settlement. Established by the Canadian government in 1950, it is only about 1,100 kilometers from the North Pole. In fact, it is closer to Moscow than it is to Toronto. From a hill near the weather station, servicemen can see the mountains of Greenland and the icy wastes of the polar cap.

◆ Land's end

Canada's most northerly point of land is Cape Columbia. The cape, at 83°06′N, is on Ellesmere Island, Nunavut, and is one of the most remote places on earth.

Skiing in a deep cavern of the Columbia Icefield.

◆ An Ice Age relic

Another vestige of the last ice age, the Columbia Icefield lies on the borders of British Columbia and Alberta, between Banff and Jasper national parks. Six major glaciers creep from the icefield, a spectacular blend of glistening ice broken by rock peaks and deep ice caverns. It blankets an area some 325 square kilometers to depths of 300 meters, making it the largest non-polar ice cap in the world. Visitors can take snowcoach tours of the glacier, which is accessible from the Icefields Parkway.

Hiking atop a glacier of the Columbia Icefield

◆ Gargantuan glacial lake

Manitoba's mighty 24,000-square-kilometer Lake Winnipeg is a remnant of giant Lake Agassiz, a glacial lake formed by the retreating Laurentide Ice Sheet. Lake Agassiz extended 1.65 million square kilometers across what is now Manitoba, northwest Ontario, eastern Saskatchewan, and parts of Minnesota and North Dakota.

◆ The tip of the iceberg

While many of the glaciers that float south off Newfoundland in the cold Labrador current originate in western Greenland, some icebergs are calved off glaciers on Baffin, Devon, and Bylot islands in Nunavut. The largest Northern Hemisphere iceberg on record was actually encountered near Baffin Island in 1882. It was 13 kilometers long, 6 kilometers wide, and had a height above water of about 20 meters. The mass of that iceberg was in excess of 9 billion tonnes—enough water for everyone in the world to drink a liter a day for over four years.

Don't feed the bears— a tundra buggy offers a chance to see Arctic wildlife up close

◆ Bears and belugas

Accessible only by plane, train, or sea, Churchill, Man. (pop. 1,000), attracts thousands of visitors each year. Many come to see the 300- to 600-kilogram bears who lumber through the area when they migrate north for the annual seal hunt, following a summer spent south of Churchill. Special "tundra buggies" take visitors up close to these unpredictable creatures. Whale watchers are also drawn to Churchill, for the largest healthy population of beluga whales in the world migrates here every summer. Thousands of the porpoise-like creatures congregate in the Churchill River estuary, singing, molting, and nursing their young. Birders are also drawn here by tremendous bird populations, numbering over 250 species. The icing on Churchill's Arctic cake is the magnificent aurora borealis displays visible at night between August and April.

marshes, minerals, and gardens

◆ From marsh to market

What was at various times an arm of glacial Lake Algonquin; a farm site for the Hurons; a haven for fish, small animals, and birds; and a source of marsh grasses used as mattress stuffing by a bedding manufacturer is now one of Canada's richest market gardens. Known as the Holland Marsh, it consists of some 2,900 hectares at Bradford, Ont., a town some 50 kilometers north of Toronto. Drained in 1925–30, the marshland revealed a layer of dead vegetation some 150 meters deep that is now a major producer of vegetables and flowers for domestic and foreign markets. Several Dutch families who settled in the Bradford area in the 1920s formed the core of the prosperous agricultural community that works there today.

◆ Potash riches

Esterhazy, Sask., a town named for Count Paul Oscar Esterhazy, a Hungarian nobleman who settled 35 families from Hungary there in 1886, is the site of what many consider the world's largest potash mine, producing 4.2 million tonnes of the prime fertilizer per year. The term "potash" dates to the 1700s, when pioneers leached wood ashes and evaporated the solution in large iron pots.

◆ Rockhound's paradise

From Scots Bay, on the tip of Nova Scotia's Blomidon Peninsula, you can hike 14 kilometers along Cape Split cliffs to a rocky beach known to rockhounds far and wide. Here Fundy's erosive tides expose glittering agates and amethysts.

◆ Honey capital of Canada

Clover and canola are abundant around Falher, Alta., a small town known as the honey capital of Canada. Some 25,000 beehives in and around this buzzing community produce 2 million kilograms of honey a year. Canada is one of the top five honey producers in the world, and 75 percent of its total annual 30,000-tonne harvest comes from the Prairie provinces. One-third of that Prairie largesse—Canada No. 1 white honey—comes from Alberta.

While the honey industry itself is a $70 million a year business, honeybees are also a key factor in pollination of many crops, and some industry experts place a $500 million a year value on this contribution by the country's 30 billion honeybees. Again, most of this apiarian workforce is to be found on the Prairies, which meets their needs for long hot summer days and extensive stretches of clover, alfalfa, and canola.

Canada also imports as many as 5 million kilograms of less expensive, lower quality honey from China, the world's leader in honey production. The imported product is used to sweeten cereals and certain baked goods.

THE ROUND GARDEN
A GARDEN FOR THE BLIND – PERTH

◆ 1000 km away from home

A thousand kilometers away from home, Subarctic plants such as Arctic wintergreen, northern liverwort, moss, and pussy willows thrive in mossy crevices near the sunless floor of 150-meter-wide, 100-meter-deep Ouimet Canyon. This great gash in the rock of Lake Superior's northern shore, some 67 kilometers east of Thunder Bay, was chiseled deep into the Canadian Shield by ice, wind, and rain. The canyon has a cool, moist habitat suitable for Subarctic foliage.

◆ Garden for the blind

Every year thousands of blind, elderly, and handicapped people wander happily through a garden in Perth, Ont., designed specifically for their needs. As they explore self-guiding pathways bordered by waist-high plant boxes, savoring the fragrances and examining leaf and flower textures and shapes, they enjoy birdsong, the whisper of gentle zephyrs, and the splashing of water fountains. Shaded benches encourage rest and conversation. Tour buses and groups are welcome, and guides will be provided for any group that wants one. The Round Garden for the Blind, which has been open to the public during every growing season since 1983, was built and is maintained by Friends of the Garden of the Blind in Perth.

Honey, amethyst, potash, and moss

◆ Open for opal hunters

Burns Lake, at the geographic center of British Columbia, is a jumping off point for one of the few known localities of precious opals in the country. Anyone making a one-and-a-half-hour hike to the nearby Eagle Creek Opal and Agate Deposits is free to hunt for some of the thousands of agates (leaf green, white, and amber) and rare opals, including fire opals, scattered there. The gem site, discovered by a local, John Shelford, is operated by the Burns Lake and District Chamber of Commerce as a recreation area for rockhounds.

◆ In celebration of peat

Île Lamèque, New Brunswick, produces most of the peat used in Canada and the U.S. It also hosts an annual Peat Moss Festival in recognition of the peat moss pioneers of the region. Peat is used as a soil conditioner, stable and poultry litter, insulation, and packing material. Île Lamèque is also where a much-celebrated international baroque music festival takes place each year.

unnatural resources

◆ Western Canada's moonscape

"The most paintable valley in western Canada" is how Group of Seven founder A. Y. Jackson (1882–1974) described southern Alberta's badlands, several vast stretches of barren gullies and eerie, mushroom-shaped buttes of sandstone and clay known as hoodoos. Years of erosion have shaped these moonscapes of winding gullies and deeply rilled rocks found in semi-arid areas of Alberta and Saskatchewan. The forbidding canyons provided a refuge from the law for turn-of-the-century horse thieves and outlaws. Southern Alberta's badlands have yielded a treasure trove of dinosaur fossil remains.

> " **The most paintable valley in western Canada** "

◆ Limestone landscape

Dramatic limestone formations are the big draw at Ontario's Bruce Peninsula National Park. The breathtaking limestone cliffs evolved over millions of years of erosion as the softer underlying limestone was washed away by the waters of Lake Huron, leaving the harder dolomite slabs overhanging the coastline. Other geological attractions include flowerpots, caves, grottos, and a dolomite beach with large chalky slabs of rock that clink strangely, like prehistoric poker chips.

◆ Sudbury's white-hot lookout

One of the most popular lookouts at Sudbury, Ont., has nothing to do with scenic vistas. Instead, it overlooks slag heaps near the Creighton Nickel Mine that become hills of fire whenever glowing tongues of white-hot slag light up their flanks at night. The area's abundant nickel is extracted by crushing the nickel-bearing ore and letting the sulphides float out. The concentrate is then smelted to produce nickel matte, which can be made into nickel products such as coins, flutes, and plating. The slag—what remains after the nickel has been melted out—is poured into copper cars, 15 at a time, and hauled by electric engine to a slag heap, where the cars are tipped over. Because factors such as wind direction have to be considered in dumping the slag, INCO—the International Nickel Company, founded in 1902 and owner of the Creighton Mine—has a special telephone number to call in order to learn where and when each day's pouring occurs.

"To look upon the falls meant death."

◆ Taming Churchill Falls

At Churchill Falls, Labrador, the Churchill River tumbles first 66 meters, then another 75 meters, before crashing 158 meters through Bowdoin Canyon. The sight and sound was so powerful that it was said among the area's Montagnais-Naskapi people that to look upon the falls meant death. Following lengthy negotiations between the governments of Newfoundland and Quebec, Hydro-Quebec set out to tame the awesome falls in 1966. It took over 30,000 people nine years to complete the massive power project, which cost $950 million. The first electricity from the project was transmitted in 1971 and the 11th and final unit was online by 1974. At the time, Churchill Falls was the largest civil engineering project in North America.

◆ Saltier than the Dead Sea

Early Plains Indians bathed their sick in what they called Lake of Good Spirit, what is now known as Saskatchewan's Little Manitou Lake. Settlers, too, found that the lake's rich mineral waters—its saline density is greater than that of the Dead Sea—offered soothing, buoyant comfort for tired and aching limbs. Fed by underground springs, the shallow saline lake lies in a deep glacier-carved valley. With a mineral content high in sodium, magnesium, and potassium, the lake has been compared to the great spas of Europe. By the 1920s, the lakeside community of Manitou Beach was one of North America's most popular spas, a tradition that continues today at the Manitou Springs Resort.

◆ Spotted Lake healed battle wounds

Just west of Osoyoos, B.C., Crowsnest Highway travelers may do a double take when they see a vast spotted lake just off the roadway. The spots, like a sea of lily pads, are salt pans, most noticeable in summers with little rainfall. Evaporation reveals cakes of crystallized minerals—magnesium, calcium, sodium sulfates, and trace minerals such as silver and titanium in the lake's muddy bottom. The lake, now in private hands, was once a mecca for various Indian tribes who found aching muscles were relieved by soaking in its mud and waters. According to one legend, warring tribes once called a truce so that both parties could bathe their wounded in the soothing waters of Kliluk, or Medicine Lake, as they called it.

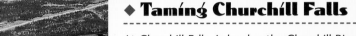

During World War I, the lake's mineral supplies were put to other uses. Chinese laborers were hired to skim it—the daily salt harvest was said to be about 1,000 kilograms—and the minerals were then shipped to munitions factories in the eastern United States.

◆ Galápagos of the north

Many of the 150 islands in the scimitar-like archipelago of the Queen Charlotte Islands, off the coast of British Columbia, are among the most isolated in Canada. Over 39 unique subspecies of plants, animals, and birds inhabit this remarkable evolutionary showcase that earns the islands their nickname "Canadian Galápagos." This isolation explains why so many species have evolved differently here than on the mainland. A prime example of this separate evolution is seen in the Haida Gwaii black bear, who, over thousands of years, developed an extremely strong jawbone to benefit from the abundance of hard-shelled sea creatures available. Today, the largest black bears in North America can be found on these islands. In addition, the biomass (or living material) found in the marine environment surrounding the islands is amongst the richest of any intertidal area in the world. Over 293 different species, including the bat star, a five-tentacled creature that comes in almost every color of the spectrum, thrive here.

1927

Second Section	THE HALIFAX HERALD	Pages 13 to 26
VOLUME 52, NO. 238	*"The People's Paper—For Nova Scotia First"* HALIFAX, CANADA, SATURDAY, OCTOBER 1, 1927	PAGE THIRTEEN

OVER EIGHTY LIVES LOST IN GREAT DISASTER

◆ Sable Island: Shipwrecks and steeds

Sable Island is a largely uninhabited crescent of shifting sand dunes in the Atlantic Ocean some 300 kilometers southeast of Halifax. It is noted for the hundreds of shipwrecks that have taken place nearby (over 350 have been recorded), and for its hundreds of wild horses. While the lifesaving stations have long been abandoned and the lighthouses now operate on solar power, the horses remain. The chestnut, palomino, and black stallions resplendent in flowing manes and tails are said to be descended from survivors of the area's many shipwrecks. However, it is more likely that they were introduced to the island in the mid-18th century by a Boston shipowner, Thomas Hancock, who was transporting Acadians deported from Nova Scotia after the Acadian Expulsion of 1755 to the United States. The Acadians were forced to abandon all livestock, so in 1760, Hancock shipped 60 of their horses to Sable Island. The horses survived and became wild. Forty to 50 herds roam the island today.

◆ Hylonomus found at Horton Bluff

Tidal bores measuring 16.3 meters, higher than a five-story building, have been recorded in Minas Basin. These massive tides' erosive action uncovers fossils which can be discovered nearly every day at Horton Bluff, near Joggins, on Nova Scotia's Parrsboro Shore.

In 1851, two geologists found 300-million-year-old fossils of Hylonomus (*Hylonomus lyelli*) here. The Hylonomus, the world's oldest, smallest, and earliest known fully adapted land vertebrate, was approximately 30 centimeters long, and closely resembled a modern lizard.

Their fossilized bones were inside large fossil tree stumps in the Fundy shore cliffs. Other early carboniferous creatures found in the tree stumps included a primitive amphibian, *Dendrerpeton acadianum*, and some of the world's oldest land snails and freshwater clams. The Joggins discovery provided the first evidence that land animals existed in the Coal Age. Joggins remains a unique archeological site and a mecca for students and scientists from around the world. At low tide, visitors can walk along the shores or the fossil cliffs.

Graveyards of the Atlantic

◆ 400 ships foundered at Anticosti

Only a few hundred people inhabit 8,000-square-kilometer Anticosti Island, at the mouth of the St. Lawrence River. Before lighthouses were established there in the 1830s, the island was known as the "Graveyard of the Gulf," with some 400 ships foundering on its treacherous reefs. Anticosti was owned at various times by English businessman Francis Stockwell, French chocolate manufacturer Henri Menier, and the pulpwood manufacturing company Consolidated Paper Corp., but none of their development plans proved viable. Today Anticosti is a hunting and fishing paradise, with 33 trout and salmon rivers, and a herd of 120,000 Virginia deer that Menier originally introduced to the island.

Headstones and crosses dot the Graveyard of the Gulf, Anticosti Island

◆ Northern lights:
The sky people's ball game

An iridescent, dancing extravaganza of green, red, yellow, and white bands appearing in the day or night skies in high latitudes of the Northern Hemisphere are known as the northern lights, or the aurora borealis. Some Aboriginal people saw the shimmering lights as spirits dancing before the Great Spirit. To the Inuit, they were *arsaniit*, sky people enjoying a ball game. Somehow the scientific explanation of solar winds interacting with the earth's magnetic field just isn't as eloquent.

◆ Canadian weather feats

◆ The lowest recorded temperature in Canada was on Feb. 3, 1937, when the mercury in Snag, Yukon, dipped to a bone-chilling –63°C. The hottest temperature recorded in Canada was a scorching 45°C in Midale, Sask., on July 5, 1937.
◆ British Columbia is the proud holder of the most Canadian weather records including amount of rainfall, highest daily and yearly average temperature, longest frost-free period, and both the most and least snowfall.
◆ One-third of all reported tornadoes in Canada have occurred in southwestern Ontario. There is a tornado risk to a major southern Ontario city, on average, once every 15 years.
◆ The highest wind speed for one hour—a stunning 201.1 kilometers per hour—was recorded on Nov. 8, 1931, at Cape Hopes Advance, Que.
◆ Canada's heaviest hailstone, weighing in at 290 grams, fell on Cedoux, Sask., on Aug. 27, 1973.

◆ Permafrost's
deep, deep freeze

Ground that remains at or below zero°C for two or more years is described as permanently frozen ground, or permafrost. Permafrost is up to 500 meters deep in many of the Arctic islands and the greatest thicknesses in Canada—in parts of Baffin and Ellesmere islands— are 1,000 meters deep. Permafrost underlies close to 50 percent of Canada.

"Spirits dancing before the Great Spirit."

◆ The windy, foggy, *and* rainy city

St. John's, Nfld., is the foggiest city in Canada, with 121 fog-enshrouded days per year. It is also the windiest Canadian city, with an average annual wind speed of 24 kilometers per hour. When it's not foggy or windy, freezing rain is probably in the forecast—38 days out of every year.

◆ Chinook magic

Temperatures can rise by 25°C in one hour, when the warm, dry, westerly wind known as a Chinook sweeps down a shallow belt along the eastern slopes of the Rocky Mountains. Early settlers named the wind for the Chinook Indians who inhabited Oregon, a region from which the wind seemed to come. Most Chinooks occur in southern Alberta, where places such as Calgary and Fort MacLeod can get 30 to 40 Chinook days a year.

◆ Pingos: A permafrost peculiarity

Pingos, conical hills of ice, are found only in permafrost regions. They are created by freezing water moving upward under hydrostatic pressure. Some of the world's largest—up to 50 meters in height and more than 300 meters in diameter—are found near Tuktoyaktuk, N.W.T.

◆ Weather capitals

- Warmest summers: Kamloops, B.C.
- Coldest winters: Yellowknife, N.W.T.
- Wettest weather: Prince Rupert, B.C.
- Driest weather: Medicine Hat, Alta.
- Sunniest winters: Winnipeg, Man.
- Sunniest summers: Yellowknife, N.W.T.
- Snowiest city: Corner Brook, Nfld.
- Least snowy city: Victoria, B.C.
- Most days with blowing snow: Chicoutimi, Que.
- Clearest skies: Estevan, Sask.
- Most humid: Windsor, Ont.

◆ Land of the midnight sun

In his Yukon ballad "The Cremation of Sam McGee," Robert Service coined the phrase "land of the midnight sun." The expression is often used to describe Arctic Canada where, in the months around the summer solstice on June 21, the sun doesn't set, and only dips below the horizon slightly

◆ We're getting warmer

Over the last 25 years Canada has increasingly experienced warmer and wetter weather, coupled with an increase in severe storms, flooding, and drought. Some climatologists attribute the latter phenomena to global warming. Whatever the cause, over the last century Canada has warmed about 1 degree Celsius, which is just about double the global rise in temperature for that period. This trend has left Atlantic regions practically unchanged but has affected Arctic regions, which are about 2°C warmer than they were in the early 1900s. This has resulted in less ice in the Arctic Ocean and less snow cover in the Northern Hemisphere.

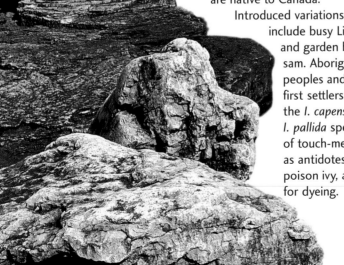

◆ 17 islands home to skinks and rattlers

Limestone cliffs, caves, archeological sites, and more reptile and amphibian species than any other national park are among the most remarkable features of Georgian Bay Islands National Park, Ont. Its 17 islands are home to the hognose snake, five-lined skink, and the massasauga rattlesnake. The latter lives on Beausoleil Island and is the only venomous snake in eastern Canada. Elsewhere in the park wind and waves have sculpted the caves and weird rock formations at Flowerpot Island (*left*). On many islands stunted, wind-twisted pines cling to shallow pockets of soil.

◆ Touch-me-not

Impatiens is the principal genus of the family of herbaceous plants known as touch-me-not, or jewelweed. Touch-me-not is so named because its seed pod, when ripe, will explode if touched. Four of some 700 species of the plant worldwide are native to Canada.

Introduced variations include busy Lizzie and garden balsam. Aboriginal peoples and the first settlers used the *I. capensis* and *I. pallida* species of touch-me-not as antidotes to poison ivy, and for dyeing.

◆ Birdman of Kingsville

American-born Jack Miner (1865–1944) was in his early teens when his family settled at Kingsville, Ont., where his father had established a tile and brick works. There for a time, Jack helped support his family by hunting moose, geese, ducks, and other wildlife.

Some days Jack and his brothers would bag ruffed grouse, other days it was rattlesnakes. Often they served as guides for hunting parties. On one such outing in northern Ontario, Jack's brother Ted was killed by another hunter's misguided shot. Hunting would never again have much appeal for Jack Miner.

In 1904, he dug ponds, planted trees, and scattered grain on his property in hopes of attracting migrating geese. He purchased seven wing-clipped geese from a neighbor, who was using them as decoys. It was 1908 before a few other geese stopped to rest at the sanctuary he had prepared. The number increased each year thereafter and before long there were thousands.

In order to learn more about migratory patterns, Miner began banding ducks and geese, and the data he assembled helped bring about the Migratory Bird Treaty adopted by Canada and the United States in 1917. Each tag had the sanctuary's address and a Bible verse. Miner supported his wildlife endeavors with lectures, sometimes several a day, all across North America. As early as 1927, he was warning about the dangers of pollution on the Great Lakes.

The 14 hectares on which migrating birds once rested has since expanded to 162 hectares and the work Miner began continues today under the auspices of the Jack Miner Foundation. As many as 125,000 visitors visit the Kingsville sanctuary annually.

◆ Come for the climate, leave because of the weather

Although blessed with unusually mild temperatures, the rainfall in British Columbia's Pacific Rim National Park Reserve amounts to more than 300 centimeters annually! Breathtaking old growth rain forests, great lengths of beach washed by Pacific swells, and rugged hiking trails characterize the park located on Vancouver Island's western shore. The reserve is in three sections: Long Beach, the 100 or so Broken Group Islands, and the West Coast Trail. Over 250 species of birds nest or migrate here, including bald eagles, dark-eyed juncos, bufflehead ducks, rhinoceros auklets, and oystercatchers. In spring, some 20,000 gray whales migrate through offshore waters. There are also over 280 native archeological sites.

◆ A-crawlin' in your whiskers, a-crawlin' in your hair

Blackflies make parts of northern Canada out of bounds to humans each summer. Forestry workers in British Columbia and northern Quebec actually have a clause in their contracts guaranteeing black-fly control. In parts of Canada, these tiny black scourges (they may be yellow-orange or gray-brown, too) make life miserable for livestock as well as people. Blackfly attacks have been blamed for outbreaks of anaphylactic shock that killed some 2,000 animals in Alberta and Saskatchewan.

The tiny black scourges were immortalized in Canadian songsmith Wade Hemsworth's 1955 "The Black Fly Song." It tells of the trials and tribulations of working on the Little Abitibi survey crew, and having to cover yourself in bacon fat and balsam gum to keep the bugs away.

◆ Okanagan Valley: Canada's fruit basket

One hundred percent of Canada's apricots, 60 percent of its cherries, 50 percent of its pears and prunes, 30 percent of its apples, and 20 percent of its peaches grow in British Columbia's Okanagan Valley. Nestled beneath the Cascade Mountains, the valley basks in a hot, dry, sunny weather. Most of the valley gets about 2,000 hours of sunlight and 35 centimeters of precipitation a year. Cactus, painted turtles, and rattlesnakes inhabit the most southerly desert-like areas of the valley.

◆ World-renowned conservation crusader made broom handles in Meaford, Ontario

Each year the town of Meaford, Ont., hosts a celebration of the life of world renowned conservationist and Sierra Club founder John Muir (1838–1914). A pacifist, Muir spent the American Civil War years in the area known locally as Trout Hollow. Among other tasks, he contracted to make his host family's mill more productive and to produce 12,000 rakes and 30,000 broom handles. He also explored the Niagara Escarpment and surrounding areas, once finding a rare calypso orchid blooming in the ice water of Holland Marsh, north of Toronto.

Muir would later devote his life to safeguarding the world's landscapes and crisscrossed the globe for this cause. Many writers and philosophers of his day were close friends, and Muir advised three U.S. presidents on wilderness preservation. His writings were a major factor in the creation of the U.S. Yosemite, Sequoia, Mount Rainier, Petrified Forest, and Grand Canyon national parks, as well as several national forests and monuments. Fittingly, a national historic site at Martinez, Calif., is now dedicated to him.

The celebration of the life of John Muir's time in Meaford (1864–66) is an annual event organized by the Canadian Friends of John Muir. Each celebration includes a flora- and fauna-rich nature walk to a nearby area. It attracts local citizens and conservation enthusiasts from around the globe.

Edmontonia, *an armored dinosaur that flourished in Alberta near the end of the Cretaceous period, unearthed in the Red Deer Valley in 1924*

◆ Giants of the past

Remains of ancient woolly mammoths, giant horned steppe bison, prehistoric horses, 180-kilogram beavers, giant short-faced bears, elephantine mastodons, scimitar cats (with fangs 7 centimeters long), monster sloths, and American lions in the Yukon Beringia Interpretive Centre at Whitehorse give some inkling of the massive creatures that inhabited Canada in pre-Ice Age times. Some of the center's exhibits were found in the Blue Fish Caves near Old Crow in the Yukon. Named for a Danish explorer, Beringia refers to a 3,200-kilometer land bridge that once linked Siberia to the Northwest Territories, and which became submerged some 11,000 years ago.

Alberta was once home to 12 families of dinosaurs

◆ Dinosaur graveyard

Fossils of clams, turtles, snails, fish, and plants are just some of the prehistoric treasures buried in the multi-hued clay of Dinosaur Provincial Park, a prehistoric graveyard beside the Red River, near Brooks, Alta. Yet it was the discovery of some 60 species of reptiles, dating back some 75 million years, that has earned it the UNESCO designation of World Heritage Site (*see page 45*).

Park visitors can take in audiovisual presentations of the park's riches, go on fossil safari trips or bone bed hikes, or partake in ongoing research at a field station of the Drumheller, Alta.-based Royal Tyrrell Museum of Palaeontology (*see page 120*). Over 150 complete dinosaur skeletons representing 12 families and 50 species of dinosaurs have been excavated at the park.

◆ Valley of Hidden Secrets

In 1991, local teacher Robert Gebhardt of Eastend, Sask., discovered dinosaur bones in the fossil-rich "Valley of Hidden Secrets" bordering the Frenchman River. Three years later, excavation of the site by Royal Saskatchewan Museum paleontologists revealed a fossilized skeleton of *Tyrannosaurus rex*, the most ferocious predator ever to walk the earth. An outstanding specimen, "Scotty" stood over 5.6 meters high, was 15 meters long, and weighed more than two adult elephants. Only one of 12 T. rex skeletons in the world, it is one of the most complete ever unearthed. It took palaeontologists and technicians two years to bring Scotty in from the hills, with help from local cowboys and a railway crew. He is now safely ensconced at a new museum, the T-Rex Discovery Centre.

◆ One-time ruler of the Prairies

The North American species of the hoofed mammal known as the buffalo is divided into two subspecies, wood bison and prairie bison. Both have curved horns, beards, shoulder humps, tails, and manes of hair around the head and neck. They live for about 20 years. In 1800, there were about 60 million bison on the Prairies, where they provided sustenance for Plains Indians, Métis, and white settlers. By 1885, the buffalo herds were practically extinct. An 1893 law prohibited buffalo hunting in Canada, and in 1922 Wood Buffalo National Park was established on the border between Alberta and the Northwest Territories in an attempt to preserve the remaining 1,500 wood bison that survived the hunting rampage of the late 19th century. Today the park protects one of the largest free-roaming, self-regulating bison herds in the world.

◆ Exquisitely preserved stone bugs

The 254-meter-high Takakkaw Falls plunging into the Yoho River is one of many spectacular waterfalls in British Columbia's Yoho National Park. The park is also famous for the Burgess Shale fossil beds, which contain some 120 species of soft-bodied creatures from the Cambrian period, some 530 million years ago.

Charles Walcott of the Smithsonian Institute, upon hearing of "stone bugs" found by Canadian Pacific railway workers, made this important discovery in 1909. Dr. Desmond Collins, one of today's leading experts on the exquisitely preserved fossils, writes: "The fossils of the Burgess Shale tell us more about how animal life appeared on Earth than any other fauna in the fossil record."

In addition to the Burgess Shale, Yoho is filled with scenic glacial lakes, stunning snowcapped mountains, pristine forests of red cedar and hemlock, and has a unique natural rock bridge over the Kicking Horse River. Little wonder why this gem of a national park derived its name from the Cree word *yoho* expressing awe.

◆ Iceberg riders

The ocean-dwelling gulls known as kittiwakes (*Rissa tridactyla*) seldom come to land and are named for their unusual piercing cry, a high-pitched, three-syllable wail. Inhabitants of the North Atlantic, they are often seen perched on icebergs off Newfoundland, and on the narrow ledges of the cliffs at Cape St. Mary.

◆ Palaeontological riches and primitive tools

Northern Yukon's unique non-glaciated landscape is preserved in Vuntut National Park, named for the memory of an ancient Gwich'in chief. Encompassing the Old Crow flats—a huge plain peppered with some 2,000 shallow lakes—the park protects the territory's most important waterfowl habitat, and contains wetlands that are home to grizzly bear, porcupine caribou, moose, and muskrat. Free of glaciers during the last ice age, the Old Crow basin served as a refuge for Pleistocene species such as woolly mammoths, giant beavers, and camels. As such it is one of Canada's richest palaeontological and archeological sites. Among the vertebrate fossils are bones that bear the distinctive marks of breakage and cutting by primitive man. Radiocarbon dating has placed the age of these bones around 25,000–30,000 years old.

◆ Salamanders thrive in Canada's smallest national park

At only eight square kilometers, St. Lawrence Islands National Park in Ontario is Canada's smallest national park. It encompasses some 21 of the Thousand Islands, which are scattered along the St. Lawrence River in the general vicinity of Kingston, Ont., and a park at Mallorytown Landing on the mainland. The park is home to a great variety of amphibians and reptiles. The black rat snake (*Elaphe elaphe*), the biggest reptile in Canada, is found here, as well as numerous species of frogs, toads, and salamanders. Ducks and geese overfly the islands during the spring and fall migrations, and great blue herons and kingfishers are regular inhabitants.

◆ "The warmest wool in the world"

Banks Island, northwest of the Coppermine Estuary in the Northwest Territories, is renowned for its muskoxen herds. In winter, the oxen dig through the snow with their powerful hooves to obtain forage. In severe storms, they remain lying down for lengthy periods. Muskoxen underwool—called *qiviut* by the Inuit—is considered the warmest in the world and can be gathered from scrub growth, boulders, and other objects they rub against. Apart from the Canadian Arctic, these shaggy, hump-shouldered, horned mammals, related to wild sheep and goats, occur nowhere else but Greenland.

◆ Turtle time

For 30 years, crowds of up to 4,000 have flocked to Boissevain, Man., to watch the drama of international turtle racing competitions. The last and final winner in 2001 was Thunder, covering the 7.5-meter run in a sprightly 23.53 seconds.

◆ An explosion of orange

Every fall, bright orange and black monarch butterflies (*Danaus plexippus*) pass through the extensive marshlands and beaches of Point Pelee National Park during their southern migration to Mexico. On early mornings, trees are an explosion of orange as thousands of monarchs hang from branches awaiting good winds and warm weather for their lake crossing. Point Pelee is at the tip of a long peninsula that juts into Lake Erie, and is in fact the southernmost tip of the Canadian mainland. Latitudinally, it is on a par with Rome, Barcelona, and northern California.

◆ Our national symbol

The beaver, the face of our nickel since 1937 and Canada's largest rodent, is largely responsible for the colonization of North America. There were some 60 million beavers in North America in the 1600s, and their fur was especially prized by fur traders, whose exploration opened up this country. Hunted almost to extinction during the fur-trade era to provide hats that were the fashion rage of Europe, *Castor canadensis* finally received official recognition as a "symbol of the sovereignty of the Dominion of Canada" in May of 1975.

The red-billed puffin, one of many cousins of the great auk

◆ Late great flightless auks

Twenty-three species of auk are found in Canada's northern polar and temperate waters. Auklets, razorbills, dovekies, guillemots, and puffins are all family members of the great auk (*Alca impennis*), an ancient flightless seabird species. But there are no extant examples of the 100,000 pairs Jacques Cartier estimated were on Funk Island off Newfoundland in 1534. Fleet in water, but clumsy and slow on land, the birds were easy prey for Cartier's men, who salted several barrels of the birds for their return voyage.

Widely distributed across the North Atlantic from the Gulf of St. Lawrence east to Scandinavia, the birds' meat and the single egg the female lays provided ready and tasty meals for generations of explorers, fishermen, and whalers. As well, the birds' feathers were in demand in the fashion world—vast numbers were slaughtered for this purpose alone.

As populations dwindled, museums and private collectors eagerly sought specimens, and great auk skins and eggs were regularly sold for huge sums at London auction houses. In June 1844, four hunters went ashore on Eldey, an island off Iceland, and clubbed to death the last two auks ever seen alive. Their skins were sold to a druggist in Reykjavik, and their pickled organs are preserved at the University of Copenhagen. In 1971, a stuffed specimen of the extinct species was sold in London to an Icelandic museum for 9,000 pounds sterling.

◆ Ookpik gives an owlish guarantee

An Inuktitut word for snowy or Arctic owl, *ookpik* was ascribed to a souvenir sealskin owl with large eyes and head created in 1963 by an Inuit cooperative. The ookpik has since become a symbol that identifies Canadian handicrafts worldwide.

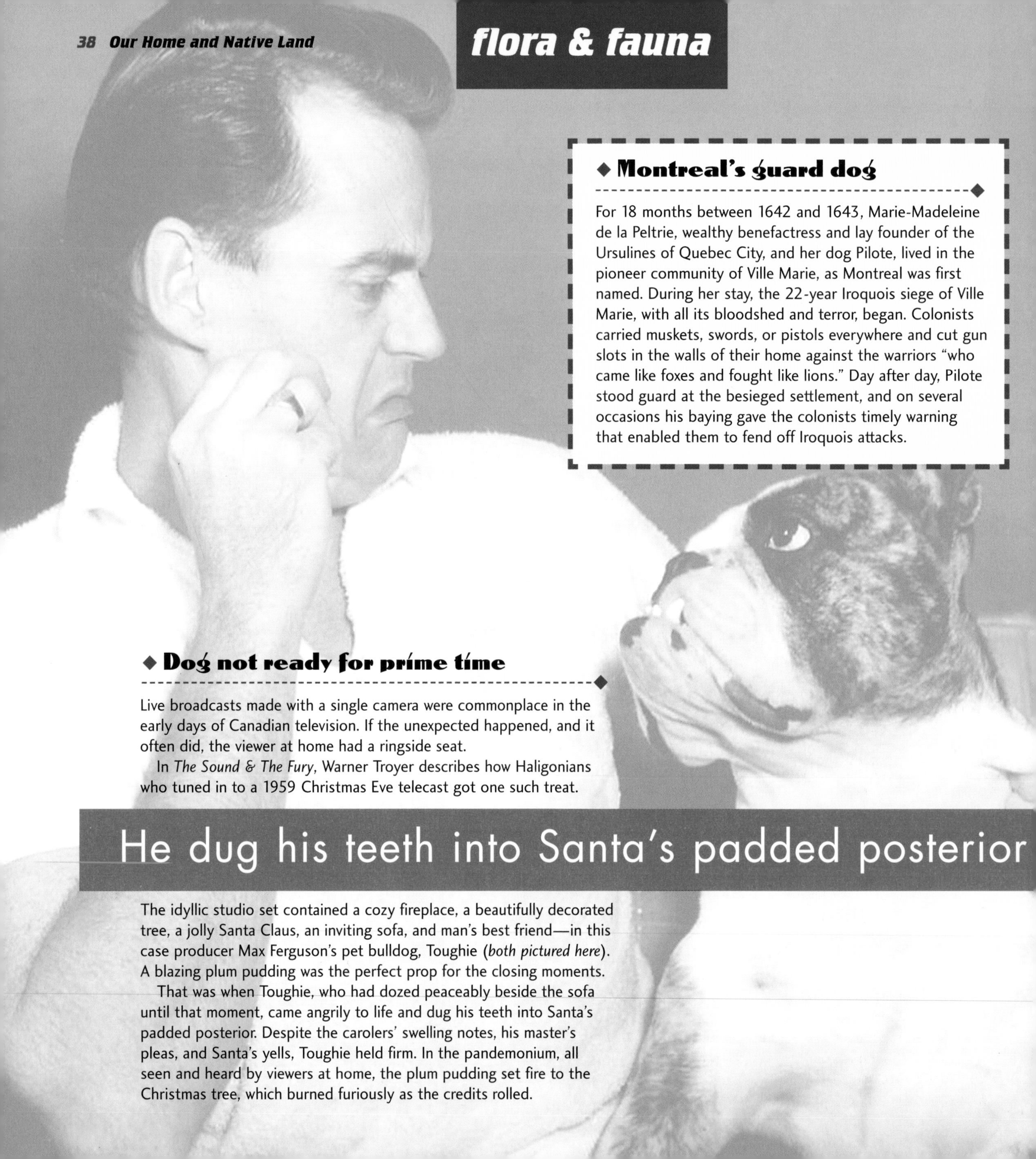

◆ Montreal's guard dog ◆

For 18 months between 1642 and 1643, Marie-Madeleine de la Peltrie, wealthy benefactress and lay founder of the Ursulines of Quebec City, and her dog Pilote, lived in the pioneer community of Ville Marie, as Montreal was first named. During her stay, the 22-year Iroquois siege of Ville Marie, with all its bloodshed and terror, began. Colonists carried muskets, swords, or pistols everywhere and cut gun slots in the walls of their home against the warriors "who came like foxes and fought like lions." Day after day, Pilote stood guard at the besieged settlement, and on several occasions his baying gave the colonists timely warning that enabled them to fend off Iroquois attacks.

◆ Dog not ready for prime time ◆

Live broadcasts made with a single camera were commonplace in the early days of Canadian television. If the unexpected happened, and it often did, the viewer at home had a ringside seat.

In *The Sound & The Fury*, Warner Troyer describes how Haligonians who tuned in to a 1959 Christmas Eve telecast got one such treat.

He dug his teeth into Santa's padded posterior

The idyllic studio set contained a cozy fireplace, a beautifully decorated tree, a jolly Santa Claus, an inviting sofa, and man's best friend—in this case producer Max Ferguson's pet bulldog, Toughie (*both pictured here*). A blazing plum pudding was the perfect prop for the closing moments.

That was when Toughie, who had dozed peaceably beside the sofa until that moment, came angrily to life and dug his teeth into Santa's padded posterior. Despite the carolers' swelling notes, his master's pleas, and Santa's yells, Toughie held firm. In the pandemonium, all seen and heard by viewers at home, the plum pudding set fire to the Christmas tree, which burned furiously as the credits rolled.

◆ Squirrels about town

Members of the squirrel family, prairie dogs (*Cynomys ludovicianus*) were once plentiful on the Prairies, where their extensive systems of burrows were known as "towns." These sociable and very vocal animals became known as dogs because they emit sounds that are remarkably like a dog's bark. Ranchers, who saw the rodents competing with them for forage, set about exterminating them and only a fraction of earlier populations survive. Today, the only prairie dog towns in Canada are found near Val Marie, Sask.

◆ Hooray for Hairy Man

Stories of the heroism and loyalty of gentle Newfoundland dogs abound, but one of the most moving occurred in July of 1828 at Isle aux Morts (Island of the Dead) in southwestern Newfoundland. (The island owes its macabre name to the number of lives lost in the treacherous waters offshore.) In 1828, the ship *Despatch* was sinking when Isle aux Morts resident George Harvey, with his son, daughter, and dog Hairy Man, rescued the passengers and crew. With a lifeline taken out to the doomed ship by the valiant dog, just about everyone on board made it to shore, where the Harveys pulled them to dry land. King George IV later awarded the Harveys a medal of honor for their tremendous feat. The family made another daring rescue in 1838, saving 25 crew members from the Glasgow ship *The Rankin*. The present day Canadian Coast Guard Ship *Ann Harvey* is named in memory of George Harvey's daughter.

Shubenacadie Sam, at the Shubenacadie Wildlife Reserve in Nova Scotia, made his first appearance in 1995, saw his shadow and predicted six more weeks of winter. Sam has always been right ever since

◆ Dog power

In July 1973, a Newfoundland dog answering to the name of Bonzo Bear dragged a 1,996-kilogram weight 4.6 meters.

◆ A touch of groundhogwash

For four decades, Wiarton, Ont., has celebrated North America's largest groundhog festival—a February weekend of indoor and outdoor family fun. (Although called groundhogs, they are actually woodchucks [*Marmota monax*].) From 1989 to 1999, festivities were built around Wiarton Willie, a rare albino groundhog whose appearance foreshadowed spring's arrival. If the sun was out and Willie saw his shadow when nudged from his burrow on Feb. 2, winter would last another six weeks. No shadow, on the other hand, meant winter was just about over. So Willie and his groundhog relatives had decreed for generations, folklore—and Wiarton folk—claimed.

But when spectators gathered for Willie's 1999 prediction, they were stunned to hear the 22-year-old furry forecaster had died two days earlier, and was lying in state in the nearby Wiarton Willie Motel. (Festival organizers later admitted the corpse was actually a stuffed understudy who had predeceased the real trouper.) However, there were assurances that Willie's "son" (Wee Willie, an albino just like the old man, was actually found in Ottawa and flown to Wiarton by a local pilot) would be on the job the following year. He was, and predicted six more weeks of winter.

Selecting the original groundhog to perpetuate centuries-old lore—and earn unbeatable publicity for the tourist town at the gateway to the Bruce Peninsula—was the brainchild of native son Mac MacKenzie. His idea served his community well; as many as 10,000 tourists fill local hotels on Groundhog Weekend.

However, Willie was not without rival prognosticators, among them Punxsutawney Phil in Pennsylvania, Staten Island Chuck in New York, and Manitoba Merv. Their accuracy is a matter of some dispute; while promoters of prognosticating groundhogs claim accuracy running around 60 percent, meteorological data suggest their predictions are right less than 40 percent of the time.

◆ Winnie, we hardly knew you

Residents of White River, a northern Ontario community, are proud of their association with Winnie the Pooh. The bear who inspired the beloved A. A. Milne books was born in the local bush. A statue of Winnie, aloft in a tree dipping into a pot of honey, has stood at the Trans-Canada entranceway to the community since 1992.

A statue in Winnipeg's Assiniboine Park Zoo also honors Winnie, as do a string of Ontario lakes named for the Pooh characters—Christopher Robin, Pooh, Piglet, Tigger, Eeyore, Owl, Rabbit, Kanga, and Roo. It all began one day in 1914 when a Winnipeg train stopped in White River to take on coal and water. On board were members of the Fort Garry Horse Regiment, one of whom was veterinary surgeon Lt. (later Capt.) Harry Colebourne. A trapper carrying an orphaned black bear cub caught Colebourne's eye and, on a whim, he bought the cub for $20.

The bear accompanied the lieutenant to Valcartier, Que., and eventually to England. When the regiment was sent to the front, Colebourne arranged for Winnie to stay at the London Zoo. There she became a favorite with visitors, including Mr. Milne and son Christopher Robin.

Winnipeg-born Lt. Harry Colebourne named his pet bear cub for his hometown

◆ Chicken chariot races

Chickens are big business in Wynyard, Sask., where the biggest employers are chicken processing and hatchery plants and related businesses. Sunnyland Poultry Products Ltd. processes more than 9 million fryers, roasting chickens, and stewing hens at its Wynyard and Saskatoon plants. The Wynyard hatchery sets more than 120,000 eggs twice a week.

Against that background it's not so surprising to find chicken chariot races among events at its annual community carnival. Each chicken contestant pulls a two-wheeled chariot—which must meet rigid size and weight specifications—down a Plexiglas-enclosed, 15 meter sloping track. Heats are limited to 48 birds and five minutes. The time limit is necessary since some birds backtrack, cross lanes, pick fights, or simply stand their ground.

Despite shouted encouragement from the young entrants, some contestants simply refuse to cross the finish line

◆ Frog jumping suspense

Frog Follies, an August celebration at St. Pierre-Jolys, a tiny community west of Steinbach, Man., features the annual Canadian National Frog Jumping Championships.

◆ Whisky, june bugs, and buttermilk

A giant, 19-kilogram frog stands out among the furniture exhibits, the World War I trench, the uniforms, and the coverlets of the Officers' Quarters of the York-Sunbury Historical Society Museum in Fredericton, N.B. Before the frog was accidentally killed in the 1800s, by dynamiting near his pond, Mr. Coleman, a local hotelier, regularly fed the amphibian whisky, june bugs, and buttermilk; then had it stuffed when it met an untimely end.

BEAUTIFUL JOE
A Dog's Own Story

ILLUSTRATED
MARSHALL SAUNDERS

CANADA'S FAVOURITE
CHILDREN'S CLASSIC

◆ A dog to remember

Beautiful Joe, a story about an abused dog, made Nova Scotia-born teacher and romance novelist Margaret Marshall Saunders (1861–1947) one of Canada's most beloved writers of children's stories. An instant blockbuster on its publication in 1894, the story became the first Canadian book to sell more than one million copies. Translated into 14 languages, the book eventually sold seven million.

Used for years in U.S. public schools for teaching children compassion toward animals and each other, *Beautiful Joe* is required reading at some Canadian universities, and is now sold on the Internet. Endorsements on Web sites tell how profoundly it affected generations of readers.

Tributes such as "That book changed my whole life," or "I became a vet because of that book" are also commonplace at The Ginger Press Bookstore, in Owen Sound, Ont., which publishes *Beautiful Joe*. The dog hero lived in Meaford. While visiting in 1892, Mrs. Saunders (*above*) met a fox terrier/bull terrier-mix puppy that had been rescued from an abusive master.

Impressed by the dog's gentle nature, she wrote a biography describing a year in the dog's life. To be eligible for an 1893 competition by the American Humane Education Society, she set the book in a fictional town in Maine. And to offset any bias against women writers, she used her middle and last names only— Marshall Saunders. The book took top prize and became a runaway success.

A lifelong champion of women's and children's rights, Saunders wrote about child labor in factories and lectured extensively on wildlife conservation and humane treatment for animals. With *Anne of Green Gables* author Lucy Maud Montgomery, she cofounded the Maritime branch of the Canadian Women's Press Club.

Mrs. Saunders spent her last years in Toronto, where she died at age 85. Her house was always filled with pets, especially canaries. Her dog, Johnny Doorstep, was a constant companion. As with many of the homeless pets she adopted, she named him for the place he was found.

> ❝**That book changed my whole life.**❞

◆ Keeping *his* memory green

Meaford, a two-hour drive north of Toronto, calls itself "the home of Beautiful Joe." It was in Meaford that Margaret Marshall Saunders met miller William Moore and the puppy whose tail and ears were axe-cropped by a brutal milkman. From this sprang her tale of a savaged puppy and his happy-ever-after life.

Buried in Beautiful Joe Park, alongside the trout-rich Big Head River, the dog hero also inspired the Beautiful Joe Heritage Society to celebrate other brave animals. The first of a series of monuments within the park honors police dogs. One day, the society hopes to have a world-class educational center on animal care, training, and nutrition and an International Canine Hall of Fame.

◆ Canada's Green Plan

Canada's national park system began with the creation of Banff National Park in 1885. Its goal, then as now, was to preserve examples of all our natural landforms, vegetation, and wildlife. There are currently 39 national parks and national park reserves in Canada, located in every province and territory. They range in size from 8.7 to 44,807 square kilometers. Under terms of the 1990 federal Green Plan, which recommended Canada set aside 12 percent of its total area as protected space, Canada was to have completed its national park system in 2000, with a national park in each of the country's 39 natural land regions. As of 2002, 14 additional national parks are still needed. (Twenty-nine marine regions have also been identified as being representative of the nation's biological, physical, and oceanographic characteristics; two national marine parks have already been created.) Creating a national park is a process of many years, and involves feasibility studies, public consultations, and negotiation with provinces, territories, individuals, and Aboriginal organizations. The Torngat Mountains in Labrador, Manitoba's Interlake region, and the Gulf Islands in British Columbia are all under consideration for future national parks.

our national parks

◆ Our oldest national park

Banff National Park, a vast wonderland of lakes and mountains in southwestern Alberta, is Canada's oldest national park. Famed for its hot sulfur springs, ice-capped peaks, glaciers, wildlife, and skiing, it started out as a small reserve established to protect warm mineral springs, discovered by chance in 1883 by railway workers Frank McCabe and brothers William and Tom McCardell. Arguments over ownership of the springs were resolved with the creation of Banff National Park two years later. The Town of Banff, now a year-round recreation center and park headquarters, began life as a railway siding in 1883. The Banff Springs Hotel, one of the loveliest of the CPR's great "château" hotels, opened five years later. Banff became one of Alberta's major cultural centers in 1933 with the creation of the Banff Centre School of Fine Arts, now one of North America's foremost schools of the visual and performing arts.

◆ Canada's largest park

The world's largest herd of free-roaming bison make their home in vast **Wood Buffalo National Park**, straddling the Alberta-Northwest Territories border. At 44,807 square kilometers, the park is Canada's largest; it encompasses an area of subarctic wilderness bigger than Switzerland. The Peace-Athabasca delta—an immense expanse of poorly drained bogs and silty channels and the largest inland delta in the world—is a staging ground for four major waterfowl flyways. Wood Buffalo is also one of the world's last nesting places for endangered whooping cranes. Scattered across the park are numerous sinkholes,

A 1950 toy train of The Canadian, which made regular stops at Banff Springs Hotel on its way through the Rockies.

depressions created when subsurface runoff causes underlying rock to dissolve. One sinkhole at Pine Lake is 5 kilometers long and 20 meters deep.

◆ Crown jewel of the Rockies

The Columbia Icefield, the largest glacier in the Canadian Rockies, straddles the Continental Divide in **Jasper National Park**, considered by many to be the crown jewel of our national parks. Every year, millions of visitors are drawn by the vast glaciers, massive mountains, flower-filled meadows, and easily-spotted wildlife. Jasper's 53 species of mammal are spread across three ecosystems—montane, sub-alpine, and alpine—and include bighorn sheep, wapiti, grizzly bears, coyotes, hoary marmot, and pika or "rock rabbit." The park contains no less than five national historic sites, including Henry House (1811) and The Yellowhead Pass.

◆ Highland splendor

The Cabot Trail, one of North America's most famous scenic drives, loops around **Cape Breton Highlands National Park**, in Cape Breton, Nova Scotia. The trail, with its villages steeped in rich Acadian, Scottish and Irish heritage, is a breathtaking way to enjoy the coastline, yet to experience the park itself, visitors should park their vehicles and explore the picturesque valleys, ocean coves, rugged highlands, and plunging cliffs. The highlands are covered in thick hardwood and evergreen forests inhabited by black bear, lynx, and a great variety of birds, including bald eagles.

◆ Where caribou outnumber residents 28 to 1

Quttinirpaaq National Park, at the northern tip of Canada (its name means "top of the world" in Inuktituk), protects a fragile permafrost environment and the muskoxen and Peary's caribou that inhabit its glacier-encrusted, mountainous terrain. The park is in Nunavut, where the temperature rarely rises above 0°C, and caribou outnumber residents 28 to 1.

◆ Springs hot and cold

At Radium Hot Springs, in the southern end of British Columbia's **Kootenay National Park**, rainwater draining through a fault in the earth's crust is vaporized by hot rock, then returns as steam that condenses to a steamy 45°C at the surface. Elsewhere in the park, brown orange mud from the Paint Pots, iron-laden cold springs, was used for decorative purposes by the Kootenay, Blackfoot, and Stoney Indians. Such is the diversity of Kootenay, which extends from glacier-clad peaks in the north, to the dry, grassy slopes of the Columbia Valley in the south, where even cactus grows.

◆ A surfeit of shipwrecks

Twenty shipwrecks—including schooners dating back to 1883—three period lighthouses, curious dolomite islands, a labyrinth of caves, and crystal clear waters provide an exciting exploration area for both novice and advanced divers at

Fathom Five National Marine Park off Tobermory, Ont. The underwater park, at the tip of the Bruce Peninsula, is Canada's diving capital.

◆ Bountiful badlands

While often looking desolate to the naked eye, the deeply dissected plateaux, coulees, and badlands of **Grasslands National Park** are actually filled with life. The Saskatchewan park is home to a unique blend of prairie-adapted common and endangered species, from the pronghorn antelope, sage grouse, and ferruginous hawk to the prairie rattlesnake and eastern short-horned lizard. Grasslands National Park and the area immediately around the park are also the only places in Canada where colonies of black-tailed prairie dogs can be found.

◆ Jewel of the Gaspé

The "Jewel of the Gaspé Peninsula," **Forillon National Park** protects a complex coastal environment embracing everything from sub-arctic plants to whales. Limestone cliffs plunge to the sea in parts of the park; in other places, beaches and coves peer through cracks in the rocks. Whales are often spotted near Forillon's shores, while large numbers of birds—including black-legged kittiwake, double-crested cormorant, black guillemot and razorbill—visit the park, many returning annually to nests built high in clefts in the windswept cliffs.

◆ A green wedge on the Manitoba prairie

A refuge for wolf, elk, moose, black bear, countless insects, and a captive bison herd, Manitoba's **Riding Mountain National Park** is like a green wedge rising from the surrounding prairie. A plateau of the Manitoba Escarpment, Riding Mountain is a crossroads where plants and animals of eastern, western, and northern Canada meet. Some 260 kilometers northwest of Winnipeg, the park has vast meadows of rough fescue grasslands, numerous lakes, and scores of hiking trails, many winding through stands of trembling aspen and white birch, others threading through forests of spruce, jack pine, balsam fir, and tamarack.

◆ Nahanni's "river of fear"

An outstanding example of northern wilderness, 4,766-square-kilometer **Nahanni National Park Reserve** sits in the Mackenzie Mountains in the Northwest Territories. The breathtakingly beautiful South Nahanni River runs through the park, crashing through three immense canyons, one 34 kilometers long. Unusual sights along the river include Rabbitkettle Hotsprings, source of the largest known tufa mounds in Canada and caves such as Grotte

Valerie, with its ancient skeletons of nearly a hundred Dall's sheep. Nahanni is famed for its spectacular waterfalls (at 90 meters, Virginia Falls is twice as high as Niagara), and its limestone cave system is a font of northern lore: giants, lost gold mines, tropical edens, decapitated prospectors and other mysterious deaths and disappearances associated with this wild "river of fear."

◆ Sandpipers & salt marshes

Secluded beaches, sand dunes, salt marshes, and hiking trails make New Brunswick's **Kouchibouguac National Park** a perfect spot for swimming, windsurfing, and pleasant strolls. The park, which has three rivers, gets its name from a Mi'kmaq word meaning river of long tides. Waterfowl rest in the park during spring and fall migrations, and sandpipers, terns, plovers, and kingfishers are among species found there. The park's waters teem with bass, eel, flounder, and trout. Grey seals lounge on offshore sandbars.

◆ A lakeland of rare species

Kejimkujik National Park at Maitland Bridge, N.S., represents the Atlantic Coast Uplands Natural Region of southwestern Nova Scotia. The park's lakes have amphibian, reptile, bird, and orchid species rarely found elsewhere in eastern Canada, while Blanding's turtle (*right*), southern flying squirrel, and the ribbon snake are also unique to this region. Hardy shrubs of the heath family, such as Labrador tea, sheep laurel, and leather leaf, grow profusely in the boggy areas.

our national parks

◆ Sculpted by time

Fascinating limestone rock formations can be found in **Mingan Archipelago National Park**, north of Anticosti Island in Quebec. The park's archipelago is

a stunning necklace of 100 forested islands, carved from sedimentary rock, and more than 2,000 islets and reefs teeming with blue whales, seals, harbor porpoises, and nesting puffins. Erosion by time, wind, and sea has sculpted spectacular rock shapes on the islands.

◆ "North of summer"

"North of summer" was how poet Al Purdy described Pangnirtung, a tiny hamlet on Baffin Island in Nunavut. Today **Auyuittuq National Park**, to which Pangnirtung marks the entrance, captures the eloquence of Purdy's words. Hikers and sea kayakers who journey to Auyuittuq (Inuktitut for "the land that never melts") are rewarded with views of jagged mountain peaks towering above sapphire blue ocean fjords. Caribou, lemmings, arctic hares, and snowy owls can be spotted on the massive, eternal glaciers, amidst fields of arctic poppies and cotton grass.

◆ A geological legacy

Spectacular freshwater fjords, salmon rivers, and the stark treeless barrens of the Long Range Mountains are the outstanding features of **Gros Morne National Park**, on Newfoundland's west coast. Continental collisions created this park's landscape by pushing to the surface massive, lava-encrusted hunks of an ancient ocean's floor. Gros Morne is one of the few places in the world where sections of the earth's mantle are readily visible. The geological legacy of volcanic cliffs, limestone breccia, and eons of marine fossils at 40 fossil sites are a scientist's delight.

◆ Canada's World Heritage Sites

Since 1972, the World Heritage Committee of the United Nations Educational, Scientific and Cultural Organization (UNESCO) has been dedicated to identifying and preserving the most outstanding examples of the world's natural and cultural heritage. Places such as the Pyramids of Egypt and Ecuador's Galápagos Islands are among some 721 such places in 124 countries around the world that are now recognized as World Heritage Sites.

Cultural sites must be unique artistic or creative masterpieces; have had long-time influence over a cultural area of the world; be a unique testimony to a lost civilization; an outstanding example of human cultural settlements; or have a tangible association with events or ideas of universal significance.

Natural sites must be outstanding examples of earth's evolutionary stages—of ongoing geological processes or biological evolution—or be an example of the foremost natural habitats of threatened animal or plant species.

Thirteen Canadian sites have met criteria for one or other of these categories. The cultural category includes the Haida Indian totem poles at Ninstints Village on **Anthony Island** in British Columbia; the oldest and best-preserved bison jump in the world, **Head-Smashed-In Buffalo Jump** in Alberta; the historic district of **Quebec City**; **Old Town Lunenburg** in Nova Scotia; and the site of the oldest known European settlement in North America, **L'Anse aux Meadows National Historic Park**, in Newfoundland.

The natural sites are **Nahanni National Park**, N.W.T.; **Kluane National Park**, Yukon; **Wood Buffalo National Park**, on the border between Alberta and the N.W.T.; **Dinosaur Provincial Park** in Alberta; the **Canadian Rocky Mountain Parks** in Alberta and B.C.; **Waterton-Glacier International Peace Park**, on the Alberta/Montana boundary; and the palaeontological site of **Miguasha Park**, on the Gaspé peninsula, Quebec. With its traces of human history in the Stone Age and unique geomorphological forms, Newfoundland's **Gros Morne National Park** falls into both categories.

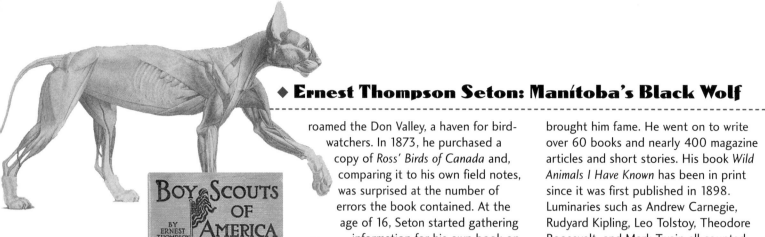

◆ Ernest Thompson Seton: Manitoba's Black Wolf ◆

Ernest Thompson Seton was an accomplished wildlife anatomist and a key figure in the Boy Scouts

A self-taught biologist, writer, illustrator, and naturalist, Ernest Thompson Seton was born on August 14, 1860, in Durham, England. When he was six years old, Seton's family moved to Canada and settled near Lindsay, Ont. Seton's fascination with nature had its roots in the wooded area around the Seton family home. In 1870, the Setons moved to Toronto and for the next nine years, young Ernest roamed the Don Valley, a haven for bird-watchers. In 1873, he purchased a copy of *Ross' Birds of Canada* and, comparing it to his own field notes, was surprised at the number of errors the book contained. At the age of 16, Seton started gathering information for his own book on the birds of Canada.

Seton started painting in 1876. At the age of 20, he won a seven-year scholarship to the Royal Academy of Art in London. In 1881, he enjoyed his first public exhibition but ill health forced him to return to Canada, where he joined two of his elder brothers homesteading in Carberry, Man. While Seton made a poor farmer, his lifelong study of animals paid off: In 1893, he was appointed Official Naturalist for the government of Manitoba, a title he held until his death.

Seton found his greatest success as a wildlife artist. His fine anatomical drawings in *Studies in Art: Anatomy of Animals* (1896) brought him fame. He went on to write over 60 books and nearly 400 magazine articles and short stories. His book *Wild Animals I Have Known* has been in print since it was first published in 1898. Luminaries such as Andrew Carnegie, Rudyard Kipling, Leo Tolstoy, Theodore Roosevelt, and Mark Twain all counted themselves fans of his dramatic wilderness stories. Through his stories, Seton forged an admiring sympathy for both wolves and native people; he eventually dubbed himself "Black Wolf."

Seton was also a key figure in the early history of the Boy Scouts of America. Chief Scout from 1910 to 1915, he helped cowrite the first Boy Scout manual with Lord Baden-Powell in 1911. Seton was at odds with the military aspects of scouting, however, and his support of the political, cultural, and spiritual rights of Aboriginal peoples was a source of friction with the organization. They parted ways in 1922. Eight years later, Seton moved to Santa Fe, New Mexico, and became an American citizen in 1931. He died in 1946.

◆ Wawaskesy, Menissawok, Nemiskam, and Buffalo: Vanishing Prairie parks

On June 24, 1938, the abolition of Wawaskesy National Park received royal assent. Abolishing a national park was a rare occurrence, to be sure, but Wawaskesy (Cree for "antelope") was not the only national park to disappear: Menissawok (Cree for "common property") closed in 1930, and Nemiskam (Siksika for "between two coulees") and Buffalo National Park in 1947. The irony behind the fate of these four Prairie parks was the very success they had in saving two threatened species: bison and pronghorn antelope.

In 1906, as part of its effort to prevent their extinction, the federal government bought North America's last wild bison herd from a Montana rancher. The herd was moved first to Elk Island National Park, then to the new Buffalo National Park southeast of Wainwright, Alta. By 1910, more than 700 bison had been brought to the latter, where they thrived. Increasing numbers, unfortunately, led to overgrazing and disease that weakened the herd.

In 1921, a slaughter of "surplus" bison took place. The public was outraged, and the park subsequently shipped surplus bison north to Wood Buffalo National Park, but this was merely the tip of the iceberg: By 1939, the original 700 bison had produced 27,000 descendants. The species may well have been saved, but many individual bison in Buffalo National Park were diseased and starving. In the winter of 1940–41, they were all killed and the park was handed over to the military.

The national park administration also took measures to save another species wildlife experts saw with extinction in its future: the pronghorn antelope. Dominion Parks Commissioner J. B. Harkin asked Ernest Thompson Seton *(see opposite page)* to help the National Parks branch identify possibl pe reserves. In 1914, Seton suggested Wawaskesy, north of Medicine Hat, and Menissawok, in Saskatchewan's Cypress Hills. A small herd of antelope was discovered near Foremost, Alta., and local landowners lent their support in helping establish pocket-sized Nemiskam National Park in 1915. All three became official national parks in 1922.

This trio of Prairie parks helped bring the antelope back from near extinction, and soon herds spread throughout the southern grasslands of Saskatchewan and Alberta. As a result, the disappearance of Menissawok and Wawaskesy raised nary an eyebrow. With free-ranging antelope nearing the 30,000 mark by 1946, there was no further need for the last park, Nemiskam.

Today, buffalo roam in Elk Island, Prince Albert, and Wood Buffalo National Parks, while antelope play in Grasslands National Park. The Preservation of the Plains Bison is an event of national historic significance, commemorated at Elk Island National Park.

Alberta

Saskatchewan

Edmonton •

Wainwright
Buffalo National Park
1906-1947
Calgary •

N. Saskatchewan River

Wawaskesy National Park
1922-1947

Medicine Hat •   Maple Creek •   Regina •

Nemiskam
National Park
1922-1947

Menissawok National Park
1922-1930

First Nations, first arrivals, first communities

HEWERS OF WOOD DRAWERS OF WATER

early explorers

◆ Newfoundland's three prehistoric cultures

Amulets, cookware, tools, and weapons found at Port au Choix National Historic Site, north of Cornerbrook, Nfld., tell of three groups of highly organized peoples who lived there more than 5,000 years ago. The site contains burial grounds of Maritime Archaic Indians who lived in Newfoundland and Labrador some 5,500 years ago. Three of their cemeteries were discovered in the early 1960s. Many of the graves contained hunting weapons such as harpoons, lances, darts, and snares. There are also vestiges of both the Dorset (1,900 years ago) and Groswater (2,800 years ago) Palaeoeskimos, whose tools for hunting seals were distinctive in their small-ness and fine craftsmanship. Port au Choix's raised coastline and alkaline soil have combined to preserve these rich, disparate traces of prehistoric culture.

◆ Cabot saw the sea awash with fish

In search of a faster route to Asia and the riches of the Far East, John Cabot crossed the Atlantic in 1497 on behalf of Henry VII of England. What he discovered was the vast coastline of North America and waters teeming with life. He returned to England with stories of a sea swarming with fish. The following year, his ship was lost without a trace on a return voyage to North America.

◆ Site of earliest occupation

The Bluefish Caves are three small caves in the Yukon's Keele Mountain Range that contain accepted evidence that they are the site of the earliest human occupation in Canada. Artifacts found there are 12,000 to 17,000 years old.

◆ Vikings among first arrivals

Norsemen such as this Viking settled the northern tip of Newfoundland in the late 11th century

Norseman "Leif the Lucky" Eriksson set foot in Canada about A.D. 1,000. He is thought to have landed here when he was blown off course as he was returning home to Norway from Greenland. Some claim he landed on the northern tip of Newfoundland, others that his landfall was in Nova Scotia. Eriksson called his short-lived settlement Vinland because it occupied a fertile plain awash in wild grapes. Vinland and the Viking explorers are featured in the narrative of two medieval Icelandic chronicles that comprise the primary written evidence of the Norse discovery of North America. The sagas tell the story of their expeditions and settlements.

Replica of a Norse Viking ship at L'Anse aux Meadows

◆ Vinland of the Norse

Remains of a settlement, discovered in the 1960s at what is now L'Anse aux Meadows National Historic Site in Newfoundland, suggest that this was the famous Vinland spoken of in Viking sagas (*see above*). The discovery proves that there is little doubt that the Vikings arrived in North America centuries before Christopher Columbus. Excavations have uncovered the remains of seven turf buildings, two cook pits, and a smithy, all similar to the remains of Viking houses found in Norway, and items such as a soapstone spindle whorl, a bronze pin, and a stone lamp.

Now a UNESCO World Heritage Site (*see page 45*), it contains the first historic traces of a European presence in the Americas. A sod house and outbuildings have been reconstructed near the site, and visitors can experience the warm smoky atmosphere of Norse huts.

◆ Cartier ended his days tippling

On his 1534 voyage around the Gulf of St. Lawrence, Jacques Cartier (1491–1557) described Labrador as "the land God gave to Cain," and Prince Edward Island as "the fairest land 'tis possible to see." He sailed for the New World again the following spring. On Aug. 15 that year, he saw the St. Lawrence River for the first time, and named it for the saint whose feast day that was. He ascended the river to what is now Montreal, then returned to spend that 1535 winter at what is now Quebec. There 25 of his men succumbed to scurvy, but the rest survived by drinking an Indian remedy, an infusion of white cedar leaves and bark.

In 1541, Cartier was back again, an advance party for the pending settlement by Sieur de Roberval. It was the great explorer's last expedition. He fell from royal favor, but settled down to life as a landowner, earning a reputation among his neighbors as a congenial tippler with a rich fund of tall tales.

◆ "False as Canadian diamonds"

When he returned to France in 1541, Jacques Cartier brought several barrels of what he thought were gold and diamonds mined by his men at Cap aux Diamants, Que. The rocks proved to be worthless iron pyrite and quartz, giving rise to the French phrase "faux comme les diamants du Canada"—as false as Canadian diamonds.

"The fairest land 'tis possible to see."

◆ Haida culture dates back two millennia

The Haida are the ancient inhabitants of British Columbia's Queen Charlotte Islands; islands they call *Haida Gwaii*, meaning "place of wonder," and according to their legend, "the place where time began." Excavations here revealed evidence of habitation dating back over 2,000 years. Their ancestors were a prosperous people, living on halibut, sea mammals, and mollusks, in addition to freshwater salmon. Abundant red cedars provided wood to make dugout canoes, ornate boxes, and woven hats. They built villages of cedar dwellings complete with spectacularly carved totem poles that told the story of each household. The rich bounty of their environment gave them leisure time to devote to art and cultural pursuits.

Today, much of this rich artistry has been preserved, along with coastal rain forests, in Gwaii Haanas National Park Reserve/Haida Heritage Site. Recognizing that their heritage must be protected, in 1981 the Haida founded the Haida Gwaii Watchmen, named after a legend where human figures on immense totem poles warned ancestors of impending danger. Today's Watchmen give visitors to the park insight into the sacredness of the sites, their history and culture, including legends, songs, and dances. The Watchmen continue their vigilance over the ancient settlements, including Ninstints Village and its hauntingly memorable group of mortuary poles (a World Heritage Site, *see page 45*).

◆ Home of the teaching stones

In 1954, over 900 finely preserved carvings of symbols and figures were discovered on rock faces at the east end of Stony Lake near the hamlet of Stonyridge, Ont. Now regarded as Canada's largest concentration of petroglyphs, they are preserved inside a building at Petroglyphs Provincial Park. The Ojibwa called the stones *Kinomagewapkong*, or "the rocks that teach," as they played a role in a warrior's coming of age. As each boy reached adolescence, he was taken here by elders who used the rocks to impart lessons on tribal mysteries and legends and the importance of harmony between man and nature. After each lesson, the rocks were covered with moss to protect the carvings from erosion.

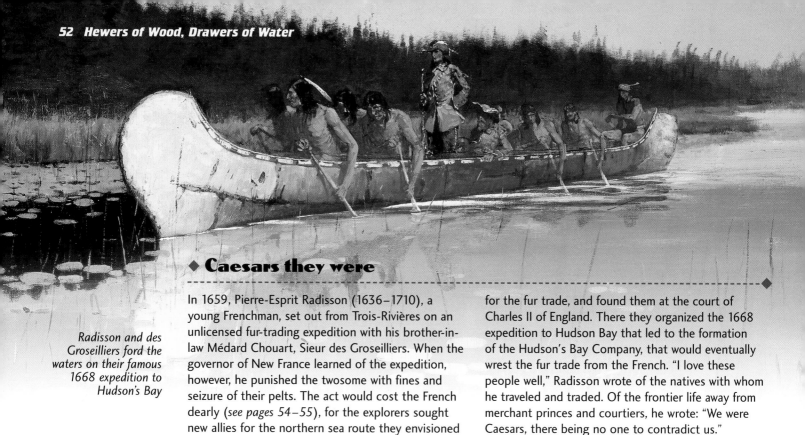

Radisson and des Groseilliers ford the waters on their famous 1668 expedition to Hudson's Bay

◆ Caesars they were

In 1659, Pierre-Esprit Radisson (1636–1710), a young Frenchman, set out from Trois-Rivières on an unlicensed fur-trading expedition with his brother-in-law Médard Chouart, Sieur des Groseilliers. When the governor of New France learned of the expedition, however, he punished the twosome with fines and seizure of their pelts. The act would cost the French dearly (*see pages 54–55*), for the explorers sought new allies for the northern sea route they envisioned for the fur trade, and found them at the court of Charles II of England. There they organized the 1668 expedition to Hudson Bay that led to the formation of the Hudson's Bay Company, that would eventually wrest the fur trade from the French. "I love these people well," Radisson wrote of the natives with whom he traveled and traded. Of the frontier life away from merchant princes and courtiers, he wrote: "We were Caesars, there being no one to contradict us."

"We were Caesars, there being no-one to contradict us."

◆ The first frontiersman

The original *coureur de bois*, Étienne Brulé (1592–1623), was the first European to see Lakes Ontario, Huron, Erie, and Superior, the sites of present-day Ottawa and Toronto, to tread the soil of what is now Ontario, and to shoot the Lachine Rapids. He was also the first European to live as an Indian. Brulé left no letters or journals and is only glimpsed through the writings of Samuel de Champlain (1567–1635) and the Jesuits, who disapproved of his actions and morals. He served France and Champlain well from 1608, when he arrived in New France, until 1629, when he deserted to the English who captured Quebec that year. Afterward, Brulé returned to Huronia, where, at age 41, he was said to have been killed by the Hurons for betraying their friend Champlain.

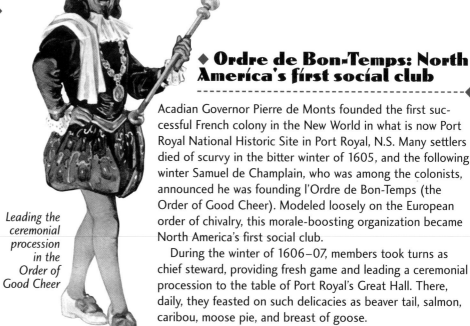

Leading the ceremonial procession in the Order of Good Cheer

◆ Ordre de Bon-Temps: North America's first social club

Acadian Governor Pierre de Monts founded the first successful French colony in the New World in what is now Port Royal National Historic Site in Port Royal, N.S. Many settlers died of scurvy in the bitter winter of 1605, and the following winter Samuel de Champlain, who was among the colonists, announced he was founding l'Ordre de Bon-Temps (the Order of Good Cheer). Modeled loosely on the European order of chivalry, this morale-boosting organization became North America's first social club.

During the winter of 1606–07, members took turns as chief steward, providing fresh game and leading a ceremonial procession to the table of Port Royal's Great Hall. There, daily, they feasted on such delicacies as beaver tail, salmon, caribou, moose pie, and breast of goose.

◆ China or bust

Because of his insistence that he could find a way across North America to China, the Quebec property owned by René-Robert Cavelier de La Salle (1643–87) was jokingly called La Chine. La Salle sold the land—where Lachine, Que., now stands—to finance an expedition to the Ohio River, which he thought led to the Orient. But the ill-planned venture never got past Lake Ontario.

La Salle turned to fur trading to raise money for further exploration and in 1679, at Lake Erie, he built the 36-tonne *Griffon*, the first commercial ship ever launched on the Great Lakes. The *Griffon* disappeared on Lake Huron in 1680. By 1681 the indefatigable La Salle had organized yet another expedition and within a year had followed the Mississippi to its alligator-infested mouth, and claimed the land he called Louisiana.

Louis XIV dismissed the find as useless but was persuaded to let La Salle colonize the Mississippi delta. Arriving by sea, La Salle could not find the river mouth, landed in what is now Texas, and began an inland search. Beset by illness, death, and native attacks, his men mutinied, and in March 1687 shot him in the wilderness he had claimed for France.

◆ Pemmican, richeau, and rubaboo

Pemmican, the great staple of the fur trade, consisted of sun-dried, powdered meat (buffalo, caribou, or moose) mixed with animal fat and berries. Packed in buffalo hide containers that held up to 40 kilograms of the mix, it was eaten in raw chunks by the voyageurs; most of these hardy men could chomp down up to two kilograms of the stuff a day. Would-be cordon bleus whipped up backwoods delicacies such as *richeau*—pemmican fried in its own grease embellished with flour, salt, and potatoes—and Northwest classics such as rubaboo—pemmican, wild onions, and salt pork simmered together in a flour soup.

◆ "Where no human beings should venture"

A fur trader from his teens, Simon Fraser (1776–1862) founded the first North West Company posts in what is now central British Columbia. "We had to pass where no human beings should venture," he wrote of his exploration of the mighty river he discovered and which now bears his name.

◆ The village that vanished

Some 1,500 Iroquois farmers in a palisaded village at the present site of Montreal greeted Jacques Cartier when he first sailed up the St. Lawrence River on Oct. 2, 1535. The Hochelagans welcomed Cartier with dancing and so much food that he said it seemed to rain cornbread and fish. Behind the circular, fortified town settlement was a mountain Cartier named Mont Royal. The town was still there when Cartier returned in 1541. But all traces of the flourishing community had disappeared when Samuel de Champlain reached the area in 1603. In 1642, a small group of people from France led by Paul Chomedey, Sieur de Maisonneuve (1612–76), founded the tiny colony of Ville-Marie which would become Montreal.

A 1565 woodcut of Hochelaga; the first printed map of a settlement in North America

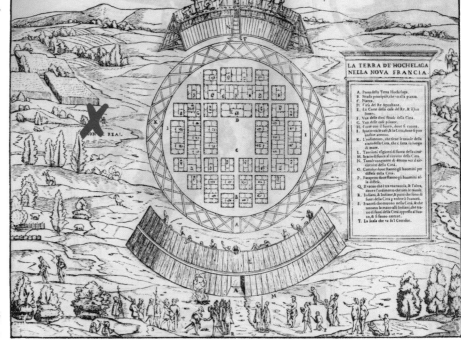

early explorers

◆ The place to meet

At the junction of the Red and Assiniboine rivers in Winnipeg, the Forks National Historic Site was once an important meeting place of Aboriginal peoples, where many of the First Nations met, camped, traded, socialized—and gambled. Games of chance often involved "gambling sticks"—sticks of maple, ash, spruce, willow, reeds, straw or bone 10 to 51 centimeters long, some intricately carved, painted, and inlaid with small pieces of shell or ivory. Ten to more than a hundred gambling sticks could be used in a game, depending on the rules and culture.

◆ Strike-Only-Once truncheon

East of Terrace, B.C., Kitwanga Fort National Historic Site was the first national historic site in western Canada to commemorate native culture. Located on the Kitwanga River, overlooking ancient trails linking the Skeena, Nass, and Stikine rivers, it features a native hilltop stronghold called Battle Hill, which burned to the ground in the early 1800s as the Gitwangak fought to defend their trade routes from encroaching clans.

According to Gitwangak legend, a warrior named Nekt ruled steep-sided Battle Hill, controlling the lucrative candlefish oil (*see* "Grease trails," *below right*) and other trade routes that passed within sight of the hilltop. Nekt's battle dress consisted of a grizzly bear skin lined with slate. His favorite weapon was a magical truncheon called Strike-Only-Once. To defend his hilltop fort, Nekt and his warriors secured huge logs to the fort's palisade. When the enemy closed in, the defenders cut the ropes allowing the logs to roll down the hillside and crush the attackers.

A Blackfoot artist's conception of a fur-trading fort, circa 1846

◆ A fur-trading empire is born

Médard Chouart des Groseilliers (1618–96) came to New France in the early 1640s and opened Lakes Michigan and Superior to the fur trade and Jesuit missionaries. His courage and his furs twice saved the colony from ruin, but its officials rewarded him with fines and seizure of his pelts. When he proposed a northern sea route for the fur trade—sailing to and from Hudson Bay—the same officials turned him down, preferring to tax furs brought down the Ottawa and St. Lawrence rivers to Montreal and Quebec.

Des Groseilliers and his brother-in-law Pierre-Esprit Radisson set about finding other backers, and found them in London. They sailed in June of 1668, des Groseilliers aboard the *Nonsuch*, Radisson on the *Eaglet*, which was battered by storms and sent limping back to shore. But *Nonsuch* sailed into Hudson Bay that September and one year later was back at its London moorings laden with furs. The northern route was not only navigable; it was eminently profitable. By May 1670, Charles II gave a royal charter to "the Governor and Company of Adventurers of England trading into Hudson's Bay," giving them a trade monopoly in the bay forever, the right to maintain a navy and to make war, and power of life and death over its subjects in Rupert's Land, a territory as large as Europe.

Médard Chouart des Groseilliers and Pierre-Esprit Radisson in a Radio-Canada TV series from the 1960s

◆ Mushrow Astrolabe

Early explorers relied on the stars to guide them through uncharted seas. Before the invention of the mirrored sextant in the 1700s (which measured longitude as well as latitude), many ships used the astrolabe, a navigational device of Arab origin. Holding the instrument at eye level, the user could sight the North Star, Polaris, through sight holes and read its altitude from the point where a slider, or *alidade*, crosses the scale.

On Nov. 26, 1981, scuba diver Wayne Mushrow, his brother Lloyd, and a friend, Michael Bennett, found a cache of artifacts near an ancient wreck off Newfoundland's Isle aux Morts. Amongst dishes, wooden bowls, a green vase, and five French coins dated 1638, was an astrolabe, dated 1628. The Mushrow Astrolabe (*above right*), as it came to be known, is especially rare in that it is in mint condition and is graduated for zenith, or overhead distance, only. While there are only 21 known sea astrolabes in the world, zenith-type astrolabes were typically Portuguese, and only three others have been recorded—the 1555 Dundee Astrolabe in Scotland, the 1609 Tenri (Madre de Desco) in Japan, and a 1675 astrolabe at Coimbra University in Portugal. The Mushrow Astrolabe can be seen at The Gulf Museum in Port aux Basques, Nfld., during the summer, and at the Newfoundland Museum of St. John's at all other times.

◆ Grease trails

Ancient trade routes known as "grease trails" in the Hazelton-Prince Rupert area of northwestern British Columbia were once followed by Bella Coola merchants trading the oil of the ooligan (*Thaleichthys pacificus*), also known as candlefish, small, smelt-like fish rich in fat. Their precious golden-colored fat was eaten, and used as medicine and lubricant for leather and tools.

◆ Frobisher found privateering to his taste

Before Sir Martin Frobisher (1539–94) was dispatched in the 1570s by London merchants to find the Northwest Passage, he preyed on French shipping in the English Channel under a privateering license from the English Crown. In 1576 he sailed into the bay which now bears his name and which he mistook for an entrance to the passage, and returned to London with black stone he mistakenly thought was gold ore. In 1577 and 1578, he abandoned his original quest to lead mining expeditions to the bay, returning to England with tons of ore that proved to be worthless pyrite. He resumed privateering in the South Atlantic, menacing Spanish merchant ships that were bringing gold from Panama.

◆ Baffin charted first longitude at sea

On his 1615–16 voyage aboard *Discovery* in search of the Northwest Passage, British explorer William Baffin (1584–1622) deduced the first longitude calculated at sea, by observing the eclipse of a star by the moon. His search ended when the *Discovery* entered the ice-choked Foxe Basin. Baffin also charted the east coast of Baffin Island, which is named for him, although Martin Frobisher had reached the island two years before Baffin was born.

◆ Round-trip passage

The second ship to sail the Northwest Passage was the RCMP schooner *St. Roch*, under Sgt. Henry Larsen. It sailed west to east in 1940–42, and east to west in 1944. It was the first to traverse the fabled passage both ways.

◆ The sea route to the Orient for which so many died

A trade route around North America to the riches of the Orient—one as far as possible from hostile Spanish ships—was the dream of many a London merchant in the late 1500s. Helped by Elizabeth I, they financed early searches for the Northwest Passage by explorers such as Martin Frobisher, Henry Hudson (1575–1611, whose crew mutinied and set him adrift in a boat never to be seen again), John Davis, and William Baffin.

Two hundred years later, with the Napoleonic wars at an end, Britain had men and ships to spare for the task, which was then assumed by the Royal Navy. In 1818, Capt. John Ross (1777–1856) repeated Baffin's voyage without success.

A year later, Lt. Edward Parry's (1790–1855) search got as far west as Melville Island, where his two ships were locked in ice for 10 months. Parry kept his crew healthy by feeding them a diet of lime juice, preserved fruits and soups, fresh bread, ship-brewed beer, and salads grown in boxes of earth over the heating pipes in his cabin.

To fight boredom, Parry kept his men busy—hunting, building a weather station, taking scientific readings. Every two weeks, the ships' officers staged a play. Crew members produced a newspaper, *The North Georgia Gazette and Winter Chronicle*. Parry himself wrote an operetta. But exploration in the short Arctic summer after they broke free of the ice failed to find the route they sought. Parry did manage to sail farther west than any previous expedition, and for this he received a 5,000-pound-sterling prize.

◆ Bernier won the High Arctic for Canada

Born on the high seas, Captain Joseph-Elzéar Bernier (1852–1934) was a ship's boy at 12, in charge of his own ship at 17, and during his life made some 260 crossings of the Atlantic. Because Canada had not explored or located many of its islands in the High Arctic, there was real danger that these might be claimed by the Americans, Norwegians, or Danes who were exploring and whaling in the region.

Bernier spent $21,000 of his own money lobbying the government, which finally sponsored four expeditions to the Arctic under Bernier's command. Between 1904 and 1911, he sailed four times to the Arctic, where he visited practically every island. On each he erected a cairn containing Canada's claim to the territory sealed in a bottle. By 1911, he had established Canada's claim to the entire region. A museum in Bernier's L'Islet-sur-Mer, Que., hometown honors the determined sailor who saved the High Arctic for Canada.

With private financing, Ross tried again in 1829, this time captaining *Victory*, the first steam-powered vessel used in the search. Two years later, the ice-locked ship was abandoned.

In 1845, it was Sir John Franklin's (1786–1847) turn. That year, he sailed from London with the best equipped expedition to date, including two ships manned by more than 130 men, and a three-year supply of food. "There is scarcely anything that would be of use that has been neglected," Franklin wrote. However, the Franklin expedition perished in the Arctic wastes amid particularly gruesome circumstances (*see page 63*). The remains of some 30 expedition members who trekked farther south were found in the 1850s in what is now Nunavut, at a place that has since been called Starvation Cove.

The elusive passage was finally discovered in 1852 by Commander Robert McClure (1807–1873), during one of scores of searches for Franklin and his men. McClure made his way from the Pacific to Banks Island, where he abandoned ship and walked across the ice to Melville Island. There he boarded another ship bound for the Atlantic.

In 1903–06, a ship finally sailed through the passage. The vessel was *Gjoa*; its captain Norwegian Roald Amundsen (1872–1928). Amundsen crossed the top of North America by sailing his ship down Peel Sound from Cornwallis Island, then passing east of King William Island through Rae and Simpson straits, and continuing on by way of Queen Maud, Coronation, and Amundsen gulfs to the Beaufort Sea.

◆ Samuel Hearne reached the northern ocean

In 1766, Hudson's Bay Company trader Samuel Hearne (1745–92) was assigned to lead a land expedition to the north to investigate native reports of a great river and large copper mines. His first two attempts ended ingloriously, but in 1770 he set off again from Fort Prince of Wales on Hudson Bay, led by Matonabbee, a Chipewyan chief. They followed the caribou migrations across The Barrens, then followed the Coppermine River to the Arctic Ocean. The fabled copper mine was a bust, but his account of this two-year expedition, *A Journey from Prince of Wales' Fort in Hudson's Bay to the Northern Ocean*, published three years after his death, left a dramatic record of his epic journey, and a vivid portrait of Matonabbee and his people.

◆ Bacchanalian revels at the Beaver Club

Although Montreal's original Beaver Club died with the last of the fur barons, many of their names live on in institutions such as Montreal's McGill University. The renowned university was founded on a 10,000-pound-sterling bequest by James McGill, one of 19 prosperous fur traders who formed the club in 1785. Members had to have survived at least one winter in the *pays d'en*

"Fortitude in Distress"

haut, as the Northwest was then known. Each received a gold medal engraved with the club's motto: "Fortitude in Distress."

The club's principal activities revolved around bacchanalian winter feasts at which guests ate roast beaver, pemmican, sturgeon, and wild rice, and club members drank toasts to the "Mother of all the Saints," the King, the fur trade, voyageurs, wives and children, and absent members. Sometimes they toasted as they sat on the floor, singing voyageur songs and paddling with walking sticks and pokers. Illustrious citizens, ships' captains, and army officers were granted honorary memberships.

◆ Henday's log

In the 1750s, former British smuggler Anthony Henday was hired by the Hudson's Bay Company to explore new territory. He traveled farther west than any European before him. Near present-day Red Deer, Alta., Henday met the Gros Ventres tribe. While courteous, the chief of the 200-lodge camp was unimpressed with Henday's sales pitch for his company, and Henday returned empty-handed. The journal he kept, however, is an important record of Aboriginal life at that time.

◆ Humphrey Gilbert had chutzpah to spare

What is now St. John's, Nfld., was a port of call for European fishermen long before Sir Humphrey Gilbert (1537–83) strode ashore in 1583 and claimed the land for England. In fact, fishing vessels from several European countries were at anchor in the bay when he arrived. A vain, tempestuous man, Gilbert was also among the first adventurers to put forward the idea of a Northwest Passage but he didn't live long enough to put his ideas to the test, or even to colonize the coast of North America, as he had been charged by Queen Elizabeth. He perished at sea a month after declaring his monarch's claim on Newfoundland.

◆ Sub-zero survival

In 1794, Peter Fidler, a Hudson's Bay company employee and one of the first weather observers in Canada, discovered some key temperatures crucial for sustaining life in the North—English brandy freezes solid at −32°C, rum at −31°C, and Holland gin at −17°C.

◆ A colony of Scottish crofters

In 1812, Thomas Douglas, Fifth Earl of Selkirk (1773–1820), established a colony of displaced Scottish crofters, or peasant farmers, on the Assiniboine and Red rivers, in what is now Manitoba. Selkirk acquired the 415,000 square kilometers of land from the Hudson's Bay Company, and called his settlement Assiniboia. Pitched to the Scots as an El Dorado of the West, Assiniboia is now downtown Winnipeg.

An HBC convoy of carts from the North arrives in Calgary in 1888, laden with furs valued at $75,000

◆ A rich mapping legacy

Hudson's Bay Company employee David Thompson (1770–1857) spent much of his life studying geography and the art of surveying. On fur-trading forays, he explored and mapped much of the western Plains and the Rockies. Frustrated by lack of recognition for his work, he left the company in 1797 and went to work for the Nor'Westers, for whom he established trading posts in what is now British Columbia, Washington, Idaho, and Montana. In 1811 he forded the Columbia River, which he followed to its mouth, thus extending the Nor'West domain from Montreal to the Pacific. On retirement from the fur trade, he completed one of his greatest mapping achievements: *The Northwest Territory of the Province of Canada*. It illustrates the posts and canoe routes by which the Nor'Westers conquered the continent from Fort Williams in the east to the Pacific.

Hudson's Bay Company gear used by David Thompson

◆ Northern numismatics

Before metal and brass tokens came into use, locally produced tokens of ivory, bone, and wood were used at Hudson's Bay Company posts. Tokens valued at 1, ¹/₂ and ¹/₈ "made beaver" (*see page 68*) were introduced in the late 1800s. Later, coins would be issued in denominations of dollars and cents (*right*).

◆ Peter Pond was dogged by murder charges

A quarrelsome man of little education, fur trader Peter Pond (1740–1807) had great confidence and an inquiring mind that served him well in his western explorations for the North West Company. Based on his own travels and native reports, he laboriously drew crude maps of the Northwest, having to thaw frozen ink for his outlines. In March of 1782, he was implicated and acquitted in the murder of a competitor. Pond drew more suspicion in the winter of 1786–87, when another of his rivals was shot and killed during a confrontation. While the killer's identity was never established, this incident effectively ended Pond's career. Replaced by a young Alexander Mackenzie, he left the company under a cloud in 1788.

hardship and defeat

◆ Battle of Fish Creek

A cairn on the Poundmaker Reserve north of Fish Creek, Sask., marks where, during the Northwest Rebellion of 1885, Crees led by Chief Poundmaker, armed only with a whip, repulsed more than 300 soldiers and policemen who were forced to withdraw east to Battleford. Poundmaker refused to let his warriors ambush the retreating force. The old battleground is now the Battle of Fish Creek National Historic Site.

◆ Out of the frying pan...

In 1604, the French founded Acadia on an island in Passamaquoddy Bay. After a winter of hardship, the settlers moved across the Bay of Fundy to southern Nova Scotia and built a fort, Port Royal, near the mouth of the Annapolis River. However, in 1613, English colonists from Virginia torched the settlement. Eight years later, James I of England granted Acadia to Sir William Alexander, setting a chain of events in motion that would lead to the expulsion of the Acadians in 1755.

Average life expectancy in 1843: 33

◆ Métis' last stand

On March 18, 1884, Métis leader Louis Riel rode into Batoche, Sask., occupied the Church of Saint-Antoine-de-Padoue, and from its pulpit proclaimed a provisional government of the Métis nation. Métis frustration and discontent had been rife for some time (*see page 69*). The buffalo on which they relied for food, clothing, and shelter were disappearing; the Métis freighting business was declining; settlers from Ontario were flooding into Métis country; and when a land survey created near panic in the community, Ottawa refused to grant land rights to the Métis.

The result was the armed resistance and bloodshed of the Northwest Rebellion, the last major battle of which was fought at Batoche between May 9 and 12, 1885. Riel was tried for treason and hanged in Regina on Nov. 16, 1885. A white wooden church, its bullet-pocked rectory, and rifle pits are all that remain of the Métis nation's headquarters. Today they are the centerpiece of Batoche National Historic Site, and a reminder that the stand made there finally won the Métis some land rights, and the acknowledgment that they were a distinct people.

◆ Canada's dark satanic mills

A Canadian Royal Commission on Child Labour in 1843 was a horrific indictment of squalid conditions in factories and mines in Canada. Millions of children, some as young as six, were forced to work 12 hours a day, often being whipped or beaten. Thousands were maimed by unsafe machinery, and hundreds were killed on the job. "Boys under 12 work all night in the glassworks in Montreal," stated the report. "In the coal mines of Nova Scotia, it is common for 10-year-old boys to work a 60-hour week down in the pits." Their average life expectancy was 33.

As late as 1910 in Canada, more than 300,000 children under 12 were still being subjected to these barbaric conditions. It wasn't until the 1920s that child labor in this country was outlawed.

"The Capture of Batoche,"
a lithograph from
Canadian Pictorial and
Illustrated War News, *1885*

◆ Cholera and typhus claimed thousands on Grosse Île

In 1832, Grosse Île, a lush green island in the St. Lawrence Estuary, 46 kilometers downstream from Quebec City, became a quarantine area in an effort to stem the tide of cholera among European immigrants, most of them Irish. Many of those who fled hardship and misery at home developed cholera on board ship and died by the thousands at sea or upon arriving in the New World.

Typhus was the killer after 1847, when millions of Irish died in the famine created when blight destroyed their mainstay crop, potatoes. Some 78,700 Irish men, women, and children sailed for Canada that year. As many as 8,000 were buried at sea during the appalling 6- to 12-week voyages. Another 9,000 were either dead on arrival at Grosse Île, or died on the island. Of ships diverted to Montreal, thousands more died.

Many doctors and French-Canadian nuns and priests who tended to the sick also died. French-Canadian families adopted scores of orphaned Irish children and let them keep their given names in memory of their deceased parents. The buildings that once served as hotels, hostels, hospitals, and Catholic and Anglican chapels, still echo with the suffering, courage, and selflessness that coexisted in that secluded sea of horrors.

Grosse Île ceased to be a quarantine station in 1937. It was off limits for several years during which it was used by Agriculture Canada as a veterinary pathology research outpost. In 1984, it was recognized as a national historic site, and 12 years later it was named Grosse Île and the Irish Memorial National Historic Site. A majestic stone Celtic cross honors the thousands of Irish immigrants who passed through a quarantine station there, and the some 36,000 who are buried on the island (*above*).

love   marriage   dowry   alliance   wedding   duty

wedding   alliance   dowry   marriage   love

Champlain

Unhappy in marriage...

◆ Champlain's child bride left her dowry and took the veil

As governor of New France, the great cartographer and explorer Samuel de Champlain (*c.* 1567–1635) shrewdly built a vast trade network he developed through alliances with various native tribes. "Our sons shall wed your daughters," he often told his native allies, "and henceforth, we shall be one people."

Yet Champlain needed money more than offspring to finance the settlement of New France. He was in his early forties in 1610 when he married 12-year-old Hélène Boullé, daughter of a wealthy secretary to Louis XIII. The marriage contract stipulated that Champlain would get a much needed dowry, but that Hélène would remain in a convent until she was at least 14 years of age.

Hélène was 22 before she finally sailed for Quebec. But after four years, she realized her heart lay elsewhere and returned to France, never to return. There had been no children from their marriage, and after her departure, Champlain adopted three native daughters he named Faith, Hope, and Charity. In 1645, 10 years after the death of her husband, Hélène realized her dream: she took the veil under the name of Hélène de Saint-Augustin. She bequeathed all her money to the Ursulines of Paris to build a new convent at Meaux, where she lived the rest of her days.

widow family money alliance children union

widow   family   money   alliance   children   union

love marriage dowry alliance wedding

◆ Franklin's wife spent fortune seeking lost husband

Arctic explorer Sir John Franklin (1786–1847), who died searching for the Northwest Passage, was the subject of 39 naval and private searches conducted over a period of 13 years. On July 26, 1845, a whaling captain saw Franklin's last expedition, the two ships *Erebus* and *Terror*, off the Baffin Island coast. Aboard were 129 officers and men—many like Franklin himself seasoned Arctic explorers—some 2,000 books, and a three-year supply of tobacco, rum, clothing, and food. It was the last time anyone saw them alive. Some scientists suspect the poisonous lead sealing some 8,000 canned goods was a factor in the expedition's failure.

Unlucky in love...

When Franklin failed to return, his wife, Lady Jane Franklin (1791–1875) petitioned the governments of Britain, France, the United States, and Russia to send expeditions to the Arctic to look for his ships. She spent most of her own fortune, even selling her house, to finance search parties. Finally, in 1859, a written record was unearthed showing Franklin had died in 1847.

Other evidence at that time hinted at cannibalism among his followers, something the British Admiralty and public refused to believe. Subsequent expeditions, however, found further evidence that this had in fact occurred, as the desperate men attempted to escape overland from ships that were icelocked for two years.

duty wedding alliance dowry marriage love

◆ Assembly of First Nations

Long before Europeans crossed the Atlantic, North America's indigenous population lived, hunted, trapped, and farmed their ancestral lands. With their unique heritage, culture, languages, and spiritual beliefs, First Nations peoples, today's descendants of these original inhabitants, were excluded from taking part in any Constitutional developments in Canada until the 1980s. In fact, it was once common for First Nations leaders to be jailed by the RCMP for organizing any form of political group.

In 1969, the National Indian Brotherhood successfully lobbied Parliament and the Canadian public to defeat a federal Liberal White Paper calling for the assimilation of all First Nations peoples into the mainstream of Canadian society. Yet organizing all the various First Nations groups across Canada into a single, cohesive lobby group proved difficult, and was only resolved in 1980, after the "Constitutional Express" arrived in Ottawa (*see page 69*) and 300

The sun spirit is a central motif in many native cultures, as shown in this Bella Coola mask

a first nations abecedary

First Nations Chiefs went to London, England, in an attempt to halt the repatriation of the Canadian Constitution.

Two years later, the Assembly of First Nations was born, with Saskatchewan Cree Dr. David Ahenakew elected the first National Chief. Ahenakew attended four First Ministers' Conferences on Aboriginal Rights in Ottawa between 1983 and 1987, marking the first time that Aboriginal leaders were represented in Constitutional talks that directly affected their people.

◆ Bella Coolas: The Nuxalk Nation

Now known as the Nuxalk Nation, the Bella Coolas were the first coastal natives to greet Alexander Mackenzie when he emerged from the interior on British Columbia's northwest coast in July 1793. Several days earlier, they had been visited by Capt. George Vancouver of the HMS *Discovery*,

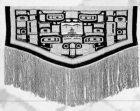

Chilkat blanket

on a mapping expedition in the area. Despite the influence of the Europeans and the Hudson's Bay Company, which set up a post at the village of Qomq'-ts (near present-day Bella Coola) in 1869, the Nuxalk retained their complex ceremonial traditions.

◆ The Beothuk genocide

Until a proclamation was passed in 1769, it was not a crime to murder a Beothuk, the Aboriginal hunters and fishermen of Newfoundland. In fact, hunting the descendants of the Maritime Archaic Indians (*see page 50*) was both popular and profitable: If an entire village could be wiped out, the hunters could confiscate their valuable furs and caribou hides. The killing went on, however, as settlers considered them a nuisance. The last Beothuk, Shanawdithit, died in 1829. A doeskin coat she made shortly before her death is in the Newfoundland Museum at St. John's.

◆ Big Bear

Small of stature and an expert Cree horseman, Big Bear (*c.* 1825–88) was the first major native chief who refused to sign a treaty with the Canadian government. Even when other chiefs signed Treaty No. 6 in 1876, Big Bear was convinced the terms were stacked against his people and feared the negotiators were lying. By refusing to sign, he became a rallying point for thousands of Aboriginal people who wanted control of their lands and for those who had signed treaty documents, but now wanted more advantageous terms.

Yet in a stunning reversal, on Dec. 8, 1882, his people near death, Big Bear entered Fort Walsh in the Cypress Hills and put his mark to Treaty No. 8. Later, he and other Cree chiefs, notably Poundmaker (1842–86), attempted to consolidate their reserves under one Cree jurisdiction. The move did not please the Indian Department, which used events surrounding the Northwest Rebellion to arrest Big Bear. Convicted of treason, he spent two years in Stony Mountain Penitentiary. Imprisonment destroyed his health and spirit, and he died shortly after his release.

◆ Joseph Brant: A prince among his people

A hereditary chief of the Mohawks, Thayendanegea or Joseph Brant (1742–1807) grew up in what is now New York State, where he was educated in a private school. He sided with the British during the Seven Years War, and again in the American Revolution. As a result, his followers lost their land and animals, and in 1783 Brant led them to Canada. They were granted land on the Bay of Quinte and along the Grand River in what is now Ontario. On a later trip to England to seek compensation for his people, Brant refused to kiss the hand of George III: "I bow to no man for I am considered a prince among my own people. But I will gladly shake your hand." The king acceded to his request nonetheless and in 1798, Brant was granted over 1,350 hectares at what is now Burlington, Ont.

◆ Chilkat blankets

Woven from mountain goat wool onto a frame of cedar bark string, Chilkat blankets of black, white, yellow, and blue were the specialty of the Tlingit tribe of northern British Columbia. Tlingit men hunted the goat, made the frame, and painted the design —typically a killer whale flanked by ravens—from which the women wove the blankets.

◆ Crowfoot: "The flash of the firefly"

Blackfoot Chief Crowfoot (1830–90) was as famed a warrior—he survived battle 19 times—as he was a skilled diplomat. Grateful to the Northwest Mounted Police for ousting the whisky traders who were exploiting his people, he used his considerable influence to bring about Treaty No. 7 in 1877, in which the Blackfoot surrendered most of southern Alberta. The Rev. Albert Lacombe (*see page 106*), whom Crowfoot once rescued from a band of hostile Cree, was with the great chief when he died at Blackfoot Crossing, near present-day Calgary, in 1890. He transmitted Crowfoot's last words to the Blackfoot. "A little while and Crowfoot will be gone from among you. What is life? It is as the flash of a firefly in the night. It is as the breath of a buffalo in the wintertime. It is as the little shadow that runs across the grass and loses itself in the sunset."

◆ Dorset Culture

From 2000–500 B.C., groups of hunter-gatherers crossed into Arctic Canada via the Bering Strait. These people are considered to be some of the earliest inhabitants of Arctic North America and ancestors of the Dorset. They lived primarily by hunting sea mammals, used dogsleds and kayaks, built homes out of snow and turf, and heated them with soapstone lamps. Because their tools— made from chalcedony and soapstone—had tiny cutting edges, archeologists often refer to the Pre-Dorset Culture as the Arctic Small Tool Tradition. Around 500 B.C., the Pre-Dorsets moved down the Labrador coast and became known as the Dorset Culture, and occupied Newfoundland for about 1,000 years.

◆ Mary "Two-Axe" Earley

Born in Kahnawake, near Montreal, Mary "Two-Axe" Earley (1912–96) lost her Indian status when she married a non-native. Undeterred, she launched a determined battle for restoration of her native rights. As a result of her efforts, Canada passed Bill C-31 in 1985, and Mary Earley became the first Aboriginal woman to have her native rights reinstated.

◆ False Face Society

Curing and the restoration of health and well-being to the individual and the community was intrinsic to the religious practices of many Aboriginal peoples and often practiced by group activity during tribal ceremonies. The best known of several curing groups among the Iroquois was the False Face Society, who carved masks on living trees. The masks would then be cut free, and used in a ritual ceremony, to scare away the spirits that caused depression or disease in a patient. After recovery, the patient could, in turn, be "spiritually called" to join the False Face Society.

Mary "Two-Axe" Earley

◆ James Gladstone: Our first native senator

The betterment of Canada's Aboriginal peoples was a lifelong passion of James Gladstone (1887–1971), a Blood Indian who was a chief scout and interpreter for the RCMP before becoming Canada's first native senator in 1958. Noted for his progressive ideas about farming, Gladstone introduced the first tractor to the Alberta Blood native reserve he grew up on, encouraging fellow natives to take up modern farming techniques.

◆ Great Turtle Islanders

Ontario Mohawk journalist and writer Brian Maracle (author of 1996's *Back on the Rez: Finding the Way Home*) suggests "Great Turtle Islanders" might be an

Ceremonial potlatches were the focus of Haida life, and their long tradition of elaborately carved totem poles, masks, war canoes, and cedar boxes continues to find contemporary expression in the intricate, colorful designs of Northwest Coast Indian art.

◆ Handsome Lake's religion

Ganeodiyo, or Handsome Lake—a name the Seneca also applied to Lake Ontario—was a respected Seneca chief who suffered a lengthy bout of alcoholism and despair before undergoing a near-death experience in 1799. Recovered, he told of seeing three angels in Iroquois regalia who had taken him on a spirit journey. They told him the Creator wanted the Iroquois people to renounce liquor and dedicate themselves to spiritual renewal.

The world is an island borne on a turtle's back

appropriate way for non-native people to refer to Canada's Aboriginal peoples. In a 1996 interview, Maracle suggested this term is preferable to "Indian," or more recent, politically correct terms such as First Nations peoples or Aboriginal peoples. Maracle's idea comes from the Iroquois explanation of the world being an island borne on a turtle's back. The Iroquois trace the beginning of human life to a time when Skywoman fell to an island created by a giant turtle, which grew into North America. There Skywoman had a daughter and so began the human race.

Haida crest, 1820

◆ Haida artistic tradition dates from antiquity

For some 8,000 years the Haida have lived in the Queen Charlotte Islands, where sea otter pelts formed the basis of a lucrative trade with China that continued into the mid-1800s. Each Haida village was an independent entity, and each family was independent of the others. All Haida belonged to one of two clans, the Eagle and the Raven, and a Haida always married a member of the opposite clan.

From then until his death in 1815, Handsome Lake traveled from reserve to reserve preaching temperance, frugality, non-violence, and family and clan values. The symbol of this movement was the Iroquois longhouse, and in time it became known as the Longhouse religion.

◆ Head-Smashed-In Buffalo Jump

Native storytellers at this Porcupine Hills archeological site in southwest Alberta describe how their Blackfoot and Crow forefathers hunted buffalo, goading them into jumping over a cliff to their deaths. Head-Smashed-In Buffalo Jump, in use until the 1870s, was used as a buffalo trap for some 5,000 years. On the nearby campsite, women quartered and "flaked" the fresh meat, slicing very thin slips which they dried on poles. Some of the dried meat was then ground with granite pestles, blended with dried berries and buffalo tallow, and tightly packed into rawhide containers for later consumption during the winter months.

◆ Indian treaties: Share, yes; surrender, no

In 1871, the Canadian government began negotiating a series of agreements with the First Nations of western and northern Canada. The "numbered" treaties—which began with Treaty No. 1 in 1871 and ended with Treaty No. 11 in 1921—covered most of the Prairie provinces, northern Ontario, and parts of British Columbia, the Yukon, and the Northwest Territories, and resulted in ornate documents written in English, even though some of the participating groups did not speak that language. Many of the issues discussed during negotiation never found their way into the treaties. As well, natives believed the treaties were sacred pacts, in which they were promising to share their land and resources with the newcomers; as far as the English negotiators were concerned, the natives were surrendering title to their lands.

◆ Inuit never said goodbye

War was unknown among the Inuit, who did not even have a word for "Chief"; the power to accept or reject an act or a person was exercised by the community collectively. Nor were there any "bad" hunters; just "unlucky" ones. When luck ran out, the unlucky died. They had numerous words for "Welcome," but not one to say "Goodbye."

In a land where weather conditions often can determine who lives and who dies, it is perhaps understandable that their most precise terminology deals with descriptions of snow conditions, with over 100 words for snow. Some examples from the Inuktitut language of the eastern Arctic:

Aniu: snow for making water.

Apigianngaut: the first autumn snowfall.

Aput: snow on the ground.

Katakartanaq: encrusted snow that gives way underfoot.

Mannsguq: melting snow.

Natiruvaaq: fine, drifting snow.

Qannik: snowflakes.

Qiqumaaq: snow with a frozen surface.

◆ Pauline Johnson gave voice to Mohawk spirit

With poems such as "The Song My Paddle Sings" and "The Cattle Thief," Emily Pauline Johnson (1861–1913), daughter of an Englishwoman and a Mohawk chief, celebrated the heritage of her father's people. Acclaimed by critics, she was much in demand in Britain and North America as a speaker and performer. She crisscrossed Canada reciting her poetry for her fans in remote settlements. In 1895, she gave a recital at Buckingham Palace for Queen Victoria.

Pauline Johnson

◆ Kabloona, Kabloonamuit

Kabloona (meaning non-Inuit) is the Inuit name for non-Inuit missionaries, teachers, police, civil servants, and their spouses living temporarily in Arctic communities. *Kabloonamuit* ("people of the white man") is how the Inuit describe their own people who adopt non-Inuit customs and ways, such as preferring manufactured food and clothing to home-made goods.

◆ Kaianere'ko:wa: The world's oldest constitution

The *Kaianere'ko:wa* (The Great Law of Peace), formed about 1390 by the Iroquois Confederacy, is the oldest constitution still in use in the world. While versions of the Kaianere'ko:wa have been reduced to written form, the Iroquois maintain that it is a law best learned through oral teachings.

◆ Lily of the Mohawks

A shrine at Kahnawake, near Montreal, honors Kateri Tekakwitha (1656–80), "the lily of the Mohawks," and the first North American Aboriginal candidate for sainthood. Converted to Catholicism by Jesuit missionaries, Kateri was baptized on Easter Sunday, 1676. Her life was devoted to teaching prayers to children and helping the sick and aged. Disfigured by smallpox as a child, it was said that the scars vanished when she died. She was beatified by Pope John Paul II in 1980.

Inuit soapstone walrus

◆ Kwakwaka'wakw relics reclaimed—45 years later

Coastal British Columbia is the ancient home of the Kwakwaka'wakw (once known as the Kwakiutl), who traditionally spent their summers fishing and hunting, then returned to their winter villages for several months of artistic and cultural activity. The potlatch that was the heart of their ceremonial life was declared illegal in 1884 (*see page 71*), and when they defied the law in 1921, some band members were imprisoned and several ceremonial masks and other religious objects were confiscated. It took the Kwakwaka'wakw 45 years to regain their relics. In 1967 the National Museum of Canada returned the part of the collection that had been previously held by the National Museum of Man.

Kwakwaka'wakw frontlet mask, 19th century

◆ The longhouse and the fireside

The family unit in Iroquois life was the "fireside," which consisted of a mother and her children. Related firesides lived together in sturdy wooden longhouses covered in elm bark, some up to 125 meters in length. A dozen or more families might share a single longhouse, living in separate areas on either side of a central aisle, and sharing a central hearth with the family opposite. (The Iroquois characterized their famed confederacy as a longhouse of five fires; *see page 72*.) Firewood was stacked at both entrances. Above each longhouse door was the clan symbol of the inhabitants. As the Iroquois were a matriarchal society, the longhouse was typically ruled by women.

A longhouse interior showing the living quarters of two Iroquois families

◆ "Made beaver"

"Made beavers" were the fur trade's units of exchange, tokens pegged to the value of a prime-quality adult male beaver pelt. Three marten skins, for example, equaled one made beaver. For decades, these tokens were the unit of currency in the fur trade, after a variety of makeshift currencies—porcupine quills, musket balls, ivory discs—had come and gone. They were designed in 1854 by George Simpson McTavish of Albany Fort. There were also smaller coins representing one-half, one-quarter, and one-eighth made beaver.

◆ Manitou: A spiritual force

Supernatural spirits or forces of the universe were part of the belief systems of many Aboriginal peoples. Virtually everything, plants, animals, even abstract things such as colors and seasons of the

A vision of a wolf

year, had spiritual counterparts. The Algonquians referred to these forces as manitous and believed they wielded a powerful influence over human events. Manitous were said to visit shamans in prophetic dreams and visions and they were invoked in ceremonies conducted to cure disease.

◆ George Manuel: "Canada's greatest prophet"

The widely respected, self-educated Shuswap Indian George Manuel (1921–89) referred to indigenous people worldwide, Canada's Aboriginal peoples among them, as the Fourth World. Manuel maintained that while Third World values were recognized throughout the world, Aboriginal values and traditions were seldom even acknowledged. Known abroad as "Canada's greatest prophet," Manuel became head of the National Indian Brotherhood in 1970 and transformed native politics from a state of voluntary activism into a well-informed forum capable of asserting and insisting on native rights. One of Manuel's strategies would forever change the state of native politics in Canada: In 1980, with other chiefs, he organized a cross-Canada train to alert native communities to the dangers inherent in the patriation of the Constitution. After "the Constitutional Express" arrived in Ottawa, the Assembly of First Nations (*see page 64*) was forged.

◆ Medicine bundles and vision quests

At puberty, most native boys set out on vision quests, a wilderness retreat during which they hoped to receive guidance from the spirit world. An initiate would undergo a purifying sweat in a bowl-shaped bath enclosed by buffalo hides, steam-heated with hot rocks splashed in water. He would then spend four days alone fasting, praying to the spirit world for guidance and an empowering vision. A vision of

consistent pattern in terms of orientation or length. Some believed them to be burial lodges, others think they were astronomical calendars set up so that important ceremonies could be timed properly: not only are there 28 days in a lunar month, but on the morning of the summer solstice, the rising sun links a stone at the center of some medicine wheels with one on its outer circle.

◆ Métis: A distinct society

In the early 18th century, marriages between Aboriginal women, mostly Cree, and European men, mostly French fur traders, gave rise to a people that was neither European nor Aboriginal, but a distinct blend of both. In time, they became the Métis nation, a culture that mixed French and Ojibwa, Scottish jigs and powwow dances. At first the Métis were centered around the Great Lakes, but following the 1763 Treaty of Paris, they moved northwest.

Métis smoked-deerskin doll

meant a young warrior had the gift of wisdom

wolves, for example, would be a sign the young warrior may have the gift of wisdom, an elk might be a sign of a harmonious family life.

On his return to camp, he would undergo another purifying bath, after which the elders would help him assemble the objects his spirit guide had told him to collect. These were known as his medicine bundle. They were wrapped in skin, to be unwrapped before any momentous undertaking so that the warrior could benefit from their protection. They were among a warrior's dearest possessions. Many tribes also had collective medicine bundles, which they opened during religious gatherings in spring and fall.

◆ Medicine wheels

There is no single explanation for the large spoked circles of stone known as medicine wheels found today across Alberta and Saskatchewan. Most are identical in design, 28 stone spokes radiating from a central point to an outer stone circle, with no

Furious with the Canadian government over what they believed were violations of their land rights, even after negotiations under leader Louis Riel (1844–85) established the new province of Manitoba in 1870, the Métis rose up in armed revolt. The Northwest Rebellion of 1885 and the defining Battle of Batoche (*see page 60*) were ruthlessly dealt with by the Dominion government, and the events drew attention to the plight of the Métis.

◆ Mukluks

The watertight boot known as the mukluk was designed by the Inuit for walking on the tundra. Traditional mukluks were soled with sealskin, which had been stripped of all hair, stretched and dried, then chewed to be pliable. The soles were attached to the caribou-skin uppers with sinew thread, with stitches passing only halfway through the skin to ensure watertightness. Several pairs were often worn simultaneously in the severest weather.

Mukluk

◆ Nisga'a reclaim their dignity

Drumming and chanting swelled triumphantly across the Nass River Valley on a July day in 1998 as federal and British Columbian ministers and Nisga'a leaders signed Canada's first Aboriginal treaty of the modern era in New Aiyanish, B.C. Some 111 years had passed since the Nisga'a's first treaty proposal had been scorned by the leaders of the day.

Under terms of the treaty, the Nisga'a received 2,000 square kilometers of land near the B.C.-Alaska border; a $190 million cash payment in compensation for releasing the rest of their traditional territory; self-governing powers with control in areas of health, education, social services, policing, and courts; return of Nisga'a artifacts held by the Royal British Columbia Museum and the Museum of Civilization; control of all resources on their lands; and the right to collect taxes. "We are no longer beggars in our own land," a Nisga'a chief told the gathering. "We now go ahead with dignity."

◆ Nuu-chah-nulth: The whaling experts

The Nuu-chah-nulth, long-known as the Nootka, were among dozens of tribal groups who enjoyed the Northwest Coast's bounty of sea and forest, fishing, feasting, and vying among themselves for power and prestige. The Nuu-chah-nulth, whose history on Vancouver Island dates back 5,000 years were renowned for their carving, crafts, and seamanship and ventured far into the ocean to harpoon their ultimate prey, the whale. They were the only Canadian native tribe to specialize in whaling and, within the tribe, the captains of their fine cedar whaling canoes held the highest prestige.

◆ Ojibwa: Medicine men who were fleet of foot

The Ojibwa (Anishinabe or "original people" to themselves) inhabited the entire Great Lakes region, and were centered at Bawating, what is now Sault Ste. Marie, Ont. The Ojibwa lived by hunting, fishing, and gathering, and traveled by birchbark canoe in summer, snowshoes in winter. Each village was an independent community with leaders selected by a council of elders. Leaders were chosen for merit from those who had proven ability in hunting and warfare, courage, stamina, oratory, and generosity. Ball games and running competitions of peacetime trained young men in methods of attack and rapid retreat needed for times of war.

Religion permeated daily life and every young man spent time praying and fasting in seclusion in quest of a guardian spirit. In the early 1700s, the Ojibwa developed an institution called the Grand Medicine Society or Midewiwin. Overseen by an organized priesthood, the Midewiwin promoted herbal medicine and advocated balance in all aspects of life.

◆ Oka crisis

In July of 1990, Kanesatake Mohawks set up barricades in an attempt to block expansion by Oka Town Council of a golf course onto ancestral burial grounds. When 100 policemen stormed the barricade, one Quebec Provincial Police officer was shot and killed. Thirty kilometers to the south, natives on the Kahnawake Reserve blocked two major highways leading into Montreal in protest, and over 100 native chiefs came from across Canada to negotiate. An armed standoff under the glare of the media continued for 78 days, ending only after intervention by 4,400 Canadian armed forces.

◆ Oneida gave us lacrosse

The Oneida dwelt in what is now Upper New York State in a single village near Oneida Lake. They were the smallest of the five nations of the Iroquois Confederacy (*see page 72*). Their town was burned by the French in 1696. Unlike most of their Confederacy brethren, the Oneida sided with the rebel cause in the American Revolution, largely because of the influence of New England missionary Samuel Kirkland. The Oneida also popularized an ancient Iroquois game of stickball, *ga-lahs*, known today as lacrosse. (*See also page 195*)

Standoff during the Oka crisis, 1990

◆ Onondaga: Keepers of the wampum records

Their position at the geographic center of the Iroquois Confederacy (*see page 72*) made the Onondaga "firekeepers" of the league on which they served as moderators at council, and keepers of the wampum records. *Thadodaho*, the most celebrated title among the 50 Confederacy chiefs, was always held by an Onondaga. The main Onondaga town served as "capital" of the Confederacy and as a hub of frontier diplomacy for 200 years.

◆ Pontiac: Victim of early germ warfare

If the Indians do not behave properly, they are to be punished, Britain's governor-general Lord Jeffrey Amherst (1717–97) ordered when he arrived in North America shortly after the 1763 Treaty of Paris. As the treaty granted most lands east of the Mississippi to England, many natives feared this would result in a surge of settlers onto their lands.

An Ottawa chief and powerful orator by the name of Pontiac (1720–69), however, had other ideas. He raised a multi-tribal force to rout the British by sending messengers to each tribe with a red-stained tomahawk and a wampum war belt. He made his move in May 1763, laying siege to the British garrison at Detroit. Within weeks several British forts had fallen to his followers. In July, acting on orders from Lord Amherst, the besieged commander of Fort Pitt on the Ohio River called for a truce. As a mark of his good faith, he presented the peace negotiators with blankets. Unbeknownst to the natives, the blankets had been infected with smallpox, which spread like wildfire through native villages in the region.

The rebellion collapsed, and Pontiac signed various peace treaties with the British in 1765. His uprising had sent shockwaves through Britain, however. Amherst was recalled and his successor set about making alliances with native peoples, as the French had done for decades.

◆ Potlatch marked joys and sorrows

Salmon fishing was the basis of a rich, affluent native culture that flourished for centuries along Canada's Northwest Coast. A few weeks' salmon fishing provided food for the year, leaving plenty of time for the elaborate potlatch ceremonies with which they marked marriages and mourning, comings of age, and chiefs' investitures. The word potlatch comes from Chinook argot, and means "to give." A really big potlatch took years of preparation and involved several days of feasting, spirit dances, theatrical presentations, and distribution of gifts.

Missionaries and government agents were frustrated at their lack of control over the mercantile and cultural aspects of these ceremonies, and condemned the potlatch. Between 1884 and 1951, potlatches were prohibited by the Indian Act, driving traditions and sacred knowledge underground. The Kwakwaka'wakw (*see page 68*) named this time "when our world became dark."

Potlatch dancer in ceremonial regalia, Alert Bay, B.C.

◆ "Sacred Feathers"

Methodism found many converts among native peoples in part because some of the most notable missionaries were themselves Aboriginals. After he was "born again" at a Methodist camp meeting in 1823,

Anishinabe: The original people

Rev. Peter Jones (1802–52, also known as Kahkewaquonaby, or "Sacred Feathers"), the son of a Mississauga woman and a Euro-Canadian land surveyor, translated the first Ojibwa version of the Bible and began preaching the gospel to his mother's people in their native tongue. The message of salvation reached the Mississauga people of what is now southern Ontario at a time when hunting, fishing, and the fur trade were declining and so no longer supporting the traditional ways of life. As a result the new message of hope spread like wildfire.

◆ Shamans: The holy ones

In Aboriginal societies, a shaman was a holy man or woman who had been initiated into trances and other altered states of consciousness, and thus possessed spiritual and mystical powers. In some tribes, people who had been struck by lightning and survived often became shamans, because they were thought to have received the power of the Thunderbird, a supernatural creature in some Indian myths who controls thunder and lightning. Shamanism, the belief system of various Aboriginal peoples, holds that good and evil spirits occupy the earth and can be summoned by a priest.

Tsimshian shaman mask

◆ Sitting Bull: North America's most renowned chief

In the decade after the Battle of the Little Big Horn (1876) in Montana, in which Aboriginal warriors annihilated Gen. George Custer and the Seventh U.S. Cavalry, Sioux chief Sitting Bull (c.1834–90)

◆ Six Nations strong

In the late 1300s, Deganawidah, a Huron holy man, and Hiawatha, a powerful Mohawk orator who had lost all his daughters to tribal strife, traveled Iroquois country forging alliances among warring groups and spreading the gospel of peace among the Seneca, Oneida, Onondaga, Cayuga, and Mohawk. The five nations agreed to an accord in 1575, forging the Iroquois Confederacy.

Matters of mutual importance such as peace and war were debated by a Grand Council which met periodically on a hilltop at Onondaga, near present-day Syracuse, N.Y. (*see page 71*). Each tribe had one vote, and decisions were always unanimous. They called themselves the People of the Longhouse, and they constituted the single most powerful confederation in recorded history of native North Americans.

The Tuscaroras joined the league in the early 1700s, after which it became known as the Six Nations. Then-journalist Benjamin Franklin studied the Iroquois system of government and his proposal

Women natives built and owned tepees, not men

was the most renowned and feared Aboriginal chief in North America. For four of those years, Sitting Bull and hundreds of his followers lived in Saskatchewan to elude American vengeance for Little Big Horn.

Fearing his presence here would incite intertribal warfare, the Canadian government refused his request for reserve lands and for food. In 1881, his people starving, Sitting Bull and some 200 followers crossed back into the United States where they surrendered to the U.S. Army. He was sentenced to two years in jail, during which time much of his tribe's lands were seized or divided up. In 1884 Sitting Bull made a U.S.-government-sponsored tour of 15 cities. A year later he began touring with Buffalo Bill Cody's Wild West Show. Cody and Sitting Bull became friends and when Sitting Bull was shot by U.S. soldiers in 1890, Cody continued to keep his memory in the public mind by displaying his "death cabin."

Sun Dance

for joining the 13 colonies into a confederacy that became the United States borrowed many of the principles of checks and balances of the Six Nations.

◆ Sun Dance

By the mid-1700s, some variation of the four-day religious festival variously known as the Sun Dance, the Thirst Dance, and the Mystery Dance was being celebrated by practically every tribe on the Canadian prairie. Ceremonies were conducted in a specially built lodge, where spectators joined the tribe's drummers, singers and dancers in a common quest for renewal. Participants hoped this would come about through a communal vision, similar to that experienced by warriors who undertook individual vision quests (*see page 69*). In some Sun Dances, participants underwent self-mutilation, piercing themselves with skewers, attaching themselves to a pole with ropes, and dancing until their skin tore free, in the hopes of one day receiving good fortune.

◆ Sunday's powerful oratory

Rev. John Sunday (1795–1875) or Shah-wun-dais ("sultry heat"), a Methodist minister, Ojibwa chief in the Belleville region of Ontario, and veteran of the War of 1812, was one of several Aboriginal clergymen of his day whose oratory packed churches throughout the United States. Of one sermon in a New York church in 1828, a member of the congregation observed that the event was "never to be forgotten."

◆ Project Surname

It wasn't until 1968 that the federal government began recording the full names of Inuit Canadians. Until that time, Inuit had been listed by number only. A typical Innu name like E6-211 (E stood for east and W stood for west), was stamped on a small disc worn about the neck. The change came about as a result of Project Surname, an Aboriginal initiative led by Inuk elder and community activist Abe Okpik (1929–97), who visited every Inuit home and asked families to choose a surname.

◆ Tepee: A 12-buffalo affair

The conical tent known as a tepee, used by Aboriginal groups that followed the buffalo hunt, measured four to six meters wide at the base and tapered to a smoke hole at the top. It was covered by up to 12 buffalo robes sewn together and spread around some 20 eight-meter-high pine poles. The cone-like structure allowed diffuse light to fill the interior, providing a place for the spirit to soar. Some tepees were enclosed in caribou skins, and some with bark, sewn together with softened and split tree roots. Women of the tribe made, erected, and owned the tepees. Men had to get their wives' consent to decorate the tepee cover.

◆ Tsimshian: Exotic traders

With roots near modern-day Prince Rupert, B.C., the Tsimshian people were notable for their highly specialized shamans (they had shamans for curing, fishing, war, and general ghostbusting) and their trade in exotic goods such as obsidian, jade, and quartz, as well as earth pigments, rare woods, preserved meats, and euchalon oil, used as both condiment and medicine. Prized among their trading partners were Tsimshian woven goats' wool blankets and raven rattles, ornamental carved rattles used by chiefs to punctuate their thundering oratory.

◆ Wampum: Symbol of events, promises, gifts

Wampum—an Algonquin term meaning "string of white beads"—consisted of bits of polished seashell or glass strung on ropes which were then bound together into belts or circles. Wampum could serve as an ornament, a trade item, a gift, a method of communication or diplomatic gesture, or a mark that a debt was paid. Particular patterns symbolized events and alliances. Runners relayed messages with wampum: White wampum meant peace; red was a declaration of war. Wampum was used to propose marriage, atone for misdeeds, or ransom captives. Iroquois councils opened with a wampum exchange. Proposals were rejected by tossing aside the speaker's wampum. Wampum belts representing treaty articles were stored at Onondaga, the heart of the Iroquois Confederacy (*see opposite page*).

A ring of tepees in Peter Whyte's 1955 painting "Blackfoot Sun Dance Camp"

◆ Whisky forts on the Whoop-Up Trail

At the end of the American Civil War in 1865, some army veterans journeyed north to cash in on the fur trade. Equipped with a new invention, the repeating rifle, they could slaughter bison on a scale not previously possible. While trading whisky to natives was illegal in Montana, the Americans knew they could make good money trading whisky for furs in lawless Whoop-Up country, what is today southern Alberta. The so-called "whisky forts" flew the American flag and had names like Ft. Slideout, Ft. Stand-Off, Robber's Roost, Whisky Gap," but the most famous was Ft. Whoop-Up.

At first the forts traded repeating rifles, but liquor quickly became the hottest commodity. For it, the natives over-hunted the bison, which were already threatened with extinction. The whisky traded was of atrociously poor quality and threatened the health of the natives. One recipe called for 26 ounces whisky, one pound chewing tobacco, one bottle ginger, red pepper, one quart molasses, and a dash of red ink. The natives became aware the whisky was being watered down to increase profits, so to test its strength, they would take a mouthful and spit it onto a fire. If the fire flamed up, the whisky was

acceptable, if it doused the flames, it was too weak. This gave new meaning to the term "firewater."

The journals of historian Paul Sharp show that a typical whisky fort population ranged from native peoples to residents of the Deep South and included "Merchants in high-collared broadcloth coats, French Canadian and Creole rivermen wearing bright-colored sashes, tough trappers and traders heavily armed, bullwhackers and muleskinners . . . pious missionaries, hunted desperadoes, speculators, miners, roustabouts and cowboys . . . immigrants from nearly every nation of Europe, as well as wanderers from China."

In 1873, the North-West Mounted Police (*see page 141*) was created to put an end to the lawlessness. NWMP Assistant Commissioner James F. Macleod hired 37-year-old interpreter Jerry Potts (*below*) to lead them to Ft. Whoop-Up. When they reached it, the Americans had fled, having heard the Mounties were on their way. Natives were greatly relieved to see the arrival of these red-coated men who would put a stop to the exploitation of their people. Jerry Potts, translating for a Blackfoot chief, later told Macleod, "Dey damn glad you here!"

◆ No whiteout could best this scout

In his 22 years as scout and interpreter to the North-West Mounted Police, Métis Jerry Potts (1840–96) never used a map or a compass. Yet he could track down a lost patrol or find a landmark in any weather. Potts educated the Mounties about the natives, and reassured the natives about the police. He was first hired in 1874 to lead the way to Fort Whoop-Up, the notorious whisky-trading post near present-day Lethbridge, Alta. Potts regularly assuaged his thirst with everything from whisky to medicinal painkillers. After drinking bouts, he and Métis buddy George Star would try to trim each other's moustaches with bullets from their six-shooters. When he died at 56, the Mounties gave him a full military funeral.

North America's first industrial plant

North America's first known industrial plant operated over 400 years ago at Red Bay, on Saddle Island at the southern tip of Labrador. There, Basque whalers rendered their catch—right and bowhead whales—into lard, which they packed in barrels for export to Europe. Over the years, archeological digs have discovered outlines of the buildings and a cemetery with 60 graves containing the remains of 140 Basque whalers. Red Bay's Basque roots deepened with the discovery in 1978 of a Spanish galleon which sank in 1565—believed to be the *San Juan*—found lying in deep silt in Red Bay Harbour. Today, the center of this once-thriving Basque whaling operation is marked by the Red Bay National Historic Site.

Whaling was a lucrative industry in Canada during the 1600s; Canadian artist Lewis Parker's famous "Beluga No. 5" details whaling among the Inuit

An 1803 shopping list

York boats, large birchbark canoes that ferried goods to and from fur-trading posts like York Factory, carried a little bit of everything. A typical bill of lading dated 1803 includes:

Bales of tobacco; kegs or casks of salt, ham, jowls, grease, gun powder, white sugar, rum, beef, butter, port wine, Madeira wine, brandy, tongue, sausage, barley, rice, cheese, raisins, figs, and prunes; boxes of iron, hats, knives, guns, traps, soap; sacks of lead, balls, peas, and Milled India Wheat, coarse and fine. Rations for the voyageurs included eight sacks of hard tack, 200 lb worth of paper-wrapped packages of pork, six bundles of spruce root, and 12-lb paper-wrapped packages of gum.

A fort resurrected from the permafrost

Located at the mouth of the Hayes River southeast of Churchill, Man., York Factory was one of the most important fur-trade supply centers in North America. Its remote location near Hudson Bay—even today it is accessible only by boat or charter aircraft—made it ideal for oceangoing vessels. Yet the ravages of war and Canada's harsh climate prompted the Hudson's Bay Company to build the fort three times: first in 1684, then in 1715, and lastly in 1788, when a third fort was built one kilometer farther upstream. While the star-shaped "Old Octagon" offered superior defense capabilities, its rigid stone-and-brick foundation was no match for frost heave, and the building crumbled in 1831. Today, all that remains is the wooden Depot Building (*shown this page*) built atop the remains of the third fort, now a national historic site. In 1991, Parks Canada archeologists working between the floor joists inside the Depot found well-preserved remains of the third fort that had heaved upward through the permafrost. The artifacts they found are on display at the site.

iron, salmon, and glass

◆ Greed was the canners' mantra

At the turn of the last century, over 500 rural salmon canneries had mushroomed on river mouths in isolated areas
of northern British Columbia. Salmon fishing was a ruth-
less business, with indigenous and immigrant workers—
Scandinavians, Italians, Englishmen, Frenchmen, Greeks,
Chileans, Hawaiians, and after 1893, the Japanese—doing
the backbreaking work of pulling in the salmon. When it
came to the owners, greed might as well have been their
mantra. J. H. Todd, an Ontarian who ran the Inverness
Cannery on the Skeena River, distinguished himself as

being a skinflint, having once attempted to pay two native
people a hardtack biscuit each for the arduous task of
paddling him upriver to New Westminster. Scottish canner
Alexander Ewen was described as "avaricious, erratic and
stubborn, a diehard liberal and a notorious drinker."
Marshall English, a Virginian who built one of the largest
canneries on the Fraser River, drank his money away. Of
him someone wrote, "He would excuse himself while walking with friends, throw up in a ditch and then resume the
conversation without showing any discomfort."

◆ Forging a new iron industry

The Saint Maurice Iron Forges, which thrived at Trois-Rivières, Que.,
from 1730 to 1883, was Canada's first ironworks, and the most tech-
nologically advanced in North America. In its day, ironmaking was the
most important industry in New France. At its peak, stokers on six-
hour shifts worked around the clock firing the cold-air blast furnaces,
and 300 men were employed producing iron bars, cauldrons, kettles,
plowshares, stoves, cannons, axes, cannonballs, and eventually railway
car wheels. The forges are now a national historic site.

Ryan Premises, Bonavista,
Newfoundland

◆ The East Coast Fishery's General Store

In 1997, to commemorate the crucial role of the East Coast Fishery in Canadian history, a once-thriving fishery site called Ryan Premises near Bonavista, Nfld., was declared a national historic site. Ryan's residence, fish store, salt shed, and retail shop have survived since 1857, when James Ryan immigrated to Newfoundland from Ireland and his family became the principal merchants on the Bonavista-Trinity Peninsula. They sent their ships to the Labrador fishery each spring, processed whale and lobster, and exported fish to Spain, Italy, and the West Indies.

Ryan's retail shop once stocked flour, molasses, sugar, butter, pork, apples, spices, tobacco, tea, coffee, thread, buttons, cutlery, shoes, leather, coal, gunpowder, cod jiggers, squid lines, and rum. According to a local saying, "If you couldn't get it at Ryan's, you couldn't get it."

Fishermen's wagons once lined up outside Ryan's to have their salt fish culled, or graded according to weight and quality. But by the 1930s, fresh frozen technology ended the demand for salt fish and fishermen began selling their catches to the new processing plants. In 1978, James Ryan closed the business that had been in his family for 100 years. At Ryan Premises, business transaction records, and furnishings from the Ryan home, offices, and store take their place beside the jigs, beams, and barrels in evoking the once-lively spirit of this pioneering fishing community.

> "IF YOU COULDN'T GET IT AT RYAN'S, YOU COULDN'T GET IT."

◆ Canada's first glassworks

The first recorded production of glass in Canada occurred in 1839 in the Mallorytown Glass Works, Ontario. Window glass was first made during the 1850s at the Canada Glass Works, Saint-Jean, Que. While most Canadian glassworks turned out industrial glassware—street light globes, lenses for railway and ship lanterns, telegraph and telephone line insulators—other glassworks specialized in more unusual items. The Dominion Glass Company listed the following industrial items in its 1926 catalog: fire extinguishers, lightning rod balls, battery jars, fishing floats, stove door plates, headlight lenses, dental cuspidor bowls, prisms, and vault lights. One company even manufactured glass burial caskets in the 1880s!

◆ Cannery recalls era of fish-rich harvests

The oldest standing cannery village on the British Columbia coast can be found on the Skeena River in the District of Port Edward. The North Pacific Cannery Village and Museum is the last remaining cannery of 19 that once operated at the mouth of the Skeena. The North Pacific Canning Company operated here from 1889 to 1958, shipping sockeye directly to England. The village has been restored to show various aspects of the canning process and the lifestyles of those involved with the work.

◆ "A little bit of England"

As the West was settled, the Prairies had its share of remittance men, well-heeled Englishmen supported by money "remitted" regularly from home. Some arrived to "do a bit of ranching," replete with expensive wardrobes and a taste for cricket, racing, and black-tie dinners.

Edward Mitchell Pierce adapted better than others. In 1882, Pierce, a retired army captain, and some fellow aristocrats settled at Cannington, some 13 kilometers north of present-day Manor, Sask., and determined to create "a little England on the prairie." There was horse racing, cricket and tennis matches, billiards, and fox hunts in full regalia, even if the hounds chased a coyote instead of a fox. The silver chalice in All Saints Anglican Church in the town of Manor used to be a racing trophy.

Many of the gentry left in the early 1890s, some lured to the Klondike, others to South Africa to fight in the Boer War. The Maltby and Hewlett houses, a carpenter's shop, and a bachelor's shack are all that remain of the remittance men's proud dreams for Cannington Manor. A museum has a model of the colony and a muzzle-loading walking stick for shooting pigeons.

◆ Bennett buggies

Cars towed by horses because owners could not afford gasoline were dubbed "Bennett Buggies," on the prairies, in contempt of Richard Bedford Bennett, the Conservative prime minister from 1930 to 1935. He won election pledging swift action against the Depression. But once in office, the wealthy lawyer did not deliver on his promises.

◆ The man who sold the Prairies

By 1896, the federal government had made recruitment of settlers a priority, and Prime Minister Wilfrid Laurier assigned the task of filling the Prairies to Manitoba MP Clifford Sifton (1861–1929). Sifton sought his first recruits among farmers in the United States, where prairie land was advertised at county fairs. For promotion purposes and especially to dispel the idea of a "frozen north," U.S. journalists were regularly taken on train junkets. Sifton pursued an equally aggressive promotion campaign in Britain, and before long he set his sights on Europe, where immigration agents were paid $5 for each farmer and $2 for each member of a farmer's family recruited. When Anglo-Saxons in Canada objected to opening the Prairies to people from eastern Europe, Sifton stoutly defended the "stalwart peasants in sheepskin coats . . . whose forefathers have been farmers for 10 generations."

◆ Isaac Barr's ill-planned venture

Alberta and Saskatchewan had not yet become provinces when Anglican clergyman Rev. Isaac Barr acquired a vast tract of land there in 1902, and recruited 2,000 Britons to settle it ("Canada for the British" was his motto). But colonists and colonizers began bickering at sea and were still at loggerheads when they docked at St. John, N.B., in April 1903. From there began the overland journey for which they were ill prepared. Not all continued west, but ongoing disputes and misery overwhelmed those who did. When they reached Saskatoon, Barr was dismissed, and Rev. George E. Lloyd (later Anglican bishop of Saskatchewan) led the others to the colony, where they would eventually prosper and name its premier community not for Barr, but Lloydminster for his rival.

◆ Bar U pioneered ranching in Canada

A working ranch for more than 100 years, the Bar U Ranch—at Longview, on Pekisko Creek in the Alberta foothills—was one of western Canada's foremost ranching operations between 1882 and 1950. One of a group of large corporate ranching enterprises that operated in this area, it was notable for open-range cattle and grain farming and for having the world's largest Percheron horse herd. Visitors to this 35-building national historic site today may take part in seasonal activities ranging from penning, branding and roping, to Percheron harnessing, haying, round-up campfires, and stooking grain.

◆ 4-H Clubs nurtured rural youth

Pioneered by the Manitoba Department of Agriculture with support from Agriculture Canada, and open to boys and girls ages 9 to 19, Canada's 4-H Clubs first bloomed in Roland, a small town some 100 kilometers southwest of Winnipeg, in 1913. "Learn to do by doing" was the motto of the movement, which aimed to develop farming, homemaking, public speaking, leisure, and other life skills in rural youth. Until 1952, the Canadian clubs were known as Boys' and Girls' Clubs, but that year they adopted the name used elsewhere in North America. (4-H comes from the pledge members recite: "I pledge my Head to clearer thinking, my Heart to greater loyalty, my Hands to larger service, my Health to better living for my Club, my Community, my Country, and my World.") Roland now hosts Canada's only 4-H Museum—a collection of uniforms, banners, trophies, books, and pony and calf displays housed in a former bank, a designated heritage building, on the village's main street.

◆ The Overlanders' odyssey

In the spring of 1862, anxious to cash in on the rush of goldseekers bound for the Cariboo goldfields, the British Columbia Overland Transit Company was wooing passengers with promises of "the cheapest, safest, and most economical route to the gold diggings." But some 200 hopefuls from Ontario and Quebec had another "overland" itinerary in mind. They planned to travel by rail to St. Paul, Minn., go from there by wagon to the Rockies, which they would cross via the Yellowhead Pass. After that, they would sail down the Fraser River to the goldfields.

Led by brothers Thomas and Robert McMicking, they set out in May. The only woman in the group, Catherine O'Hare Shubert, was pregnant and accompanied by her three children. On arrival at Lower Fort Garry in early June, they creaked across the Prairies on oxen-pulled Red River carts to Fort Edmonton, where, in late July, they switched to packhorses. Led by native guides they crossed the Rockies. Most made their way to the Fraser River, but a smaller group struck off for the Thompson River. Both groups built rafts, and many drowned. The Fraser group arrived at Fort George in September, while the Thompson party reached Fort Kamloops in October, hours before Mrs. Shubert's child was born. After their arduous odyssey, only a few Overlanders made it to the goldfields, and only one found gold.

◆ She conquered the Yukon

Abandoned by her first husband enroute to the Klondike, 32-year-old Chicago socialite Martha Louise Black (1866–1957) hiked over the Chilkoot Pass in 1898, sailed down the Yukon River to Dawson in a homemade boat, bore a child in a log cabin, raised money to buy a sawmill, and operated a mining claim before marrying George Black, the Yukon's Member of Parliament and later Commissioner of the Yukon. After the Second World War, when her husband became too ill to continue in politics, she ran for and won his seat in Parliament, becoming the Yukon's first and—after Agnes Macphail—Canada's second woman MP.

◆ Diamonds in the rough at Ekati

Lac de Gras, N.W.T., was so named because white granite outcrops along its shoreline glistened like caribou fat. Now this lake some 300 kilometers northeast of Yellowknife and 200 kilometers south of the Arctic Circle is the site of what many believe will become one of the world's top diamond producing centers. Geologist Charles Fipke started the rush when he discovered diamonds there in 1991. Ekati, North America's first operating diamond mine, began at the site in 1998, and now outputs some $1.7 million of top-quality white diamonds every day. A second mine, Diavik, hopes to be in production by 2003. Diamond deposits in other northern sites, including Baffin Island, also look promising and mining companies are planning operations. When these open, the annual value of mined diamonds will run into billions of dollars.

A "sourdough" was a Yukon survivor, a "cheechako"

◆ Sourdoughs and cheechakos

A "Sourdough," named for the fermented bread eaten by locals, became the term used to describe a Yukon old-timer during the Klondide gold rush, while a "Cheechako" was a newcomer. The only way for a cheechako to become a sourdough was to watch the river freeze in the fall and still be there for the thaw in spring. The terms were immortalized in Robert Service's *Songs of a Sourdough* (1907) and *Ballads of a Cheechako* (1909).

◆ Camels of the Cariboo

Between 1862 and 1864, large sections of British Columbia's Cariboo Road—a 650-kilometer wagon route to the Cariboo goldfields in the B.C. interior—had to be blasted from solid rock. As construction lurched along, prospectors continued to stream along the tortuous trail to the goldfields. The going was slow and some entrepreneurs decided to speed things up with camel power.

Sure of foot, able to carry half-tonne loads and go days without water, camels made ideal freight transport, and 23 two-humped beasts were imported from Manchuria at a cost of $6,000. But the entrepreneurs hadn't counted on the camels' smell, which caused mules and horses on the trail to panic. Things came to a head when one animal and his load of Scotch whisky fell over a cliff. The Manchurian beasts were thereafter banished from the Cariboo Trail.

◆ A pink diamond for a royal princess

The largest diamond deposit outside South Africa was discovered by a Canadian in 1939 in Mwadui, Tanganyika (present-day Tanzania). John Williamson (1908–82), a geology graduate from McGill University, Montreal, was down to his last cent when he found the mine that would yield up to $10 million worth of diamonds a year. Mwaudi also yielded Tanzania's most famous diamond: the Williamson Pink, a 23.60 carat gem cut from a 54.50 piece of rough diamond, with a value of $280,000. Williamson set it in a brooch and gave it to then-Princess Elizabeth as a gift for her forthcoming wedding to Prince Philip. Today, it remains one of her favorite brooches.

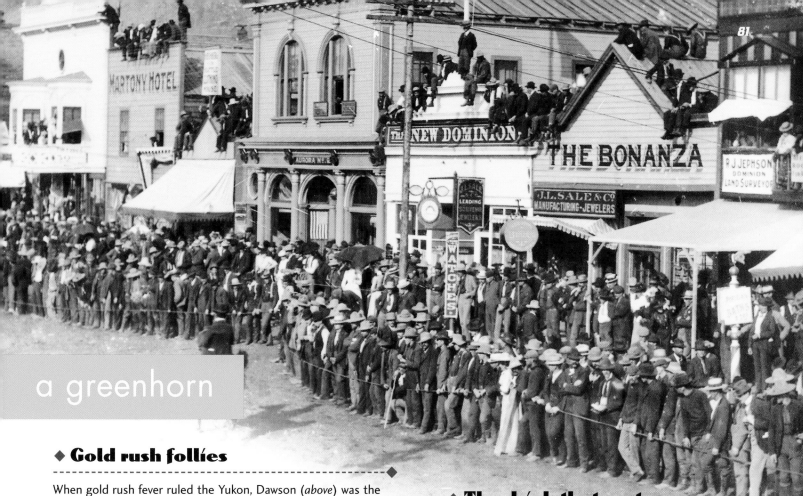

◆ Gold rush follies

When gold rush fever ruled the Yukon, Dawson (*above*) was the good-time capital of North America. The bare-bones burlesque follies that passed for frontier entertainment at Dawson's first theater and dancehall, the Opera House—an 1899 log building with stage curtained in blue denim and lit by candles—encompassed everything from dancing to variety to melodrama. When it came to props and special effects, improvisation was the name of the game: ice floes were represented by newspapers; a pack of bloodhounds was a lone husky dragged across the stage. At the end of each night's stage show, the benches were cleared away and dancing began. Dance hall girls with ribald stage names like "Snake Hips Lily" were paid commission on every bottle of liquor a man bought. One redhead by the name of Cad Wilson persuaded a Klondike miner to spend $1,740 on champagne in one night. Another time, she sweet-talked another miner into filling her bathtub with wine—at $20 a bottle. Cad spent only one season in Dawson, but she left $26,000 richer than when she arrived.

Yukon dancehall girl, circa 1900

◆ The drink that cost a miner $230 million

In 1909, at the height of northern Ontario's gold rush, prospector Sandy McIntyre (1869–1943) discovered the mine near Timmins that would later bear his name, and would eventually produce $230 million in gold. Yet McIntyre had sold his stake for $25 to buy liquor. He spent his later years in area beverage rooms bemoaning his bad luck.

◆ Diamond Tooth Gertie

Yukon dance hall queen Diamond Tooth Gertie (née Lovejoy) made a fortune mining Stampeders of their hard-won gold nuggets, reasoning "The poor ginks have just gotta spend it, they're scared that they'll die before they have it all out of the ground." Her nickname came from the sparkling diamond she had wedged between two front teeth. Her name lives on in a gambling hall in Dawson City.

The Hurdy Gurdy Girls, German dancers at Barkerville in the 1860s

◆ From a golden fortune to a pauper's grave

By 1862, the trail into British Columbia's Cariboo Mountains was clogged with packers, merchants, and gold seekers all seeking their fortune and panning gold from the streams and sandbars of the Fraser River. One of the hopeful was a 38-year-old English seaman named Billy Barker, who was flat broke until he dug a crude, 24-meter shaft beside Williams Creek and came upon gold nuggets as big as hen's eggs. His find triggered a rush of fortune seekers, and the town of tents, shacks, and stores that sprang up along the creek within days was known as Barkerville. At its peak, Barkerville had 10,000 inhabitants.

The gold petered out, however, and the gold seekers moved on. Most had left by 1868 when a fire leveled the community. The man whose find triggered the rush was reduced to buying and selling candles. Barker lived on to 1892, when he died in poverty, having long since squandered his fortune in Barkerville's dance halls and saloons. He was buried in a pauper's grave. Today, staff in period costume and more than 120 restored or reconstructed buildings bring the frenzied days of the pioneer mining town to life.

◆ Mile of gold

Kirkland Lake, Ont., can truly say its streets are paved with gold. In its heyday, the town produced more than 20 percent of the gold ever mined in Canada. When mining was at its height, a construction crew building a section of Government Road, the main road through town, mistakenly took ore from a pile waiting to be milled instead of from a waste pile, and poured the gold-rich ore into the road bed in 1930. The ore was then sealed under a coat of pavement, giving Kirkland Lake its famous "Mile of Gold."

◆ Tonnes of talc

Canada's only pure talc mine is located in Madoc, a tiny logging and farming community in eastern Ontario. The basic ingredient in talcum powder, talc, or soapstone, is also used as a lubricant and electric insulator, and is an ingredient in the manufacture of rubber, paper, and soap. The mill has produced 1,260,000 tonnes of talc since 1906.

◆ The hammer that opened the Canadian Shield

One dark September night in 1903, Cobalt, Ont., blacksmith Fred LaRose threw his hammer at what he thought was a fox's eyes, but what was in reality a 1.5-meter-wide vein of raw silver, several thousand meters long. His discovery—the world's richest vein of silver—touched off a mining boom that opened up exploration of the Canadian Shield. By 1908, the small town on the edge of Lake Temiskaming near the Quebec border had become the cradle of Canadian mining, with 50 mines operating and a population near 30,000. Drilling in surrounding districts led to gold strikes in nearby Porcupine in 1909 and Kirkland Lake in 1912. Mining machinery, tools, and a 570-kilogram hunk of raw silver in the Cobalt Northern Ontario Mining Museum commemorate the boom.

An original stamp mill used in 1910 to crush ore into powder at Hollinger Mines

◆ It was the world's biggest gold mine

Timmins, Ont., "The City with the Heart of Gold," can trace its origins to a large vein of the precious metal found in 1909 when prospector Harry Preston slipped on a rocky knoll, his heel stripping moss from the rock exposing the rich ore below. The city itself was established in 1911 by Noah A. Timmins (1867–1936), one of the founders of the LaRose silver mine in Cobalt (*see opposite page*).

One of Timmins' first operational mines was the Hollinger Mine, first staked in 1909 by a young barber named Benny Hollinger. With its massive industrial mining equipment right out of Jules Verne and over 965 kilometers of tunnels, it was once the richest gold producer in the Western Hemisphere, yielding a total of $400 million in gold over its lifetime—at prices of around $35 an ounce.

Today, at the Timmins Underground Gold Mine Tour, visitors can don hard hats and journey into the deeps with seasoned miners for a mining demonstration that includes a mock explosion and rescue operations. At the surface, they can pan for gold and keep their findings.

◆ Radium's bloom led to a Curie Medal

When Manitoba's Eldorado Gold Mines was in its final days in 1930, one of the owners, Gilbert LaBine (1890–1977), began prospecting in the Great Bear Lake area of the Northwest Territories. From a plane window on one of his forays, he spotted a purple-yellow bloom on rocks below, a telltale sign of pitchblende, the source of the prized radioactive elements uranium and radium. When he reached the remote site the following spring, LaBine not only found pitchblende, but rich veins of silver, nickel, bismuth, cobalt, iron lead, and copper.

Gilbert and his brother Charles borrowed $950,000 to mine the ore and transport it to a refinery they established 6,400 kilometers away at Port Hope, Ont. There, in 1936, they produced their first ounce of radium. The Great Bear Lake discovery literally trebled the world's radium supply, forcing the price from $70,000 to $20,000 a gram, and helped usher in Canada's atomic age. Of the fame and honors that followed, LaBine treasured most the Marie Curie Medal for radiation research he was awarded in 1938.

GOLD

◆ Sibley's silver lining

When nuggets of pure silver were found in 1869 on a rock 24 meters square that rose barely 2.5 meters out of the water off the Sibley Peninsula near Thunder Bay, Ont., the thriving community of Silver Islet was born overnight. The rock was enlarged to a tiny island that eventually became Ontario's first silver mine, producing $3.2 million in silver from 1869 to 1884.

◆ The legendary Lost Lemon Mine

A mythic motherlode of gold allegedly discovered in 1870 by prospectors "Blackjack" and "Lemon," the Lost Lemon Mine is said to lie in southwest Alberta, somewhere between the Highwood River and the Crowsnest Pass. In one of many versions of the tale, Lemon went mad and murdered Blackjack at the mine. Two Stony Indian witnesses were sworn to secrecy by their chief, but the story leaked out. But Lemon was never able to recall the mine's location, and many have since tried—and died trying—to find it.

the past preserv'd

◆ Our longest historic site

A 386-kilometer "highway" of lakes, rivers and canals, the Trent-Severn Waterway is Canada's longest national historic site. It took 87 years for this inland navigation route from Lake Ontario to Georgian Bay to become a reality, starting with the first small wooden lock at Bobcaygeon, Ont., in 1833. Today, 45 locks carry boaters through communities like Peterborough, Lindsay, Orillia, and Fenelon Falls. Archeological sites found along the waterway point to the importance of this transportation and migration route.

◆ "Are you receiving?"

A Wireless Hall of Fame is among attractions at the Marconi National Historic Site at Baddeck, N.S. It was from here that the first official wireless message to cross the Atlantic was sent to England in 1902. The site is dedicated to Marconi's role in global communications.

◆ Montreal's Masonic Temple

More than 70 years after its official opening in 1930, Royal Victoria Lodge No. 57, a Masonic Memorial Temple in downtown Montreal, Que., was designated a national historic site in 2002. Designed by John S. Archibald, a Montreal architect of Scottish descent, the Beaux-Arts building's ornate façade and detail represents how Freemasonry utilized architecture to convey its elaborate system of codes, signals and Enlightenment ideas.

◆ Motherwell's model estate

A national historic site since 1966, the Motherwell Homestead near Abernethy, Sask., has been restored to

the estate-like standards that applied when it was first occupied in 1882 by William Motherwell, agrarian activist and federal and provincial agricultural minister. Motherwell, who grew up in Perth, Ont., was a tireless advocate of scientific techniques for cultivating the dry prairie, and adopted the Ontario settlers approach to farmstead design, dividing the Motherwell farmstead into four quadrants, domestic, garden, water supply, and barnyard. Motherwell homesteaded here for 60 years.

◆ The easternmost light

The oldest surviving lighthouse in Newfoundland, the Cape Spear lighthouse is the easternmost light in Canada. It was built in 1835 to offer a shining beacon to mariners negotiating its rocky coasts. The light, shipped from Scotland, rotated slowly to produce a 17-second flash of white light, followed by 43 seconds of darkness. First lit by oil, the lights adopted acetylene in 1916, and electricity in 1930. Cape Spear was briefly used as a coastal defence battery during World War II.

◆ World's biggest historical reconstruction

The most elaborate example of an 18th-century North American fortification, and the world's biggest historical reconstruction, Fortress Louisbourg stands southeast of Sydney in Cape Breton, N.S. Founded in 1713 by the French, it soon became an important military base and substantial seaport supported almost entirely by the export of cod. It was besieged in 1745 during the War of the Austrian Succession by New England troops and the Royal Navy, and again in 1758 by the British Army and Navy. It was finally leveled by the British in 1760. Canada's first lighthouse, a 70-foot circular stone tower, stood at this site. Its light, provided by wicks set in cork floating in a tub of whale oil, shone through a lantern containing 400 panes of glass, and was visible 29 kilometers out to sea.

◆ Rocky Mountain House

Once the base of explorer David Thompson's mapping expeditions (*see page 59*), Rocky Mountain house, 90 kilometers west of Red Deer, Alta., was a key settlement in the exploration of western Canada. Five different fur-trading posts took in pelts at this location between 1799 and 1875, bought from Thompson and other explorers who pushed west looking for new routes to the West Coast. The first two posts were erected by the North West Company and the Hudson's Bay Company. Blackfoot-speaking peoples, namely the Peigan, Blood, and Blackfoot, were the principal customers at the posts. Today an interpretive centre at this national historic site has exhibits on the fur trade, while trails follow the banks of the North Saskatchewan River leading past fort remains, a Red River cart, a York boat, fur press, and cemetery.

◆ Hodgepodge and succotash

King's Landing Historical Settlement, in the Saint John River Valley west of Fredericton, N.B., is one of Canada's most outstanding pioneer villages. This living history museum contains some 70 restored buildings, including a school, church, forge, carpenter's shop, and inn, depicting life in New Brunswick from Loyalist to Victorian times. Costumed "residents" carry out daily tasks—farming, making crafts, and working at chores—in homes, barns, stores, and mills. Early "housewives" demonstrate how to make rhubarb and raspberry wines, and dishes such as hodgepodge (a mix of baby carrots, beans, peas, and potatoes, butter and cream) and succotash (corn, pole beans, onions, and potatoes, all richly blended with butter and cream).

◆ HQ for musical horses

Headquarters of the North-West Mounted Police in 1878–93, Fort Walsh—a national historic site since 1925—served as the breeding ground for horses for the force's Musical Ride between 1942 and 1968. The Saskatchewan location contains the fort buildings, two cemeteries, and a reconstructed whisky trading post.

Louisbourg Fortress, Nova Scotia

◆ "Splendor without diminishment"

The motto of Canada's westernmost province is *Splendor sine occasu*, or "Splendor without diminishment." British Columbia covers 946,011 square kilometers of rugged northwestern wilderness, 91 percent of which is uninhabited. Its deep forests fuel its prosperous forestry and paper industries. Specialty and fruit crops dominate its agricultural sector; salmon and herring its fishery, Canada's largest. The province has three-fifths of its mountain goats, and one-quarter of its bald eagles and grizzly bears. As Canada's gateway to Asia and the Pacific, B.C. is home to people of many different origins, cultural traditions, languages, ethnicities, and religions. There are 197 First Nations bands in the province, including Gitxsan, Haida, Nisga'a, and Squamish. Mandarin is B.C.'s second-most spoken language.

◆ Canada's heartland

The name Manitoba comes from the Cree words *Manitou bou*, or "the narrows of the Great Spirit." Scores of rivers and thousands of lakes cover huge chunks of the province, many are remnants of glacial Lake Agassiz that buried this region 12,000 years ago. Canada's geographical heartland, Manitoba has an economy built on agriculture in the southwest—which basks in as many as 2,300 hours of sunshine a year, almost as much as California—and mining in the Canadian Shield underlying the northeast, where the province is a world leader in the production of nickel.

◆ Home to 1 in 3

One in three Canadians live in Ontario, a founding member of the Dominion of Canada and Canada's most populous province. Ontario has a freshwater shoreline on the Great Lakes, and saltwater shorelines on Hudson and James Bays. Half the province's population, some 5 million people, live in an area known as the Golden Horseshoe that encircles Lake Ontario. Toronto, the capital, is Canada's largest city with over 4 million inhabitants. Ontario has the largest farming sector of any province, is second in mineral production, and accounts for about one-half of Canada's manufactured goods. Leading industries are manufacturing (steel, motor vehicles, electronics, processed foods, and lumber), agriculture (livestock, grain, dairy, fruit, and vegetable farming), and mining.

10 provinces + 3 territories = Canada

University of Montreal

◆ Named for Victoria's daughter

The colors of the Alberta tartan represent the green of its forests, the gold of its wheat fields, the blue of its clean skies and sparkling lakes, the pink of its wild rose (the official flower), and the black of its coal and petroleum. Joining Confederation on Sept. 1, 1905, the province was named for Queen Victoria's daughter, Princess Louise Caroline Alberta. Because of its abundant petroleum, natural gas, and coal deposits, the province accounts for about half the value of all minerals produced in Canada.

◆ Bread basket to the country

The only province with entirely man-made boundaries, Saskatchewan is Canada's great bread basket. The province grows over 54 percent of the country's wheat, and its dynamic agriculture sector also produces canola, rye, oats, barley, and flax. Saskatchewan is also the world's leading exporter of potash. While the province has a reputation as being thoroughly flat, the highest point between the Rockies and Labrador, in the Cypress Hills, towers 600 meters above the surrounding landscape in southwestern Saskatchewan.

◆ A distinct society

Three times the size of France, Quebec, Canada's largest province, extends from the St. Lawrence River north to Hudson Strait. Montreal, its largest city, is the third largest francophone city in the world, after Paris and Kinshasa, and has the largest French-language university outside Paris, the University of Montreal. Quebec's leading industries are manufacturing (textiles, newsprint, aircraft parts, telecommunications, automobiles), forestry, mining, and agriculture. Harnessing hydroelectricity from mighty rivers like the Eastmain, Manicouagan, and La Grande has been a powerful factor in the provincial economy.

◆ Home of the Mi'kmaq

The ancient home of the Mi'kmaq, New Brunswick is known for its serene, marsh-like coastlines. It's also famed for Ganong's chocolate, Sabian cymbals, the world's longest covered bridge (390 meters, in Hartland), and salmon angling in the Miramichi River. The province has a dynamic economy based on pulp and paper and food processing—McCain, one of the province's largest employers, produces over 450,000 kilograms of potato fries an hour.

◆ Nova Scotia's red, green, and blue

The world's largest producer of lobster, Christmas trees, and wild blueberries, Nova Scotia is surrounded by water. Its fishery—lobster, cod, scallop, and haddock—is the largest in the North Atlantic. Halifax, the provincial capital, sits on the world's second largest natural harbor (after Sydney, Australia). Nova Scotia is also synonymous with great salmon fishing and apple farming.

◆ The province with its own dog

Our most easterly and youngest province, Newfoundland joined Canada in 1949. Its rugged, barren, rocky terrain is dotted with bogs and swamps, and communities ringing its coastline trace their roots to ancient seafarers. Labrador, a mosaic of rocks, wetlands, and lakes, is the largest part of Newfoundland, and lies across the Strait of Belle Isle, stretching 750 kilometers inland. Pulp and paper, mining, hydroelectricity, fishing, offshore oil production, and tourism are its major industries. Newfoundland has no frogs, porcupines, snakes, or skunks, and is the only province with its own breed of dog—Newfoundlands, large, gentle swimming heroes of many a sea rescue.

Nunavut crest

◆ Cradle of Confederation

The ocean is never more than 16 kilometers away on Prince Edward Island, Canada's smallest province. Bays and inlets stud its coastline, which boasts some 800 kilometers of smooth beaches. Agriculture (including turnips, mixed grains, hay, and 32 varieties of potatoes), fishing (mackerel, mussels, lobster, clams, oysters), and tourism are the province's main industries. Charlottetown, the provincial capital, is renowned as the site of the 1864 conference that led to Confederation in 1867. However, P.E.I. itself didn't join the Dominion of Canada until 1873.

◆ The land that never thaws

The Northwest Territories (N.W.T.) is a mixture of rocky taiga and vast, frozen tundra home to 40,000 Dene, Inuvialuit, and Métis. Diamond mines, the biggest territorial industry, are clustered around Great Slave Lake. Only the Mackenzie Delta and the Great Slave Lake areas are accessible by road. Permafrost in many of the Territories' Arctic islands can reach up to 500 meters deep.

◆ Our newest territory

On April 1, 1999, Canada's map was redrawn to create Nunavut, a territory of more than 27,000 people, 85 percent of them Inuit. The population is scattered over 28 communities, ranging from Bathurst Inlet (pop. 18) to Iqaluit (pop. 4,500), the capital. Inuktitut, the mother tongue of some 70 percent of the population, is compulsory for kindergarten to Grade 4 students. Comprising some 60 percent of the old Northwest Territories, Nunavut covers almost 2 million square kilometers—about one-fifth of Canada's total landmass.

◆ "Great River"

Established in 1898, the Yukon Territory takes its name from the Gwich'in Indian name Yu-kun-ah, or "Great River." At 3,185 kilometers long, the Yukon River is one of North America's longest. Mining and tourism around the historic gold rush town of Dawson City are its main industries. Canada's highest point, Mount Logan (5,959 m) is one of several mighty peaks in the spectacular St. Elias Mountain range.

highways and byways

◆ The world's longest national highway

Canada's national highway system is over 25,000 kilometers in length, the longest stretch of which is the Trans-Canada Highway (National Highway 1), extending 7,821 kilometers from Victoria, B.C. (Mile 0) to St. John's, Nfld.—the longest national highway in the world. Building commenced on April 25, 1950, at a cost of $1 billion. The highway opened on Sept. 3, 1962, even though it wasn't fully complete until June of 1965.

◆ Ontario's pleasure canal

A scenic waterway known for its museums, wildlife, hiking, fishing, and of course boating, Ontario's Rideau Canal was originally built amid the threat of invasion. After the War of 1812, Britain embarked on a massive defense program to prevent another American invasion of Canada, part of which included this canal. Built in 1826–32 by Lt. Col. John By of the Royal Engineers, the canal was part of a water route joining Kingston with Bytown (present-day Ottawa). An engineering marvel in its day, the exquisite stone-masonry of the control dams and hand-cranked wooden locks are still admired by waterway travelers.

◆ The longest street in the world

Toronto's main street since the late 18th century, Yonge Street is considered by some to be the longest street in the world. The street was surveyed in 1793 by Lt. Col. John Graves Simcoe, who named the street after Sir George Yonge, Secretary of War. The first segment of the street was built in 1796 and was about 55 kilometers long. Today Yonge Street measures 1,896 kilometers long, running north from downtown Toronto's Union Station and following Highway 11 to the Ontario-Minnesota border.

◆ Beloved Bruce Trail

The Bruce Trail, a continuous, 725-kilometer footpath from Queenston to Tobermory, Ont., follows the entire length of the Niagara Escarpment from Niagara Falls along the Bruce Peninsula to Georgian Bay, preserving distinctive geological landforms and unique ecosystems. The idea for the trail was first put forward in 1960 by Hamilton metallurgist Ray Lowes. Public-spirited landowners gave permission for the trail to cross their properties, and volunteers formed the Bruce Trail Association, which now organizes and maintains the beloved trail that attracts hikers by the thousands.

◆ Billion-dollar bridge

The world's longest continuous marine span bridge, the $1 billion, 13-kilometer Confederation Bridge (*shown below*) opened to motorists on May 31, 1997, arching over the Northumberland Strait and linking Borden, P.E.I., to Jourimain Island, N.B. Some 2,000 cars can cross the bridge every hour, which is curved to eliminate the hypnotic effect of a straight bridge. The steel-and-concrete bridge has 44 spans, each weighing 7,500 tonnes, 310 streetlights, and 7,300 drain ports to allow runoff of rainwater and snow. Piers supporting the bridge descend 35 meters into the water. Each of the bridge's cone-shaped pier supports is capped with a bell-shaped concrete ice shield, which is meant to act like the bow of an icebreaker when pack ice clogs the strait. Cruise ships can pass easily underneath the bridge, parts of which stand 60 meters above the water.

◆ A monumental feat

On April 25, 1959, the icebreaker *D'Iberville* began the first through transit of the Great Lakes-St. Lawrence Seaway, the world's longest inland waterway open to ocean shipping. A monumental engineering and construction feat, the 3,790-kilometer seaway was a joint project of Canada and the United States, and was officially opened by Queen Elizabeth and President Eisenhower on June 26, 1959. From Anticosti Island to Duluth, Minnesota, each of the 19 locks along the seaway fills with over 90 million liters of water and is capable of raising ships more than 180 meters above sea level, or as high as a 60-storey building. Since then, more than two billion tonnes of cargo estimated at $450 billion has moved through the seaway.

◆ $40 creates a meter of Canada's longest trail

The longest shared-use recreational trail in the world, the Trans Canada Trail will span a total of 17,250 kilometers when complete in the fall of 2005, covering all provinces and territories from Saint John's, Nfld., to Iqaluit, Nunavut. Mostly built on existing trails and disused rail corridors, it will accommodate walking, cycling, horseback riding, skiing and snowmobiling. Canadians are helping to build the trail by donating money; every $40 donated builds one meter of trail. Names of donors will be permanently inscribed on trail pavilions in the province or territory of one's choice. Thus far, Ontario has contributed the most of any province or territory, with $3.9 million worth of donations, followed by Alberta with $1.7 million.

◆ Biggar than the Big Apple

Visitors entering Biggar (est. 1911), a small town in central Saskatchewan, are greeted by a sign saying "New York is Big, but this is Biggar." (Legend has it a survey crew in their cups one night wrote the slogan on a sign as a prank; the townspeople liked it so much they adopted it.) Named for W. H. Biggar, a railway lawyer, the community began as a divisional point on the Grand Trunk Pacific Railway.

◆ Sealed with a kiss

Each February, postmasters at the tiny communities of Saint-Valentin, Que. (pop. 550), and Love, Sask. (pop. 100), are flooded with thousands and thousands of plain brown envelopes—some originating as far as Japan—containing stamped love letters the senders want canceled with the town's postmark. The senders want the letters delivered to their loved ones for St. Valentine's Day, Feb. 14. Tour buses have now taken to visiting Saint-Valentin, where each spring the villagers festoon their houses and streets with hearts and flowers and light up their village at night.

community spirit

◆ In honor of a sci-fi grocer

The Manitoba town of Flin Flon just may be the only city named after a science fiction character. Josiah Flintabbatey Flonatin was a grocer in J. E. Preston-Muddock's obscure 1905 sci-fi novel *The Sunless City*. Apparently, one of the prospectors who was excavating in what is now the Flin Flon area was reading the novel at the time. The town's reputation for the bizarre was cemented in 2002 when disused parts of the Flin Flon mine were chosen as the site for Canada's first medicinal marijuana crop.

◆ Discovered by chance

Come by Chance, Nfld., a community at the head of Placentia Bay on the Avalon Peninsula, was originally called Passage Harbour. The first recorded reference to the present name dates from 1706, when it was described as "Comby Chance," an indication that the harbor was likely discovered by accident.

◆ Nouvelle Ukraine

In 1739, the great explorer La Vérendrye named a Manitoba post "Dauphin" for the heir to the French throne and the name stuck. But the area was the site of one of the earliest rural settlements by Ukrainian immigrants, and special occasions, particularly the National Ukrainian Festival in August, are marked not by reminders of Versailles but by balalaika music, Cossack dances, and Ukrainian culinary delights.

◆ Hats off!

The name of Medicine Hat, Alta., has many possible origins, all are steeped in native lore. In one, a Cree medicine man lost his headdress fleeing a battle rout by Blackfoot warriors. Another involves the rescue of a female Cree from the South Saskatchewan River by a brave, upon whose head a medicine man placed his own headwear in recognition of his act of bravery. Still another explanation ties the name to a hill east of the town, shaped like the famous headdress.

◆ Kicking open the West

In 1858, on the Palliser expedition in the Rocky Mountains, an unruly pack horse kicked geologist Sir James Hector senseless, breaking three of his ribs and leaving him unconscious for so long that he was pronounced dead. When he came to, he dubbed the twisting river Kicking Horse River, and the mountain pass they found themselves in Kicking Horse Pass, future path of the Canadian Pacific Railway and gateway to the West.

◆ Named by Portuguese?

The name Labrador is thought to be from the Portuguese *lavrador*, or landowner; explorer and lavrador João Fernandes was among the earliest to chart Labrador's coastline in the early 1500s.

◆ The red, red deer of home

The river for which Red Deer, Alta. (est. 1913), was named was known to natives as the Elk River. But the Scottish settlers who built a community there mistook elks for the red deer of their homeland, and so the river and the town became Red Deer.

◆ A symphony of streets

There are musical notes on every street sign in Mozart, Sask., the only town in the world to so honor the great composer. Julia Lund, an early Swedish settler and a music lover, named the town settled by Icelanders in the early 1900s. Other composers are also honored, including such luminaries as Gounod, Haydn, Liszt, Schubert, and Wagner.

◆ Plaster, not Paris

Paris, Ont., a picturesque town 50 kilometers west of Hamilton, Ont., is named not for Paris, France, but for the local gypsum, source of plaster of Paris. The town was founded in 1822 when Hiram "King" Capron began developing gypsum deposits at a site then known as Forks of the Grand River. Capron's home, Penmarvian, is now a local landmark.

◆ Qu'appelle Valley's poignant legend

Saskatchewan's Qu'appelle River and river valley are named for a poignant Cree legend recounted in a poem by Pauline Johnson (*see page 67*). After a long journey, a young brave was crossing one of the lakes that dot the valley when he heard someone call his name. "Qu'appelle?" ("Who calls?") he replied, but no sound broke the stillness. When he reached the other side he learned his bride-to-be had fallen ill in his absence and died before his arrival. It was only then he realized she had called out to him in death.

◆ Dreams of utopia

Sointula, a tiny community on Malcolm Island off the British Columbia mainland, takes its name from a Finnish word meaning "place of harmony." Finnish political refugee Matti Kurikka (1863–1915) hoped an economically independent utopian community would emerge when he and his followers settled the area at the turn of the century. Unhappily, prosperity eluded the settlers, and this romantic utopia lasted only three years. Today, third and fourth generation Sointula Finns make up the backbone of this tiny Scandinavian island paradise community of about 700.

◆ A town that wouldn't die

The name of Aklavik, a Northwest Territories hamlet near the Mackenzie River mouth, comes from an Inuit word meaning "where there are bears," but to the Inuvialuit and Gwich'in who still live in Aklavik, it is "the town that wouldn't die." The community was an important center in the 1950s, but continuous and serious flooding led to all government offices being moved to nearby Inuvik in 1961.

◆ Seldom-Little Seldom

This picturesque fishing village on Newfoundland's Fogo Island, first settled in the mid-1700s, was named by schooner captains fishing in the area. As the village is blessed with a sheltered bay, the community adopted the name Seldom Come-Bye because schooners or fishing crews seldom passed by without dropping in for a visit.

A
nation's
people and
their
stories

OUR SOCIAL
MOSAIC

◆ The children's friend

In the early 1900s, J. J. Kelso (1864–1935) was recognized as Canada's leading expert in child welfare, and widely revered as "the children's friend." As a reporter, the Irish-born Kelso had seen firsthand the awful living conditions of Toronto's poor. During his years as Superintendent of Ontario's Neglected and Dependent Children, Kelso won public support for closing down reformatories and instituting many facets of the social safety net—youth courts, family allowances, legal adoptions, and recreation programs—in place today. He also founded various organizations to prevent cruelty to children and animals, such as the Toronto Humane Society and the Santa Claus fund.

◆ Child labor activist

Craig Kielburger was only 13 years old in 1995 when he confronted world leaders, including the Team Canada trade delegation led by Prime Minister Jean Chrétien, about the plight of enslaved child laborers. Craig, the younger son of Thornhill, Ont., schoolteachers, credits an older brother's influence for his activist nature. As an impressionable six-year-old, he watched brother Mark devote his time and energies to environmental issues. A garage sale provided the initial funding for Craig and some friends to set up an anti child-labor group that has now expanded internationally. Following his 1995 Asia trip, where he crossed paths with Team Canada in India, Craig became much in demand as a speaker across North America. He chronicled his Southeast Asia experiences in *Free the Children* (1999), which he co-wrote with novelist Kevin Major.

◆ Coast to coast wept when this courageous hero died

A native of Winnipeg, Man., Terry Fox (1958–81) grew up a keen athlete in Port Coquitlam, B.C. A student at Simon Fraser University, he was planning on a career in physical education when in 1977 he learned he had bone cancer, which necessitated amputation of his right leg. Shortly afterward, Terry began planning his Marathon of Hope, a cross-Canada odyssey to raise money for cancer research. At first the run attracted little attention, but within a short time the televised images of the courageous one-legged athlete had captured the imagination of the country. Canadians from coast to coast wept when he announced in Thunder Bay, Ont., that he was abandoning the run because the cancer had spread to his lungs. The Marathon of Hope that Terry Fox began in Saint John's, Nfld., in April 1980 was never completed. But like the young heroic runner who planned it, the Marathon of Hope continues to raise money for cancer research as well as inspire Canadians by the thousands.

◆ The renegade economist

"In economics, the majority is always wrong," wrote John Kenneth Galbraith (born 1908). A native of southern Ontario, the world-renowned Harvard University economist has been an adviser to Prime Minister Trudeau and to American presidents dating back to Franklin Roosevelt. A renegade in the field of economics, one of his lifelong tenets is that governments should create jobs by directly intervening in the economy. In 1997 Galbraith was invested as an Honorary Officer of the Order of Canada.

◆ Thwarted musician enriched the prairies

"He contributed more to the wealth of his country than any other man," London's *Daily Express* wrote on the death of Charles Saunders (1867–1937), the London, Ont., chemist who developed Marquis, an early-maturing, rust-resistant strain of wheat capable of surviving early prairie frosts. But Saunders' achievement came at a terrible personal price.

His father, the dictatorial founder of an Ottawa experimental farm, insisted his son study chemistry rather than music, which was Charles' wish. When he refused to become a full-time assistant on his father's plant hybridization research, Saunders Senior named him Experimentalist (the title later became Cerealist, then Dominion Cerealist) to the Experimental Farms Service, and Charles, who was teaching music in Toronto, docilely moved to Ottawa. Years of careful seed selection, crossbreeding, and harvesting followed. Charles chewed kernels from various varieties to test their glutenous strength. Milling and breadmaking qualities were also tested. By 1904, Marquis wheat was clearly superior. The first crop of the new strain was harvested in Saskatchewan in 1909, and by 1920, Marquis represented 90 percent of the wheat grown in western Canada and throughout much of the United States. Saunders was knighted in 1934.

◆ Lonergan's drive to know

Quebec-born Bernard Lonergan (1904–84), Jesuit philosopher and theologian, taught at Rome's Gregorian University, Harvard, and Boston College. In his studies of the mind in action, Lonergan demonstrated the interaction of the natural and social sciences, philosophy, and theology. "Deep within us all," he wrote, "emergent when the noise of other appetites is stilled, there is a drive to know, to understand, to see why, to find the cause, to explain."

◆ Human rights pioneer

Born in Hampton, N.B., in 1905, John Peters Humphrey did not have an easy childhood. He lost both parents by the time he was 11, and his left arm was amputated when he was six because of a severe burn. Undeterred by these setbacks, Humphrey earned four degrees at McGill University and later became a professor and Dean of Law. As first director of the Human Rights division of the United Nations, he drafted the U.N.'s Universal Declaration of Human Rights, passed on Dec. 10, 1948. Humphrey was also instrumental in helping launch Amnesty International Canada and the Canadian Human Rights Foundation. He died in 1995.

◆ Dean of naturalists

Canada's foremost field naturalist, Irish-born John Macoun (1831–1920), amassed a comprehensive collection of flora and fauna which became the basis of Canada's National Museum of Natural Sciences. "The Professor," as Macoun was popularly known, also championed the agricultural possibilities of the West, so much so that Canadian Pacific Railway directors opted to build the railway across the southern prairie via Calgary and Kicking Horse Pass, rather than along its original northerly route through Edmonton and Yellowhead Pass. In 1882, Macoun was appointed Dominion Botanist to the Geological Survey of Canada and began a comprehensive study of the range and distribution of flora and fauna across Canada. He later established The Dominion Herbarium, to which he donated more than 100,000 specimen sheets. Over 75 species ranging from plants to butterflies have been named for him.

Oxytropis macounii, or locoweed

◆ She brought the bar to justice

It was 1941 before women could study and practice law in every Canadian province. Some 49 years earlier, the Law Society of Ontario refused to permit Clara Brett Martin (1872–1923) to study law. With the support of women's groups, Martin mounted a massive lobbying campaign that bore fruit in Ontario legislation allowing women to study law. But Martin's problems didn't end there. After her studies were over, the Law Society refused to call Martin to the bar. She had to lobby Ontario lawmakers to pass more enabling legislation, and in 1897, the feisty Torontonian finally became a lawyer.

◆ Canada's first female professor

One year after graduating from Montreal's McGill University, Carrie Matilda Derick (1862–1941) became Canada's first female instructor when McGill appointed her a professor of morphological botany in 1912. A dozen years earlier, the outspoken women's rights activist had filed a government report demanding a greater say for women in matters of higher education. As a McGill professor, Derick was able to play a significant role in that area. She actively fought to have domestic service recognized as a profession, and compulsory school attendance, care for handicapped children, and industrial education were also lifelong causes.

> **66 Whatever women do, they must do twice as well as men to be thought half as good. Luckily, this is not difficult. 99**
> — Charlotte Whitton

◆ Ottawa's no-nonsense mayor

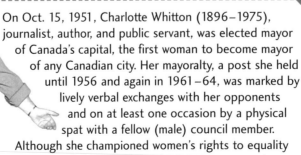

On Oct. 15, 1951, Charlotte Whitton (1896–1975), journalist, author, and public servant, was elected mayor of Canada's capital, the first woman to become mayor of any Canadian city. Her mayoralty, a post she held until 1956 and again in 1961–64, was marked by lively verbal exchanges with her opponents and on at least one occasion by a physical spat with a fellow (male) council member. Although she championed women's rights to equality in politics and the workplace, the feisty mayor spoke out against married women who worked and was opposed to more liberal divorce laws. Whitton's repartee was legendary. When a visiting dignitary asked, "If I smell your corsage, will you blush?" Charlotte shot back, "If I pull your chain, will you flush?"

◆ A hen for hubby's birthday

Despite bitter opposition from the medical community—Sir Charles Tupper took out advertisements warning the public against "these female quacks"—Lady Ishbel Aberdeen (1857–1939) founded the Victorian Order of Nurses in 1897.

The VON was her compassionate response to pitiful stories of women dying in childbirth for lack of trained help and settlers dying unnecessarily from accidents and epidemics.

Lady Aberdeen's social and philanthropic legacy to Canada, from the years she spent here in the late 1800s with her husband, Governor General Lord Aberdeen, included both the VON and the National Council of Women of Canada, which she helped found in 1893.

A woman of great poise and action, Lady Aberdeen was an excellent public speaker, but considered herself deficient in small talk. She also possessed an unusual sense of humor: On her husband's 50th birthday, she gave him a hen, so that even when traveling he could enjoy fresh eggs.

◆ First woman in Parliament

Canada's first female Member of Parliament, Agnes Macphail (1890–1954) won her seat in 1921 in the first federal election in which women had the vote. The Ontario schoolteacher held her seat in Ottawa until 1940. Three years later Macphail was elected to the Ontario legislature, where she served until 1945, and again from 1948–51. Though rural issues led her to politics (she represented a farmers' organization), women's issues were also close to her heart. She founded the Elizabeth Fry Society of Canada, was an active participant in the Women's International League for Peace and Freedom, and played a major role in Ontario passing its first equal pay legislation in 1951.

◆ Suffragette seamstress

The daughter of a schoolteacher, Flora MacDonald Dennison (1867–1921) began work at 18 teaching in a one-room school near Belleville, Ont. After marrying traveling salesman Howard Dennison, Flora settled in Toronto, where she designed ball gowns and trousseaus for a major department store. Later she opened her own dress-making business. An outspoken advocate of women's rights, she saw how poorly seamstresses were paid, and began to speak out in favor of unions seeking better pay for women. One of her forums was a weekly column in the *Toronto Sunday World*, where divorce, birth control, pacifism, and women's suffrage were among her favorite subjects. Eventually she became president of the Canadian Suffrage Association.

Queen of Siam

◆ Canada's most famous governess

Before she was made famous in Hollywood's *The King and I*, Canada's most famous governess, Anna Leonowens, spent four years as governess to the children at the Court of Siam (present-day Thailand), where she is said to have persuaded the Siamese King to liberate one million slaves.

Born Anna Harriette Crawford in Wales in 1834, she was raised in the Far East, where she married Maj. Thomas Leonowens of the Indian Army. They had two children and were living in Singapore when Leonowens died in 1858. Two years later, King Somdetch P'hra Paramendr Mongkut invited her to tutor his 64 children, and she spent the next four years at his court. She wrote two books about the experience: *The English Governess at the Siamese Court* and *Siamese Harem Life*. When she left Siam she moved to New York and then to Halifax to live with her daughter and son-in-law, Thomas Fyshe. In Halifax, where she lived from 1876-97, Leonowens worked to improve conditions for women prisoners and was instrumental in founding what is now the Nova Scotia College of Art and Design. In 1897, the family moved to Montreal where Fyshe was manager of the Merchants Bank.

Leonowens died in 1915. The inscription on her grave, marked by a Celtic cross in Montreal's Mount Royal Cemetery, reads: "Duty was the guide of her life and the love of her heart. To her life was beautiful and good. She was a benediction to all who knew her, a breath of the spirit of God."

Anna Leonowens, age 44

Alberta's famous five

◆ They courted change for women ◆

History has called Nellie McClung, Emily Murphy, Irene Parlby, Louise McKinney and Henrietta Muir Edwards "Alberta's Famous Five" for their 1928 petitioning of the Supreme Court of Canada to rule on the status of women under the British North America Act. At the time, women were not deemed persons, and were thus barred from certain federal posts and positions. When the court ruled against the women, the five appealed the case to the British Privy Council (then the court of last resort), which in the famous "Persons" Case of 1929 ruled that women were indeed persons. "The exclusion of women from public office," declared the court, "is a relic of days more barbarous than our own."

Ontario-born **Nellie McClung** (1873–1951; *see opposite page*) was a best-selling writer and activist who campaigned for many reforms including women's suffrage and dower rights, prohibition, and legislation to make factory work safer.

Writer and journalist **Emily Murphy** (1868–1933) was a self-taught legal expert who in 1916 became the first woman magistrate in the British Commonwealth. On her first day on the bench, a lawyer challenged her right to the position, saying she was not a person under British law. From then on she fought to have women declared legal persons, and was instrumental in the passing of the Dower Act and the Married Women's Protection Act of 1910–11.

A strong proponent of women's rights, **Louise McKinney** (1868–1931) gave up her teaching career to become an organizer for the Women's Christian Temperance Union. With her election to the Alberta legislature in 1917, she became the first woman member of a legislative assembly in the Commonwealth.

Farm issues and women's welfare were a lifetime cause of British-born **Irene Parlby** (1868–1965), founder of the United Farm Women of Alberta. During her 14 years as member of the Alberta legislature, she became the first woman cabinet minister in Alberta, sponsored the Minimum Wage Act for Women in 1925, and was Canada's delegate to the League of Nations in 1930.

Daughter of a wealthy Montreal family, **Henrietta Muir Edwards** (1849–1931) helped found the National Council of Women and the Victorian Order of Nurses. Vocational training for young women, divorce on equal grounds, dower rights, mothers' allowance, and prison reform were all causes she championed.

Larger-than-life bronze statues of the Famous Five have been created by Edmonton artist Barbara Paterson. One set was unveiled by Governor General Adrienne Clarkson on Oct. 18, 1999, in Calgary's Olympic Park; 70 years to the day of their landmark case. The second set was unveiled on Parliament Hill in 2000.

W. L. Mackenzie King at a ceremony unveiling a plaque to the Famous Five in the Senate Antechamber, June 11, 1938. Although not all five could be present, attendees included: Back row, left to right: Senator Iva Campbell Fallis, Senator Cairine Wilson. Front row, left to right: Henrietta Muir Edwards, Mrs. J. C. Kenwood, King, Nellie McClung

*Nellie McClung (far right)
and friends, June 17, 1916*

"Never retract, never explain, never apologize"

◆ "Get the thing done and let them howl"

Ontario-born Nellie McClung (1873–1951), militant feminist, fiery author, and rural schoolteacher, was the first woman member of the Alberta legislature. Growing up in Manitoba, she became acutely aware of the disparity between men and women. She once wrote if pregnancy-related morning sickness were a man's disease, it would have been subject to scientific research "and relieved long ago."

"Never retract, never explain, never apologize. Get the thing done and let them howl," was her motto. A prolific writer, her first book, *Sowing Seeds in Danny* (1908), went through 17 editions and 100,000 copies. A humorous and engaging speaker, she led parades and made fiery speeches in quest of the vote for women, which Manitoba granted in 1916. By then she was living in Alberta and fighting in Emily Murphy's fight to have women recognized as persons. The Prairie crusader also served six years on the CBC board of governors and was Canada's representative to the League of Nations in 1938.

◆ Wilfred T. Grenfell's medical mission

In the 1890s, a British doctor, Wilfred T. Grenfell (1865–1940), established hospitals, nursing stations, schools, and orphanages in remote coastal communities of Newfoundland and Labrador. He arrived on the scene in 1892 on behalf of Britain's Mission to Deep Sea Fishermen. Even though the evangelical Moravian Brethren had been laboring in the area since the 1770s, Grenfell was shocked at the rampant poverty and disease he found there.

Working with the Moravians, he hired doctors and nurses to look after the health and general well-being of the local people. Grenfell organized cricket matches and concerts to lift their spirits, cottage industries such as rug making to bring them some income, and fought to replace "trucking," a bartering system that kept the fisherfolk forever in debt to cooperative stores. Grenfell publicized his cause through his books (he wrote 20) and lecture tours that brought willing, unpaid summer volunteers and outside financial support. It also earned him considerable criticism for being a self-promoter.

In his later years, Grenfell was knighted and honored with awards from various medical and geographical organizations.

A tombstone commemorates three of Grenfell's beloved sled dogs who gave their lives for his when he was lost at sea

TO THE MEMORY OF THREE NOBLE DOGS. MOODY. WATCH. SPY. WHOSE LIVES WERE GIVEN FOR MINE ON THE ICE. April 21st 1908. WILFRED GRENFELL, ST. ANTHONY.

◆ Public triumphs spurred by private grief

In the 1880s, one in every five Canadian children died from what their stricken parents called "the summer complaint." Most of the bereaved accepted the loss as "God's will." Not Adelaide Hoodless (1857–1910). The wife of a wealthy Hamilton, Ont., furniture manufacturer, Mrs. Hoodless went looking for answers in 1889 when her 18-month-old son succumbed to the dreaded summer illness. Her child, like scores of other infants of her day, had died from drinking milk contaminated by the sun, flies, and bacteria to which it was exposed on its way to market. From that day on, Hoodless campaigned tirelessly for the pasteurization of milk and for home economics programs in schools.

Because of her efforts, many colleges and universities introduced home economics programs. Hoodless headed the Hamilton branch of the fledgling YWCA, founded the first Women's Institute (at Stoney Creek, Ont., in 1897), and helped Lady Aberdeen found the National Council of Women and the Victorian Order of Nurses (*see page 98*). An indefatigable campaigner for women's causes to the end, she collapsed and died at age 52 while addressing the Federated Women's Institute in Toronto in 1910.

> " **Real joy comes not from ease or riches or from the praise of men, but from doing something worthwhile.** "
> — **Wilfred T. Grenfell**

◆ Nursing pioneer

From the earliest days of New France, Canada had known many dedicated nurses, but apart from orders of nuns and the occasional dedicated laywoman such as Jeanne Mance (1606–73), founder of Montreal and founder of the country's first hospital, nurses all too often were uneducated, poorly paid, and the lowest of servants. Mary Agnes Snively (1847–1933), a native of St. Catharines, Ont., changed all that. On graduating from New York's Bellevue Hospital in 1884, she became superintendent of Toronto General Hospital, a position she held for the next 25 years. In that time she established a school of nursing, graduates of which started nursing schools elsewhere in Canada and throughout the world. Miss Snively was the first president of the Canadian Nurses' Association, which she had helped found.

◆ Doctors without borders

In 2001, the Canadian chapter of Médecins Sans Frontières/Doctors Without Borders marked 10 years of providing medical assistance to populations in dangerous, war-torn and disease-ridden regions of the world. Ten years ago, Dr. Richard Heinzl, a young Toronto doctor who helped found the Canadian chapter of the international humanitarian organization, was one of the first volunteers Canada sent overseas. He traveled to Cambodia to assist in the rehabilitation of a provincial hospital and helped Kurdish refugees in Turkey, where in one day Heinzl recalls treating 300 patients.

Passport of a doctor with Médecins Sans Frontières

Since its founding in 1991, Doctors Without Borders Canada has sent more than 700 volunteers into the field, as doctors, nurses, logisticians, administrators, water and sanitation experts and coordinators. The international group won the Nobel Peace Prize in 2001.

◆ The "Conscience of Canada"

Fired for opposing conscription, arrested during the Winnipeg General Strike (*see page 166*) and accused of being a communist when he organized the Manitoba Independent Labour Party, James Shaver Woodsworth (1874–1942) may be one of Canada's most unlikely heroes. A social worker and Methodist minister, Woodsworth is generally credited with persuading Mackenzie King to adopt the Old Age Pension Plan, the cornerstone of Canada's social welfare legislation, in 1926. In 1933, he was the first leader of the Cooperative Commonwealth Federation (CCF), the forerunner of today's New Democratic Party.

◆ **Honest Ed: The man with the midas touch**

Canada has many millionaires, but none as unique as Edwin "Honest Ed" Mirvish. The son of Russian Jewish immigrants, Mirvish was born in Colonial Beach, Virginia, in 1914, and came to Toronto when he was nine. He became famous as Honest Ed, of discount department store and restaurant fame. He rescued the Royal Alexandra Theatre from receivership in 1962, bought London's Old Vic Theatre in 1982, and built Toronto's Princess of Wales Theatre in 1993, reinventing himself as a theatrical impresario and producer of such hit shows as *Les Misérables*, *Miss Saigon*, and *Rent*. An Officer of the Order of Canada and Commander of the Order of the British Empire, Mirvish has also been awarded the Freedom of the City of London, which gives him the right to walk his sheep, untaxed, across London Bridge, and, in the event of his execution by hanging, the use of a silk rope.

Massey-Ferguson tractor, 1958

◆ **Suzuki took science to the people**

Demystifying science has been a lifelong avocation of David Suzuki (born 1936), an internationally respected geneticist who believes science is too important a subject to be left to the experts. His accessible science and sense of humor on television series such as *Suzuki on Science* (1971–72) and *The Nature of Things* (1979 on) has made him a household name in Canada. Interned with his parents like thousands of Canadians of Japanese ancestry during World War II, Suzuki has since become a role model for tolerance and knowledge, teaching at university, writing widely on science and science policy, and creating the non-profit David Suzuki Foundation in 1990 to explore human impact on the environment.

◆ **Parsimonious to employees, philanthropic to the world**

Through acquisition of patents, mergers, and aggressive advertising, Hart Massey (1823–96) transformed his father Daniel's Cobourg foundry and plow-making shop into the giant agricultural machinery manufacturer Massey-Harris Company Limited. In the 1890s, the company was the largest of its kind in the British Empire. (Further mergers in the 1950s changed the company into Massey-Ferguson Limited.) A devout Methodist who regarded his business as a trust from God, Hart Massey contributed to many charitable, religious, and educational institutions. He promoted the pasteurization of milk and numerous cultural endeavors. Yet to many of his workers, he was a parsimonious employer who got enormously wealthy on their backs. His company was one of the first to have its own staff magazine, *Massey Magazine*. The industrialist's philanthropy built Toronto's Massey Hall, and the University of Toronto's Hart and Massey colleges.

◆ The candy man

Known to his employees as "Mr. A.D.," confectioner Arthur D. Ganong (1877–1960) was an avid angler who often cast his line in the St. Croix River near his family's sweet factory in St. Stephen, N.B. Ganong and factory supervisor George Ensor (a gum and jelly whiz from Baltimore) were tired of returning from their fishing trips with pocketfuls of sticky chocolate, and created a wax paper-wrapped chocolate bar as a convenient snack. The first five-cent chocolate nut bar went on sale in 1910.

◆ Oracle of the electronic age

The medium is the message

The *Oxford English Dictionary* lists 346 references to Edmonton-born English professor and communications theorist Marshall McLuhan (1911–80), who first attracted international attention in the 1960s for his ideas on the way mass media affects how people think and behave. McLuhan emphasized the connectedness of things—the underlying ideas of the Internet and our wired world can be traced to McLuhan's best-selling books *The Gutenberg Galaxy* (1962), *Understanding Media* (1964), and *The Medium Is the Massage* (1967). Controversy raged around much of his work but his basic message was that how we communicate is as important as what we communicate, that in fact, "the medium is the message."

◆ McCurdy piloted first Canadian flight

On Feb. 23, 1909, Nova Scotia-born J.A.D. McCurdy (1886–1961) flew the *Silver Dart* (*above*) over the Bras d'Or lakes in his native province in what was the first airplane flight in Canada. McCurdy was reported to have said the flight felt like downing two shots of whisky, and that he wanted to do it three or four more times. McCurdy would go on to set other aviation records: the first transmission of a radio message in flight in 1910; and, in 1911, the longest overwater flight up to that time from Key West in Florida to Cuba. From 1947 to 1952, he was lieutenant-governor of Nova Scotia.

◆ An "animated cash register"

Rejected for military service because of poor eyesight, Toronto-born press baron Roy Thomson (1894–1976) began work as a clerk at age 14 for $5 a week. He died the enormously wealthy Lord Thomson of Fleet, owner of several newspaper chains and a string of radio and television stations. Once described as "an animated cash register," the future press baron's fortune was secured in 1931, when, as a lone radio salesman in Northern Ontario, he bought an unused radio license (for $1) and transmitter and set up a radio station in North Bay, Ont. He bought his first newspaper, the weekly *Timmins Citizen* in 1934, and turned it into a daily. It was the first of many print acquisitions, leading up to the purchase of the prestigious *Times* of London in 1967. When asked by Nikita Khrushchev what good all his money would do him, since he couldn't take it with him, Thomson replied "Then I'm not going."

Thomson had a reputation for being kind to dogs and small children, and for eating journalists for breakfast

◆ "The apple of God's eye"

From 1776 to 1783, itinerant evangelist Henry Alline (1748–84), a Puritan who had moved from Rhode Island in the 1760s, rode and tramped through the Nova Scotia countryside holding revival meetings for his New Light religious movement. God, he thundered, had led His faithful from sinfully rebellious New England to Nova Scotia, "the apple of God's eye," where His church would be reborn. Although the basic thrust of Alline's message—"There shall be no frolicking, drinking, or horse racing"—would have little appeal to the average Nova Scotian today, he was a major influence in establishing the Baptist Church in the Maritimes.

◆ Cree clergyman and lexicographer

Anglican clergyman Edward Ahenakew (1885–1961), spent his life trying to give his fellow Cree a sense of their worth as native people. A gifted writer and speaker in Cree and English, Ahenakew traveled from reserve to reserve in his native Saskatchewan, spreading his message of hope and respect. He collaborated in the creation of a Cree-English dictionary, wrote a monthly newsletter in Cree syllabics, and in the 1920s worked to form the League of Indians of Western Canada.

in God's service

◆ A Jesuit martyr

A tall, powerfully built man, Jean de Brébeuf (1593–1649) learned the Huron language within two years of arriving in Canada in 1625, and worked among the Huron for two decades. In the 1630s, he supervised the preparation of a Huron grammar and dictionary. Around 1640, he wrote "Ahatonhia" (Jesus Is Born), a carol in the Huron language describing a Nativity scene in which angels summon hunter braves to visit the infant, wrapped in "a ragged robe of rabbit skin," lying within a lodge made of bark. In 1649,

he was captured by the Iroquois, who subjected him to hours of appalling torture. He is buried near the Martyrs' Shrine at Midland, Ont.

◆ The Children of Peace

Between 1825 and 1830, David Willson and his followers, the Children of Peace, built the impressive, square, three-story Sharon Temple that dominates the village of Sharon, Ont. The pioneer religious sect consisted of former Quakers, and the architectural features of their temple symbolize many of their beliefs. The square shape denoted unity and justice to all. Doors on all sides were a sign that everyone entered on an equal footing from all directions. To ensure that the light of the Gospel fell equally on all members of the congregation, all walls had an equal number of windows. The temple was made a national historic site in 1990.

◆ The cardinal who served lepers

For years French Canada's leading churchman, Cardinal Paul-Émile Léger (1904–91) was also one of the most liberal of the church's princes. A native of Valleyfield, Que., Léger became a Sulpician priest in 1929, after which he worked as

rector of the Pontifical Canadian College in Rome. In 1950, he was consecrated Archbishop of Montreal, an office in which he was much admired for his support of the poor and disadvantaged and his willingness to increase the laity's role in the church, particularly in such times of social upheaval. Named a cardinal in 1953, he decided it was "time for deeds," and stepped down from his see in 1967 to become a missionary to a leper colony in the Cameroons. In 1968, he was made one of the earliest Companions of the Order of Canada.

◆ Doukhobors: "Spirit wrestlers" helped by Tolstoy

More than 7,000 Doukhobors ("spirit wrestlers") settled in western Canada in 1899. Originally a pacifist religious peasant group in southern Russia who believed God dwells in people, not buildings, they rejected liturgy and secular governments. Novelist Leo Tolstoy and Quakers from Britain and America helped many Doukhobors flee to Canada.

Most Doukhobors arrived penniless, and the men went to work building railways to earn money to feed their families and stock their farms. Without horses or oxen to pull their plows, women harnessed themselves to the plows to get the first year's crop in the ground. As many as 60 communities soon flourished around Yorkton, Sask., but some dispersed in 1903, angry at government regulations that would break up their communal farms into individual homesteads. A zealous few protested through civil disobedience, disrobing in public and burning buildings. Many moved on to British Columbia, others established individual farms in Saskatchewan.

◆ Montreal's street priest

In 1988, with $20,000 from a private foundation and a van donated by a local Kiwanis Club, Montreal Roman Catholic priest Emmet Johns launched Le Bon Dieu Dans la Rue ("The Good Lord on the Street"). With a small band of volunteers he began patrolling the streets nightly between 8 p.m. and 4 a.m., offering homeless young people free coffee, hot chocolate, hot dogs, cigarettes, bus tickets, condoms upon request, and above all, friendship. Winning the young people's trust was not easy, but Johns and his team persisted and within 10 years the van was receiving 30,000 visits a year.

Known to his clientele as "Pops," Johns always wanted to be a priest, but felt his calling was to the missions. Nevertheless in 1952, at age 24, he was ordained for the diocesan ministry. For the next 30 years he was involved in parish work and served as a chaplain. One of his most distinguishing features, his silver goatee, dates from those years. He grew it, and has vowed to wear it all his life, in memory of two young nurses who went for an evening stroll and died from exposure on a spiritual retreat he conducted during his hospital chaplaincy.

◆ The kidnapping of Sister Aimee

Sister Aimee knew the value of good publicity. She once visited California's Luna Park Zoo and, before the cameras, faith healed an elephant and a lion

Aimee Kennedy of Ingersoll, Ont., was only 17 when she married Robert Semple, a Pentecostal missionary bound for China. Widowed four years later, she left China in 1912 and sailed to the United States with her baby daughter. There she married H. S. McPherson, with whom she began holding tent revival meetings along the Atlantic seaboard, and with whom she later had a son.

Enormously successful as an evangelist, Sister Aimee, as she was known, built the Angelus Temple of the Four Square Gospel in Los Angeles in 1923. Each night its 5,000 seats were filled by the faithful who came to hear her preach. Sought after worldwide, she toured North America, Britain, and Australia. All this proved too much for her marriage and she and McPherson divorced in 1926. Shortly after, Aimee disappeared while swimming at Long Beach, California, and was presumed drowned.

Weeks later she reappeared in the Mojave Desert, claiming to have been held captive by kidnappers in a remote mountain cabin, but her story was too full

of holes to be convincing. Rumor held that the alleged kidnapping was a ruse to cover up her affair with a radio station manager. Her career never rebounded. In 1944, at the age of 54, she died from an accidental drug overdose.

◆ A Methodist conductor on the Underground Railway

Between 1830 and 1860, as many as 30,000 fugitive slaves are thought to have found freedom in Canada, having made their way here via the Underground Railroad, a network of people and safe houses extending from the slave states in the southern U.S. Perhaps the most famous of these saviours was Methodist minister and author Josiah Henson (1789–1883), who was born on a Maryland plantation and escaped with his family to Canada in 1830. He later wrote: "When my feet first touched the Canadian shore, I threw myself on the ground, rolled in the sand, seized handfuls of it and kissed them." Settling near Dresden, Ont., he first worked as a farm laborer, but went on to found the 1842 British American Institute, a vocational school for escaped slaves. His memoirs, published in 1889, provided the main inspiration for Harriet Beecher Stowe's explosive anti-slavery novel *Uncle Tom's Cabin.*

◆ The "man of good heart"

"The man of good heart" was how the Cree and Blackfoot peoples described Catholic missionary Albert Lacombe (1827–1916). Lacombe spent years as an itinerant missionary in Alberta before serving at various Manitoba and southern Alberta parishes. Known as "the Apostle of the Cree," he wrote a Cree grammar and dictionary, and often served as intermediary between the government and native peoples. In 1883, when the Canadian Pacific Railway came into conflict with the Blackfoot, who threatened to block the route across one of their reserves, Lacombe successfully negotiated on behalf of the railway with Blackfoot chief Crowfoot (*see page 65*).

◆ An Irish pilgrimage in Quebec

The Shrine of Our Lady of Knock, a small church in the Outaouais town of Mayo, Que., is a replica of one that once stood at Knock, Ireland, the site of a miraculous apparition at the turn of the century. The Irish Knock is now a major pilgrimage site and an impressive basilica stands at the site of the original church. The Mayo church also attracts pilgrims in the thousands—from Montreal, Ottawa, and communities in between. Many of them are Irish, and have been making the pilgrimage on the Sunday closest to August 15, the Feast of the Assumption, for some three decades. It began in 1956, when a young Galway man, days after arriving in Canada, was killed in a construction accident on his first day on the job. When his friends got together to plan his funeral, someone offered them a burial site in Mayo, and the church next to the cemetery reminded them of home. News spread among the Irish community, and they began making a pilgrimage to the site. Many of the original funeral party have been regulars ever since.

◆ Mennonites' Old World order

The Mennonites, a Protestant religious group that developed from the 16th-century Anabaptist movement in Europe, first came to Canada in the 1780s via the United States, and bought land in the Niagara Peninsula and Kitchener-Waterloo areas of Ontario.

That first migration was followed by a more conservative group known as the Amish, who also settled in what is now the Waterloo region. Later, in the 1870s, large numbers of Mennonites left Russia for Saskatchewan and Manitoba.

Even today, the Old Order Mennonites continue their traditional farming existence, rejecting modern ways and conveniences, in favor of simple, un-adorned clothes (*below, left*), elaborate hand-made quilts, and traveling by bicycle and horse-drawn buggies (albeit ones with hydraulic brakes, pneumatic tires, and battery-operated lights).

"What you lack in lightnin' you make up for in thunder."

◆ Templeton journeyed from evangelism to agnosticism

Toronto-born Charles Templeton (1915–2001) began his working life as a sports cartoonist, but he abandoned journalism for evangelism. In 1936, he converted through the Church of the Nazarene, a denomination Templeton felt had low academic standards: After reading six books and taking an oral exam, he was ordained. One local preacher said to him: "You'll do fine, Chuck. What you lack in lightnin' you make up for in thunder."

Templeton introduced the Youth for Christ movement to Canada in 1945, and later to Europe and Japan. Templeton began to doubt his faith. Reading Thomas Paine's *The Age of Reason* challenged everything he believed about Christianity. He nevertheless went to Princeton and became an ordained Presbyterian minister, yet increasingly he found his mind at war with his spirit. Evangelism eventually gave way to agnosticism and he quit the ministry in 1957.

Templeton returned to journalism, working for the *Toronto Star*, *Macleans*, and the CTV Network, and wrote three best-selling novels, including *The Kidnapping of the President* (1974).

◆ A miraculous statue comes to life?

From mid-May to mid-October, candlelight processions are held nightly at Cap-de-la-Madeleine, Que., (popularly known as "Le Cap") at Notre-Dame-du-Cap National Shrine to the Virgin Mary. After St. Joseph's Oratory in Montreal and Ste. Anne de Beaupré near Quebec City, it is the most important pilgrimage site in Quebec. The shrine became Canada's national shrine to Mary in 1909, but pilgrims have been flocking there since 1888, when three people are said to have seen a statue of the Virgin come momentarily to life. The miraculous statue (*right*) is housed in a stone chapel that dates from 1714. Its belfries are believed to be the oldest in Canada. A nearby magnificent octagonal Basilica of Our Lady of the Rosary seats 2,000.

◆ Slave legacy put abolitionist on the spot

Irish-born Presbyterian clergyman Rev. William King (1812–95), an active abolitionist, was a missionary in Ontario in the late 1840s when he inherited 14 American slaves. The unusual bequest was from his father-in-law; King had married an American wife during an earlier ministry in the United States. He promptly went to Ohio, where he freed his inheritance. He then proposed that the group found their own Elgin Settlement at North Buxton, a village near Chatham, Ont., where King had some land.

By 1846 the group had cleared fields, built houses, and established a flourishing community that served as a haven for many fugitive slaves. Eight years later, as many as 300 black families were established in the area. Even though many returned to the United States when the Civil War ended, the settlement survived. Today, its pioneers are honored with a Black Historical Settlement exhibit in the Raleigh Township Centennial Museum.

in loving memory

◆ Joseph Guibord's seven-year funeral

During his life, Montreal printer Joseph Guibord (1806–69) had fallen afoul of the Roman Catholic Church by joining the free-thinking Institut Canadien, which was anathema to Montreal's powerful Bishop Ignace Bourget (1799–1885). So the church decided it wanted no part of him in death, and halted his funeral procession at the gates of the Catholic Côte-des-Neiges cemetery, which contained the Guibord burial plot.

The deceased free thinker was temporarily placed in a vault in the Protestant Mount Royal Cemetery, and his wife Henriette and lawyer Joseph Doutre took the bishop to court. In 1870, the court ruled in favor of Henriette, but an appeal court reversed the judgment, which in turn was upheld by the Court of Queen's Bench. In the meantime, Henriette died and was buried without fanfare in Côte-des-Neiges Cemetery. Doutre, however, carried on with the case and won. In London, the Empire's highest court ruled that Guibord must be buried in his family plot. The court also awarded the Guibord family $6,000 costs against the Catholic church.

On Sept. 2, 1875, the Joseph Guibord cortege retraced the funeral journey it had begun six years earlier, but a club-wielding mob barred the way to the cemetery. Once more the corpse had to find

Ashes to ashes

rest in Mount Royal's vaults. Another funeral was planned, this time with police and armed militia on hand, and interment finally took place on a drizzly Nov. 16. The coffin, placed atop that of Henriette's, was encased in cement to ensure it would not be removed by the hostile crowd watching from a distance. The mayor ordered police to remain on guard until the cement dried.

Yet the wily bishop had the last word; after the cement was dry he promptly deconsecrated the ground surrounding his old adversary.

◆ Canada's first national historic cemetery

Halifax's Old Burying Ground, once known as St. Paul's Cemetery, is Canada's first national historic site cemetery. The tree-lined grave-yard was used from 1749 to 1831, with the first burial taking place the day after Halifax was founded. Members of the ship-owning Cunard family and British Major General Sir Robert Ross, who in 1813 ordered that Washington, D.C., be burned, are buried here. The cemetery is also notable for having the Sebastopol Arch, North America's lone memorial to the Crimean War of 1854–56.

◆ Hopewellian burial mounds

Extensive earthworks in Serpent Mounds Provincial Park, just south of Keene, Ont., are Canada's best example of the elaborate, serpentine burial mounds—some up to 61 meters in length—created by the Hopewellian culture that flourished for some six centuries up to about A.D. 500. Hopewellian tradition was not confined to any single native people or language group; Hopewellian peoples stretched from Ontario to Florida, living in fairly permanent villages and trading staples and luxury items. Different groups had their own styles of material goods but all shared a fascination with earthworks, in which animal effigies and geometric shapes figured prominently. They expended great energy and resources on burying their dead and furnishing their tombs with a large array of tools, ornaments, and food for the journey to the next world.

◆ Violent ends etched in stone

The words "murder," "murdered," "shot," and "killed" have appeared on many early Canadian headstones. "Murdered" appeared after each of James, Johannah, John, Thomas, and Bridget Donnelly's names on the imposing granite tomb-stone erected at their gravesite in Lucan, Ont. All were violently slain by vigilantes, because of a dispute over land, on the night of "The Biddulph Horror," Feb. 4, 1880 (*see page 131*). Because of continuing vandalism, the Roman Catholic diocese of London removed the original monument in 1964, and replaced it with a simpler stone which gives the dates on which they "died."

abracadabra

◆ Tribute to a young magician's final disappearing act

Always believe in the magic of your dreams is the motto of a museum of magic and illusion in the village of Giroux, Man. The museum is Gordon and Marilyn Hornan's memorial to their son Philip, a magician who died of cancer at age 15, and whose dying request was that his magic collection be housed in a special room, so others could see and enjoy what had given him never-ending delight.

The Hornans did more than that. In 1991, five years after their son's death, they opened Philip's Magical Paradise in a former church renovated to look like a castle. Magicians from around the world have donated books, posters, and magical apparatus to Philip Hornan's original collection. Among items on display is a 50 cent piece that once belonged to Harry Houdini, a water torture cell used by Doug Henning, trick swords, and lock and key collections.

◆ Hanged for a goose?

A sketch on a rock near Churchill, Man., depicts the hanging of John Kelley, a native of the Isle of Wight, who was rumored to be hanged for stealing a salted goose. In actual fact, Kelley left Churchill very much alive on Aug. 20, 1764, on the London-bound *Seahorse*.

◆ Bean cryptogram eulogizes "2 better wives a man never had"

There is probably no other place where loves and hates, tragedies and treacheries are proclaimed so unabashedly as on weathered tombstones in cemeteries across the land. Mostly poignant, sometimes provocative, often whimsical, they can stop us in our tracks. In his final address to the American people, U.S. president Richard Nixon mused, "Grief, pride, pathos, guilt, gratitude, love: headstones express all of them."

One of the most puzzling headstones ever made has to be a 15-character-square, 225-word cryptogram on a white marble slab in Rushes Cemetery in Crosshill, Ont. (*A replica is shown at right.*) It tells most of what is known of Henrietta and Susanna Bean, but little of the mysterious husband who buried them side by side.

The decoded cryptogram reads (punctuation added for clarity): "In memoriam, Henrietta, 1st wife of S. Bean MD, who died 27th Sep. 1865, aged 23 years, 2 months, and 17 days, & Susanna, his 2nd wife, who died 27th April, 1867, aged 26 years, 10 months and 15 days. 2 better wives a man never had. They were gifts from God, and are now in heaven. May God help me, SB, to meet them there." An invitation beneath the cryptogram says "Readers meet us in heaven."

According to local lore, the cryptogram's author arrived in the nearby hamlet of Linwood in 1865 with Henrietta, a woman half his age. Before the year ended, Henrietta had died. At her funeral, the grieving husband handed out black-bordered cards inscribed with a second cryptogram, this one 19 characters square.

Reading counterclockwise from a specific letter on the 10th line, the card's cryptogram said: "In memoream (sic) Henriettah (sic) Furry Bean, born in Penn., married in Philadelphia to Samuel Bean MD & went with him to Canada, leaving all her friends behind. Died in Linwood the 27th of Sep. 1865, after an illness of 11 weeks. Aged 23 years 2 months and 17 days. She was a model wife, 1 of 1,000—much regretted by her sorrowing husband & all who knew her. Was married 7 months and 10 days. Lived a godly life for 5 years & died happy in the Lord. Peace be to her ashes. So mote it be."

Before long Bean it seems found another love, Susanna, believed to be Henrietta's sister. (How soon this happened after his first wife's death is not known. Provincial records date only from July 1, 1869.) But 19 months to the day of Henrietta's death, Susanna, too, was dead. Soon after, Bean left the area and was never heard from again. Even during his stay in Linwood, there were some doubts as to whether or not he was a medical doctor.

The Bean cryptograms continue to intrigue historians and scholars alike. In 1973, Prof. G. A. Noonan had students in his writing course at Waterloo Lutheran University, now Wilfrid Laurier University, write fictional accounts of the Bean entourage. One student, Margaret Williams of Delhi, Ont., came up with a novel plot in which Bean and his wives—natives of Utah, not Philadelphia—came to Canada to escape the U.S. polygamy prohibition of 1862.

◆ Epitaph to his horse

In a Rosemary, Alta., cemetery, prairie scenes and a cowboy-and-rider image adorn the headstone marking the gravesite of poet and cowboy Roland Roy Eastman, who died in 1990, aged 73. One of Eastman's poems is also reproduced on the marker. It reads:

*"We roamed the range together,
Undaunted, unfettered, so free.
Over trails that are now forgotten,
My brown pony and me.
Over the hills and valleys,
Out where the wild sage grows
Oh give me back that life so free,
That only a cowboy knows."*

◆ His last bedroom

*"Here lies Petter de Broidair
in his last and best bedroom."*

reads the inscription on a grave marker in St. James Anglican Church in Pictou, N.S. The man beneath the slab is thought to be a crusty itinerant schoolteacher who invariably complained to his landladies about the quality of the sleeping accommodation he rented from them. What is not clear is who designed the marker: Did the teacher plan a final putdown of his old nemesis, or did one of his long-suffering landladies finally get the last word?

◆ Western brevity

In the Earleville Rutherford graveyard near Ponoka, Alta., a headstone succinctly sums up the life of Hulbert (Hullie) Henry Orser, who died in 1981, aged 84:

*"He feared God,
did nothing mean,
shot straight and stayed clean."*

Briefer still, but hinting at a wonderful life, is Nellie Chapman's inscription in a Vernon, B.C., cemetery:

"She loved, was loved, and died."

◆ In a few words—or less

Contrasting sharply with the ornate obelisks, imposing angels, and towering monuments in many of Canada's older graveyards are the simple slabs, bearing only the deceased's initials, in Amish cemeteries of southwestern Ontario.

Not quite as down-to-earth as the apocryphal epitaph

"I told you I was sick"

but nevertheless pithy and to the point is an Edam, Sask. grave marker that tells only that

"Big Jack has gone upstairs."

In Greenwood Cemetery in Owen Sound, Ont., a tombstone gives dates when the deceased was

"Born" and *"Born Again."*

And in Picton, Ont., Wm. Pierce's grave marker doesn't give his birth date, but does note that he died on Feb. 31, 1860.

◆ A final plea

In Toronto's Mount Pleasant Cemetery, a tree is carved onto a gravemarker that invites passersby to

"Please walk on the grass."

The memorial is to Thomas "Tommy" Thompson (1913–85), Toronto's first commissioner of parks.

◆ The tired woman

Once Upon a Tomb author Nancy Millar calls the following "the tired woman's epitaph." It reads:

*"Weep not for me now.
Weep not for me never.
For I'm going to do nothing
for ever & ever."*

The inscription marks the grave of Harriet Elizabeth Connell, a centenarian when she died in 1989. The marker is in a cemetery at Okotoks, Alta.

◆ Broken tribute

Echoes of Canada's bloody rebellions of the 1830s—when Canadian revolutionaries attempting to overthrow English rule were sheltered and armed by American sympathizers—are found in a Windsor, Ont., cemetery where one huge flat tombstone reads in part:

*"SACRED
to the memory of
John James Hume
Esqre M.D.
Staff assistant Surgeon
who was inhumanly
murdered and his bo
dy afterwards brutally
mangled by a ga
ng of armed
ruffians from
the United States
styling themselves
PATRIOTS
who committed this
cowardly and shameful
outrage on the morning
of the 4th of
December 1838."*

Up to the mid-1900s, it was not unusual to use the available space on grave markers by dividing even one-syllable words, such as "body" and "gang" above, something unheard of today.

◆ A common epitaph

An obelisk in Quebec City commemorates the Marquis de Montcalm and James Wolfe, generals of the Plains of Abraham battle. The 12-minute encounter on a drizzly Sept. 13, 1759, altered Canadian history and cost both men their lives. The obelisk inscription is written in Latin. Translated it reads:

*"Valor gave them a common death,
history a common fame,
posterity a common monument."*

◆ A royal wife?

If there was a marriage to Edward VIII—as she claimed—and a royal son—as was whispered—schoolteacher Millicent Milroy of Rockwood, Ont., took the details to the grave. But even in death she stuck to her guns about the marriage. The monument that marks her grave in Mount View Cemetery in nearby Cambridge says: "Millicent Milroy, A.M.M.M.; P. St.; Daughter of James and Helen Jane Milroy; 1890–1985; Wife of Edward (VIII), Duke of Windsor; 1894–1972."

The A.M.M.M. in the epitaph is said to stand for Agnes Mary Maureen Marguerite, her other given names, and the P. St. is to indicate a princess of the royal House of Stuart, a title she claimed through her father. The headstone, however, makes no mention of Wallis Simpson, whom Edward is also said to have married, and for whom he gave up the throne.

Apart from her alleged links with the royal houses of Stuart and Windsor, Millicent Milroy led an unspectacular life for all of her 95 years, 35 of them teaching in Ontario. She would have been in her late 20s in 1919 when a Canadian visit by the Duke of Windsor included visits to Ontario schools. Or they could have met four years later when he spent some time in Alberta, where her sister Bessie lived, or in 1924, when the Duke also visited Canada.

Though she claimed to have married the prince, and did not squelch rumors of a son taken to England by his father, Millicent was not forthcoming with details. "They don't want me to tell," she told anyone who pressed for specifics. She promised all would be revealed after her death. Meantime, some people claimed to have seen not only photographs of Millicent with the duke, but their marriage certificate as well. Others said letters arrived regularly from England.

The proof Millicent promised was never found. Shortly after she died in 1985, her house was broken into and several pieces of furniture and other items were removed. While most saw this as just another burglary, Millicent believers saw it otherwise; they remembered how *"they"* would never let her tell.

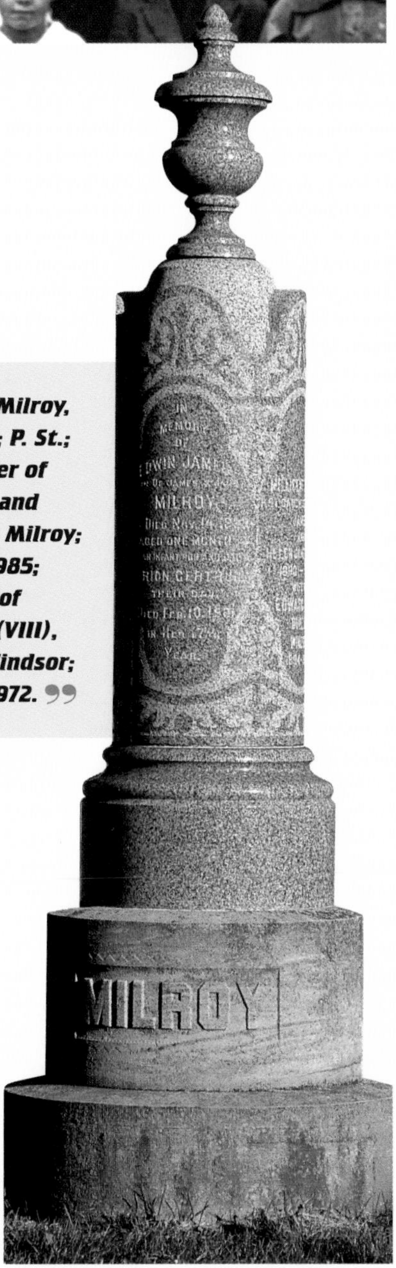

Millicent Milroy, seen here with some of her pupils, at the time Edward, then Duke of Windsor, visited Canada

66 **Millicent Milroy, A.M.M.M.; P. St.; Daughter of James and Helen Jane Milroy; 1890–1985; Wife of Edward (VIII), Duke of Windsor; 1894–1972.** 99

This imposing headstone to the "Wife of Edward VIII" marks the grave of Millicent Milroy and was in place for years before Millicent died

their homes were their castles

◆ The house on the hill

Toronto industrialist Sir Henry Pellatt (1858–1939) made his millions in transportation ventures and hydroelectric power. In 1911, armed with a fortune of $17 million, Pellatt drew up plans to build a dream castle with Canadian architect E. J. Lennox. The land on which he planned to build had been given a name by its previous owner: "House on the hill," or Casa Loma. The result was an opulent, 98-room medieval castle with 30 bathrooms, 25 fireplaces, three bowling alleys, a 50-meter shooting gallery, an indoor swimming pool, hidden panels and secret staircases, and an electrically operated elevator—an unheard-of luxury for its day. The castle's interior is finished in teak, walnut, and marble. The conservatory doors are of bronze. A 245-meter tunnel leads to palatial stables which have mahogany stalls and floors of Spanish tile.

Casa Loma was Pellatt's home for a dozen years, but the upkeep proved too much for him—annual taxes were above $12,000, heating fuel cost another $15,000, and 40 servants added a further $22,000—and he abandoned the castle shortly after his wife's death in 1923. Unable to pay his taxes, he was forced to turn it over to the City of Toronto, which auctioned off most of its contents.

The building was considered for a luxury hotel, a high school, an art gallery, a war veterans' convalescent home, and later, a permanent residence for the Dionne quintuplets. None of the projects proved feasible and Toronto even considered demolishing the castle. In 1936, The Kiwanis Club proposed that they operate the castle as a tourist attraction. The city agreed and a year later Casa Loma opened to the public after extensive refurbishment.

◆ An auto tycoon's showroom mansion

Magnificently landscaped gardens and a splendid 55-room Greek revival mansion in Oshawa, Ont., were part of the estate of Col. R. S. McLaughlin (1871–1972), founder of General Motors of Canada. Parkwood Estate, designed by Darling & Pearson—designer of Canada's Parliament Buildings—was built in 1917 and renovated in the 1930s.

Parkwood's rooms are furnished in Louis XIV, Chippendale, Queen Anne, and Art Deco pieces. Some walls and ceilings are decorated with hand-painted murals; others are covered in exquisite tapestries. Among the furnishings are an Aeolian organ with pipes concealed by silk panels, and a gilded, hand-painted grand piano. The house contains an indoor swimming pool, a bowling alley featuring one of the earliest automatic pin-setters, a squash court, and a billiard room. The grounds contain pools, fountains, an Italian water garden, a Japanese garden, and a formal garden.

◆ Castle fit for a laird

Dundurn Castle, an Italianate Regency villa in Hamilton, Ont., was built in 1832–34 by Sir Allan Napier MacNab (1798–1862), land agent, builder, lawyer, and member of Upper Canada's legislative assembly. From the black walnut paneling of the library to the gleaming mahogany dining room furniture, the house epitomizes the elegant, privileged lifestyle of the 19th-century ruling class. Cockfights are said to have been held in the nearby Cockfight Theatre.

◆ Days of wine and chaperones

The business and banking elite of 19th-century Canada socialized and did business at Glanmore House, a Belleville, Ont., French rococo-style mansion built in 1883 by wealthy local financier John Philpot Curran Phillips. Now open to the public as Hastings County Museum, the house features magnificent ceiling frescoes, Wilton carpets, ornately carved furniture, and an angled ballroom sofa, intended for a couple and their chaperone. Among museum exhibits is the Couldery collection of fine European and Oriental furniture, silver, jewelry, and some 200 paintings. The museum's Dr. and Mrs. William Paul lamp collection is considered the best in North America.

◆ A trompe l'œil masterpiece

An Italianate Victorian mansion, built in 1877 at Baden, Ont., and known locally as Castle Kilbride, was the home of James Livingston, local flax mill king, who named it for his birthplace in Scotland. Unique ceilings and wall paintings, many in a trompe l'œil style, are among its many striking features. The uniqueness and quality of these paintings were largely responsible for the building to be designated a national historic site. The castle's location between Kitchener and Stratford has made it a popular destination with Stratford Festival visitors.

◆ Dalvay-by-the-Sea

A remarkable example of Queen Anne revival architectural style, Dalvay-by-the-Sea Hotel on Prince Edward Island, was once the summer home of Cincinnati oil tycoon Alexander MacDonald, a business associate of John D. Rockefeller's. Sitting on grounds kissed by the Atlantic, this elegant building, characterized by bays, gables, and dormers with contrasting colors and textures, cost $50,000 when it was built in 1896. Furnished with beautiful articles of furniture, pottery and draperies from England, France, Egypt, and Italy, Dalvay also boasted stables, a covered bowling alley, and a billiard room. The MacDonald summer home was usually filled with guests. It cost $10,000 a year to operate Dalvay, a huge sum at the time.

◆ Craigdarroch: The coal miner's castle

Coal baron Robert Dunsmuir (1825–89) arrived penniless in British Columbia, and had gone from mine worker to millionaire, the first millionaire in the province. He built an opulent, four-story, 39-room Scottish-style manor in Victoria, B.C., over thirteen years starting in 1887, but died shortly before he was to move in.

Craigdarroch Castle—named for the birthplace of Annie Laurie—was the tallest building in Victoria in its day. Its 30-meter-high tower room, at the top of 87 steps of stairs, offered a spectacular view of the city. After Dunsmuir's death, his widow, Joan, and three of their 10 children moved in, and Mrs. Dunsmuir regularly took her afternoon tea in the tower room.

Dunsmuir's widow lived in the castle until her death in 1908, at which time the contents were auctioned off. The castle subsequently served as a military convalescent hospital, a college, school board offices, and a music conservatory.

Extensive renovations and restorations were undertaken in 1979, when the castle became a museum, open to the public. Now a national historic site, it attracts some 150,000 visitors a year. Standing imperiously in Victoria's historic Rockland district, the castle features the West Coast's finest collection of residential stained and leaded glass, magnificent wood paneling and carving, gold-leaf trimmed rooms, 17 fireplaces, and outstanding period furnishings.

Pink pills

◆ A magnificent lifestyle financed by a miracle cure

A $3 million investment by the Ontario government has restored the original grandeur of Fulford Place, a 35-room mansion built in 1889 beside the St. Lawrence River in Brockville, Ont. One of the few completely intact Edwardian homes in North America, its opulent design was largely inspired by the summer "cottages" of the Vanderbilts, Rockefellers, and other rich-and-famous dynasties of the day. (In 1983, the Gloria Vanderbilt story, *Little Gloria, Happy at Last,* was filmed at Fulford Place.)

At the turn of the century, world leaders and captains of industry frequented Fulford Place, then the home of patent medicine king George Fulford (1852–1905). When Prime Minister Mackenzie King visited, the mansion's chatelaine reminded him so much of his late mother that, while there, he began the first of his many conversations with his dead parent.

The man who built Fulford Place made a fortune selling Pink Pills for Pale People, a patent he bought from a local doctor in 1890 for $53.01. His marketing know-how made his pink pills the third best-selling patent medicine of the day, and made him a millionaire many times over. Packaging on the iron, starch, and sugar concoctions—"Recommended by the Liberal Minded Doctor and Trained Nurse"—claimed the pills make "Weak People Strong," and mail-order customers in 82 countries bought the spiel—at 50 cents a box.

Today, the grand hall, Louis XV drawing room, the library, and the ornate dining and billiard rooms the pills paid for contain many of the original family furnishings— exquisite tapestries and paintings, French bronzes, Japanese lacquerware. In Fulford's day, it took 30 servants to care for the house, grounds, and yacht. Some, it seems,

George Fulford I | Mary Fulford | Martha | Dorothy | George II

In 1991, descendants of the original occupants (George and Mary Fulford, and their children, Martha, Dorothy, and George II), donated Fulford Place to the Ontario Heritage Foundation

for pale people

The Fulfords traveled extensively—George is seen here astride a camel at one of the pyramids of Egypt—often returning with elegant objets d'art, such as the Russian bronze below. They entertained on a grand scale, regarding this as a duty of their class. Guests in their 50-seat baronial dining room (right) included prime ministers Wilfrid Laurier and Mackenzie King, British prime minister Stanley Baldwin, and Edward VIII (in his Prince of Wales days)

Miracle-cure testimonials figured prominently in promotions that claimed pink pills were a cure-all for everything from anemia and paralysis to pale and sallow complexions. Up to $9,000 weekly—about $90,000 by today's standards—was spent on advertising in Canada alone. Such marketing made George Fulford a fortune that financed this magnificent Edwardian mansion, now a national historic site

benefited little from the pink pills that made weak people strong. Local lore claims that some Fulford Place servants never looked their employers in the eye, turning their faces to the wall if they and family members met on the stairs.

Appointed to the Senate in 1900, Fulford suffered fatal injuries five years later when his chauffeur-driven car hit a streetcar in West Newton, Conn. He is thought to be the first Canadian to die from an auto accident.

Prompted in part by a *Collier's Weekly* exposé of patent medicine scams, the pink pill business began to go downhill shortly after its founder's death. Its demise became inevitable when patent medicines began to be regulated in the early 1900s.

◆ Jessop raised the bar in B.C. schools

When John Jessop (1846–1901) first came to British Columbia on New Year's Day in 1860, the school system was in a state of acute disorganization. At the time, most schools in British Columbia were makeshift affairs erected by canneries, logging camps, and mines for the children of employees. Schools were scattered, attendance fitful, buildings mean and dilapidated, blackboards scarce, the curriculum crude.

Jessop had initially come west from Ontario to seek gold, but failed to find the motherlode and turned back to his original profession, teaching. Born in the English cloth town of Norwich, Jessop emigrated to Canada at the age of 17 when his family settled in Toronto. After completing his teacher's certificate, Jessop taught in several small communities before the lure of

the goldfields in British Columbia disrupted the tranquility of his schoolmaster's life.

After an unsuccessful stint in newspapers in Victoria, Jessop went back to the boards. He opened a school of his own in the old Assembly Hall at the foot of View Street, and called it the Central School. In the first year of its operation, the school enrolled 75 pupils.

Jessop's friendship with the Provincial Secretary for the new government in 1871 led to his appointment as the province's first Superintendent of Education. In 1872, Jessop visited all the schools of the province—on foot and horseback, by canoe and paddle steamer—blazing a trail that would one day be followed by school buses. Jessop noted that some schools were so poorly equipped that they didn't even have a globe. Jessop made sure each had a set of maps and a globe, and made arrangements for textbooks to be bought and distributed. He advertised for teachers in Toronto's *Globe and Mail*, and outlined his dreams for a new provincial education system in his reports to the government.

When Jessop left the education office in 1878, he left 51 elementary schools and one high school enrolling 2,734 scholars all learning a standard curriculum, the foundation for an educational system which would endure virtually unaltered for a century.

*Mission, B.C.,
school bus, 1923*

◆ Montreal's first schoolmistress

Montreal's first schoolmistress, Marguerite Bourgeoys (1620–1700), opened her first school in 1658 in a tiny stable. She would later found a girls' boarding school, a school for native girls, and a domestic arts school. She also chaperoned the *filles du roi*, the young girls sent from France as brides for settlers. Her French and Canadian recruits—her teaching "sisters"—began teaching in rural parishes, founded domestic arts and primary schools in Quebec City, and in 1698, the Congrégation de Notre-Dame de Montréal. Sisters and colonists alike already regarded Marguerite Bourgeoys as a saint at the time of her death, but it was another 182 years before the Roman Catholic Church made it official.

◆ Equal education for all

In 1899, Rev. Alfred Fitzpatrick (1862–1936) was concerned over the plight of Canada's frontier laborers, most of whom were uneducated, illiterate, and often exploited by their employers. Fitzpatrick began teaching out of a log cabin in Nairn, Ont., with no staff, some parish assistance, and little money. Today Frontier College is a beacon for universal education, offering literacy programs for remote communities, ex-convicts, and people with learning disabilities; working with teens, children, and families in urban centers, and offering programs to promote reading. UNESCO gave international recognition to the now Canada-wide college's work by awarding it the 1977 Literacy Prize for its "meritorious work in the field of adult education."

◆ The Antigonish Movement

Thousands of community organizations world-wide have been influenced by the Antigonish Movement, an adult education program designed to improve social conditions through cooperatives. The movement was born in 1928 when Nova Scotia's St. Francis Xavier University created an extension department under Father Moses Coady (1882-1959). A charismatic leader with superb oratory and organizational skills, Coady argued that the essence of genuine community development was that participants became masters of their own destiny.

Coady quickly put his philosophy to the test in the impoverished Antigonish region of Nova Scotia. In the late 1920s, he traveled 13,000 kilometers in 10 months, organizing up to four meetings a day in fishing villages. By the summer of 1930, he was able to bring together more than 200 delegates from fishing communities to a meeting in Halifax, at which they founded the United Maritime Fishermen, a marketing cooperative. Not only did the members gain skills in fish conservation, marketing, refrigeration and the like, but the cooperative rapidly grew and unexpectedly expanded into other areas such as housing and banking.

After his death, St. Francis Xavier University created the Coady International Institute to train adult educators from developing countries based on the theories and practices of the Antigonish Movement. More than 22,000 people have since attended courses and seminars organized by the Institute.

◆ A Canadian university quiz

1. Which university has a Department of Icelandic Language and Literature?
2. Which university has a campus in Essex, England?
3. Which university takes pride in having Bertrand Russell's papers in its library?
4. Which university began its history in 1663?
5. What university's library includes the Hall of the Clans?
6. Which university has an institute specializing in wine-making research?
7. Which university competes in American athletic leagues rather than Canadian ones?
8. What institution was once called simply The Provincial University?
9. Which college has igloo building as an accredited course?
10. Which university adopted the martlet, mascot of McGill University, as its own?
11. Which institution calls itself "Canada's only women's university?"
12. Which university has a course on casino and gambling law?

See answers below

◆ CN's school-on-rails

Living up to its motto as "The People's Railway," Canadian National Railways ran medical, dental, and school cars during the Great Depression. One of CN's four school cars was run by Fred Sloman, the son of a railwayman who offered a mobile education to children of loggers, trappers, and remote railway workers along a 75-kilometer stretch of track between Foleyet and Capreol, north of Sudbury, Ont. A boxcar was furnished as a schoolroom in one part, and a living quarters for Sloman and his family in the other. Children would arrive to class on snowshoes or skis. Fred Sloman retired after 40 years of teaching approximately 1,500 children in car No. 15089.

◆ **Answers**

1. University of Manitoba
2. Memorial University of Newfoundland
3. McMaster University
4. University of Laval
5. St. Francis Xavier University
6. York University
7. Simon Fraser University
8. University of Toronto
9. Nunavut Arctic College
10. Trent University
11. Mount St. Vincent University
12. Queen's University

wonder cabinets: our unique museums

◆ From Model Ts to Bricklins

One of the 2,880 Bricklins manufactured before New Brunswick's ill-fated auto manufacturing plant closed is among automobile treasures displayed in the **Antique Auto Museum** in Les Jardins Provincial Park near St-Jacques, N.B. Most of the prized exhibits—including a 1916 touring Model T Ford in mint condition and a 1910 Detroit Electric three-passenger coupe designed to cover about 65 kilometers on a 40-cell Edison storage battery—came from the private collection of Melvin Louden.

◆ A highly developed museum

A disused Grand Trunk Railway tunnel between Parliament Hill and the Chateau Laurier Hotel in Ottawa is the home of the **Canadian Museum of Contemporary Photography**, Canada's only museum dedicated exclusively to photography. It houses the visions of Canada's foremost photographers of the last 50 years, some 160,000 photographic transparencies, negatives, prints and other photography-based works. The museum was created in 1985 to take over the National Film Board's vast still photography collection.

◆ Napoleon's black silk socks

A pair of black silk socks worn by Napoleon in exile on St. Helena, is among exhibits in Toronto's **Bata Shoe Museum**. After Napoleon's death, the socks were acquired by William Dickson, assistant surgeon on HMS *Carmel*, which took Napoleon's entourage from the island after his death. The museum boasts over 10,000 shoes in its collection, from Chinese bound foot shoes and ancient Egyptian sandals to chestnut crushing clogs and Elton John's platforms.

◆ 100 years of 20/20 vision

The **Museum of Visual Science and Optometry** at the University of Waterloo, Ont.—the only one of its kind in Canada and one of only four in North America—has a collection of eyeglasses dating back to 1700. Displays include many instruments used in the examination of eyes and vision over the last century, optometrist office furnishings of the past, and a Hall of Frame with spectacles of celebrities.

◆ A millennium's history on display

Noted architect Douglas Cardinal designed the **Canadian Museum of Civilization**, a magnificent waterfront building in Hull, Que. Once known as the Museum of Man, the museum houses close to four million artifacts chronicling 1,000 years of Canada's history. Ottawa's Parliament Buildings across the river are framed in the windows of the building's central Grand Hall. Exhibits range from a grain of rice bearing an engraving of a map of Canada to a huge plaster model of the sculpture *The Spirit of Haida Gwaii*. There are archeological, ethnological, folk culture, and historical collections, as well as a postal museum, a children's museum (*see opposite*), and a Virtual Museum of New France.

◆ Ghostly hosts and haunts

At Gananoque, Ont., a ghostly host will guide you and your family unharmed through 20 amazing displays in the **House of Haunts**, a building dating from 1883. The "hauntings" are a relatively recent addition. The attraction is open from mid-May to mid-October.

◆ A five-alarm fire museum

Dedicated to the history of firefighting in Nova Scotia, Yarmouth's **Firefighters Museum of Nova Scotia**'s extensive collection includes several horse-drawn pumpers and historic firefighting equipment from the 19th and early 20th centuries. The rare collection includes one of Canada's oldest steam pumpers, an 1863 Amoskeag; examples of almost every type of fire engine ever used in Nova Scotia; many smaller items like antique toy fire engines.

From teeth to toonies

Teeth, glass beads, shells, fish hooks, grain, cattle, cocoa beans, paper, metal, and playing cards have all been legal tender at various times in 18th-century New France. Many examples are displayed in the **Currency Museum of the Bank of Canada** in Ottawa, where exhibits trace the development of money in Canada and around the world.

Canada's oldest museum

A full-size model of a right whale and a Reynolds Elevated Railway Car are just a few of the items housed in **The New Brunswick Museum**. Officially incorporated in 1929, this Saint John institution is Canada's oldest continuing museum, and began with a collection of rocks, minerals and curiosities of Provincial Geologist Dr. Abraham Gesner (1797–1864), inventor of kerosene (*see page 188*).

No adults allowed

Part of the Canadian Museum of Civilization (*see opposite*), **The Canadian Children's Museum** offers children 14 years of age and younger an interactive, hands-on way of learning, sharing, creating, and having fun. In this 10,000-artifact museum, young visitors can ride an elaborately decorated Pakistani bus, trek through deserts, play chess on a larger-than-life gameboard, unload cargo boats in exotic ports, and learn how to make foods that are favorites of children in other countries.

A totemic village

An authentic native Gitksan village has been reconstructed at the confluence of the Skeena and Bulkley rivers near Hazelton in northern British Columbia, a region where the Gitksan people have lived for 8,000 years. At '**Ksan Indian Village Museum** visitors can tour six cedar longhouses, glimpse Aboriginal culture through performances of native dancers and exhibits of Gitksan regalia, carving, jewelry, beadwork, and other crafts, and visit the Gitanmaax School of Northwest Coast Indian Art, an institution which has fostered world-renowned native artists. Groupings of totem poles, many on their original sites, are in the neighboring villages of Kitwanga, Kitwancool, and Kispiox.

Our flagship museum

A spectacular dinosaur gallery, world famous Chinese treasures including the only Chinese tomb in the western world, and an evolution gallery that traces the history of life on earth are all among the wonders of Toronto's **Royal Ontario Museum**, Canada's flagship public museum. The museum has begun a startling facelift, scheduled to open in 2005. Its new crystal-shaped glass wing (*right*) was designed by German architect Daniel Liebeskind.

Toys in the attic

The Dalziel Barn Museum in Toronto's Black Creek Pioneer Village contains the largest collection of 19th-century toys in Canada. The village, which depicts life in Ontario before 1867, is built around five log buildings that were erected here in the early 1800s. Some 25 other buildings—an inn, school, church, gristmill, weaver's and blacksmith's shops, and general store—were moved from other sites. Educational tours enable students to try their hand at carding wool, churning butter, and hooking rugs.

A Columbian bilboquet, or ring-and-pin game from the Elliott Avedon Museum and Archive of Games

◆ Jurassic Park north

The **Royal Tyrrell Museum of Palaeontology** in Drumheller, Alta., contains not only one of the most extensive collections of dinosaur specimens in the world—some 800 fossils in all—but it also has numerous models of the prehistoric creatures, and thousands of specimens of plants and other ancient remains, including a Burgess Shale exhibit (*see page 35*). Some 400,000 visitors annually visit the museum, named for Joseph Burr Tyrrell (1858–1957), the Geological Survey of Canada geologist who, in 1884, discovered the area's fossil-rich beds.

◆ Time in a bottle

Vintage neon clocks from the 1930s and 1940s, a rare Dutch hooded clock, and a 350-year-old British clock are among timepieces from three continents in Thornhill, Ont.'s **Antique Clock Museum**. Another museum of timekeeping is **The Canadian Clock Museum**, in Deep River, Ont. Dedicated to preserving the products of Canada's many clock manufacturers and sellers since 1800, the museum has more than 600 clocks and watches, including retro novelties such as the "Snider Spider" (*right*). The collection was provided by Allan Symons, a long-time resident of Deep River and the museum's founder.

◆ Games people played

The **Elliott Avedon Museum and Archive of Games** at the University of Waterloo in Waterloo, Ont., is the only museum in the world dedicated to the study of games and game playing. The collection includes 5,000 items and an archive of related research materials. Games range from those played in ancient Egypt to computer games, including puzzles, board and war games, pinball machines, and logic games. Many of the games were brought to Canada by various immigrant groups. Visitors are encouraged to try their hand at the games.

◆ Western Canada's largest museum

A settler's trunk of Austrian silverware, a 17th-century rapier, a 1920s wedding dress, a Paul Kane painting. These disparate historical items are among more than one million objects housed in Calgary's **Glenbow-Alberta Institute**, western Canada's largest museum, and one of the country's foremost museums of art and western history. Visitors can try on cowboy chaps or a suit of armor or research their family tree at this renowned institution, which was created in 1966 when oilman and philanthropist Eric Harvie (1892–1975) donated his vast personal collection of memorabilia and historical material to the people of Alberta. The provincial government built an eight-story downtown building to house the collection.

◆ Lilliputian village

Topiary displays, flower festivals, nature walks, wildflower and bird sanctuaries, and 250 miniature replicas of local historic homes, churches, and area resorts are among attractions at **Cullen Gardens and Miniature Village** in Whitby, Ont. At a scale of 1:12, the homes on its miniature main street even have working, five-centimeter television sets! Elsewhere, the Lynde House Heritage Home, originally built in 1812–14 by one of Whitby's first settlers, offers a glimpse into a typical day in 1856 Canada.

◆ Antiques and philanthropy

Housed in a 100-year-old barn, **Madonna House Pioneer Museum** at Combermere, Ont., contains a workshop, farm implements, household furnishings, clothing and crafts of early settlers of this area. Home of a lay religious community, Madonna House was founded by the late Russian Baroness Catherine de Hueck (1896–1985), a writer and social activist. Proceeds from the sale of antiques, collectibles, fabrics, jewelry, and book collections on sale in several adjoining gift shops go to the world's needy.

◆ Saluting the spud

The history and culture of the noble spud is on display at **The P.E.I. Potato Museum**, located in the community of O'Leary, P.E.I. The whimsical museum, marked by a 4.2-meter giant potato at the entrance, contains the largest exhibit of potato artifacts in the world, including horse-drawn farm machinery once used to plant, cultivate, and harvest potatoes, a heritage chapel, log barn, and schoolhouse.

◆ Valley of the dolls

Canadian doll museums offer something for everyone, from the young in age to the young at heart. The **House of International Dolls** at DeSable, P.E.I., houses a popular collection of handmade porcelain Anne of Green Gables dolls.

First Nations dolls, from as early as the 18th century, made from corn cobs, husks, beeswax, and leather with porcupine quillwork and beads, are among the treasures at The Canadian Children's Museum (*see page 119*), where **The Forster Dollhouse** resides. It contains some 900 furnishings and miniatures, some dating back to the 1830s. The house, complete with electricity, has children's and servants' quarters, a parquet-floored, silk-paneled dining room, a tool shed, and a folding garden stand. Before coming to the museum, the house belonged to six generations of Forsters who immigrated to Canada from Dublin, Ireland, in 1868.

Eaton's beauties, bisque babies, and a Charlie McCarthy ventriloquist's doll are among more than 160 antique and character dolls in the **Kleinburg Doll Museum** in Kleinburg, Ont., while the **Carousels and Dolls Museum** near Brandon, Man., houses a bevy of Barbie dolls dating back to the 1960s. Doll-lovers will also appreciate the over 1,250 dolls from 1850 onward on display at **Dolls in Toyland** in Tillsonburg, Ont.

◆ No "Do Not Touch" signs here

One of the country's leading interactive, hands-on cultural centers, the **Manitoba Children's Museum** in Winnipeg has a grain elevator, a sun gallery, and a working television studio. Youngsters can prepare and star in a newscast, climb on board a 1952 diesel engine, explore an underwater beaver dam, and study wildlife from a treetop vantage point—with nary a "Do Not Touch" sign in sight.

◆ We'll meet again

The glory, the horror, and the legacies of war dominate exhibits and dioramas in the **Canadian War Museum** in Ottawa. Pistols, swords, breastplates, tanks, uniforms, ceremonial military dress, and heavy artillery reveal stories of conflict involving Canadians from the days of New France through to present-day peacekeeping missions abroad. Visitors to the Discovery Room can try on a Viking warrior's garb or don the uniform of a modern air force pilot. One of its most popular exhibitions ever, *We'll Meet Again*, was built around 24 stories of wartime loves and loses dating from World War I to the Bosnian peacekeeping mission. It was mounted in the late 1990s with the help of the Royal Canadian Legion.

Jack Nichols' 1946 oil painting Normandy Scene, Beach in Gold Area, *at the Canadian War Museum*

◆ Moose Jaw's tunnels of "Little Chicago"

Deep below downtown Moose Jaw, Sask., a mysterious labyrinth of underground tunnels preserves the checkered past of one of the Prairies' wildest frontier towns. Widely believed to have been dug in the late 1800s by Chinese railway workers, the tunnels and adjoining basements became the sunless domain of Chinese immigrants who lived and toiled in steam laundries and gunnysack factories, seeking a hiding place for relatives unable to pay the "head tax" required for Canadian citizenship.

The tunnels got a new lease on life in the Roaring Twenties, when speakeasies, prostitution, gambling, and "blind pigs" flourished in Moose Jaw, particularly on notorious River Street, and when the local liquor trade went underground—literally— to escape enforcers of Saskatchewan's Temperance Act. Then, Moose Jaw became the hub of a huge liquor distribution network funneling booze south into an America parched by Prohibition. One tunnel ran straight under the CPR railyards,

making it easy to load and unload illegal booze. It also helped that the local police chief, Walter Johnson, was the bootleggers' friend, and ran the town with little interference from the mayor.

Many Chicago mobsters, Al "Scarface" Capone among them, were said to hightail it to Moose Jaw on the old Soo Line railroad when things got too hot on home turf. Suits made to measure, Turkish baths, and high stakes poker were just a few of the underground amenities allegedly offered to the bootleggers, gamblers, and gangsters who sought refuge in the tunnels. This accounts for the present moniker of the subterranean passageways, the tunnels of "Little Chicago."

The existence of the tunnels was denied for years, but the collapse of part of Main Street revealed them to the world. Today, the tunnels are Moose Jaw's most popular tourist attraction, drawing more than 100,000 visitors to date curious to see the city's "The Chicago Connection."

◆ The Brandy Parliament

Drunkenness was becoming such a problem in the nascent colony of Quebec that in 1668 Intendant Jean Talon (1625–91) built Canada's first brewery in the desperate hope of getting colonists to drink beer instead of brandy. A decade later, Bishop François de Laval declared it a mortal sin to sell brandy to the natives, putting the church on a collision course with Governor Frontenac (*see page 126*), who insisted such sales were essential for the fur trade.

In 1678 King Louis XIV established what became known as the Brandy Parliament to resolve the impasse. Frontenac managed to select the members, however, and they ruled along with Frontenac. They declared such a prohibition would result in the Indians trading with the English at Albany, in what is now New York State. They feared that Protestantism and English rum, instead of Roman Catholicism and French brandy, would become the order of the day. Nonetheless, the king later issued an edict limiting the sale of liquor to native peoples in French settlements and forbidding the transport of liquor to French villages. Frontenac, unshaken in his beliefs about the deal-making merits of brandy, did little to enforce the order.

◆ Burrowing out behind bars

With around 800 residents, Greenwood, B.C., boasts of being "Canada's smallest city." In the 1890s, when it was a mining boom town, Greenwood also had a boisterous nightlife that included gambling halls frequented by notorious figures with such colorful names as Pie-Biter Smith, Two-Fingered Jack, and Dirty George.

With citizens like that, an imposing courthouse was in order, and the one architect George Dillon Curtis designed lived up to expectations. Completed in 1902, it was the area's finest building. Woodwork in the courtroom was of clear-grained coast cedar. Stained glass windows depicted the original seven provinces of Confederation. A staircase led straight from the prisoner's box to cells in a basement constructed of granite masonry. This seems to have been the only flaw in Curtis' design, however. Incarcerated miners experienced in hard rock mining techniques had no trouble digging their way through the foundation walls. Eventually the cells had to be lined with a steel casing that remains to this day.

◆ Will the real Betsy Bigley please stand up?

No one had to tell Betsy Bigley (1859–1907) to dream big; she always knew the world was her oyster. The Eastwood, Ont., railway worker's daughter was blessed with abundant good looks. But she was also an accomplished forger, convincing liar, and a conniving charmer. She bewitched some of the wealthiest men of her day into marriage, then, under a variety of names, spent their fortunes with abandon. One millionaire, however, proved that he was not such an easy touch: Andrew Carnegie turned up in court to deny she was his daughter and to swear his purported signature on a $250,000 check to Betsy (then masquerading as Cassie Chadwick) was not his.

Betsy was only 13 when she first ran afoul of the law for passing bad checks. Three years later she had become Emily Heathcliff and was running a brothel in London. She was working as clairvoyant Lydia deVere in Cleveland in 1882 when she met Wallace

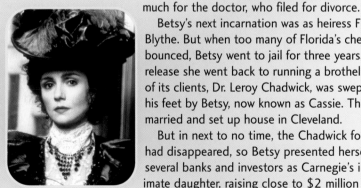

Jennifer Dale as Betsy Bigley in 1985's Love and Larceny

Springsteen, a physician, whom she married. But the speed with which his wife went through his money proved too much for the doctor, who filed for divorce.

Betsy's next incarnation was as heiress Florida Blythe. But when too many of Florida's checks bounced, Betsy went to jail for three years. On release she went back to running a brothel. One of its clients, Dr. Leroy Chadwick, was swept off his feet by Betsy, now known as Cassie. The pair married and set up house in Cleveland.

But in next to no time, the Chadwick fortune had disappeared, so Betsy presented herself to several banks and investors as Carnegie's illegitimate daughter, raising close to $2 million using a check bearing a signature remarkably like Carnegie's. But during a sensational six-day trial in 1904, Cassie failed to convince the court of her innocence. She went from millionaire's row to a jail cell, where she died two-and-a-half years later.

The Dionne quints at three years of age (left to right): Émilie, Annette, Marie, Cécile, and Yvonne

DIONNE QUINTUPLETS PICTURE ALBUM

THE COMPLETE STORY OF THEIR ...

DIONNE QUINTS MUSEUM ♦ NORTH BAY ONTARIO ♦

Dionne Quints North Bay

A cash cow to the Ontario government, the Dionnes were used to sell everything from plates to diapers

◆ Quintuple quandary

The world's first quintuplets to survive birth were born May 28, 1934, in a small farmhouse in the village of Corbeil, in northern Ontario. The five identical little girls, Yvonne, Émilie, Cécile, Annette, and Marie Dionne—whose combined weight was slightly more than 6 kilograms—were taken from their parents soon after and raised in Quintland, a nursery complex custom built for them by the Ontario government. Dr. Allan Roy Dafoe (1883–1943), the country doctor who delivered them, was made their guardian.

During their first nine years, The Dionne sisters were Canada's and indeed one of the world's greatest tourist attractions. As many as 6,000 people a day came to see the little girls. This, combined with income from souvenirs, public appearances, and endorsements

of products—corn syrup, cod liver oil, diapers, milk, soap, toys, and children's clothes—was netting the Ontario government up to $20 million a year. At the height of the Depression, Quintland created thousands of jobs in the Corbeil-North Bay area. Hotel keepers, restaurateurs, tourist operators, merchants, souvenir producers and transportation companies all got a piece of the action.

At nine years of age, the girls were returned to their parents, with whom they lived until they grew up. They had not been prepared for the transition to regular family life, however, and the ensuing years were anything but happy. At age 18, they moved to Montreal. Émilie became a nun and died from epilepsy when she was 20. Marie also died young. In the 1980s, the surviving

quints sued the Ontario government, demanding compensation for using them as a tourist attraction and pocketing the proceeds. At the time the sisters were living on a combined $746 a month.

The $10 million suit remained unsettled until 1998, when public pressure forced the Ontario government to give the sisters $4 million for the exploitation they endured. Part of the settlement was earmarked for Marie's two children. Ontario Premier Mike Harris, who grew up in North Bay, was widely criticized for how he dealt with the suit. He flew to Montreal to apologize in person to the sisters for the treatment they received from the government of Ontario. Yvonne died three years later.

The quints' birthplace, now the Dionne Quints Museum, still attracts visitors from around the world.

◆ Millar kept the stork busy ◆

Ontario lawyer Charles Vance Millar (1853–1926) loved a practical joke. So when details of his will became public, many former associates believed the sole purpose of an unusual clause in the will was to amuse his legal friends. Instead, it touched off a contest among Toronto women that drew interest around the world, and litigation that went all the way to the Supreme Court of Canada.

In the famous "Stork Derby" clause of his will, Millar, a bachelor, left the bulk of his considerable estate to the Toronto mother who would have the most children within 10 years of his death. Within the decade, several claimants came forward, and several court cases ensued. While magazines and newspapers ran box scores of leading contenders, Millar's relatives contested the will. Some parties sought to break the will on the grounds it encouraged immorality; others charged that some of the claimants were ineligible or not married.

However, the courts upheld the will, and in February 1938 the derby funds—some $500,000—were divided between Annie Smith, Kathleen Nagle, Lucy Timleck, and Isabel MacLean, each of whom had given birth to nine children within the 10-year limit. Pauline Clarke, who had 10 children, and Lillian Kenney, who had 12, failed to make the final cut. Mrs. Clarke was disqualified because all her children did not have the same father; some of Mrs. Kenney's children had died and she could not prove that they were not stillborn. Both were awarded $12,500 for their "effort."

Although the stork derby garnered the most publicity, it was not Millar's only last laugh. His will also left racetrack shares to a judge and several clergymen who were outspoken opponents of betting and gambling, and shares in the O'Keefe Brewing Company to Toronto clergymen known as temperance advocates.

The Nagle family (top) and the Timleck family (middle) were two of four families that won the stork derby. At left, Pauline Clarke with twin boys

capers, cons, and curiosities

◆ Foot doctor saw 4,000 feet a day

With a degree in medicine from Queen's College in Kingston, Ont., Dr. Mahlon William Locke (1880–1942, *pictured at right*) took a year's postgraduate training in Scotland in 1905, and two years later began practicing in Williamsburg, Ont.

Before long, his many successes treating foot problems were the talk of the country. One of the first to sing Locke's praises was the local blacksmith, who

suffered severely from arthritis. Dr. Locke tried various treatments and eventually designed shoes, fashioned by a local shoemaker, that greatly helped the stricken man. Other successes followed and by 1919, Dr. Locke was seeing 200 patients a day, mostly for fallen arches. Notices of his work published in U.S. newspapers swelled his clientele to 2,000 a day by 1932.

◆ Landowner laird sued for libel

Scottish families settling on the Ottawa River near present-day Arnprior, Ont., in the early 1820s soon discovered that they were dealing with a landowner who would put most of today's slum landlords to shame. Archie Macnab (1781–1860), a Scottish laird, wouldn't let his tenants leave the land without his permission. Those who got his permission had to pay quit rents, and anyone who dared complain about the unpleasant state of affairs got thrown in jail.

For some 20 years, tenants who complained to the authorities got short shrift, as Macnab had friends in high places and the ruling Family Compact ignored all complaints against him. Finally Francis Hincks (1807–85), Reform leader and publisher of the Toronto *Examiner*, published a Macnab exposé, and the outraged laird promptly sued for libel. He lost the case and with it his power over the settlers. He left Canada and died in poverty in France.

◆ Bible Bill's $25 promise

Albertans suffering through the Great Depression were captivated by radio evangelist William "Bible Bill" Aberhart's promise to give every citizen $25 a month for basic necessities. They elected him premier in 1935, and he formed Canada's first Social Credit government. Although Bible Bill (1878–1943) was never able to make good on his payout promise, he remained premier until his death.

> **"*I do not want a dead heart which, when beating, did not belong to me.*"**

◆ Frontenac the flamboyant

Louis de Buade, Comte de Frontenac (1622–98), the flamboyant governor of New France from 1672–82 and 1689–98, was a 26-year-old spendthrift army officer when he fell in love with Anne de la Grange, a 16-year-old heiress. They married against her parents' wishes, then ran up enormous debts which he sought to evade by taking on the governorship of New France. During his time in Canada, the haughty, autocratic Frontenac ruled the colony as if it were his private kingdom, while his comtesse worked tirelessly in Paris keeping his creditors at bay, restoring his reputation, and encouraging support of his undertakings. But although the marriage lasted 50 years, she never saw New France. In 1699 she learned her husband had died the previous year. Handed a silver chest containing his heart, she rejected it saying: "I do not want a dead heart which, when beating, did not belong to me."

◆ Prairie ghost writer

Frederick Philip Grove (1879–1948) first got a job as school teacher in Manitoba in 1912 and over the next few years earned a well deserved reputation for *Over Prairie Trails* (1922), *Fruits of the Earth* (1933), and other novels of prairie life. His friends were also impressed by his distinguished background as the son of rich Russian parents who maintained a castle in Sweden, a life he described in a 1946 "autobiography," *In Search of Myself*, that won a Governor General's Literary Award.

But the autobiography was as fictional as everything else about Grove, whose real name was Felix Paul Greve, the son of German parents. Before coming to Canada, Greve earned a precarious living in Europe translating English and French authors into German, was in debt and briefly imprisoned for fraud. The mysterious writer spent his last years in Ontario.

Rascals & rogues

◆ St. Thomas founder was no saint

Cantankerous, hard-drinking, Irish-born Thomas Talbot was anything but a saint. Nevertheless, St. Thomas, Ont., was named for him. Talbot (1771–1853) was secretary to Gov. John Graves Simcoe in 1803 when he was granted 2,000 hectares of land on Lake Erie, south of present-day London. Talbot kept plans to his settlement in pencil, so he could erase the names of settlers who displeased him, and kick them off their land. Often he would only speak to his tenants through a window. Nevertheless he got the land cleared and roads built: Talbot Settlement grew to cover over 26,300 hectares of southwestern Ontario, and the Talbot Trail linking towns is now Highway 3. But eventually his eccentric behavior became a hot political issue, and he was forced to surrender the township's plans.

◆ Oak Island's elusive buried treasure

For more than 200 years, rumors have persisted that a fantastic buried treasure lies somewhere on Nova Scotia's legendary Oak Island. No one, however, is sure just what or whose treasure the island is hiding. Pirates were active in the area in the 17th century, and many think the mythical treasure may have belonged to Captain Kidd, or Henry Morgan, or maybe even Blackbeard. Others suspect that it contains Marie Antoinette's jewels, or tell tales of Mayan treasure deposited by Incas fleeing Spanish conquistadors.

Although no trace of the legendary hoard has ever been found, a maze of underground tunnels and shafts on the island have attracted adventurers down the centuries, including a teenaged Franklin Roosevelt and actors such as John Wayne and Errol Flynn. Serious searching began in 1795, when a teenager exploring the then uninhabited island found an unusual depression under the sawn-off limbs of a huge oak tree. He and two friends began digging, and 75 centimeters down came upon a huge layer of stone covering a circular shaft. More digging revealed platforms of oak logs crisscrossing the shaft at three-meter intervals. At nine meters, the trio gave up.

Eight years later, another, more determined group went to work. At a depth of 27 meters they found a slab of stone imprinted with what seemed to be an inscription of some kind. Feeling this was the key to the "money pit," they attempted to bring it to the surface and in the process tripped a booby trap that flooded the shaft with water. Subsequent investigation showed that an ingenious series of tunnels linked the shaft to the ocean. Vast sums of money have since been spent trying to overcome the flooding, which hampered further exploration and caused several accidents. Three treasure hunters died in one accident in 1965.

Oak Island is now privately owned and any gold seeking under way is kept well out of view of prying eyes. The current exploration company, Triton Alliance, has consulted scientists from the Woods Hole Oceanographic Institute in Massachusetts, who have explored the area with camera probes and high-tech equipment similar to that used to explore the wreck of the *Titanic*. So far, Captain Kidd is still having the last laugh.

larger than life

◆ The Giantess of Nova Scotia

By the time she was five, Anna Swan (1846–88) was already 1.42 meters tall. When she went to school at Mill Brook, N.S., she couldn't fit in the standard desks, and her parents couldn't find shoes to fit her. Anna (right) soon became known as the "Giantess of Nova Scotia."

At 16 Anna went to work for American showman P. T. Barnum, where she was paid $1,000 a month to let people marvel at her statuesque beauty. While touring with Barnum, Anna met the Kentucky giant who became her future husband, Capt. Martin Van Buren Bates. At 2.28 meters and 2.19 meters respectively, Anna and her husband were billed by P. T. Barnum as "the largest married couple in the world."

Together they toured Europe and North America, then settled down in a specially built home at Seville, Ohio. On Anna's death, her husband erected a magnificent monument to her memory that still stands in the Seville cemetery. Memorabilia of the famous couple can be seen in the Anna Swan Archives at the Fraser Cultural Centre in Tatamagouche, N.B.

◆ Too tall to ride

At 2.5 meters tall, Edouard Beaupré (1881–1904) of Willow Bunch, Sask., may have been too tall to ride horses, but he could pick one up with one hand. Beaupré was 17 and wore size 25 shoes when he joined the P. T. Barnum Circus, where he remained until his death six years later. A life-size papier-mâché figure of the native son, his clothes, ring, and bed are displayed in the Willow Bunch Museum.

Edouard Beaupré's shoes, size 25

◆ McAskill sipped his rum in threes

Cape Breton's Angus McAskill (1825–63), a 2.4-meter-tall mill operator from St. Anns, N.S., was credited with singlehandedly lifting huge logs and pulling heavy wagons. Born a normal-size baby in the Scottish Hebrides, McAskill grew to his enormous height and a weight of 193 kilograms. He had a 102-centimeter waist and wore 37-centimeter boots, was reputed to have smoked a mallet-sized pipe that held 77 grams of tobacco, and drank brandy and rum from a huge wooden bowl that held the equivalent of three glasses. Hard times in Cape Breton forced McAskill to tour North America, Europe, and the West Indies in 1849–53, during which he amazed and delighted thousands with feats of strength and his kindly manner. He later returned to Cape Breton and his mill. He died in 1863 at age 38 at St. Anns.

Too tall to ride horses, but he could pick one up

◆ Faster than a speeding stagecoach

In 1865, Peter Loler, a Maliseet native from New Brunswick, outran four teams of horses and tore into Woodstock five minutes before the stagecoach that refused to let him get on board in Fredericton, 96 kilometers away. Angry at the stagecoach driver who wouldn't allow him on the coach, Loler vowed to get to Woodstock ahead of the coach and raced ahead of the team of horses that had to be changed four times on the journey.

◆ He lifted 18 fat men aloft

Louis Cyr (1863–1912), a turn-of-the-century Montreal tavern owner, weighed 166 kilograms, sometimes ate a 13.5 kilogram pig for lunch, and thought nothing of lifting a barrel of cement onto his shoulder with one hand. In London, England, Cyr once lifted in succession 250 kilograms with his finger, 1,860 kilograms on his back, and 124 kilograms above his head with one hand. His most spectacular achievement, however, took place in Boston in 1895, where he lifted a platform holding 18 fat men, a total of 1,967 kilograms, thought to be the greatest amount ever lifted by any man. When Cyr died of kidney disease in 1912, at age 49, Montreal gave him a hero's funeral.

◆ Heavyweight gold

Surgery corrected the club foot and withered leg Doug Ivan Hepburn (1926–2000) was born with, but the experience left him a weakling. His Vancouver schoolmates would ridicule him shamelessly, so Hepburn responded as scores of other bullied boys in similar situations have: he took up bodybuilding.

Hepburn had his first big success at 22, when he pressed 136 kilograms, the greatest weight pressed by a Canadian athlete since official records had been kept. The following year, he beat the U.S. champion, but this feat brought him little fame at home. It took his friends to raise the money to send him to Stockholm in 1953, where he lifted 468 kilograms and was acclaimed the strongest man in the world. Later that year, he was awarded the Lou Marsh Trophy as outstanding athlete of the year. The following year, he won the heavyweight weightlifting gold medal at the British Empire Games.

◆ Twelve-foot Davis

Vermont-born trader and prospector Henry Fuller "Twelve Foot" Davis (1820–93) was much beloved by his neighbors in Alberta's Peace River country. Davis established trading posts at Dunvegan, Fort Vermilion, and Lesser Slave Lake, where his honesty, generosity, and pumpkin pies were legendary. The epitaph on the wooden statue marking his final resting place above the town of Peace River reads: "He was every man's friend and never locked his cabin door."

The statue gives the impression that Davis was a physical giant. In fact he was a small man; it was his spirit that was mighty. As for the nickname, it dates back to 1861, when Davis found two claims exceeding the regulation width, claimed the 3.6 m (12-foot) space in between, and extracted $15,000 in gold.

Doug Hepburn hoists his training partner, Johnny Irving, in an over-head handstand

tall tales & unsolved mysteries

◆ A terrible price for a stray cow

Food was scarce on the the reserve near Batoche, Sask., on the October day in 1895 when Almighty Voice (1874–97), a young Cree, spotted a stray cow and shot it for his wedding feast. It was the young man's second marriage and his first wife's family did not approve. His former brother-in-law told police about the cow.

Almighty Voice was arrested, but escaped from jail, and killed the Mountie who tracked him down. It was May the following year before the police caught up with Almighty Voice. The fugitive, together with a cousin, and ex-brother-in-law, with whom he had reconciled in the meantime, took refuge in a poplar grove in Saskatchewan's Minichinis Hills. There they were surrounded by police and civilians—the number would eventually reach 100. When two Mounties and the Duck Lake postmaster were killed in the ensuing skirmish, the police called for reinforcements including cannon, one seven-pounder and one nine-pounder. Heavy shelling followed, and when the attackers finally rushed the grove all three natives were dead.

Field guns were never again used in action in Canada.

◆ The sheriff who stopped CNR in its tracks

In 1907, Stony Plain, Alberta, appointed Israel Umbach its first sheriff and tax collector. The new sheriff discovered that while most citizens were conscientious about paying their taxes, the Canadian Northern Railway was more than a little in arrears. Umbach purchased a sturdy padlock and length of chain from the local hardware store, seized the next CNR train that stopped in town, and padlocked the locomotive to the tracks. The CNR paid up promptly and Sheriff Umbach released his "prisoner." *The Strong Arm of the Law*, a 74-square-meter mural painted by Calgary artist Doug Driediger on a downtown Stony Plain building, commemorates the event.

◆ Pirate of the St. Lawrence

From his hideout in the Thousand Islands, Bill Johnston (1782–1870), "Pirate of the St. Lawrence," amassed a sizable fortune from seizing and looting Canadian vessels plying the St. Lawrence. Johnston claimed it was all honorable. His forays took place during the War of 1812, and he insisted his attacks were all in support of the loyalty he had suddenly developed toward the United States. Johnston later became famous for his exploits during the Canadian rebellion, or so-called "Patriot War" of 1838. On May 29 of that year, Johnston led 22 self-styled patriots in plundering and burning the British mail steamer *Sir Robert Peel* anchored at Wells Island. In 1841, Johnston journeyed to Washington and received a pardon from President Harrison.

◆ Newfoundland's diabolical duo

Between 1740 and 1760, shipping in the Gulf of St. Lawrence was at the mercy of British pirate Eric Cobham and his wife, Maria Lindsay. From their base in Newfoundland, they plundered ships plying the Gulf waters, then murdered the crews, and sank the vessels to ensure there were no living witnesses. Thus they managed to escape capture for some two decades. With their vast booty and terrible secret safe, they settled down on an estate in France, where Cobham was named a magistrate.

Maria, reputed to be the crueler of the two, with a fondness for bizarre executions, went insane and met a violent death, whether by her own or her husband's hand is not clear. Cobham dictated his life story for posthumous publication, but his heirs were partly successful in having it suppressed. A fragmentary copy survives in the Archives Nationales in Paris.

◆ The Biddulph horror

The "Black Donnellys," an immigrant family from County Tipperary, Ireland, were regarded by some as the scourge of Lucan, in Biddulph Township, a farming district near London, Ont. Jim and Johannah Donnelly had seven sons (James Jr., William, John, Patrick, Michael, Robert, and Thomas) and one daughter, Jennie. Many believed the Donnellys were responsible for barn burnings, cattle maimings, and beatings that terrorized the neighborhood. Others claimed that because the poor Catholic family were land squatters, they were victimized by a group of affluent Protestant landowners.

What is known is that Jim Donnelly did serve time in jail for killing a neighbor in an argument over land in 1858. Released in 1865, he returned to Biddulph. Early on the morning of Feb. 4, 1880, a group of masked men broke into the Donnelly home and murdered the entire family as well as a niece, Bridget. A visiting 13-year-old boy witnessed the attack, and survived by hiding under a bed. Six neighbors were accused of the massacre, but were never convicted. The Donnelly story spawned hundreds of books and decades of controversy.

◆ The mad trapper of Rat River

Little is known of the origins of Albert Johnson (*right*), the man known to history as the "Mad Trapper of Rat River." In 1932, Johnson shot and wounded a Mountie who visited his Yukon cabin investigating complaints that Johnson had stolen from Indian traplines. Thus began an epic 48-day manhunt involving dog teams and bush planes (*above*), and January and February temperatures that often plunged below 40°C. But another Mountie was wounded, and a third was shot dead before Johnson was gunned down on the Yukon's frozen Eagle River.

◆ Bill Miner: The gentleman bandit

On a foggy September evening in 1904 near Mission, B.C., three masked men held up the CPR's Transcontinental Express, scooped up cash and gold dust totaling $7,000, then disappeared into the mist without a trace. According to the train crew, the leader of the trio was

Bill Miner, a polite, soft-spoken silver-haired older man. The audacity of robbing the all-powerful CPR—which many westerners despised as overbearing and

exploitative—captured the imagination of British Columbians.

At the time he took on the CPR, Miner, then 56, had four decades of holdups under his belt. Indeed, he is said to have coined the phrase "Hands up." His politeness on the job (he always apologized to his victims for the inconvenience) had caused him to be nicknamed "the gentleman bandit."

When not in jail, the Kentucky-born Miner lived elegantly, earning a reputation for kindness to children and for being a superb dancer. His good manners and wealthy aura

endeared him to society matrons. When he left one community, there was a civic sendoff in his honor.

Miner bungled his second CPR holdup, this time near Kamloops, B.C., in 1906. Although the train carried some $70,000 in cash and bullion, Miner's take was a measly $15. An $11,500 reward was offered for Miner and his cohorts, a massive search was mounted, and they were quickly captured. Miner escaped from Westminster Penitentiary the following year and with local help made his way back to the United States, where he took part in a series of robberies and escapes. His last days were spent as a model prisoner in a Georgia jail, where he died in 1913.

◆ An unfinished canvas

Music, literature, hunting, and fishing were all family passions in the Leith, Ont., farmstead where Tom Thomson (1877–1917) grew up, one of a family of 10. In his twenties, he worked for several photoengraving houses, earning a reputation as a designer-illustrator. In 1906 he took art lessons and began working in oils. He spent the spring of 1912 sketching in Algonquin Park. He later painted "Northern Lake," which was purchased by Ontario for $250, a huge sum to Thomson, who was then earning 75 cents an hour as an illustrator.

Determined to spend more time painting, Thomson made Algonquin his home in the summer months, sketching scenes he would paint in Toronto in the winter. An expert canoeist and fisherman, he worked as a forest ranger in the park and also acquired a guide's license. On the afternoon of July 8, 1917, he was seen leaving Mowat Lodge on Algonquin's Canoe Lake. Later that day his empty upturned canoe was recovered from the water. A week later his dead body was found floating in the lake. Like an unfinished canvas, his suspicious death left many unanswered questions; no satisfactory explanation was ever found.

◆ Wilbert Coffin may have been innocent

On Feb. 10, 1956, still affirming his innocence, 41-year-old Wilbert Coffin went to the gallows in Bordeaux Jail in Montreal for the murder of one of three American bear hunters. The three men disappeared in Quebec's Gaspé Peninsula, where Coffin was prospecting. By the time the bodies were found it was evident that one had been shot, but cause of death could not be established for the others.

Coffin was on death row for three years, during which time he had seven stays of execution. Then, as now, controversy swirled around the case. Many people believed he was innocent and that he had not received a fair trial. The lawyer hired to defend him promised to call 100 defense witnesses, but at the crucial moment called not one. There was widespread belief the Quebec government, concerned about the tourist trade, put pressure on local police and Crown prosecutors to get a conviction.

Long after the trial, but before the hanging, the Toronto *Star* interviewed a man who confirmed seeing a jeep and two other Americans in the area at the time of the disappearances—information that matched Coffin's statements. When the story appeared several other witnesses surfaced, among them a Montreal doctor and a New Brunswick policeman, both of whom called the Gaspé police about their sightings, but nothing was ever done about the matter.

Even though the federal Parliament had referred the case to the Supreme Court before Coffin's execution, public concern was not allayed. In 1964, the Quebec government appointed a Royal Commission to investigate the affair. It, too, found that Coffin had received a fair trial.

◆ Mining magnate's murder still unsolved

A leading figure in early Ontario mining history, American-born Harry Oakes (1874–1943) abandoned medical school at age 24 to prospect in the Klondike. After, he worked in mining in Alaska, Australia, and California. In 1911, he got off the train in Swastika, Ont., with $2.65 in his pocket. He left 24 years later with $200 million.

In 1912, Oakes staked the Lakeshore and Tough-Oakes properties near Swastika (*below*). He became immensely wealthy because of the famous Lakeshore mine, one of 12 great gold producers along Kirkland Lake's Golden Mile (*see page 82*).

Miffed at rising taxes and failure to get a Senate seat, and concerned about his health, Oakes moved to the Bahamas in 1935. There he became a major real estate developer and a member of the Bahamian legislature. In 1939 he was knighted for philanthropic work in England, but four years later he was brutally murdered at his home near Nassau. His son-in-law was charged, but acquitted, and the crime was never solved. One rumor was that the murder was the work of a Mafia don whose casino plans Oakes opposed. Others whispered that he knew too much about a wartime plot involving the Duke and Duchess of Windsor.

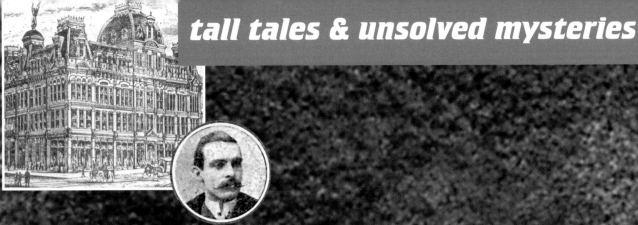

◆ Millionaire vanishes without a trace

More than eighty years after walrus-mustachioed Ambrose Small (1863–1919) vanished from downtown Toronto, his disappearance remains one of Canada's most intriguing mysteries.

On Dec. 1, 1919, the theater magnate, part-time gambler, and self-made millionaire sold his theater chain to Trans-Canada Theatres for $1.7 million. Included in the sale were the Grand Theatre in Toronto, the Grand Opera House in London, Ont., and theaters in Kingston, St. Thomas, and Peterborough, all in Ontario. Motion pictures were beginning to edge out the lavish touring shows Small mounted in his own theaters and some 60 others where he controlled bookings, and so he wanted out.

On the afternoon of Dec. 2, he deposited Trans-Canada Theatre's downpayment—a $1 million certified cheque—in a downtown bank, then had lunch with his wife Theresa (for whom he had already ordered a $10,000 limousine, a $10,000 pearl necklace, and a $3,500 chinchilla-trimmed sealskin coat), and their lawyer, E. W. Flock.

Later, in the Globe Theatre office, Small and his lawyer finalized some business details, after which Flock left. As far as could be positively proved, Small was never seen again.

Mrs. Small did not get unduly alarmed when her husband didn't show up for supper that evening; his business and other interests often kept him away for days at a time. It was two weeks before he was reported missing, and then by one of his theater managers.

Rewards for information were duly posted— $50,000 if he were found alive, $15,000 if

dead—and tips poured in. He was buried beneath the local dump; aliens had taken him aboard their spacecraft; he was spotted playing roulette in Mexico; his body was burned in a Montreal furnace; several hospital patients even claimed they were Ambrose Small.

The search moved briefly to London where the showcase Grand Opera House was gutted in search of his body. But it yielded no trace of Small. (His ghost is said to appear, however, on opening nights at the Grand Theatre, as the Grand Opera House is now known. Many of the theater staff have reported seeing his apparition in the building.)

Meantime, Small's unmarried sisters Florence and Gertrude, were chagrined that Theresa Small inherited their brother's fortune. (She missed out on Trans-Canada Theatres' outstanding $700,000, however, for the company later went bankrupt.) Small was the sole support of the sisters and now they sued the estate for $200 a month. In 1924, a judge awarded each of them the interest on $100,000. Mrs. Small remarked that they could have had that at the outset, plus the $100,000, if they had only asked.

Although she had traveled extensively, led a busy social life, and been active in several charities before her husband's disappearance, Mrs. Small became a semi-recluse after he vanished. She died in 1935 leaving numerous bequests after which the residue of her estate was to go to the Roman Catholic Church. But her lifetime of generosity, the litigation with her sisters-in-law, and succession duties had taken their toll and there wasn't even enough money to pay the bills.

Ambrose Small as seen in the 1998 film Sleeping Dogs Lie

a canadian grimoire

◆ Phantom schooner of Northumberland Strait

On a stormy night in 1786, the lighthouse keeper at Seacow Head Lighthouse in Prince Edward Island saw a three-masted schooner out in Northumberland Strait, sails ablaze in the terrible winds of a nor'easter. The eerie phantom ship has since been spotted by ferry captains, fisheries patrols, even by people from their bedroom windows overlooking the Strait. In January of 1988, a burning ship was spotted just off Borden from the ferry, but did not show up on the radar. Many have set out to the ship to solve its mystery, but the ghost vessel has remained elusive. Legend has it that a pirate, his ship under fire and sinking rapidly, made a deal with the Devil to protect his booty from being discovered. In return, the captain and his crew were to sail forever on the burning ship.

◆ Keeping the wee folk at bay

Stories about the "little people" and "changelings"—fairy children left in place of stolen earthly ones—often figure in Newfoundland folklore. Most tales warn of crossing the paths of these netherworld folk, and island lore offers some novel suggestions to avoid just such a meeting:

Never go into the woods or lonely places on your own, but if you must, don't wear odd socks; turn your sweater or jacket inside out; and carry bread or silver in your pocket. If, despite all these precautions, you still encounter the wee wizened folk, curse loudly or make the sign of the cross, and they will disappear.

The chopping was so loud it knocked plaster off the

◆ Tabor Light of Esterhazy

One night in 1938, a resident of Esterhazy, Sask., was walking near the Tabor cemetery, when a mysterious light about 40 centimeters in diameter began bouncing along the road in front of him. As news of the phenomenon spread, people began making midnight excursions to the site. Eventually many people found the light bobbing in front of them. But as they approached it, it would disappear, then reappear behind them later on. Many theories were put forward, but a true explanation has never been found.

◆ Gruesome goings-on in Griffintown

For more than a century, folklore in the old Griffintown area of Montreal holds that every seven years a headless woman is seen wandering the neighborhood. The spirit is said to be that of Mary Gallagher, in search of the head she lost shortly after midnight on June 26, 1879. As the story goes, Mary and her best friend, housemate, and fellow prostitute Susan Kennedy, had spent the previous afternoon drinking and carousing in Place Jacques Cartier in what is now Old Montreal. Mary picked up a client named Michael Flanagan and the trio returned to the apartment the women shared in Griffintown, an area then occupied by many Irish families.

A downstairs neighbor later testified that she was awakened shortly after midnight by the sound of a body falling, and this was followed by 10 minutes of chopping sounds. The noise was such that it knocked plaster off her ceiling. Mary Gallagher was subsequently found decapitated, her head set in a pail of water by the kitchen stove.

At first Kennedy and Flanagan were considered suspects, but police became convinced that only Kennedy was guilty, since only her clothes were bloodied and a bloody hatchet was found concealed in a dresser in her bedroom. The prosecution's argument was that Kennedy was angry her friend had found a client when she hadn't, and, in a fit of drunken rage, she hit the sleeping Gallagher with an axe. Kennedy offered two alibis. In one version a strange man, who had broken into the apartment in the early morning hours, had done the killing, and she neglected to report the deed "because he was good looking." In the other, she left the house briefly and returned to find her friend decapitated.

Found guilty, Susan Kennedy was at first sentenced to hang on Dec. 5, but Prime Minister John A. Macdonald commuted this to life imprisonment. Released after 16 years in jail, she died in 1916.

In 1998, a Griffintown bar celebrated the apparition with a Bloody Mary special.

◆ Deadly do-it-yourself exorcism

Of the thousands of exorcisms performed in Canada each year, most are by untrained, self-taught exorcists, and some turn deadly. A two-year-old baby girl was accidentally killed by her mother and a neighbor in 1995 when she was force-fed water during an attempted exorcism. In Jan. 2002, Walter Zepeda, 19, of London, Ont., died of dehydration after being tied to a chair for three days without food or water in a botched exorcism. Police charged the dead man's parents and a family friend with murder.

ceiling...

Journalist Kathryn Newman (right) tried to meet the mysterious tenant of the third floor of Legion Hall No. 217

◆ The ghost of Legion Hall 217

Practically every community in the country has its Royal Canadian Union Hall, where veterans of Canada's wars gather for camaraderie and occasions to remember and honor the wars that were and their comrades who made the supreme sacrifice and perished in them. They are not forgotten.

But one Legion Hall stands out from the rest because it is said to be haunted. Here one dead person is certainly not forgotten. It is Legion Hall No. 217, Mimico and Humber Bay Branch, which is located in Etobicoke in western Toronto. Its third floor, it is maintained, is the haunt of the spirit of a young soldier. Only the first name of the soldier is known. It is Henry, and he is believed to be trapped in the top floor of the hundred-year-old building.

Journalist Kathryn Newman learned of the building's reputation in 1987 and convinced the Legion steward to permit her and a friend to spend a night in the building. On the second floor, they kept their eyes peeled on the stairway that led to the third floor, where together they saw what Newman described as "a ghostly green glow." They heard the sound of footsteps coming from the third floor and started to climb the stairs. "Somewhere between the second and the third floor, I lost my courage," Newman later wrote. "I tried not to notice the room getting colder. I switched on the light and then I heard footsteps and thumping right behind me." That was all that it took. They fled, leaving Henry to his haunt on the third floor.

◆ The ghost in the wings

Since it opened in 1912, the Empress Theatre in Fort MacLeod, Alta., has served as a vaudeville house, a concert and lecture hall, and a center for live theater. The decorative neon tulips on the pressed tin ceiling look as good today as they did when prominent Fort MacLeod citizen Daniel Boyle added them to please his wife during major renovations in 1937.

A more unusual reminder of the 1930s is a janitor named Ed, long deceased, but still frequently sensed—and seen—in the building. Ed is said to have carried out a lengthy crying jag in the dressing rooms, when there was a possibility the theater would close down. (He had little to fear—the Empress was eventually purchased and renovated in 1982 by the Fort MacLeod Provincial Historic Area Society.) To this day, Ed is thought to be behind many unexplained happenings about the theater: slamming doors, seats that move up and down on their own, fire alarms that do not register with the security company, coffee cups that move across tables, and garbage cans that empty themselves.

Ed even appears to have a somewhat mischievous nature. Staff have seen him sitting in the same balcony seat, show after show. Occasionally, he appears on stage or in the men's washroom, or is heard racing up and down the aisles. A patron who once purchased admissions from an elderly man inquired next day about the identity of the ticket salesman, and was told that only women were on duty the night before. In death, as in life, Ed seems to be a busy but fun-loving guy.

◆ A sea monster named for a music hall song

Ogopogo, British Columbia's great aquatic monster said to inhabit Lake Okanagan, is described as having the head of a horse and the body of a serpent. In native lore, the monster was "the snake in the lake" and figured often in prehistoric petroglyphs. Monster watchers say Ogopogo inhabits an underwater cave on the east side of the lake.

Recorded sightings, which date back to the 1800s, describe Ogopogo as several humps moving through the water, dark green in color, and up to 15 meters long. The B.C. government took Ogopogo seriously enough to announce in 1926 that a new Okanagan Lake ferry would be equipped with special "monster repelling devices." The beast's name is a palindrome from an old English music-hall crowd-pleaser, "Ogopogo Song."

◆ Two good whacks

She took an axe and gave her husband two good whacks, and on April 15, 1763, Marie-Josephte Corriveau (1733–63) was hanged for murder. Enclosed in an iron cage, Corriveau's body went on public view at Lauzon, Que. Legend says her cage-rattling spirit still waylays travelers on lonely Quebec roads, stories which stem from the mid-1800s, when a cage containing some bones was unearthed in a Lauzon cemetery.

◆ In search of sasquatch

For centuries the sightings around Sasquatch Provincial Park, west of Harrison Lake in British Columbia, have remained uncannily similar: a huge ape-like creature, with a short neck, flattened nose, sloping forehead, and long swinging arms, who leaves a trail of sulphur and footprints up to 45 centimeters long. While Courtenay, B.C., biologist John A. Bindernagel believed most sasquatch sightings were misidentified bears, he firmly believed bigfoot was real. His book, *North America's Great Ape* (1998), examines the elusive creature from a biological and behavioral perspective. Weighing evidence from over 150 sasquatch sightings, Bindernagel makes a strong case for a lost breed of North American gorilla, related to the great apes of Africa and Asia.

◆ Dance with the devil

A popular Quebec folk tale warns of dancing with handsome strangers. While partying with her fiancé, one Rose Latulippe was smitten by a handsome new arrival to the party, and danced with him all night. As the evening drew to a close, the unknown man produced a necklace he told her would bind her to him forever. As he set about putting it around her neck, Rose became aware of the claws inside the velvet gloves she had so much admired. Before the clasp closed, the local curé, alerted by the distraught fiancé, rushed in and placed his stole about the young girl's shoulders. With that, the dark stranger fled on his horse, from whose nostrils flames erupted as they sped into the night.

◆ The Fernie curse

At the foot of Mount Hosmer, near Fernie, B.C., the Elk Valley is a pristine Rocky Mountain preserve dotted with meadows and thick with pine, fir, and spruce. Sometimes, at sunset on summer evenings, shadowy figures—a ghostly horse and rider, the horse led by a native Indian chief—appear on Mount Hosmer's rocky face. Old-timers say the ghost rider is a jilted native maiden who enjoyed less idyllic times in this tranquil, picturesque valley.

According to legend, William Fernie (1837–1921), for whom the city is named, was prospecting near Crowsnest Mountain in the 1890s when he encountered a band of natives. One of the chief's daughters sported a necklace of black stones that Fernie recognized as coal. The chief agreed to share the source of the coal, provided Fernie marry his daughter. Yet once Fernie was shown the source of the coal, he deserted his bride-to-be. When the chief heard his daughter's sobs, he cursed future Elk Valley inhabitants, who would "suffer from fire, flood, strife, and discord, and die from fire and water."

Fernie has since suffered more than its share of disasters: more than 300 men lost in a series of mining accidents; ordeals by flood and fire (including a 1908 fire that leveled the city); rock and snow slides; epidemics of sickness and famine. By the late 1950s, Fernie seemed on the way to extinction. The mayor appealed to Kutenai chief Ambrose Gravelle, known as Chief Red Eagle, and in a solemn song, dance, chant, and drum ritual on Aug. 15, 1964, Red Eagle finally lifted the Fernie curse.

The man who started it all, Fernie, escaped the curse entirely. In fact, not long after jilting the maiden, he found a brand new coal market in Japan. He eventually retired to Victoria, where he died at the age of 84, leaving a $300,000 estate.

◆ Legend of the white horse

On the Trans-Canada Yellowhead Highway at St. François Xavier, Man., a 3.7-meter statue of a white horse recalls the native legend of the White Horse Plain. As the story goes, a young Cree brave from Lake Winnipegosis asked for the hand of an Assiniboine chief's daughter in marriage. To seal the deal he offered the chief a beautiful snow-white steed, a Blanco Diablo, from the famed breed in Mexico. This sent another suitor—a Sioux brave from North Dakota—into a jealous rage. The young couple fled on the snow-white horse, whose gleaming coat was to be their undoing—the Sioux brave was easily able to catch up with the lovers and kill them. The horse escaped—and with him, some say, the spirits of the dead lovers. To this day, the steed is said to haunt the plains surrounding St. François Xavier.

◆ Trotsky's Halifax connection

Nova Scotia once kept famous Bolshevik Leon Trotsky (1879–1940) cooling his heels in an Amherst prisoner-of-war camp. Trotsky was in the United States in 1917, and when he learned the Russian revolution had begun he boarded the *Kristianiafjord*, bound for Norway, in an attempt to return home.

In April 1917, a British naval intelligence official, Admiral Reginald Hall, ordered the ship intercepted in Halifax, where they took Trotsky prisoner. Held briefly, he was interrogated but released in time to continue his journey to his date with destiny.

◆ Trailblazing editor sued for libel

Straight-talking editor Joseph Howe (1804–73) was a staunch champion of his native Nova Scotia and the freedom of the press. In 1835 he was sued for libel for attacking Halifax magistrates and police for corruption and levying excessive fines. His criticisms were published in *The Novascotian*, which he owned and edited. Howe conducted his own defense before a packed courtroom, outlining over six and one-quarter hours the suffering caused by official corruption and the press' right to know. The jury acquitted him and jubilant Haligonians, most of whom were Howe supporters, celebrated for two days.

◆ Masterless Men of Newfoundland

According to oral tradition, the "Masterless Men of Newfoundland" were a society of outlaws who hid out in the Butter Pot barrens, near Ferryland on the Avalon Peninsula, in the late 18th and early 19th centuries. Mostly they were Royal Navy deserters and indentured servants who had run away from the harsh life of the coastal fisheries.

Under the leadership of Irish-born folk hero Peter Kerrivan, they survived by hunting, fishing, trading illegally in isolated villages, and when desperate, by stealing. To the authorities they were criminals, and though a few of them were captured and hanged, most eluded police until conditions improved in the 19th century, and Newfoundlanders won the right to fish independently. Then the remaining Masterless Men moved to outports and began to earn their living as fishermen.

Hanged as a group— the notorious (left to right): Archie, Charlie, and Allen McLean and Alex Hare

◆ McLean gang died in group hanging

British Columbian brothers Allen, Charlie, and Archie McLean, and their partner-in-crime Alex Hare were well-known outlaws in 1879, when Kamloops police officer John Tannatt Ussher crossed their path. The group was suspected of stealing horses, and when Ussher tried to arrest them, they shot him, as well as John Kelly, a shepherd who witnessed the shooting. A posse sent out to bring them in surrounded them in a cabin near Douglas Lake, and after a short siege the four surrendered. Tried and found guilty at New Westminster, they were executed in a rare group hanging on Jan. 31, 1881. Allen was 24 at the time, Charlie and Alex Hare were 17, and Archie was only 15 years old.

◆ Raven's bomb brings down a DC-3

On Sept. 9, 1949, 23 people died when a Quebec Airways DC-3 (*left*) blew apart in mid-air near St. Joachim, Que. One of those killed was Rita Guay, wife of a Quebec City jeweler, Joseph Albert Guay, who had taken out a $10,000 insurance policy on her life moments before she boarded the plane. Tried and convicted, Guay was sentenced to death.

Shortly before his execution, he implicated two accomplices, wheelchair-bound watchmaker Généreux Ruest, who worked for Guay, and Ruest's sister, Marguerite Pitre, a black-clad woman known as the Raven. In return for Ruest making the bomb, and Marguerite putting the package containing the bomb on board, Guay had forgiven the pair a $600 debt.

Guay went to the gallows on Jan. 12, 1951, Ruest on July 25, 1952, Marguerite Pitre on Jan. 8, 1953. She was the last woman Canada executed.

◆ Dr. Dolittle he wasn't

When Peter Lerat appeared in a Toronto courtroom in May 1997 to answer extortion charges, court staff and spectators did a double take: Mr. Lerat arrived completely nude. According to police, Lerat had once demanded customers in a doughnut shop give him money to keep him from killing the Canada goose he carried under his arm. Another time, with a raccoon in tow, he accosted pedestrians and threatened to hurt the animal unless they forked over some money. Charges against Lerat were dropped for lack of evidence.

◆ "Lord Somerset" hanged

One of Victorian Canada's most sensational murder trials ended with an 1890 hanging at Woodstock, Ont. For months before the trial, the accused, a man named Birchall, had duped the town into believing he was "Lord Somerset." Those who had befriended the titled gentleman farmer were incredulous to find out that he was arrested for murdering a young man named Benwall, whom he had defrauded and lured to Canada with promises of non-existent land.

Birchall's demise was not a public event, however. When Thomas Cook was hanged in 1862 for murdering his wife, he was decapitated and his head rolled into the crowd. The uproar that ensued put an end to public hangings in Woodstock.

◆ The priest who couldn't be collared

It took four trials, but on an October day in 1924, a Montreal jury finally acquitted Father Adélard Delorme of murdering his half-brother, Raoul. When the 24-year-old University of Ottawa commerce student's bullet ridden body was dumped on a Montreal street some 2½ years earlier, the priest had offered a $10,000 reward for the killers, and said he hoped they would be executed by public hanging. But Adélard himself became the prime suspect when police discovered he had recently taken out a $25,000 insurance policy on Raoul's life. Their suspicions hardened when they learned that Raoul had inherited their father's considerable fortune, which Adélard administered, often in his own favor. Adding to the circumstantial evidence was the priest's bloodied car, and the fact that the bullets that killed Raoul came from Adélard's gun.

Charging a Roman Catholic priest with murder in a province then very much under the thumb of a Roman Catholic hierarchy was not something taken lightly. Nevertheless Father Delorme was arrested within weeks of the murder. In court, seven psychiatrists testified he was insane, and he was declared unfit to stand trial.

Delorme spent a year in an institution for the criminally insane, but found himself back in court a year later when the institution's medical superintendent certified him sane. From the dock, he blessed those who would save him, and cursed anyone who would dare convict him. That trial, and a subsequent one, ended in hung juries. Finally, the jury at trial number four acquitted him.

◆ David Milgaard: A travesty of justice

In 1999, 44-year-old David Milgaard (*left*), was awarded a $10 million compensation package ($6 million by the Province of Saskatchewan, and $4 million by the federal government) for his wrongful conviction and 23 years behind bars. Found guilty at age 18 of the 1969 murder and rape of Saskatoon nursing aide Gail Miller, Milgaard, who had always insisted he was innocent, was exonerated in 1997 by DNA analysis.

Throughout his incarceration, his mother, Joyce, had worked ceaselessly to clear his name, at one time even buttonholing then Prime Minister Brian Mulroney. Largely because of her detective work, the Supreme Court recommended in 1992 that he be given a new trial. But police and justice officials refused to do so, choosing instead to release Milgaard. As a result he remained under a cloud until 1997, when his lawyers successfully presented DNA evidence clearing him of Gail Miller's death.

The genetic evidence that cleared Milgaard linked Larry Fisher, a serial rapist, to Miller's death. A week later, Fisher was arrested, charged with her murder, and eventually convicted. He had never figured in the original investigation, even though he had an apartment in her home at the time she was killed.

◆ Pot luck

A 60-year-old Ontario man fined $25,000 in a London, Ont., court in June 1998 for growing marijuana for purposes of trafficking didn't have to worry about coming up with the fine. In March of that year, shortly after the marijuana charges were laid against him, a $22.5 million lottery windfall made Bernie Nauss the largest single-ticket lottery winner in Canadian history.

◆ Innocent man jailed for 11 years

Donald Marshall of Sydney, N.S., a Mi'kmaq Indian, was falsely convicted of the 1971 stabbing death of Sandy Seale and served 11 years in Nova Scotia's Dorchester Penitentiary. Marshall, who always maintained his innocence, was finally cleared in 1983 when new evidence came to light. He was released and another man charged with the murder.

A subsequent inquiry revealed that prejudice against native peoples was a factor in Marshall's wrongful conviction. He was awarded $1 million in compensation.

◆ DNA detectives

DNA fingerprinting has been used in many sensational murder trials since it was first used in England in 1986. In Canada, the RCMP first started using DNA analysis in criminal investigations in 1988. Ontario's Centre of Forensic Sciences' DNA Unit, which opened in 1990, has helped settle many court cases, including the conviction in 1993 of Johnny Terceira for the 1990 murder of a six-year-old Toronto girl, Andrea Atkinson. DNA evidence has also been used in Canada to exonerate those wrongly convicted of murder, of whom David Milgaard is the most famous case.

◆ Newfoundlander Gregory Parsons was 19 years old in January 1991, when he found his mother murdered in her St. John's home. For Parsons, the tragedy became even more unbearable when police charged him with his mother's death. In 1994 a jury convicted him of second degree murder, a verdict which was overturned by the Court of Appeal in 1998 when it was shown that DNA material under the dead woman's fingernails did not match Parsons'.

◆ In 1995, DNA tests proved that Guy Paul Morin was wrongfully convicted of the 1985 sex slaying of his next-door neighbor, nine-year-old Christine Jessop of Queensville, Ont. Morin, acquitted of the crime in 1986, was retried and convicted in 1992, largely on the evidence of a cellmate that psychiatrists later characterized as a pathological liar. At the 1997 inquiry into his wrongful conviction, police officers who had earlier balked at conceding Morin's innocence, finally admitted they had helped convict the wrong man. Christine Jessop's killer was never found.

◆ 14-year-old sentenced to death

On June 9, 1959, 12-year-old Lynne Harper got a bike ride from her friend and neighbor 14-year-old Steven Truscott (*left*). When her raped and strangled body was found two days later on the RCAF base at Clinton, Ont., where they both lived, Truscott became the principal suspect. Charged as an adult, he was sentenced to be hanged, but the Diefenbaker government later commuted this to life imprisonment.

In *The Trial of Steven Truscott* (1966), Toronto writer Isabel LeBourdais presented impressive arguments why Truscott could not have committed the crime. The

book struck a guilty chord in the Canadian psyche and the case was reviewed, but eight of the Supreme Court judges upheld the original conviction.

After serving 10 years, Truscott was paroled in 1969 and given a new name. Then, in 2001, he went public, and proclaimed his innocence on the CBC's *Fifth Estate*. A year later, he petitioned the Minister of Justice to clear his name. To date, there has been no reply to his brief. It claims that police and prosecutors knew all along he was innocent. Today, he is married with two children and lives in Ontario.

They always get their man

◆ Forerunners of the Mounties

The North-West Mounted Police (NWMP) is the forerunner of the force known today as the Royal Canadian Mounted Police (RCMP). A paramilitary police force, the NWMP was established in 1873 to bring law and order to the West. Violence and lawlessness were prevalent at that time around the whisky forts that were disrupting the traditional Aboriginal way of life (*see page 74*). The force's next big challenge came two decades later when tens of thousands of prospectors invaded the Yukon during the Klondike Gold Rush. In 1907, King Edward VII gave the force the right to add "Royal" to its name.

◆ The Mounties' musical mounts

Canada's national police force, the Royal Canadian Mounted Police (RCMP) provides policing in all provinces and territories except Ontario and Quebec, both of which have provincial police forces, and is the local police force for some 200 municipalities. It got its present name in 1920, when the government extended its jurisdiction to the whole country.

Horses have always played a major role in the history of the RCMP, as their method of transportation in the early days, and later as entertainment—part of a unique display of riding ability known around the world as the RCMP Musical Ride. Their first performance took place in the Regina barracks in 1887. Interestingly, while the stallions in early days of the Musical Ride were often brown (*below*), today's RCMP mount is always black, approximately 16 hands in height, and weighs between 545 and 590 kilograms.

Hit by the flood of the century—twice

◆ Manitoba's rampaging Red River

Lawson Alfred Ogg drowned in his basement on May 5, 1950, when the flooded Red River invaded his home. Bizarre as this may be, it was even more extraordinary that his was the only death in a $100 million disaster in which 107,000 Winnipeggers had to be evacuated and 5,000 homes and businesses were destroyed (*left*).

When the river finally crested on May 18, it was more than 9 meters above normal. By May 25, the waters were clearly subsiding. City Engineer William Hurst later acknowledged the work of the sandbag brigades, pointing out that Winnipeg was saved by "a million fingers in the dikes."

Nine years after that awful flood, a 51-kilometer canal system was built to handle all future Red River overflows. But that was well before 1997 and what became known as "the flood of the century." When the 180-meter-wide Red overflowed its banks in the spring of that year, Manitobans fought it back farm by farm. But in spite of their ferocious efforts, the river became a massive 30-kilometer-wide torrent. It eventually formed an 1,800-square-kilometer lake that stretched from the U.S. border to the very outskirts of Winnipeg.

Canada's single largest military operation since the Korean War was deployed against the raging river, and 8,500 members of the Canadian Forces formed sandbag brigades alongside thousands of civilians. "It's a war. The enemy is at the gates," observed one army officer. Some 28,000 residents of the affected areas fled to safer ground. But when the Red's crest finally rolled into Winnipeg on May 2, the city was spared.

◆ Regina's twister

Just before 5 p.m. on June 30, 1912, a tornado hit Regina, Sask., slicing a six-block swath of death and destruction. People, houses, pianos, bathtubs, loaded freight cars, trees, horses, and grain elevators were hurled through the air. Five people drowned when winds formed a whirling waterspout at Wascana Lake. Within minutes it was over but in its wake were 28 dead, hundreds wounded, and $56 million in damage.

◆ Hurricane Hazel walloped Ontario

Born in the Caribbean in October of 1954, Hurricane Hazel was all but spent nine days later, when she suddenly sprang to life to become Canada's worst storm, lashing Toronto and southern Ontario with 113-kilometer-an-hour winds and dumping 10 centimeters of rain over a 12-hour period. Hazel hit on Oct. 15, 1954, and when she was finished 83 persons were dead and damage ran into the millions of dollars.

In suburban Toronto, Hazel washed out 40 bridges on the Don, Humber, Highland and Etobicoke rivers and forced 3,000 residents to flee their flooded homes. Outside Toronto, the fierce storm cut a 320-kilometer-wide swath of destruction. A flotilla of boats was pressed into service to help 1,000 Dutch farmers escape from the Holland Marsh, where 2,830 reclaimed hectares of land and vegetable crops worth millions of dollars were inundated.

◆ Ice storm '98 left millions in the dark

On Jan. 5, 1998, massive waves of freezing rain began falling on eastern Canada and the northeastern United States. Four days later, 80 to 100 millimeters of ice rain had turned an area greater than the Great Lakes into a frozen wasteland, where 1,673,000 Canadian hydro customers had neither heat nor light.

The worst hit area extended from Kingston, Ont., through Ottawa and Montreal, to Granby, Que. Over 1,300 giant hydro towers and 35,000 hydro poles buckled like matchsticks under 30 times their own weight in ice. In the largest military peacetime mobilization in Canadian history, some 16,000 troops were rushed to move people to generator-powered shelters; deliver stretchers, blankets, and cots; operate field kitchens; and clear trees.

Other assistance and supplies poured in from across the country, prompting Prime Minister Jean Chrétien to note that "the darkness was being lighted by thousands of individual acts of kindness." Hydro crews from other provinces and the United States worked 16-hour shifts in frigid temperatures to restore power over 3,000 kilometers of fallen transmission lines. In the western part of Montreal Island, the power was out between 3 and 12 days, but for some 100,000 people south of Montreal, the frigid blackout did not let up for more than a month.

When the power finally came back on, 35 people were dead, from hypothermia, carbon monoxide poisoning, and falling ice. Insurance claims totaled $1.5 billion. Hydro Québec's reconstruction bill was estimated at $500 million; Ontario Hydro's over twice that. For families, governments, and companies, the loss was estimated at more than $2 billion.

◆ Hail to Calgary

One of Canada's most expensive natural catastrophes was a violent hailstorm that hammered Calgary on Sept. 7, 1991. Insurance claims paid out for damage to cars, homes, businesses, and aircraft exceeded $400 million.

◆ Barrie tornado

Twelve people died, some 450 were injured, and property damage totaled $100 million when a tornado cut a swath through southern Ontario on the afternoon of June 1, 1985. Within minutes, 300 houses were destroyed, leaving thousands homeless (*left*).

Gander, 1985

◆ Airborne atrocities

None of the 256 passengers and crew survived when a chartered Arrow Air DC-8 crashed on takeoff after refueling at Gander, Nfld., on Dec. 12, 1985. Aboard were members of the U.S. 101st Airborne Division who were heading home to Hopkinsville, Ky., for the Christmas holidays. The tragedy was Canada's worst air disaster.

◆ A cockpit fire made Swissair Flight 111 attempt an emergency landing at Halifax International Airport on Sept. 3, 1998. The plane crashed into the sea off Peggy's Cove, killing 215 passengers and 14 crew.

◆ On Nov. 29, 1963, four minutes after takeoff from Montreal's Dorval Airport, a Trans-Canada Air Lines DC-8 jet crashed at Sainte-Thérèse-de-Blainville, Que., killing 118.

◆ Loss of life totaled 109 when an Air Canada DC-8 enroute from Montreal to Los Angeles crashed at Toronto International Airport on July 5, 1970. The co-pilot inadvertently deployed the plane's flight spoilers on approach, causing the plane to touch down with enormous force, detaching the starboard engine from the wing. Believing he was dealing with an engine fire, the pilot followed normal flight procedure in pulling up for a second landing attempt but the plane crashed minutes later.

◆ Sixty-two people died in a Trans-Canada Air Lines North Star that disappeared on Dec. 9, 1956, enroute from Vancouver to Calgary and was discovered on May 13 the following year on Mount Slesse near Chilliwack, B.C.

◆ Ocean Ranger found a watery grave

An entire 84-man crew—68 Canadians, 15 Americans, and one Briton—went to a watery grave in the early morning hours of Feb. 15, 1982, when the *Ocean Ranger* (*above*) sank in a fierce winter gale. The world's third largest oil drilling rig, *Ocean Ranger* had been anchored in the Hibernia Oil Field, some 300 kilometers southeast of St. John's, Newfoundland. But 145-kilometer winds and 18-meter-high waves proved too much for the oil rig's emergency ballast system, and she overturned. Twenty-two workers escaped from the sinking platform but perished in the icy waters before the first rescue aircraft reached the site eight hours after the sinking. Thirty months later, an investigation concluded that inadequate safety equipment and training procedures contributed to the loss of life.

◆ New Year's avalanche

Four Inuit adults and five children died on Jan. 1, 1999, when an avalanche from a steep hill crushed the school gym where some 500 Kangiqsualujjuag residents were celebrating the New Year. Another 25 residents of this small Ungava Bay community (pop. 700) some 2,400 kilometers north of Montreal were injured in the avalanche. The slide came 90 minutes after a ceremonial gun salute to the New Year. After a similar slide five years earlier, a study commissioned by the local school board—a study not made public until the 1999 tragedy—recommended protective fencing at the school.

◆ End of the *Empress* ◆

Canada's worst marine disaster occurred on May 29, 1914, when the *Empress of Ireland* sank in the St. Lawrence River, 16 kilometers east of Pointe-au-Père, Que., with the loss of 1,014 lives. The *Empress*, a floating palace with her library (*above*) and her own cricket pitch, had left Quebec the previous afternoon bound for Liverpool. Radar that might have warned of the Norwegian collier *Skorstad* approaching in the fog had not yet been invented, so by the time both vessels saw each other no reversal of engines or helm order could stop them.

Once thought unsinkable, the *Empress* was sliced open in the high-speed impact, and she was gone within 14 minutes. Because it went down so quickly, passengers and crew had no time to enter its lifeboats and 1,014 of 1,479 people aboard were lost. The cries of the drowning were like "one long moaning sound," according to *Skorstad*'s captain. None of his crew was lost.

Many of the victims were never recovered. Eighty-eight unclaimed bodies, 68 never identified, are buried in Empress of Ireland Cemetery at Pointe-au-Père. Another 167 victims, all Salvation Army members enroute to a congress in London, were buried in Toronto's Mount Pleasant Cemetery.

◆ St-Jean Vianney's killer mudslide ◆

The signs had been there. During April of 1971, a month of exceptionally heavy rains, most residents of St-Jean Vianney, a small village 220 kilometers north of Quebec City, had seen cracks in village streets, or noted that houses and driveways suddenly settled inexplicably, often by as much as 20 centimeters. Even a 12-meter-high hill had simply disappeared. Neighbors traded stories of loud thumps and sounds of running water beneath their basements.

Yet no-one was prepared for the night of May 4. While hockey fans watched a Montreal-Chicago Stanley Cup playoff game on television, local dog owners were mystified when their dogs began sniffing at the ground or barking. They thought their pet was just acting up; there was no inkling that pets across the village were similarly distressed.

At about 11 p.m. there was a crackling noise, the power went out, and one of the worst landslides ever to occur in Canada swept the sleeping town away in a river of liquid clay flowing at 25 kilometers per hour toward the Saguenay River. Many saw their homes and loved ones slide out of sight. In the dark terror and confusion, no one knew where to run. One family opened its front door to find a yawning abyss where the front porch had been, then pushed and pulled each other to safety through a window as their house melted away. A bus driver and his passengers narrowly escaped when their bus plunged into a 30-meter-wide crater. By midnight, the landslide was over. The gaping muddy hole had swallowed 31 people (most of them children), 44 homes, several cars, and a bus. St-Jean Vianney was gone.

This famous photo is often mistaken for the Empress of Ireland. It is actually her sister ship the Empress of Britain; the name on the ship was retouched on the original photo

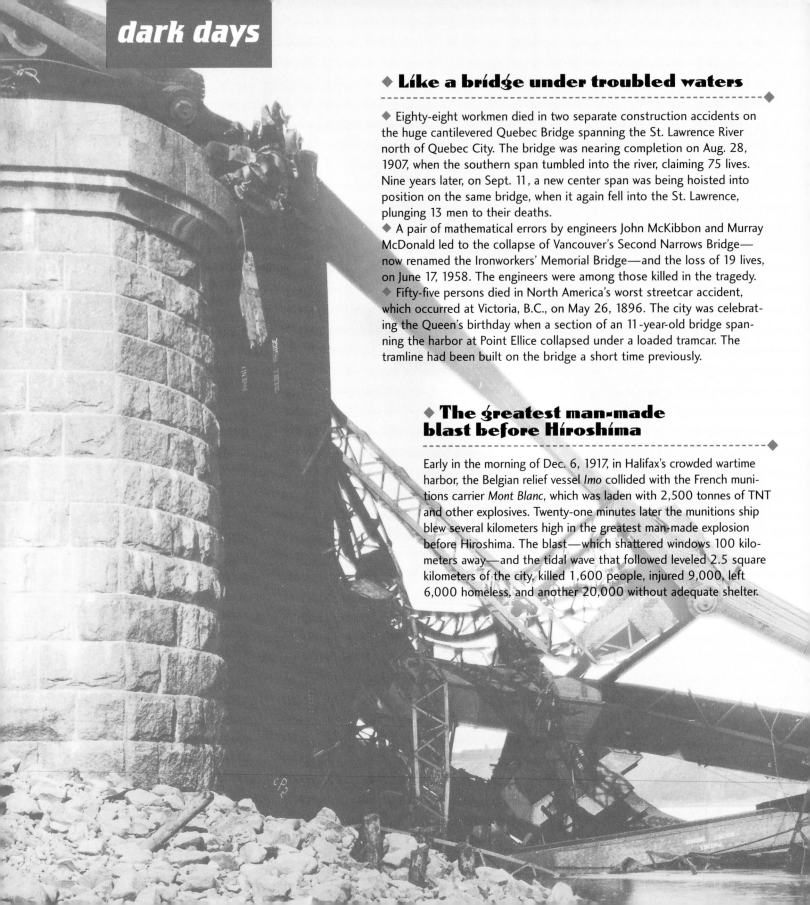

◆ Like a bridge under troubled waters

◆ Eighty-eight workmen died in two separate construction accidents on the huge cantilevered Quebec Bridge spanning the St. Lawrence River north of Quebec City. The bridge was nearing completion on Aug. 28, 1907, when the southern span tumbled into the river, claiming 75 lives. Nine years later, on Sept. 11, a new center span was being hoisted into position on the same bridge, when it again fell into the St. Lawrence, plunging 13 men to their deaths.

◆ A pair of mathematical errors by engineers John McKibbon and Murray McDonald led to the collapse of Vancouver's Second Narrows Bridge—now renamed the Ironworkers' Memorial Bridge—and the loss of 19 lives, on June 17, 1958. The engineers were among those killed in the tragedy.

◆ Fifty-five persons died in North America's worst streetcar accident, which occurred at Victoria, B.C., on May 26, 1896. The city was celebrating the Queen's birthday when a section of an 11-year-old bridge spanning the harbor at Point Ellice collapsed under a loaded tramcar. The tramline had been built on the bridge a short time previously.

◆ The greatest man-made blast before Hiroshima

Early in the morning of Dec. 6, 1917, in Halifax's crowded wartime harbor, the Belgian relief vessel *Imo* collided with the French munitions carrier *Mont Blanc*, which was laden with 2,500 tonnes of TNT and other explosives. Twenty-one minutes later the munitions ship blew several kilometers high in the greatest man-made explosion before Hiroshima. The blast—which shattered windows 100 kilometers away—and the tidal wave that followed leveled 2.5 square kilometers of the city, killed 1,600 people, injured 9,000, left 6,000 homeless, and another 20,000 without adequate shelter.

◆ Montreal theater blaze claims 78 lives

Seventy-eight children ages 4 to 18 died mostly by suffocation in one of North America's most disastrous theater fires on Jan. 19, 1927. As petrified youngsters rushed to escape a fire at Montreal's Laurier Palace Theatre, one child fell at the bottom of a stairway blocking the exit and others tripped over her. The children were trapped and later were found piled eight deep in a solid mass one on top of the other. Firemen were on the scene almost immediately and, within 10 minutes, 78 young bodies were pulled from the theater and laid in rows on the snow-covered sidewalk. Twelve were crushed to death; all the others died from asphyxiation.

The Gazette.

WEATHER FORECAST
Fresh to strong northerly winds partly cloudy and cold or, with light local snowfalls.

TEMPERATURE YESTERDAY
Max. 13; Min. 4

SAME DAY LAST YEAR
Max. 14; Min. 1

CLVI. No. 8   LATE EDITION   MONTREAL, MONDAY, JANUARY 10, 1927.—TWENTY-TWO PAGES   PRICE FIVE C

SEVENTY-SIX CHILDREN KILLED IN PANIC ON STAIRWAY AT FIRE
IN EAST ST. CATHERINE STREET MOVIE THEATRE SUNDAY AFTERNOO

◆ St. John's plague of fires

St. John's, Nfld., has had more than its share of horrendous fires. In 1816–17, three fires left a third of the city homeless. Another fire in 1846 destroyed 2,000 of the city's buildings. Twenty years later, fire devastated the downtown again, leaving over 10,000 people homeless. Then, on the bone-chilling night of Dec. 12, 1942, disaster struck one more time.

It was Saturday night and many residents were enjoying *Uncle Tim's Barn Dance Troupe*, a regular weekend radio show. Some 400 Canadian and American servicemen and their dates were at the site of the broadcast, the Knights of Columbus hostel, a popular spot with military personnel. Listeners at home suddenly heard screams of "Fire!" Within two minutes of receiving the alarm, firemen were on the scene. But those in the auditorium quickly discovered they were locked in a fire trap—the two emergency doors had been locked to ensure compliance with the wartime blackout—and 99 persons burned to death, and as many were seriously injured.

◆ Saguenay flood

In July 1996, two days of torrential rain caused catastrophic flooding on four rivers in Quebec's Saguenay-Lac St-Jean region. Damages were such that insurers regard the tragic event as Canada's first billion dollar natural disaster. Up to 280 millimeters of rain fell, driving some 12,000 residents of Alma, Chicoutimi, Jonquière, La Baie, and other area communities from their homes. When the deluge subsided, 10 people were dead and more than 2,600 homes and cottages had been destroyed. Miraculously, a little white house in the historic Basin Quarter (*above right*) survived. Oddly enough, the house's owner, Jeanne d'Arc Lavoie-Genest, had prayed to the mother of the Virgin Mary to save her little house. The house withstood the flood and became a symbol of resilience to Canadians. Although it was damaged by fire in April 2002, possibly by an arsonist, the little white house remains standing.

The Quebec Bridge collapses for the first time on Aug. 28, 1907

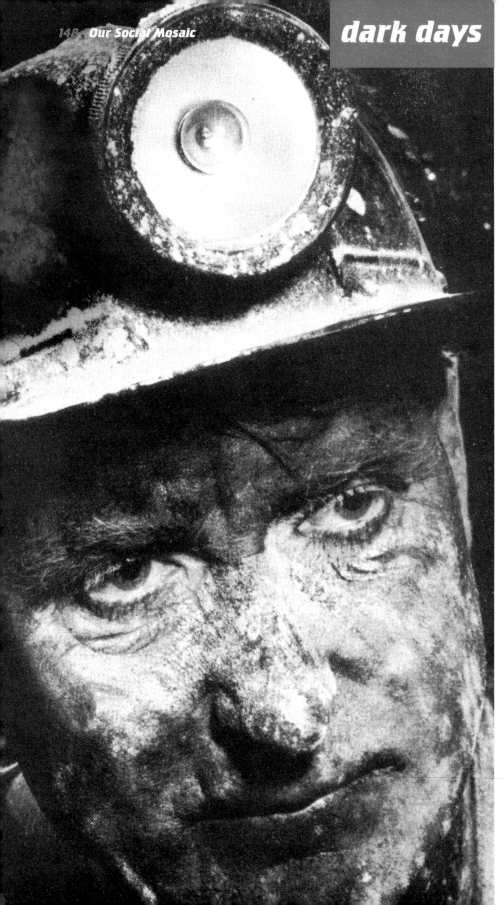

dark days

◆ Tragedy from the deep

Whether coal, silver, gold, or uranium, mining has been one of Canada's most lucrative industries—and also one of its deadliest. Mining accidents have exacted a terrible toll on Canada's miners and their families. One of the worst disasters occurred at Hillcrest, Alta., in 1914, when a rock fall set off an explosion of black damp, or coal dust, that led to the loss of 189 lives.

◆ Coal Creek catastrophe

An underground explosion in the No. 2 Mine at the Coal Creek Colliery outside Fernie, B.C., took the lives of 128 men on May 22, 1902. While the blast killed many of the miners working the night shift in the No. 2 mine, many more in the No. 3 mine were asphyxiated by gas and coal dust. The force of the explosion was so great that the roof of the fan house was torn off, shooting a column of coal dust and rocks nearly 300 meters high.

◆ Gone in 90 seconds

In April 1903, from 70 to 100 people died in what is now Frank, Alta., when 74 million tonnes of limestone crashed down from Turtle Mountain, blocking a mine entrance and in 90 seconds wiping out the outskirts of this Crowsnest community. Sweeping almost two kilometers across the valley, the slide swallowed roads, railways, houses, and farms in its path. After being trapped for 13 hours, 17 miners dug their way to safety. Elsewhere, 23 persons were pulled from the rubble alive.

◆ Springhill sorrow

After being the major industry in the area since the 1870s, large-scale mining ended in the Springhill area of Nova Scotia after the tragic accidents of October 23, 1958, when 174 men, some entombed for up to nine days, were rescued from the mines following an accident that claimed 75 other lives. Today, a monument downtown honors 125 men and boys lost in an 1891 tragedy, 39 miners lost in a 1956 explosion, and the 75 who died three kilometers underground in 1958.

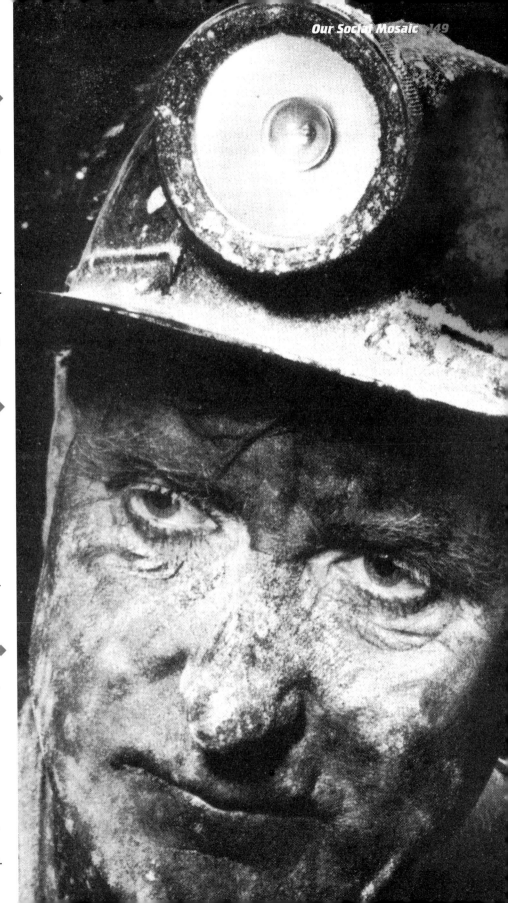

◆ The Westray inquiry

A monument outside New Glasgow, N.S., honors 26 men who died in a May 9, 1992, underground explosion at the Westray Mine in nearby Stellarton. The memorial takes the form of a miner's lamp from which 26 beams of light emanate.

In 1997, a public inquiry concluded the disaster was "the result of incompetence, of mismanagement, of deceit, of ruthlessness, of cover up of apathy, and of cynical indifference," and that management was "significantly derelict in its duty to the workforce and seemed actively to promote a disdainful and reckless attitude to safe mining practices." Following the report, charges of manslaughter and negligence were pressed against two former mine managers. But in July 1998, charges were dropped because of insufficient evidence.

◆ Mass murder in the mines

One of Canada's ugliest labor disputes ended in 1992 with an underground bombing that claimed nine miners' lives in one of the largest mass murders in Canadian history. The blast and the strike that precipitated it divided Yellowknife, pitting neighbor against neighbor. It began when miners who struck at the Giant Mine were locked out by owners Royal Oak Mines. Violence was commonplace on the picket line in the months leading up to the tragedy. Two years later, former gold miner Roger Warren was convicted of the crime and sentenced to life.

◆ Bre-X: Fool's gold

Shareholders around the world lost their shirts when what had been touted as the world's largest gold mine turned out to be one of mining's biggest hoaxes. In 1994, after samples from an Indonesian mine controlled by the Calgary-based Bre-X company were reported to be extraordinarily rich in gold, Bre-X stock soared. When questions about the soundness of the samples were raised, the mine's geologist, fell, or was pushed, from a helicopter flying over the Borneo jungle. Bre-X stock crashed, but before it did, major Bre-X promoter David Walsh sold $45 million of his stock. Walsh subsequently died at home in the Bahamas.

Our
enterprise
and
expertise

MOVERS AND
SHAKERS

ships and shipping

◆ The world's fastest sailing ship

Neighbors of shipbuilder James Smith did not like the look of the triple-masted, triple-decker vessel taking shape in his Courtenay Bay yards, east of Saint John, N.B., in 1850. The fat-bodied, narrow-keeled ship, something of a cross between a cargo ship and a yacht, was unlike anything they had seen before. When a sudden Fundy storm swept in, crushing the giant frame, they took it as a sign the ship didn't want to be built. Shipbuilder Smith had no such qualms. He set about replacing the bent and broken ribs, securing the hull timbers, and planting a figurehead of Marco Polo on the bow.

He launched his 56-meter, 1,625-tonne clipper, *Marco Polo*, on April 17, 1851, but it hit the water at falling tide and remained mired in mud for two weeks. Naysayers murmured darkly that this was a ship that didn't want to go to sea. Freed eventually, she sailed for England with a cargo of lumber, reaching Liverpool in a record 15 days.

As was his plan, Smith sought buyers—a broom tied to her mainmast served as a For Sale sign. *Marco Polo*'s new owners converted her hold into paneled cabins and lounges to accommodate the thousands seeking passage to the Australian goldfields. Captained by James Nichol "Bully" Forbes, she made the 46,000-kilometer round trip to Melbourne and back—then an eight- to nine-month undertaking—in five months and 21 days.

To make this happen, Forbes had his crew jailed in Melbourne on trumped-up charges, lest they desert to join the gold rush, and pistol drove his half-frozen sailors to perform their hazardous duties throughout the gales and ice blizzards of the return trip. But on Boxing Day 1852, she sailed triumphantly into Liverpool docks with a banner that read: "*Marco Polo*, Fastest Ship in the World."

On her next voyage, Forbes vowed he would "astonish God Almighty," but

although *Marco Polo* retained her status as fastest ship, she failed to beat her own record. She continued to ply the Australian route for another 14 years. Then, bought by a Norwegian firm, she reverted to carrying cargo, mostly lumber. Her end came in July 1883, when, leaking heavily, she ran aground off Cavendish, P.E.I. A week later, her fittings were auctioned off for $8,000.

Lucy Maud Montgomery, eight years old at the time, was among those on shore when the once-proud ship met her end. Lucy Maud's recollections of the event were a third-prizewinner in an 1890 essay competition and her first major newspaper breakthrough when published in the *Montreal Witness* in 1891.

The figurehead of the Marco Polo, on display in the New Brunswick Museum. In the background: A. Chidley's "Full Rigged British Ship Marco Polo"

◆ Banks brought strong-arm tactics to the waterfront

Harold Chamberlain "Hal" Banks (*right*) had the blessing of Canada's shipping industry and anti-Communist labor leaders when the 40-year-old American union organizer and convicted felon arrived in Canada in 1949 to oust the Communist-controlled Canadian Seamen's Union (CSU). Using a combination of blackmail, intimidation, and secret accords with the shipping companies, he decimated the CSU. By the early 1950s, Banks ruled the competing Canadian District of the Seafarers' International Union (SIU) with an iron fist. Thirteen years of corruption, turbulence, and violence ensued, during which the careers of thousands of Canadian seamen were destroyed. In his 1963 Industrial Inquiry Commission on the Disruption of Shipping report, Hon. Justice T. G. Norris said of Banks: "He is the stuff of the Capones and Hoffas . . . a bully, cruel, dishonest, greedy, power hungry, contemptuous of the law." Convicted in 1964 of conspiracy to assault, Banks fled his lakeside home in Pointe Claire, Que., in the middle of the night and crossed the border into the United States. The American government refused Canada's request for his extradition. Banks died in California in 1985.

"He is the stuff of the Capones and the Hoffas."

◆ Christened with cider, not champagne

On Oct. 27, 1874, some 4,000 Nova Scotians were on hand at Maitland to witness the launching of the *William D. Lawrence*, the largest wooden-hulled, full-rigged ship ever built in Canada. It was named for its builder, a passionate Nova Scotian who felt that, by approving Confederation, his province's politicians had sold out to central Canadians. Being a teetotaler, Captain Lawrence christened his ship with cider instead of champagne. With a carrying capacity of 2,500 tonnes, she made Lawrence a wealthy man in the nine years he sailed her. Then, in 1883, he sold her to a Norwegian company for whom she also proved profitable for another 15 years. In 1890, she put into Parrsboro, N.S., for a cargo of lumber and the people of Maitland organized an excursion across Minas Basin to see her. The great ship ended her days as a lowly barge.

The stately Victorian home where Lawrence designed his great ship is now a museum containing many of the shipbuilder's fine furnishings and exotic souvenirs of his voyages. Local folklore claims that on stormy nights, the captain can be heard wandering through the house playing his fiddle.

◆ Royal William steamed into history

Royal William, a Quebec-built paddlewheeler, was the first ship to cross the Atlantic under continuous steam power. Pressed into transatlantic service after an outbreak of cholera in the Maritimes, the ship sailed from Pictou, N.S., to London, England, in 1833.

◆ Shipping magnate knitted his own socks

As a youth, Samuel Cunard (1787–1865), son of a Halifax carpenter, knitted his own socks. Later he ran a government soup kitchen for immigrants, and auctioned tea he imported from China. He had already made a fortune in lumbering and shipping when the steam era arrived. Cunard out-bid his rivals for the contract to take mail across the Atlantic and in 1840 launched the first transatlantic mail service.

In time, his company became one of the great passenger lines, launching the luxurious cruise ships *Queen Mary*, *Queen Elizabeth*, and *Queen Elizabeth II*. The line was responsible for many shipping firsts, including the first passenger ship to be lit by electricity (*Servia*, 1881); the first gymnasium and health center aboard a ship (*Franconia*, 1911); and the first indoor swimming pool on a ship (*Aquitania*, 1914).

Left: The Queen Elizabeth II, *a Cunard Line ocean liner that has ferried many dignitaries across the Atlantic, including HRH The Prince of Wales, King Hussein of Jordan, and President Nelson Mandela. Below: A posh night-club on the Cunard White Star superliner* Queen Mary

◆ The *Bluenose*: No dime-a-dozen schooner

Canada's most famous ship, the schooner *Bluenose*, was launched at Lunenburg, N.S., on April 26, 1921. She won the International Fishermen's Trophy that October and for each of the next four years. Immortalized on the dime in 1937, *Bluenose* was also a working ship and once brought home a 136,000-kilogram catch, the largest ever landed at Lunenburg to that date. Sold in 1942, she was used to ferry freight in the Caribbean, where she perished on a reef off Haiti in 1946. A replica, *Bluenose II*, was built in Lunenburg in 1963.

◆ Financed by penny banks

The brigantine *Dayspring* was a pure white missionary ship built in 1863 in New Glasgow, N.S., by James W. Carmichael, whose family built hundreds of sailing vessels. Financed from the penny banks of schoolchildren in Canada, Scotland, and Australia, *Dayspring* served Presbyterian missions on many South Sea islands, where church members christened it a "Dayspring from Heaven." The Carmichael-Stewart House Museum in New Glasgow preserves memorabilia of the famous shipbuilding family.

Schooners and scandals

◆ The mystery of the *Mary Celeste*

Built in 1861 on Spencer's Island, N.S., and originally named *Amazon*, the brigantine *Mary Celeste* remains one of shipping's great unsolved mysteries. On Nov. 7, 1872, she left New York for Italy. On board was Capt. Ben Briggs, his wife and two-year-old daughter, seven crewmen, the ship's cat, and a cargo of industrial alcohol. A month later, another vessel, *Dei Gratia*, found *Mary Celeste* adrift in the Azores with no one on board. A lifeboat and some navigational instruments were missing, but table settings, money, and everything else seemed to be in place. In the open log book, the last entry was a week old.

The *Dei Gratia* took the deserted ghost ship to Gibraltar, but no one there or elsewhere could find a plausible explanation for the mystery. Piracy, mutiny, sea monsters, and alien abductors were all suggested. One of the more plausible theories is that an alcohol leak forced a speedy abandonment in a lifeboat that broke away from the mother ship in a ferocious storm.

◆ Shipping sultan cost John A. an election

In 1872, a syndicate organized by shipping sultan Sir Hugh Allan (1810–82) as the Canadian Pacific Railway won the contract to build the first transcontinental railway to British Columbia. When it was revealed that Allan had contributed $400,000 to the Conservative Party, the resulting cries of patronage cost Sir John A. Macdonald the 1873 election.

Allan made his fortune in shipping. On emigrating from Scotland at age 16, the future captain of industry went to work clerking for a Montreal general merchandising firm. A decade later, when he had become a partner in the firm, his family in Scotland provided financing that enabled him to buy sailing ships and steamers to expand his business. Allan then convinced the Canadian government to support steamship lines by contracting with them to deliver mail between Canada and Britain, making sure his Montreal Ocean Steamship Company got all the contracts. In 1879 Allan was the first to launch the first all-steel steamship on the Atlantic. Later he expanded into coal mining, textiles, tobacco, and paper interests.

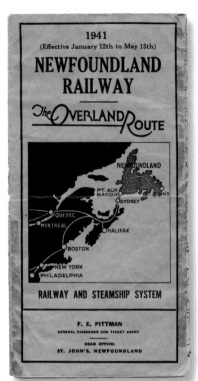

◆ Newfoundland Rail's human wind gauge

Newfoundlanders nicknamed the trans-island passenger railway that operated in that province from 1898 into the 1960s "the Newfie Bullet." The narrow-gauge train ran, none too speedily, some 900 kilometers around the lakes and mountains between St. John's and Channel Port aux Basques.

Because howling, gale-force winds would often disrupt highway traffic and occasionally derail trains along the Bullet's route, the Newfoundland Railway had a contract with a man called Lauchie MacDougall. He grew up in the valley below Table Mountain and had a keen sense of the region's weather. He was known locally as the human wind gauge because of his ability to determine whether the rail line was passable on any given day. If the gusts were too high, Mr. MacDougall notified the railway and service was suspended until conditions were again favorable. Mr. MacDougall died in 1965 and his wife took over the task until 1972.

A bus service eventually replaced the Bullet.

◆ Railway stood still for Van Horne funeral

William Cornelius Van Horne (1843–1915) had worked for various railroads in his native United States before Canadian head hunters came calling in 1882. He had started out as a telegraph messenger and was acting general manager when Canada hired him to push through the Canadian Pacific Railway.

"All I can say is that the work has been well done in every way," he said at Craigellachie, B.C., 46 months later.

Between then and his retirement in 1910, he built branch lines, hotels, and transatlantic and transpacific steamships. All traffic on the railway he created came to a five-minute stop to mark his funeral in 1915. His cortege left Montreal's Windsor Station, bound for his native Joliet, Ill., where he is buried.

An iron ribbon from sea to sea

◆ CPR star of the world's first travelogues

The Canadian Pacific Railway (CPR) played an important role in Canadian cinema. In 1898–99, it showed British audiences a film of Prairie life, produced in 1897 by James Freer of Manitoba. The goal was to encourage immigration to Canada, essential if the CPR was to prosper. To this end, the company's colonial agent commissioned Charles Urban of London to make additional films, and in 1902–03, Urban's cameraman traveled Canada by train, filming the scenic wonders of Quebec, northern Ontario, Banff, Kicking Horse Pass, the Rocky Mountains, and other attractive places. These 35 short "Living Canada" films were probably the world's first travelogues.

◆ Turbo sets speed record

On April 23, 1976, CN's experimental Turbo passenger train set a Canadian speed record, clocking a top speed of 224.3 kph. It was powered by gas turbines, and its streamlined aluminum body was designed to cut wind resistance. The Turbo was intended for the high-traffic corridor between Montreal and Toronto, yet was plagued by mechanical problems and excessive fuel consumption. It was mothballed in 1980.

◆ The spike that joined a nation

It had cost almost $250,000 to drive home a golden spike to complete the American Northern Pacific Railroad in 1883. But when it came time to complete the Canadian Pacific Railway at Craigellachie, B.C., on Nov. 7, 1885, the CPR could not afford such a fancy ceremony. Instead, Donald Smith (later Lord Strathcona) hammered home a practical iron spike without pomp or oratory, and in so doing, united Canada as a nation. "A nebulous dream was a reality," reads the commemorative plaque. "An iron ribbon crossed Canada from sea to sea." Smith's first tremendous blow actually bent the spike, but a new one was put in place. The bent spike now rests in the Glenbow Museum in Calgary.

◆ An eccentric pianist's hymn to the rails

Pianist Glenn Gould (*right*) was famed for his virtuoso, idiosyncratic approaches to Bach and Beethoven, yet his ears were also attuned to the rhythm of the rails. After his first retirement from the public stage in 1965, Gould took a railway trip to Hudson Bay on the *Muskeg Express*, a train that runs from Winnipeg to Churchill. On the ride, Gould met W. V. "Wally" Maclean, a wizened surveyor, and the two men philosophized at length about what the Arctic meant to Canadians.

Maclean unwittingly became the muse for an unusual radio documentary Gould produced for the CBC called *The Idea of North*. Gould interviewed Maclean and four other people who had spent time in the North: Frank Vallee, a professor of sociology in Ottawa; Marianne Schroeder, a nurse; James Lotz, a British anthropologist, and Bob Phillips, assistant secretary of the cabinet, Privy Council Office.

Broadcast on Dec. 28, 1967, *The Idea of North* was hailed as a new form of radio art. Using the hypnotic clatter of a train's wheels as a ground bass, Gould wove the spliced voices of his interview subjects together in an overlapping, contrapuntal symphony, a sonic portrait of rail travel and the beautiful isolation of the Canadian Arctic.

◆ Flying ace "Billy" Bishop claimed 72 kills

"The courage of the early morning," was how one writer described William Avery "Billy" Bishop's one-man dawn sorties to search out and rake enemy air bases. A World War I flying ace with Royal Flying Corps, Bishop (1894–1956) was credited with shooting down a phenomenal 72 planes.

Not quite so, challenges historian Brereton Greenhous. He claims Bishop's record is full of lies and exaggerations launched by Bishop's superiors to overshadow the exploits of Germany's fighter ace Manfred von Richthofen, the Red Baron. In *The Making of Billy Bishop* (2002), Greenhous even charges that Bishop's June 2, 1917, early morning flight into enemy territory and his downing of three planes at a German aerodrome never happened. The exploit won Bishop the Victoria Cross.

Questions about Bishop's record are not new. They were featured in the popular 1979 musical *Billy Bishop Goes to War* and

in *The Kid Who Couldn't Miss*, a 1982 National Film Board docudrama. (It was originally called a documentary but was renamed under criticism by veterans' groups and pressure from the Senate.)

The charges do not faze Bishop admirers at countless Legion halls, schools, and the Winnipeg air force headquarters named for him, nor at the Billy Bishop Heritage Museum in his native Owen Sound, Ont. All vigorously defend the pilot's record, as do historians such as David Bashow. During three years' research for his book *Knights of the Air* (2000), Bashow found nothing to cast doubt on Bishop's claims.

Bishop's record was never challenged in his lifetime. Between wars, Bishop was successful in aviation and oil businesses. During World War II, he was made an honorary air marshal and was extremely successful in signing up recruits to the Royal Canadian Air Force.

◆ The hero of Malta

Quebec-born "Buzz" Buerling (1921–48) had a passion for flying. He flew his first plane when he was 14, and won an aerobatic competition three years later. But even in wartime, Buzz couldn't find a home in the Royal Canadian Air Force: he hadn't enough education. Instead, he emigrated to England and joined the Royal Air Force, where he became one of their star fliers. During five months in the fierce 1942 battle for Malta, Buerling shot down 27 enemy aircraft. As a hero of this engagement, he transferred to the RCAF, which hoped his star image would boost recruitment. But Buerling, unhappy away from the action, resigned in 1944.

Four years later he was enroute to Israel when his plane caught fire over Italy. The hero of Malta was dead at 26.

◆ Pilots of the purple twilight

Most of Canada's early bush pilots were young veterans of World War I, confident, unceremonious, fearless risk takers, as famous in their time as today's hockey stars. Using water-based craft in summer, ski-equipped planes in winter, they landed and took off from lakes and rivers, flying into makeshift airports (*above*) in remote areas of the Canadian Shield or the Arctic. They ferried mail, food, fuel, and equipment to remote communities and mining operations, providing services for medical teams, geologists, missionaries, trappers, surveyors, and miners. Their skill and courage opened up the North, where one trader dubbed them "Pilots of the Purple Twilight."

◆ Barker beat the odds, 60 to 1

World War I flyer William George "Billy" Barker (1894–1930, *left*) is credited with shooting down 53 enemy aircraft. The fuselage of the Sopwith Snipe with which he won the Victoria Cross in a single-handed battle with 60 German planes is preserved in the Canadian War Museum in Ottawa. The battle happened in the skies above Cambrai in northern France on Oct. 27, 1918, when the Manitoba-born pilot was headed to England to take up an instructor's job. Spotting a heavily armed German reconnaissance plane, he attacked and shot it down. Within seconds Barker found himself fighting off three Fokker squadrons, each 20 aircraft strong. Seriously wounded and drifting in and out of consciousness, he blasted four of the attacking craft from the skies before crashing his bullet-ridden Sopwith upside down behind Allied lines.

After the war, he and Billy Bishop (*see opposite page*) joined forces in a commercial aviation business. When it folded, Barker served briefly as first director of the RCAF. He was fatally injured in 1930 when his aircraft stalled above Uplands air station in Ottawa. Some 2,000 uniformed service personnel marched in his funeral procession, one of the largest ever seen in Toronto.

◆ Royal air

The Canadian Air Force (CAF) was established in 1920, enlisting 1,340 officers and 31,905 airmen. King George V officially bestowed the designation of "Royal" four years later.

◆ "Punch" Dickins helped usher in the atomic age

Clennell Haggerston "Punch" Dickins (1899–1996) first gained glory as a 19-year-old World War I flying ace. In the 1920s he became one of Canada's premier bush pilots, flying for Western Canada Airways, covering thousands of kilometers of unmapped country, often in temperatures nudging 50 below. Dickins was the first pilot to fly the full length of the Mackenzie River in just two days, and the first to land at Aklavik. He also delivered the mail by air to Winnipeg, Regina, Calgary, Edmonton, and Saskatoon.

One historic flight occurred in 1929 when he flew prospector Gilbert LaBine along the eastern shores of Great Bear Lake. LaBine spotted an area of scrub and muskeg glowing purple and yellow in the afternoon sun, a sign of rocks containing pitchblende (the mineral source of uranium and radium). That flight led to the Eldorado Mine, a discovery that broke the world monopoly on radium and ushered in the atomic age (*see page 83*).

Wilfred "Wop" May received the U.S. Medal of Freedom with Bronze Palm (right) in 1947 for his pioneering work in the field of aerial search and rescue

◆ Barnstorming pioneer of aerial search and rescue

On his first World War I combat flight, flying hero Capt. Wilfred Reid "Wop" May, guns jammed, was being chased by the legendary Red Baron seconds before the German flier was blown from the skies by Ontario-born Roy Brown. After the war, May (1896–1952) was one of the bush pilots whose flying skills opened up the Canadian North. In 1929, May flew the first official mail service to the Arctic Coast, and he later helped the Mounties track down the Mad Trapper (*see page 131*). In his spare time, May took to barnstorming at fairs and rodeos, once swooping three meters above Edmonton's baseball diamond so the mayor could pitch the season's first ball from the air.

May's most famous exploit was a 1,900-kilometer round-trip mercy flight from Edmonton north to Fort Vermilion on Little Red River in January 1929. Told that a diphtheria epidemic was threatening an entire settlement, May and his partner Vic Horner set out in a two-seater Avian with open cockpits to deliver inoculation serum. They battled blizzards, icy headwinds, and ground temperatures of –40°C, but returned safely to Edmonton, where thousands swarmed onto the airfield to welcome them home.

◆ Zurakowski broke the sound barrier

The first test pilot to fly a Canadian-made plane faster than the speed of sound, Russian-born Jan Zurakowski (*being hoisted, above*) emigrated to Canada in 1952. He grew up in Poland, and was commissioned an officer in the air force in 1937. After the conquest of Poland in World War II, he managed to escape to London where he flew with the RAF as a Spitfire pilot in the all-Polish squadron and fought in the Battle of Britain. Shortly after arriving in Canada, he flew the Canadian-made CF-100 jet fighter. Zurakowski then test flew the Arrow extensively, pushing the envelope and exceeding the speed of sound on his third flight, when he reached Mach 1.1 at an altitude near 13,000 meters.

◆ Blueprint for a new Arrow

Peter Zuuring, a Dutch-born University of Toronto engineering graduate and 30 years under his belt as an entrepreneur, is spearheading a $50 million plan to build a fully functional, working replica of the Avro Arrow. Zuuring's Arrow Alliance is using aircraft parts and blueprints that some Avro employees had taken home. Zuuring hopes to see the Arrow fly, like a phoenix rising from the ashes, on Feb. 23, 2009, the 100th anniversary of powered Canadian flight.

◆ The world's fastest interceptor

The CF-105, a twin-engined, supersonic, interceptor jet known as the Avro Arrow was developed in the 1950s by A. V. Roe of Canada. The sophisticated planes were a source of national pride during the Cold War, and were intended to counter Soviet bombers over the Canadian North. Test flights reaching over Mach 2 indicated the planes could well be the world's fastest interceptor. But with costs per aircraft at $12.5 million and rising rather than the $2 million originally projected, the Diefenbaker government canceled the project, and all Avro Arrow plans and prototypes were subsequently destroyed. The grounding of the Arrow was both a bitter blow to Canada's aircraft industry and an incalculable brain drain—scientists and engineers who flocked to the United States because of 14,000 job losses at A. V. Roe helped launch the U.S. space program. Some claimed that as many as 50,000 people were left without work, when suppliers and other Avro-related services were factored in. Yet the Arrow refuses to die, and lives on as an example of Canadian innovation and expertise.

◆ Project Silver Bug: Hovercraft or UFO?

Sponsored by the United States Air Force and developed in 1954 under a blanket of secrecy at Avro's Malton, Ont., plant, Project Silver Bug turned the heads of even the most open-minded of the aircraft manu facturer's engineers.

Approximately 5.5 meters in diameter, Silver Bug (*right*), or the Avrocar as it came to be known, was a circular vertical-takeoff-and-landing (VTOL) craft that could hover and fly above the ground. The first of two prototypes was unveiled in May of 1959. At a test flight that November, Avro pilot

Mladyslaw "Spud" Potocki managed to raise the 2,575-kilo gram Avrocar 90 cm off the ground and fly the strange-look-ing saucer at 55 kph for a short distance.

Despite the fact that Avro had stumbled across the principle of the modern hovercraft, the USAF was not keen on the Avrocar's insta-bility and power problems, and did not renew Avro's contract. One of the prototypes ended up in a warehouse at the Smithsonian Institute in Washington, D.C., while the other is mounted on a pedestal at U.S. Army Transportation Museum at Fort Eustis, Virginia.

◆ Shooting down a popular myth

For decades, popular mythology claims then-prime minister John Diefenbaker ordered the cancellation of the Avro Arrow project and the destruction of all planes and blueprints at the behest of the United States military, who were worried that the Arrow would challenge the supremacy of their U2 spy planes. In fact, recently declassified top-secret memos from 1958 discovered by Peter Zuuring (*see* Blueprint for a new Arrow, *opposite page*) reveal Gen. Charles Foulkes, Canada's chairman of the chiefs of staff for the Department of

Avro Arrow

Defense, pressured Diefenbaker to scrap the plane, citing not only its exorbitant cost but the worrisome lack of Canadian military control over Avro and the Arrow project.

According to Pierre Sévigny, the associate defense minster in John Diefenbaker's cabinet from 1959 to 1963, the Americans actually offered to help save the program. Documents obtained by Zuuring corroborate this, revealing that American secretary of the air force James Douglas floated the idea of purchasing and using a squadron of Arrows on behalf of the United States as a line of defense against possible Soviet attack in the Arctic. The Canadian gov-ernment turned down the offer.

As for the actual destruction of the planes, Sévigny has gone on record claiming that Crawford Gordon, head of A. V. Roe, ordered the destruction of all 37 Arrows and their blue-prints out of spite when the program was scrapped in 1959.

◆ The race to recover Avro's sunken treasure

After five years of searching Lake Ontario, Belleville marine mechanic and Arrow buff Dave Gartshore dis-covered one of nine scale models of the famous jet in 1999, beating out aviation conservation groups hot on his trail. With a wingspan of two meters and a weight of 180 kilograms, the test models were fired over Lake Ontario from 1954 to 1957 at Point Petre, and had lain at the bottom of the lake, encrusted with mussels, for four decades. Unfortunately, Gartshore did not have a required permit, and could not claim credit for his find. The non-profit (and licensed) Avro Arrow Model Recovery Project found a second test model days after Gartshore. Four of the nine models have been recovered to date.

◆ Canada's astronauts

Only a few Canadians belong to that exclusive club of men and women who have made it to outer space. Those who have had that honor have gone into orbit either as payload or mission specialists. Payload specialists conduct experiments aboard the space shuttle; mission specialists supervise and operate orbiter systems, including Canada's famous contribution to the U.S. Space Program, the Canadarm, first used on the space shuttle *Columbia* in 1981. Before blasting off, Canadian astronauts must undergo basic training at the Canadian Space Agency in Saint-Hubert, Que., then mission specialist training at Johnson Space Center in Houston, Texas.

◆ Marc Garneau

Over eight days in 1984, Quebec City native Marc Garneau (*right*, born 1949), became the first Canadian astronaut in space, traveling some 5.5 million kilometers around the earth as a payload specialist on the space shuttle *Challenger*. Afterward, Garneau went to work for the Johnson Space Center, where he was in charge of verbal communications with astronauts on shuttle missions. Aboard *Endeavour* in 1996, he helped deploy two satellites. On his third foray into space in 2000, Garneau helped install solar-powered batteries and radiators in the $63 billion International Space Station, due for completion in 2004. Garneau is currently retired from active flight status, and was elected President of the Canadian Space Agency in 2001.

◆ Roberta Bondar

In 1997, Canada's first woman astronaut, Roberta Bondar (born 1946), was named head of Canada's newly formed Science Advisory Board. Five years

earlier, she went into space as a payload specialist in charge of the microgravity laboratory in the shuttle *Discovery*. Among her qualifications: a medical degree, a doctorate in neurobiology, and post-graduate training in neuro-ophthalmology. She left the Canadian Space Agency in 1992 to pursue her research.

◆ Steven "Steve" MacLean

A one-time member of the Canadian National Gymnastics Team, physicist Steve MacLean was one of six astronauts selected by the Canadian Space Agency in 1983, and as a payload specialist made an 11-day flight aboard the shuttle *Columbia* in 1992. Born in Ottawa in 1954, he holds a doctorate in physics from York University. In 1994–95, he was director of the Canadian Astronaut Program. Afterward, he took mission specialist training at Houston, Texas, where he later worked for the Astronaut Office Robotics Branch and became the capsule communicator between Mission Control and crews during space flights. In April 2003, MacLean is scheduled to become the second Canadian to walk in space when he visits the International Space Station as a crew member aboard the *Endeavour*.

◆ Chris Hadfield

A native of Sarnia, Ont., engineer and colonel in the Canadian Armed Forces since 1978, Chris Hadfield (*below*) became the first Canadian to walk in space on his 2001 assembly mission to the International Space Station. In all he floated for nearly 15 hours in two space walks to supervise installation of the 17.6-meter-long Canadarm 2. His first space trip took place in 1995 when, as a mission specialist, he used the Canadarm to install a docking module to the Russian space station

Mir. Currently, he is stationed at the Yuri Gagarin Cosmonaut Training Center in Russia, as the Director of Operations for NASA.

◆ Dafydd "Dave" Rhys Williams

In the sixties, the Americans and Russians seemed to have cornered the market on space. Dafydd Williams (*above*, born 1955) was growing up in Pointe Claire, Que., at that time, and dreamed of being an astronaut. But it was an impossible dream, or so he thought, so he got on with his life—scuba diving, sailing, canoeing, skiing, becoming a specialist in emergency medicine, starting a family. But the buried dream sprang to life in 1992, when he heard the Canadian Space Agency had four vacancies. He was among four recruits chosen from the 5,330 who applied. A few years later, he was nominated for training as a mission specialist, and in 1998, from Cape Canaveral, Florida, he was blasted off in the space shuttle *Columbia*. Many of the mission's scientific experiments had to do with problems encountered by the elderly—balance and sleeping difficulties, disorientation, and hand-eye coordination.

◆ Robert "Bob" Brent Thirsk

Among degrees held by British Columbia native Bob Thirsk (*below*, born 1953) are a master of science degree in mechanical engineering from the Massachusetts Institute of Technology (MIT), a doctorate of medicine degree from McGill University, Montreal, and a master of business administration degree from the MIT Sloan School of Management. In 1996 he completed a 17-day mission aboard the space shuttle *Columbia*, investigating changes in plants, animals, and humans under spaceflight conditions.

◆ Bjarni Tryggvason

Engineer Bjarni Tryggvason was 51 in 1997, when he embarked on an 11-day mission in space on the shuttle *Discovery*. Born in Iceland, the astronaut emigrated to Canada at age 7, and grew up in Nova Scotia and British Columbia. During the investigation into the sinking of the Ocean Ranger (*see page 144*), it was Tryggvason, an expert on wind effects on structures, who designed and led the aerodynamics tests that established the wind loads that battered the sunken rig. His job in space: to test a Canadian-made shock-absorbing device for protecting experiments in zero gravity, a device which he had helped invent.

◆ Julie Payette

As a child, Montrealer Julie Payette (*right*, born 1964) was fascinated by the Apollo moon landings and thought it would be fun to drive a spacecraft. She surpassed her childhood dreams in May of 1999 when she blasted into space to help construct the International Space Station. Payette was responsible for overseeing the transfer of tons of food, clothing, medical supplies and other equipment for the first permanent crew members, who boarded the station in 2000. An engineer, a pianist, and a classical singer, Payette speaks English, French, Spanish, Italian, German, and Russian. Also, she has a commercial pilot license, and has logged more than 800 hours of flight time, including 450 hours on jet aircraft.

from picket to post

1780.
2 PAIRS A DAY.

THE OLD STYLE.

1880.
300 PAIRS A DAY

THE NEW WAY.

◆ The right to strike

For most of the 1800s, trade unions in Canada were small, local, and often illegal. In 1816, for example, the government of Nova Scotia enacted legislation enabling it to jail workers who bargained for better hours or wages.

After violent putdowns of striking workers on Ontario's Lachine and Welland canals in the 1840s, small unions began uniting with each other and with their British and American counterparts. By the 1850s, most skilled workers had banded together. Despite the advances of industrialization, 12-hour workdays were commonplace then, and the Nine-Hours Movement, an international push for a shorter working day, found ready support among Canadian workers. Beginning in Hamilton, Ont., Nine-Hour leagues attracted union and non-union workers in other Ontario towns, Montreal, and Halifax.

Employer antagonism to the growing labor movement was seen when 100 Toronto printers stayed off the job for two months in 1872. This and a defiant march that year by 1,500 Hamilton, Ont., workers gave a public presence to the labor movement that politicians could no longer ignore. As a result, the right to associate in trade unions became law with the Trade Union Act of 1872. With this legislation, Canadians got the right to strike, although picketing remained illegal until a 1934 amendment to the Criminal Code.

◆ The formula that paid its dues

The Rand Formula was devised in the 1940s by labor specialist Mr. Justice Ivan Rand of the Supreme Court of Canada. At the time, Rand was arbitrating a labor dispute between the Ford Motor Company and employees of its Windsor plant. Justice Rand's premise was that where unions exist, they must be responsible for all employees, members or not. Accordingly, he devised a formula whereby an employer deducts union dues from all employees, union members or otherwise, within a bargaining unit. Variations of the Rand Formula now apply to most collective bargaining units across Canada.

◆ The mother of all strikes

Massive unemployment and inflation were widespread when western labor leaders met to plan collective bargaining strategies in March 1919. On May 15, the Winnipeg Traders and Labour Council called a general strike, and more than 22,000 factory workers, clerks, telephone operators, firefighters, policemen, and other workers walked off the job. A strike committee of leaders of the unions involved began negotiating with employers and coordinating essential services.

Determined not to give in to the workers' demands, many of the city's businessmen, manufacturers, bankers, and politicians also rallied together and formed the Citizens' Committee of 1,000. Supported by local press, the committee spread word that the strike was a revolutionary conspiracy. On June 17, a dozen strike leaders were arrested. Four days later a force of North-West Mounted Police charged a group of strikers, killing one and injuring 30. The strike ended on June 25 amid bitterness and controversy. In the chaos that followed, federal troops occupied Winnipeg's streets.

International Chemical Workers Union Strike at the St. Lawrence Starch Company, Port Credit, Ont.,1947

◆ From snail mail to e-mail

Postal services of one kind or another have existed in Canada since 1693, when the government of New France hired Portuguese immigrant Pedro Dasilva to deliver mail between Montreal and Quebec for 20 sous per letter.

BE **RIGHT** WHEN YOU **WRITE**

FOR FASTER MAIL DELIVERY ALWAYS INCLUDE YOUR POSTAL CODE IN YOUR RETURN ADDRESS

CANADA POST OFFICE

Canada Post introduced the postal code in 1971. The possible unique number of addresses under the code runs over seven million

Canada's first official post office (providing links to England and other Atlantic colonies) opened in 1755 in Halifax, which already had an office for local mail.

Cross-country railway development was a major factor in helping set up a national mail service within two decades of Confederation. In 1948, Canada became the first country in the world to introduce domestic airmail letter service at regular rates.

To expedite delivery and sorting of an increasing volume of mail (49 billion letters annually by 1966), Canada Post introduced a six-digit alphanumeric postal code in 1971. The job losses caused by automated reading of postal codes prompted numerous strikes by postal unions throughout the 1970s.

Today, Canada Post has crossed another Rubicon, and is finally fully wired into the digital age, offering a full range of electronic mail services while still handling some 40 million pieces of snail mail every day.

Mail sorting case from Trappist Monastery, Oka, Que.

◆ H0H 0H0

Each year Canada Post assigns more than 16,000 employees to handle mail addressed to one of the country's most popular addresses—Santa Claus, North Pole, H0H 0H0. Diligently they read and reply to the million plus letters mailed to this address by young hopefuls worldwide. While many letters are mere wish lists for the latest toys and entertainment gadgets, others are heart-rending appeals for such things as health for a parent or sibling dying from cancer. To ensure that Santa is able to reply to every letter no matter which language it was written in, Santa's elves pride themselves on being polylingual. In 2002, postal elves responded to over a million letters in more than 26 different languages, including Braille.

◆ Postal facts

◆ 1693: Pedro Dasilva transports packets of letters between Montreal and Quebec City.

◆ 1755: First Canadian post office established in Halifax.

◆ 1851: First Canadian stamp, the Three Penny Beaver, designed by Sir Sandford Fleming.

◆ 1868: An Act for the Regulation of the Postal Service creates a uniform postal system throughout the new Dominion.

◆ 1884: The Eaton Company issues its first mail-order catalogue.

◆ 1896: Electric mail marking machines introduced.

◆ 1898: World's first Christmas stamp, a multicolored stamp features a map of Canada.

◆ 1918: First official airmail flight in Canada, from Montreal to Toronto. Mail consists of 124 special envelopes.

◆ 1971: Postal code is introduced.

◆ 1999: Canada Post offers e-mail delivery services.

business titans

◆ Bonds seeded Lord Beaverbrook's wealth

Born in Ontario, William Maxwell "Max" Aitken (Lord Beaverbrook, 1879–1964) was raised in Newcastle, N.B., where he worked as a journalist, salesman, and bowling alley operator. While still in his twenties he became immensely wealthy selling bonds, and through businesses he established, including Stelco and Canada Cement.

In 1910, Aitken emigrated to England, and was elected a Conservative Member of Parliament. Awarded a peerage in 1917, he chose the name Beaverbrook for a small waterway near his childhood home. He acquired a number of newspapers in the 1920s and served as minister of aircraft productions during World War II.

Yet Lord Beaverbrook never forgot his home and it benefited greatly from his largesse. It is estimated that he donated some $16 million to various New Brunswick causes. To the University of New Brunswick, to which he was named chancellor in 1946, he contributed generously, including first editions of Charles Dickens, James Joyce, and H. G. Wells. In 1959, he gifted the Beaverbrook Art Gallery in Fredericton to the people of the province along with works by Dali, Turner, and Gainsborough.

◆ Jack Kent Cooke: Major league millionaire from A to Z

Hamilton, Ont.-born, high-school dropout Jack Kent Cooke (1912–96) peddled encyclopedias door-to-door during the Depression before going to work for newspaper baron Roy Thomson (*see page 103*). Cooke learned well from the thrifty entrepreneur and was a millionaire in his own right when he went into business for himself in 1944. He acquired several radio stations and magazines as well as his first sports venture, the Toronto Maple Leafs' minor league baseball club. Foiled in his attempt to buy *The Globe and Mail* and Canada's first television license, Cooke went to live in the United States. By the early seventies, he controlled three major-league sports franchises: the National Hockey League's Los Angeles Kings, the National Basketball Association's Los Angeles Lakers, and the National Football League's Washington Redskins. At the time of his death in 1996 he had sold all but the Redskins. Cooke left his money in a Foundation to help young people of exceptional promise reach their full potential through education.

◆ Izzy Asper: Street-smart media mogul

The son of Russian Jewish immigrants and a scrappy, larger-than-life, chainsmoking jazz buff who resolutely refuses to leave his hometown of Winnipeg, Manitoba, media mogul Israel "Izzy" Asper (born 1932) used his considerable street smarts to build CanWest Global Communications Corporation, a western media empire rich in television and newspapers. From his first job—scraping gum from under the seats of his father's movie theater—Asper was dazzled by the lure of showbusiness. In the early 1970s, he helped establish Winnipeg independent television station CKND. After bailing out Toronto's Global Television in 1974, he turned the station into the cornerstone of a successful Canadian TV network of the same name.

In 2001, he bought much of Conrad Black's Canadian holdings (*see opposite page*) in the biggest media deal in Canadian history, $2.3 billion. Asper now controls 148 newspapers from coast to coast, including such high-profile dailies as *The Vancouver Sun*, *Ottawa Citizen*, and Montreal's *Gazette*.

Cyrus Eaton

Lord Beaverbrook

Timothy Eaton

Izzy Asper

Pierre Péladeau

◆ Péladeau shot from the hip

In 1950, newly graduated Montreal lawyer Pierre Péladeau (1925–97) borrowed $1,500 from his mother to buy a community newspaper. Over the next 47 years, he parlayed that sum into Quebecor Inc., a $6.2 billion printing, publishing, communications, and forestry products empire employing 34,000 people on three continents. Péladeau was a brusque businessman, known for speaking his mind and shooting from the hip, and his words got him in trouble more than a few times with the media. *Le Journal de Montréal*, the tabloid Péladeau founded in 1964, is now Quebec's biggest newspaper, and the French daily with the largest circulation in North America.

◆ Conrad Black: Lord of the press

At its peak, financier and newspaper tycoon Conrad Black's Hollinger, Inc. was the planet's third largest newspaper empire. *The Vancouver Sun* and the Montreal *Gazette* were once among 60 Canadian newspapers owned by Black (born 1944). His international holdings still include the *Jerusalem Post*, *Chicago Sun-Times*, and *The Times* of London. A thorn in the side of Canada's political left, he annoyed Jean Chrétien's Liberal government which blocked his admission to England's House of Lords. In response, Black renounced his Canadian citizenship in 2001 and sold his interest in the national newspaper he created in 1997—*National Post*. He was subsequently appointed a life peer to the House of Lords as Lord Black of Crossharbour.

◆ Timothy Eaton: Father of "The Wish Book"

Conrad Black

Jack Kent Cooke

A native of County Antrim, Ireland, Timothy Eaton (1834–1907) apprenticed in a general store before emigrating to Canada in 1854. Two years later, he and his brother opened a small store, first in Kirkton, in the Huron Tract of Upper Canada, then in St. Mary's near Stratford. When Timothy opened his own store on Yonge Street in Toronto in 1869, he introduced a policy of cash sales and a fixed price, a revolutionary notion to customers used to credit or bargain and barter methods.

His employment practices raised eyebrows— 6 p.m. evening closings, summer Saturday afternoons off, and a cheerful, airy workplace. He introduced Eaton's mail order catalogue in 1884, revolutionizing the retail sales business with his "Goods satisfactory or money refunded" slogan. The catalogue was so popular with settlers in western Canada that it was known as the "Prairie Bible." To others it was simply "The Wish Book."

For many years, Timothy Eaton wrote his own advertisements. When an advertising department was eventually formed, he supplied it with a handwritten directive that said in part: "Use no deception in the smallest degree." At the time of his death, his company employed 8,000 persons in Toronto, and in branch stores in Winnipeg, Oshawa, Hamilton, and Montreal. When the mail-order catalogue ceased publication in 1976, it had grown to a 900-page book featuring 15,000 items and with a circulation of two million.

Canadians were shocked in 1997 when, seemingly out of touch with the Canadian consumer, Eaton's filed for bankruptcy protection. Sears bought the foundering chain and tried to reposition it as a high-end retailer. Six Eaton stores were to be spared, including the sprawling Eaton Centre in downtown Toronto. Losses continued to mount, however, and Sears shut Eaton's doors for good in 2002.

◆ Eaton's Pugwash conferences tempered Cold War fears

Steel magnate Cyrus Stephen Eaton (1883–1979) is best known for the conferences he sponsored in his Pugwash, N.S., hometown. When first established, the conferences were intended to ease Cold War tensions and foster international understanding by bringing together public figures and scientists from East and West. For his efforts, Eaton was awarded the Lenin Peace Prize in 1960.

◆ Fortunes made from facials and foals

Founder of the Red Door cosmetics empire, Florence Nightingale Graham (1884–1966) was born in Woodbridge, Ont. Her first career choice was nursing, but she gave it up to work for a New York cosmetics firm. At first she gave massages and facial treatments, but within a few years she was a partner in the business. Later, with $8,000 borrowed from a relative, she opened her own beauty salon on Fifth Avenue and changed her name to Elizabeth Arden. She then hired druggists and challenged them to make beauty products better than anything then on the market. "I only want people around who can do the impossible," she told her staff.

Elizabeth Arden

On a business trip to Europe, Arden met Thomas Lewis, an American silk manufacturer, whom she married in 1915. He became her European sales manager, but they divorced in 1934, after which he went to work for her rival, Helena Rubenstein. Like her first, Arden's second marriage, to a Russian prince, was all business, and also ended in divorce.

Elizabeth had grown up tending her Scottish father's horses, and in the 1930s she bought a farm in Kentucky, where she operated racing stables under the name Elizabeth Graham. This endeavor, too, was highly successful, and her string of prizewinners earned her some $2 million dollars. Her horse "Jet Pilot" won the 1947 Kentucky Derby.

When she died in 1966, Elizabeth Arden left an estate valued at $30 million, much of it bequeathed to her family and faithful employees. She left special instructions for disposing of her horses, including a specification that mares and foals be sold together.

◆ A billionaire and the Bermuda tax angle

Speaking in the Senate during the 1970 Davey Commission on newspapers and mass media in Canada, New Brunswick Senator Charles McElman once said that the corporate empire of Kenneth Colin "K. C." Irving (1899–1992) "had the appetite of a vulture . . . the instinct of a barracuda . . . and the principles of an alley cat." Some of the competitors "K. C." put out of business while building said empire might well have agreed.

Born into a well-to-do New Brunswick family, Irving was running an automobile dealership and a gas station in 1924 when a dispute with Imperial Oil prompted him to found Irving Oil and a chain of gas stations. Later came oil refineries, pulp and paper industries, shipbuilding interests—one of his most profitable deals was a $9.3 billion federal contract to build frigates for the Canadian navy—and publishing and communications ventures. At one point, every English-language newspaper and just about every television and radio station in New Brunswick were Irving owned. With some 300 companies, stretching across the Maritimes and the northeastern United States, he became one of the world's richest men.

Taxes were something of a fixation with "K. C.": he just couldn't bring himself to pay them. In fact to avoid doing so, he became a non-resident of Canada, and ran his empire from Bermuda for his last 20 years. And to make sure that Ottawa got nothing even when he was dead, the $7 billion inheritance he willed his three sons was conditional on their not making their homes in Canada either.

◆ Some playing cards were real trumps

In 1685, when the supply ships from France failed to arrive in Quebec, there was a great shortage of coin in the colony. To offset the crisis, government notes made of playing cards (*left*) were circulated as legal tender and remained an accepted form of money until 1720, when they were withdrawn from circulation for a decade. They were re-established again in limited amounts in 1730.

◆ Canada's other official currency

In 1958, Canadian Tire co-founder A. J. Billes needed to convince Esso and Shell customers —who were being plied with dinner plates and toasters—to come to his gas pumps. His wife Muriel suggested store coupons that could be reimbursed for merchandise at any time. The vouchers, picturing Sandy McTire, an amiable, bearded gent with a tam-o'shanter at a jaunty angle, were an instant hit. (Scots, Billes reasoned, were famed for their frugality.) Today Canadian Tire money is virtually a second form of currency for many Canadians, and accepted in lieu of money in many charity drives.

The royal flush you could spend

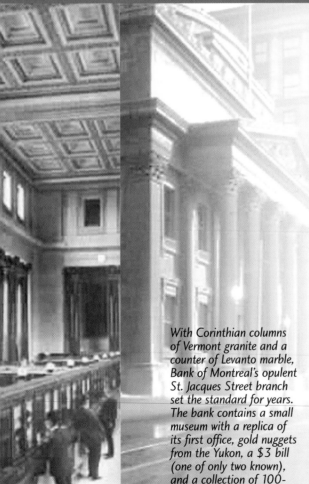

With Corinthian columns of Vermont granite and a counter of Levanto marble, Bank of Montreal's opulent St. Jacques Street branch set the standard for years. The bank contains a small museum with a replica of its first office, gold nuggets from the Yukon, a $3 bill (one of only two known), and a collection of 100-year-old mechanical banks

◆ Canada's first bank

Bank of Montreal, Canada's first permanent bank, opened for business on Nov. 3, 1817. The bank provided Canada's first sound and plentiful currency, issuing national bank notes, and has since played a major and continuing role in the development of the country. The bank took part in the financing of the first transcontinental railway in the 1880s, the creation of Confederation in 1867, and served as Canada's central bank until 1935. The first Canadian bank to open branches abroad, Bank of Montreal has built a worldwide reputation, being active in European, Latin American, and Asian markets. Today it is one of Canada's flagship financial institutions and a significant presence in the United States.

◆ Dentist's son's formula wins Nobel Prize

Whenever bankers make investment decisions, approval often hinges on whether the investment passes the Black-Scholes equation. This formula, a method of assessing the soundness of complex financial deals, won the 1997 Nobel Prize for Timmins, Ont.-native Myron Scholes (born 1941) and Robert C. Merton, a Harvard economics professor. Scholes, son of an Ontario dentist, was teaching at the Massachusetts Institute of Technology in Cambridge when he and fellow economist Fisher Black developed the model in 1973. (Black died in 1995, and the formula was refined by Merton.) By enabling investors to accurately predict how certain securities will perform regardless of fluctuations in share price or interest rates, the Black-Scholes formula has taken much of the guesswork out of complex investments. The formula works by bundling securities and/or assets together in such a way that one hedges the other against potential losses.

dollars and nonsense

◆ Credit for workers was Desjardins' goal

Determined to bring economic emancipation to French Canadians and make credit available to working-class Quebecers, journalist and Hansard reporter Alphonse Desjardins (*right*, 1854–1920) founded the first *caisse populaire*, or credit union, in his own home in Lévis, Que., in 1900. The savings and loan operation opened for business on Jan. 23, 1901, and the first savings deposit, all of 5 cents, was made on Feb. 7 that year. But before year's end savings in the Lévis branch totalled $9,556.63, and by the late 1900s, Quebec's *caisses populaires* counted billions of dollars in assets.

A caisse populaire in a Quebec school during the 1950s

◆ The devil was in the details

Architect Ludwig Mies van der Rohe once commented that "God is in the details." It is unlikely, therefore, that he would have wasted time looking for Mephistopheles in the intricate details of the Queen's hair.

When Elizabeth II ascended the throne in 1952, the Bank of Canada busied itself with creating new plates for a new series of bank notes scheduled for issue in 1954. The bank hired George Gundersen of the British American Bank Note Company to design the bill. Gundersen  based his engraving of the Queen on a portrait photo taken by Peter-Dirk Uys, one of Her Majesty's official photographers. The bills were printed and put in circulation.

In 1954, a complaint at the Bank of Canada touched off a storm of controversy. It seems that behind the Queen's left ear, the outline of a devil's face was visible (*above right; enlarged at left*). Gundersen was grilled, but claimed he had merely worked from the Uys photograph. Theories about who was responsible ranged from a prankster at large in the Bank of Canada to French-Canadian nationalists to IRA sympathizers. New bills for all denominations were quickly engraved, with highlights darkened to mask the illusory face. The original photographic negative went missing, and as time went by, the scandal died down. The so-called "Devil's Head" are worth a considerable amount of money among numismatic collectors.

◆ Jumbo liked his boilermakers

A life-size statue of an elephant opposite the Elgin County Pioneer Museum in St. Thomas, Ont., is the town's memorial to a much loved circus animal that met an untimely end here in 1885. Jumbo, who weighed about 7,000 kilograms and was said to have a taste for whisky and beer, was one of the stars of the P.T. Barnum Circus, which had just finished playing St. Thomas. The circus train was rolling out of town when it collided with another train, and when the dust settled, Jumbo lay dead.

◆ Make mine a double-double

Located halfway between Regina and Saskatoon, Davidson, Sask., is a popular meeting place for denizens of both cities. So it's natural Davidson would build the world's biggest coffeepot as a symbol of their hospitality. If needed, the 7.3-meter-high sheet metal sculpture—decorated with different murals painted on each side—could hold 150,000 225 mL cups of joe.

◆ Canada's very own Big Apple

George Boycott saw firsthand the business generated by The Big Pineapple, a theme park in his native Australia, and The Big Kiwi, a similar tourist attraction in New Zealand. So The Big Apple seemed a natural when he moved to Canada. In 1987, at Colborne, Ont., he built the structure that now—at three stories and some 11 meters high—is reputed to be the world's biggest apple. Boycott later sold the business. Now family-run and open year-round, The Big Apple has welcomed as many as 600,000 visitors in one year. A major attraction is a "pie factory" with observation windows, where visitors can watch bakers turn out some of the thousands of apple pies sold each year.

◆ The Big Cheese of Ingersoll

Ontario produces nearly one-half of Canada's cheeses, and much of the Ontario production is centered around the village of Ingersoll. Canada's first cheese factory was built near there in 1840, and 26 years later Ingersoll cheesemakers devised a plan to put their cheese on the world stage. They produced a mammoth 3,330-kilogram cheese that stood one meter high, which they first showed at the New York State Fair in Saratoga, N.Y. (*below*), then shipped to Britain for exhibition at several fairs there. When the tour ended, a 135-kilogram slice was brought back to Ingersoll to treat the townspeople, many of whom had a hand in producing the giant cheese.

◆ They stand on guard

Countless communities across Canada have adopted symbols to represent them. A curious sampling:

◆ Selkirk, Man., economic and social hub of the province's Interlake recreational district, calls itself the catfish capital of the world, led by a nine-meter Main Street statue of Chuck the Channel Cat.

◆ A six-meter-long, functioning pipe, allegedly the world's largest smoking pipe, is the symbol of St. Claude, Man., a reminder of the pioneers who established the community—immigrants from Belgium, Switzerland, and Saint-Claude au Jura in France, a town noted for pipe-making.

◆ A six-meter-high statue of Mi'kmaq warrior Glooscap watches over Parrsboro, N.S. According to local lore, Glooscap created the Fundy tides and scattered the gems of his grandmother's jewelry along the Minas Shore.

◆ Built in 1967, a UFO landing pad at St. Paul, Alta., patiently awaits interplanetary visitors. In part, its plaque reads, "The area under the World's First UFO Landing Pad was designated international by the Town of St. Paul as a symbol of our faith that mankind will maintain the outer universe free from national wars and strife."

◆ The grandfather of community monuments

George Barone (1916–95) could never be accused of not thinking big. The Italian-born sculptor, known as the grandfather of community monuments in Manitoba, ran a Winnipeg studio that was responsible for many memorable outsized statues in that province, including Sara, the seven-meter Camel overlooking the Spirit Sands in Glenboro; a 4.6-meter Viking in Gimli, Man.; the white horse in St-François-Xavier (*see page 137*), and a seven-meter turtle in Boissevain. Barone also sculpted the famous statue of Winnie the Pooh in White River, Ont. (*see page 40*).

Josiah Flintabbatey Flonatin (right) is the mascot of Flin Flon, Man., a town named by gold miners for a fictional character (see page 90). The 7.5-meter statue at the entrance to town was designed by cartoonist Al Capp, creator of L'il Abner

◆ "Like a meteor passing"

To Henry Norman Bethune (1890–1939), no medical text could possibly equal the learning experience of working in the trenches. He interrupted his medical studies to become a stretcher-bearer during World War I. When he finally graduated, he worked among Detroit's poor, where he caught tuberculosis, then an incurable disease. He volunteered for a new treatment and was among the first patients treated with artificial pneumo-thorax, a procedure that involved collapsing the affected lung. On his recovery, he introduced the technique to Montreal, where he devoted seven years of his life to TB patients.

Confronted daily by poverty, undernourishment, and overcrowded tenements where the wasting disease flourished, Bethune crusaded for better medical care and health service reforms. He urged people to demand government-sponsored health care, and organized parades of the sick for this cause. The changes Bethune fought for didn't happen for another three decades, but his outcry played a major role in creating the national health care programs Canadians would later enjoy.

In 1936, the Spanish Civil War beckoned. In Spain that year, Bethune founded the world's first mobile blood transfusion service to aid Republican forces. When Japan invaded China two years later, Bethune became a surgeon with the Northern Chinese Communist forces of Mao Tse-tung. Before long his battlefront surgery had made him a hero to the Red Army. When he died a year later—of septicemia from an infected finger nicked during surgery—he was buried in China's Martyrs' Tomb. A Montreal friend of Bethune said of him that like him or dislike him, "he was like a meteor passing."

◆ Canada's Renaissance man

Hamilton native George J. Klein (1904–92) may not be a household name, yet some consider him to be the most prolific inventor in Canadian history. A 20th-century Renaissance man, Klein's enthusiasm for how things worked was likely sparked in the endless hours he spent in his father's watch and jewelry store as a boy. Klein applied his enthusiasms and unique problem-solving skills to inventions that were elegant in their simplicity and practicality, such as the motorized electric wheelchair for quadriplegics and the microsurgical staple gun.

Klein's pioneering research at the National Research Council made it practical to use skis on aircraft, and his later inventions included the STEM (Storable Tubular Extendible Member) antenna which was a hallmark of not only Canada's first satellite, *Alouette I*, but the Gemini and Apollo space programs as well. At the age of 72, Klein was called out of retirement to act as chief consultant on gear design for the Canadarm project (*see page 179*). Klein never became rich off his inventions, but that bothered him not one jot. He would rather spend time with students in elementary school woodworking shops, sharing the simple wonders of discovery.

◆ Penfield charted the brain's mysteries

World-renowned neurosurgeon, philosopher, and best-selling author, Dr. Wilder Graves Penfield (1891–1976) is probably Canada's most distinguished medical scientist. He had degrees from Princeton, Johns Hopkins, and Oxford universities, before he founded Montreal's Neurological Institute, of which he was director from 1934 to 1960. There he charted the mysteries and intricacies of the human brain, how it learns movements and language, how it receives sensations, and how it remembers.

Our medical and

Penfield also became the world's leading authority on the surgical treatment of epilepsy. Before his retirement from surgery, Penfield started what he liked to call his second career—writing historical novels in his spare time.

◆ Bigelow kept hearts beating

Millions of people world-wide owe their lives to Manitoba-born William Bigelow. A heart surgeon, Bigelow invented the pacemaker, and was the first to develop a procedure by which hypothermia is used to lower the temperature of patients undergoing open-heart surgery. Both developments took place at Toronto General Hospital, where Bigelow was head of heart surgery for some 20 years. The first pacemaker was large (about 30 centimeters long) and was powered by 60 Hz household current. It wasn't until transistors and batteries got smaller that a pacemaker was implanted in the chest of a Swedish man in 1957. Collaborating with Bigelow on the pacemaker invention were his research fellow John Callaghan and J. A. Hopps of the National Research Council, Ottawa.

◆ Toronto surgeon invented artificial kidney

North America's first artificial kidney, featuring an electric motor-driven pump, was invented by Dr. Gordon Murray (1894–1976), an Ontario surgeon who had fought in World War I and built a brilliant career in surgery in England. Murray's artificial kidney was used in the first hemodialysis performed in North America, at the Toronto General Hospital in 1946. Dr. Murray would later perform the world's first human heart valve transplant (1955) and Canada's first kidney transplant (1958).

scientific milestones

◆ Nobel-winning physicist came to Canada with $2.50

German born astrophysicist Gerhard Herzberg (1904–99) endured many a lean year on his quest to discover the building blocks of the universe. A bright pupil from a penniless family, he learned from the great Danish physicist Niels Bohr, whose atomic theories laid the foundation for quantum mechanics. One of the world's leading physicists by the age of 30, Herzberg, whose wife was Jewish, was forced to flee Germany in 1935. He emigrated to Saskatoon with only $2.50 in his pocket. He studied at the University of Saskatchewan for 10 years, then accepted a position in Chicago. In 1948, he accepted the National Research Council's invitation to establish a laboratory for research in spectroscopy (the study of molecular structure and dynamics through the absorption, emission, and scattering of light). He won the Nobel Prize in Chemistry in 1971 "for his contributions to the knowledge of electronic structure and geometry of molecules, particularly free radicals."

◆ They helped diabetics worldwide regain their lives

Insulin, a hormone manufactured by the pancreas, was introduced as a drug in 1922 by a University of Toronto team, acting on a research idea by London, Ont., orthopedic surgeon Dr. Frederick Banting (1891–1941, *pictured right*). Banting worked with physiologist Charles Best (1899–1978, *pictured left*) and U. of T. professors J. J. R. Macleod and J. B. Collip. The drug provided an immediate treatment for diabetes mellitus, then a fatal disease afflicting some one million North Americans.

The big breakthrough—discovering the link between insulin and diabetes—had been made the previous summer by Banting and

Best. Macleod, who was responsible for supervising the experiments, was overseas for much of the work. Banting, whose idea sparked the research in the first place, was widely credited with the discovery, yet was aghast when he and Macleod were named joint winners of the 1923 Nobel Prize for medicine. Publicly crediting Best as his co-discoverer, he shared his prize money with him, and assigned all financial interest in insulin to the University of Toronto. Macleod shared his prize money with Collip, who had produced the first insulin suitable for human use.

◆ A prankster who revolutionized medicine

His clergyman father had hoped his son would follow him into the church, but influenced by a high school teacher, William Osler (1849–1919; *below*) turned to medicine instead.

The greatest physician of his day, Osler is considered by many to be the father of psychosomatic medicine. From 1874 to 1888, he was on the staff of the medical school at Montreal's McGill University. During that time he became a voluntary pathologist at the Montreal General Hospital, where he often volunteered to conduct other doctors' autopsies. Later he taught at the University of Pennsylvania in Philadelphia and Johns Hopkins University in Baltimore, Maryland. During his Baltimore years, he continued teaching medicine at the bedside, as he had formerly done in Montreal. Later he joined the staff of Oxford University, England. Osler was a prolific writer—his landmark 1907 work *The System of Medicine* ran to seven volumes. He revolutionized hospital treatment and exerted a profound influence on medical education. He was particularly expert at diagnosing diseases of the heart, lungs, and blood.

An outgoing man, Osler was also given to practical jokes and pranks. He worked at dispelling gloom from the sickroom, and inspiring hope in his patients. He is infamous for a fake letter written to *The Philadelphia Medical News* of Dec. 13, 1884, under his pseudonym of Egerton Y. Davis, describing an exotic malady he called *penis captivus*. Thinking better of it, Osler tried to pull the letter before publication, but to his dismay it ran—and the phony condition continues to live on in urban legends to this day.

◆ Polyani's laser chemistry

As a student at Manchester, England, John Charles Polanyi (born 1929) was interested in politics and writing—he edited a newspaper and got his poetry published in *The New Statesman*—but only peripherally interested in science. Yet the Berlin-born Polyani was soon to follow in his chemist father's footsteps, even if he disdained the rigorous empirical testing that was the foundation of chemistry.

In the late 1950s, Polyani came to Ottawa to work as a Postdoctoral Fellow at the National Research Council, undertaking research in chemical reactions in gases. He was awarded the 1986 Nobel Prize for the discovery of laser chemistry, lasers based on the movement of molecules in chemical reactions that could be the most powerful sources of infrared radiation in existence.

The Nobel laureate has always been aware of the potential misuse of new technology, particularly in his field of subatomic research, and has consistently exhorted scientists to involve themselves in public affairs. He has been an active member of the Canadian Centre for Arms Control and Disarmament, and in 1978 he chaired an international symposium on "The Dangers of Nuclear War," and published a book of the same title. Polyani is presently a faculty member in the Department of Chemistry at the University of Toronto.

◆ The long arm of Canadian science

Tested and used extensively since its space debut in 1981, the Canadarm, Canada's contribution to the U.S. Shuttle Program, played a key role in retrieving, repairing, and redeploying the first satellite ever repaired in space. In April 1984, Canadarm plucked the malfunctioning *Solar Max* satellite from space, then returned it to orbit after its repair aboard the spaceship *Challenger*.

A $110 million project, Canadarm was developed by an industrial team led by Spar Aerospace Limited of Montreal, and directed by the National Aeronautical Establishment, a division of the National Research Council. With *Solar Max*, it met the two-pronged purpose of its design: to enable astronauts to take satellites from their orbiter's cargo bay and position them accurately in space, and to grapple satellites already in orbit and place them in the cargo bay for repair.

The arm—about 15 meters long and 40 centimeters in diameter—is designed for manual and automatic operation, and is controlled by hand from within the ship's cabin. A TV camera, or "eye," located on the arm's wrist provides visual cues of an astronaut's grappling maneuvers. The Canadarm made its space debut in 1981 on the second flight of the orbiter *Columbia*. Canada donated the initial Canadarm system to the U.S. space program. Subsequent Canadarm purchases by NASA were in the area of $25 million each.

◆ Hyslop identified Alzheimer's gene links

In 1968, at age 15, Kenyan-born Peter St. George Hyslop and his family immigrated to Canada. Working in Toronto 27 years later he identified two genes responsible for causing Alzheimer's-type memory loss in people as young as 30. The findings may be crucial in arresting a disease that afflicts some 300,000 Canadians. A graduate in medicine from the University of Ottawa, St. George Hyslop studied at Harvard Medical School before undertaking research into Alzheimer's at the University of Toronto, where he heads the Center for Research in Neurodegenerative Diseases. Hyslop received the Gold Medal in Medicine from the Royal College of Physicians of Canada in 1994.

◆ CIA's Montreal brain drain

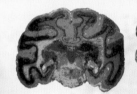

World-renowned Scottish psychiatrist Dr. Ewen Cameron was long dead when evidence of his CIA-funded mind-altering experiments conducted at Montreal's Allan Memorial Institute emerged. Cameron used massive doses of electroshock and injections of LSD and curare on unsuspecting psychiatric patients, many of whom suffered permanent brain damage.

Ewen's goal was to "depattern" his patients' minds, then reprogram the blank slate with healthier attitudes delivered by way of endlessly repeating taped messages. Between 1957 and 1960, the CIA channeled money to Cameron's experiments. In 1980 nine of Cameron's victims sued the CIA for damages.

Eight years later, one of the claimants was dead and the remaining eight each accepted a $100,000 out-of-court settlement from the CIA. Some time afterward 78 other Cameron victims also received $100,000 each from the Canadian government. But neither Ottawa nor the CIA ever admitted culpability.

Cameron's treatment and his victims' suits against the U.S. and Canadian governments are the subject of Anne Collins' *In the Sleep Room: The Story of the CIA Brainwashing Experiments in Canada*. The work won the 1988 Governor General's Award for non-fiction, and was later made into a CBC-TV mini-series.

◆ Men duelled over laywomen's right to be nurses

Nursing in Montreal had been the preserve of religious communities until the Montreal General Hospital, an English Protestant institution, staffed by laywomen opened in 1819. Not everyone took kindly to the change: Some, including Michael O'Sullivan, a member of the Quebec Legislature, objected to "hirelings" taking care of the sick. "Patients," O'Sullivan declared, "should be served by nuns devoted to the service of God." Meanwhile, the Montreal General's Dr. William Caldwell, a respected surgeon, published a spirited defense of his hospital and its use of lay nurses in the newspapers.

Feelings ran so high on both sides that O'Sullivan actually challenged Caldwell to a duel on the issue. He foolishly believed a dedicated physician would refuse to settle any dispute in such a manner on principle.

Caldwell, however, welcomed the challenge. As an ex-army surgeon, Caldwell's skill with firearms gave him the upper hand, and he swiftly put three bullets into O'Sullivan while taking one himself. While both men were seriously wounded, both survived.

The lay nurses stayed. O'Sullivan may have had the final word, however; Caldwell would later die of typhus in his own hospital.

"Patients should be served by nuns, not by hirelings."

◆ McGill extends M.D. olive branch ◆

In 1910, over 20 years after refusing her application to study medicine because of her sex, Montreal's McGill University conferred pathologist Maude Elizabeth Seymour Abbott (1869–1940) with an honorary doctorate in medicine. By then, Dr. Abbott, curator of the university's medical museum, was an internationally recognized authority on cardiac disease. The reputation was partly based on her groundbreaking research into congenital heart defects, which was published in Dr. William Osler's *System of Medicine* in 1907.

◆ Dr. "James"

The meteoric rise of Scottish surgeon Dr. James Barry (c.1790–1865) to the very top of the army medical service in Canada baffled many in military and medical circles. His high-pitched voice, short fuse, and mysterious demeanor weren't exactly officer material. At his autopsy in London, part of the mystery was solved—a nurse saw Barry unclothed and was shocked to discover he was a woman. The reason for Barry's lifelong masquerade, however, has long been a subject for conjecture.

◆ Canada's first woman doctor

The first Canadian woman to become a doctor, Emily Stowe (1831–1903), was also a driving force in the struggle to get women the vote. Raised in a Quaker family, Stowe believed in the equality of men and women. A teacher and school principal, she only decided to study medicine after her marriage to a physician. The University of Toronto refused to admit her, so Stowe enrolled in the New York Medical College for Women, and graduated as an M.D. in 1867. Even then, she was refused licensing in Canada until 1880.

The privilege withheld from Emily Stowe was later granted to her daughter, Dr. Augusta Stowe-Cullen, who was permitted to study at the Toronto School of Medicine and in 1883 became the first woman doctor to graduate in Canada. However, the discriminatory treatment Augusta had to endure from her fellow students convinced her mother that medical schools for women were essential, and in 1883 she founded the Ontario Medical College for Women—now known as Women's College Hospital—in Toronto.

◆ Licensed to heal

In 1875, Jennie Trout (1841–1921), the daughter of Ontario settlers, became the first woman in Canada licensed to practice medicine. She did so by passing the registration examinations of the Ontario College of Physicians and Surgeons. Jennie had had to train at the Women's Medical College in Pennsylvania, as no Canadian university admitted women medical students. In 1883, in association with Queen's University, she founded the Women's Medical College in Kingston, Ont.

◆ Prolific baby doctor was birth control pioneer

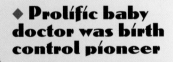

Hamilton, Ont., obstetrician Elizabeth Catherine Bagshaw (1881–1982) delivered some 3,000 babies in her 71 years of practice. In 1932, she courageously founded Canada's first birth control clinic, dispensing information and contraceptives. Illegal at the time, the clinic became legal in 1969.

◆ He created the lingua franca of the Web

When he was a child on a farm near Calgary, James Gosling (born 1955) was always interested in taking things apart. At the age of 12, he built a tic-tac-toe game from discarded telephone and TV parts. Two years later he discovered computers at the University of Calgary, and memorized the combinations of the door locks so he could let himself in to experiment after hours. After the sorcerer's apprentice graduated with a B.Sc. in Computer Science, his first job was with IBM, writing software. Gosling joined Sun Microsystems in 1984, where he created Java, a programming language that has become the lingua franca of the World Wide Web. Java allows Web pages to come alive with animations, stock market tickers, and games, no matter what type of computer is being used.

◆ Rare computer a pioneer in the Canadian industry

The Ferranti-Packard 6000, built in Toronto in 1961, filled an entire room, required an air conditioner, and had a total memory of 32K, but it was still years ahead of IBM and other computers. Not only was the FP 6000 capable of multitasking, it was the first computer that used programming via punch cards rather than hard-wiring to execute instructions. The largest unit was bought by the Saskatchewan Power Corporation in 1962, who used it for 20 years. Only five FP 6000s were built before the British government bought Ferranti-Packard in 1964 and shut down the project.

◆ The first Canadian Internet address

In 1981, Henry Spencer, in charge of the zoology department's computer facility at the University of Toronto, typed in the following address on the command line of his PC:

duke!duke34!utzoo!henry

His computer then dialed a computer at Duke University in North Carolina over UUCPnet, at the time the largest computer network in the world. (The World Wide Web was still a decade away.) Spencer's computer was the network's first international node from Canada, qualifying "utzoo" as the first Canadian Internet address.

◆ Waterloo's Father of Computing

James Wesley Graham (1932–99), the Father of Computing at University of Waterloo, had a reputation for doing things fast and without too much paperwork. The former statistician saw the enormous potential of computers outside the ivory towers of academia, and championed them to business. His software WATFOR (WATerloo FORtran), written in 1965, put Waterloo on the map, making it known as "MIT North" in the industry. Graham taught computer science at Waterloo for 40 years, and was a key figure in negotiating a partnership deal that brought $17 million worth of IBM hardware to Waterloo. He was awarded the Order of Canada in August 1999.

Internet privacy architect

phanie Perrin does not see privacy as a luxury, particularly
n age when our personal information can be easily har-
ed or hijacked online. "We are framing the information
," she told *The New York Times*, "and . . . privacy [is]
man right." The internationally recognized privacy and
tography expert spent five years engineering Canada's
sonal Information Protection and Electronics Documents
(PIPEDA), which came into force in 2002. She is now
ef Privacy Officer (CPO) of Zero-Knowledge Systems, a
ntreal-based company that sells services allowing people
urf the Internet safely and anonymously.

> e are framing the information age."

Archie does the search

In 1990, before the days of the World Wide Web,
connected Internet users were finding it impossible to wade through information and resources
on their networks. That year, two McGill graduate
students, Peter Deutsch and Alan Emtage, developed a software application they called Archie as
part of their graduate work. Archie (a play on
"archive") automatically searched File Transfer
Protocol (FTP) sites on the Internet and collected available file names in an archive of its own.
Users could log onto an Archie server hosted at
McGill and then search the database for key-
words or phrases, in the same way one would use
an Internet search engine such as Google today.
Archie was an unprecedented success, so much
so that McGill's servers were inundated with connections. Not long after its introduction, Archie
became available on dozens of mirror servers
around the world, reducing some of the pressure
on McGill.

Dude, you brought down the Internet

In February of 2001, several large Internet
portals and e-commerce websites such as
Yahoo, Amazon.com, eBay, and CNN.com were
brought to their knees by a new form of electronic sabo-
tage called a
Distributed
Denial of
Service
(DDoS) attack. A 17-year-old Montreal hacker
nicknamed "Mafiaboy" had commandeered a
host of computers to mount a simultaneous
attack on the websites, effectively locking
them up so that they could not be accessed.
When the RCMP and the FBI traced the attacks
to him, Mafiaboy (who cannot be identified
under the Young Offenders Act) pleaded guilty
to 56 counts of mischief and
was sentenced to eight
months in a youth
detention center.

world firsts

The Ganong candy factory in St. Stephen, N.B., produced the first Canadian-made lollipop (1895), the first chocolate bar (1906), and the first heart-shaped packaging for Valentine's Day candies (1932). Products from Stephen Ganong's family business (see page 103) are now sold around the world

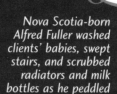

Nova Scotia-born Alfred Fuller washed clients' babies, swept stairs, and scrubbed radiators and milk bottles as he peddled his wares door to door

The world's first panoramic camera was patented in Elora, Ont., in 1887 by John Connon

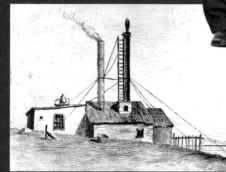

Invented in 1997 by Ontario farmer Lance Matthews, iWALKFree (right), an adjustable, hands-free crutch, greatly facilitates mobility of land-mine victims or anyone with below-the-knee injuries

Before radar, sailors approaching land relied on steam fog horns to warn of rocks and shoals. Steam fog horns were invented in Saint John, N.B., by Robert Foulis. The first one (right) was installed on Partridge Island in Saint John harbor in 1859

◆ Made-in-Canada originals—

Door-to-door sales and green garbage bags, five-pin bowling and zippers are just some of the everyday activities and objects created by Canadians or made in Canada. Some inventions, such as the telephone (*see page 187*) or the snowmobile (*page 192*) were inspired by one person's vision. Other breakthroughs, such as the Canadarm (*page 179*) were the culmination of hundreds of talented people working to a common goal. But whether by individual or collective effort, Canadian inventiveness and ingenuity has sparked many thriving industries worldwide.

◆ Green ink, used since 1862 for printing U.S. banknotes, (and source of the term "greenback"), was developed by Thomas Sterry Hunt (1826–92), then a chemistry professor at McGill University in Montreal. Because it was difficult to duplicate, the invention was a major blow to counterfeiters.

◆ A Halifax marine biologist, Dr. Archibald G. Huntsman (1883–1973), developed a product called "Ice Fillets," the first packaged quick-frozen food.

◆ We owe batteryless radios to Edward Samuel Rogers (1900–39), who perfected the alternating current tube in 1925. The invention helped create the Rogers communication empire—the RB in the call letters of Toronto's CFRB station stand for Roger's Batteryless.

◆ Door-to-door sales originated with Nova Scotian Alfred C. Fuller (1885–1973), who launched his Fuller Brush Company in 1906 and pounded the pavement, visiting homes to demonstrate the efficiency of his product.

McIntosh apple   screw propeller   washing machine

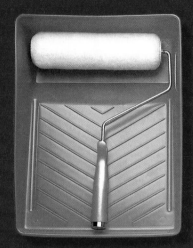

In 1940, Norman Breakey of Toronto devised the roller that revolutionized the paint industry, but failed to find financial backing for his invention and died a poor man

Toronto businessman Thomas F. Ryan downsized 10-pin bowling in 1909 after his patrons complained that the large bowling balls were too heavy. Five-pin bowling became a hit around the world, but because Ryan failed to patent his invention, he didn't see a penny

Walter Chell was working in a Calgary hotel when he developed the Bloody Caesar

worldwide winners one and all

◆ Montenegro-born Walter Chell was working for the Westin Hotel chain in Calgary in 1969 when he hit upon a recipe for a new cocktail. He mixed mashed clams, tomato juice, vodka, Worcester sauce, and salt and pepper, and called it the Bloody Caesar. Chell later worked for the Mott company, which began making Clamato juice in the 1970s.

◆ Around 1905, Thomas F. Ryan (1872–1961) opened the first 10-pin bowling alley in Canada. When patrons, many of them prominent Toronto businessmen, complained the ball was causing arm strain, Ryan fashioned a smaller ball, and his father whittled down five pins to match. Five-pin bowling was born in 1909.

◆ Hooks and eyes were the niftiest fasteners around in the early 1900s, when Swedish-born Gideon Sundback, president of the Lightning Fastener Company of St. Catharines, Ont., produced the hookless gadget now known as the zipper. The fastener was the big selling point in rubber galoshes manufactured by the B. F. Goodrich Company, who sold the overshoes under the Zipper trade name.

◆ While there's no dispute that green garbage bags are 1950s Canadian originals, it isn't entirely certain whether the first one was made in Winnipeg by Harry Wasylyk or in Lindsay, Ont., by Larry Hanson.

◆ Laser sailboats, too, got their start in Canada. The boat itself was designed and built by Bruce Kirby and Ian Bruce; the sail was designed by Hans Fogh, who skippered the first model in a 1970 regatta in Pointe Claire, Que.

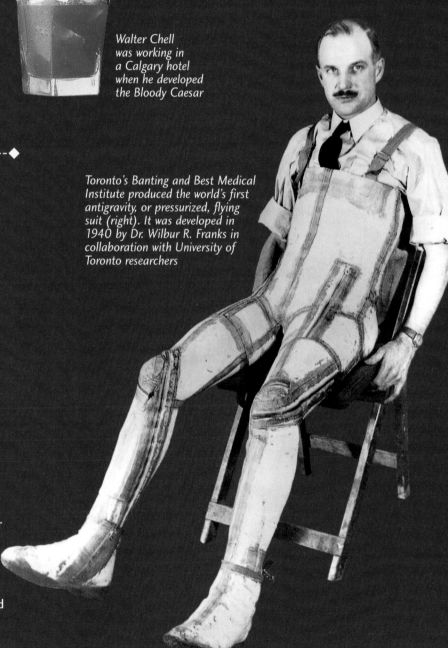

Toronto's Banting and Best Medical Institute produced the world's first antigravity, or pressurized, flying suit (right). It was developed in 1940 by Dr. Wilbur R. Franks in collaboration with University of Toronto researchers

newsprint   kerosene   undersea telegraph cable

◆ Wasps inspired paper pioneer

Pulp and paper is one of Canada's biggest industries today, thanks in part to entrepreneurial paper pioneers such as Charles Fenerty (1821–92), a Nova Scotian farmer and lumberman who claimed to be the first person in the world to make paper from wood. Fenerty began experimenting in the late 1830s; by 1844 he had produced usable white paper by grinding sprucewood fiber, but his invention attracted little attention. Up to this point, paper was ordinarily made from rags. Fenerty's inspiration came from watching wasps build their nests: from the wood fiber they chewed, they produced a fine paper for lining their nests.

Some 30 years later, John Thompson of Napanee, Ont., followed Fenerty's lead and became the first person in North America to produce paper on a commercial scale from wood pulp. North America's first pulp mill was opened at Valleyfield, Que., in the late 1860s.

◆ Ontario bush yielded the apple of McIntosh's eye

In 1811, John McIntosh (1777–1845) settled on a farm in what is now Dundela, Ont. Over the next few years he transplanted apple trees that he found growing wild in the bush. The cultivated trees produced crops of red apples that proved immensely popular with McIntosh's neighbors, and by 1900 McIntosh apples were well established in eastern Canada. Eventually McIntosh's son, Allen, started a nursery and from there McIntosh-bearing apple trees were dispersed all over North America.

The original apple tree continued to bear fruit until 1908. Two years later it was toppled by a storm. A granite monument erected on the McIntosh property in 1912 commemorates John McIntosh and his famous apple trees.

◆ Into the mouths of babes

In the pre-antibiotic days of the early 1900s, Dr. Alan Brown (1887–1960), Physician-in-Chief of Toronto's Hospital for Sick Children, had few resources against the infectious diseases and other illnesses that took the lives of many of his tiny patients. Because poorly nourished children were especially vulnerable, Dr. Brown set up a nutrition research laboratory at the hospital.

Two young Ontario doctors, Theodore Drake and Fred Tisdall, whom Brown hired to work there, soon discovered that many babies were being fed finely milled grain cereals from which the bran and wheat germ—the source of vitamins, minerals, and protein—had been removed. So they developed a cereal containing wheat meal, oatmeal, cornmeal, wheat germ, bonemeal, brewer's yeast, alfalfa, iron, calcium, and copper.

When they saw that the babies who were fed the cereal grew stronger, Drake and Tisdall patented the product, directing all royalties to the Hospital for Sick Children. By 1931 Mead Johnson had the product ready for market as Mead's Cereal, but its creators renamed it Pablum (from *pabulum*, Latin for food). By the time the patent expired in the 1950s, the hospital had received more than $1 million in royalty fees.

◆ Bell invented the "world's rudest instrument"

Scottish-born Alexander Graham Bell (1847–1922) called his most famous invention one of the world's rudest instruments, noting that no one but a telephone user would interrupt you while you were at dinner, or sleeping, or having a bath.

A teacher of the deaf, Bell visualized his invention during a summer visit to his childhood home, Tutela Heights, near Brantford, Ont. It took him two years to build the instrument, and on Aug. 3, 1876, in a Dominion Telegraph Company office in Mount Pleasant, Ont., Bell heard his uncle David—three kilometers away in a telegraph office in Brantford—recite Shakespeare's "To be or not to be . . . " This was the first intelligible telephone transmission from one building to another. On Aug. 10, it was followed by the first intelligible long-distance call—made from Brantford to Paris, Ont., 13 kilometers to the northwest.

Bell had a summer home and laboratory at Baddeck, N.S., where he eventually retired. His other inventions include the phonograph (1889) and an artificial respiration device he called a vacuum jacket (1881), a forerunner of the iron lung.

Few Canadians could afford a telephone in the late 1800s; telephone booths (left) were often luxurious, paneled affairs that befit the new invention's glamor

◆ World's first radio broadcast beamed at sailors

Marconi may have been the first to send wireless messages, but Reginald Fessenden (1866–1932) invented radio as we know it today. Born in East Bolton, Que., the clergyman's son grew up in Fergus and Niagara Falls, Ont. Electricity was a lifelong fascination for Fessenden, and in his twenties he became a student at the Edison Laboratories in New Jersey.

Marconi had used Morse code for his famous transatlantic radio transmission of Dec. 12, 1901, but a year earlier Fessenden had found a way of transmitting voice over radio. In 1902, on Cobb Island in the Potomac River near Washington, D.C., he became the first to successfully transmit the human voice, when he asked his assistant more than a kilometer away, "Is it snowing where you are, Mr. Thiessen?" In 1906 he became the first to achieve two-way voice radio transmission, and later that year he beamed the world's first radio broadcast—a Christmas concert in which Fessenden played Holy Night on the violin—to United Fruit Company ships in the Atlantic and Caribbean.

Although many of his radio patents were adopted without his consent, The U.S. Radio Trust awarded Fessenden $2.5 million in 1928 for his contribution to radio.

◆ Kerosene fired the oil industry

Kerosene inventor Dr. Abraham Gesner (1797–1864) first unveiled his new product at a lecture in Charlottetown, P.E.I., in 1846. Most lighting of Gesner's day came from whale oil and seal oil lamps, which gave off almost as much smoke as they did light. So even though Gesner's kerosene, or coal oil as it became known, smelled awful, his audience was impressed with the clear flame it produced. Gesner, a geologist as well as a physician, had distilled his kerosene from hydrocarbons such as asphalt and petroleum. North America's oil refining industry was based on his distillation method, which enabled oil industry pioneers to refine petroleum into a saleable product.

◆ The electron microscope's powerful eye

A native of Brantford, Ont., James Hillier was a lecturer at the University of Toronto in 1937 when he and Albert Prebus, a research student from Alberta, invented the electron microscope (*left*). Their breakthrough resulted from work originally begun by another Alberta research student, C. E. Hall. Used today worldwide, its powerful magnification lets scientists examine structures thousands of time smaller than anything visible through an ordinary microscope. Interestingly, the two scientists had personalities of different polarities; with Hillier outgoing and Prebus introspective, they complemented each other and made the seemingly impossible project a reality.

◆ Dropping the cobalt bomb

Treatment by cobalt bomb radiation took place for the first time on Oct. 27, 1951, at the War Memorial Children's Hospital attached to Victoria Hospital, London, Ont. Cobalt 60 beam radiation therapy worked by bombarding cancer cells with neutralizing X-rays, enabling doctors to successfully treat a wide spectrum of cancers located deep in the body. The "bomb" was the outcome of pioneering radiation studies at the University of Saskatchewan by one of the founders of medical physics, Dr. Harold Elford Johns (1915–88), and atomic research begun during World War II at Atomic Energy of Canada's nuclear laboratories in Chalk River, Ont.

◆ Itinerant Ontario tool seller no square head

One of Canada's best-selling tools resulted from a decidedly unhandy do-it-yourselfer's awkwardness. The Robertson screwdriver (*above*) might never have been invented if a Cayuga, Ont., street vendor hadn't gashed himself with a sharp-tipped screwdriver while setting up his stall on a Montreal street corner. The accident got itinerant tool seller Peter Lymburner Robertson (1879–1951) thinking about tools that could be handled safely—square-slotted screws with matching screwdrivers, for example.

Before long, Robertson perfected and patented his idea, found backers, and by 1908 was manufacturing his socket-head screw in a Milton, Ont., plant. His first customers, boatbuilders, told other tradespeople how the Robertson system speeded up their work. Electricians liked his system for difficult-to-reach areas: The Robertson screw-and-driver system does not slip and requires only one hand. But Robertson's big break came when Model T Ford manufacturers in Detroit began using his products. Before long, the street hawker had become a millionaire.

◆ "Bottled sunlight" lit the way for early autos

Even as a teenager, Thomas "Carbide" Willson (1860–1915) was obsessed with inventions. Many of his early projects were conducted in the basement of his parents' home in Hamilton, Ont. History now knows him as the man who, in 1892, discovered how to mix lime and coal tar to produce carbide, which in turn produces acetylene gas.

Willson's "bottled sunlight" would later light construction sites, fuel lighthouses, and provide the lighting on early automobiles (*left*). Willson was unable to interest Canadian investors in his invention, which was eventually bankrolled by an American company, Union Carbide. Although most lighting eventually switched to electricity, the acetylene industry survived in the form of acetylene torches for cutting and welding steel.

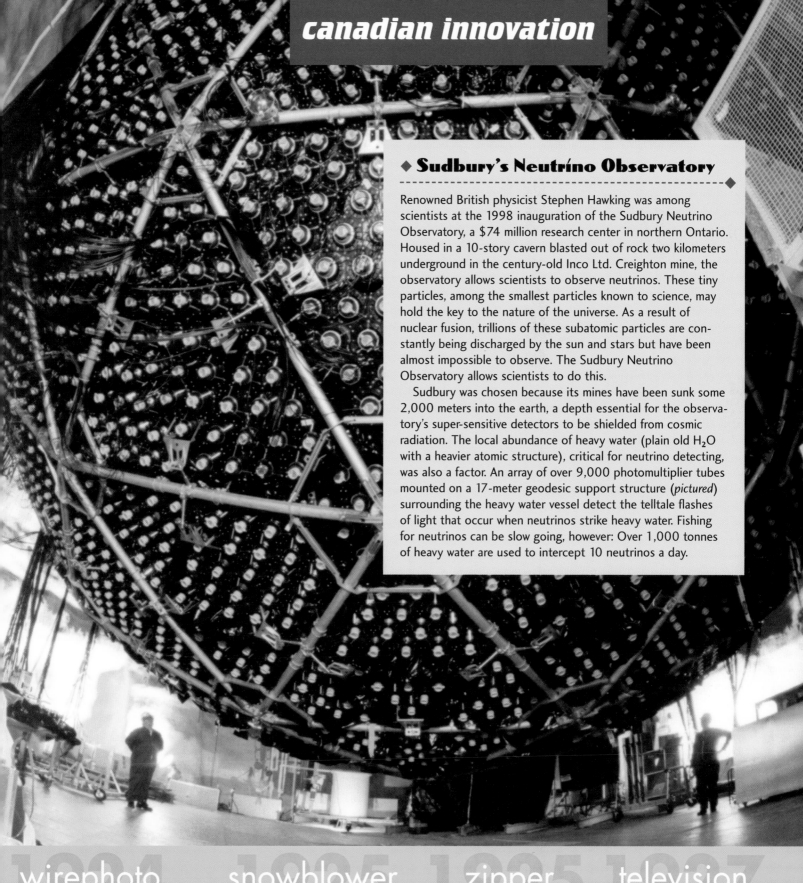

◆ Sudbury's Neutrino Observatory ◆

Renowned British physicist Stephen Hawking was among scientists at the 1998 inauguration of the Sudbury Neutrino Observatory, a $74 million research center in northern Ontario. Housed in a 10-story cavern blasted out of rock two kilometers underground in the century-old Inco Ltd. Creighton mine, the observatory allows scientists to observe neutrinos. These tiny particles, among the smallest particles known to science, may hold the key to the nature of the universe. As a result of nuclear fusion, trillions of these subatomic particles are constantly being discharged by the sun and stars but have been almost impossible to observe. The Sudbury Neutrino Observatory allows scientists to do this.

Sudbury was chosen because its mines have been sunk some 2,000 meters into the earth, a depth essential for the observatory's super-sensitive detectors to be shielded from cosmic radiation. The local abundance of heavy water (plain old H_2O with a heavier atomic structure), critical for neutrino detecting, was also a factor. An array of over 9,000 photomultiplier tubes mounted on a 17-meter geodesic support structure (*pictured*) surrounding the heavy water vessel detect the telltale flashes of light that occur when neutrinos strike heavy water. Fishing for neutrinos can be slow going, however: Over 1,000 tonnes of heavy water are used to intercept 10 neutrinos a day.

wirephoto   snowblower   zipper   television

Money¢ent$ (near left) is used in 20,000 Canadian classrooms. Proud To Be Me! (far left) has become a valuable aid for parents, teachers, and psychologists. Trivial Pursuit (above) has been issued in over 100 different editions and is sold in 16 languages around the world

◆ Canadian board game champions

Inquisitive Canadian minds are behind some of the greatest board game successes of all time, whether the subject is trivia, money, or murder.

◆ **Yachtzee** had its origins in a game called "The Yacht Club," invented by a Canadian couple in the 1920s who later sold the rights to it. The popular dice game sells millions of copies each year.

◆ The world's most popular board game, **Trivial Pursuit** was invented in 1979 by Christopher Haney, a Montreal *Gazette* photo editor, his brother John, and Scott Abbot, a Canadian Press sportswriter. Lawyer Edward Martin Werner helped the Montreal-based trio get the trivia blockbuster off the ground. Each now has personal fortunes estimated at more than $50 million. David Wall, a Sydney, N.S.,

plumber, has been trying to sue the threesome for years. Wall claims he shared his idea for a trivia board game with Chris Haney, with whom he once hitched a 10-minute ride.

◆ **Balderdash**, a brilliant game of bluff invented by seasoned Toronto parlor game players Paul Toyne and Laura Robinson in 1984, requires players to come up with credible definitions of over 2,500 obscure words.

◆ Vancouver native Rob Angel hit upon a novel twist on charades while working in Seattle, Wash., in 1985. In **Pictionary**, players must guess words not from gestures but from sketching clues.

◆ Would you take money from a broken phone booth? Ethical conundrums are the heart of **A Question of Scruples**, the

1986 creation of Henry Makow, an English professor in Winnipeg.

◆ **Hummzinger** was the name of a 1986 game where players tried to stump each other by humming the tunes of popular songs—not as easy as it sounds.

◆ **MindTrap** challenges whodunnit fans with murder-mystery scenarios and mind-bending puzzles. First released in 1991, it was created by Richard Fast of Kingston, Ont., in collaboration with artist Garnett Plum and lawyer Tibor Sarai.

◆ The 12,000-question **The Reel to Reel Picture Show** was created by school principal Kathy Cargill, teacher Pauline Harley, and engineers Sandy Cherry and Bill Lewochko, all of Toronto. The movie trivia game was the biggest selling new board game in Canada in 1996.

frozen food   Pablum   paint roller   walkie talkie

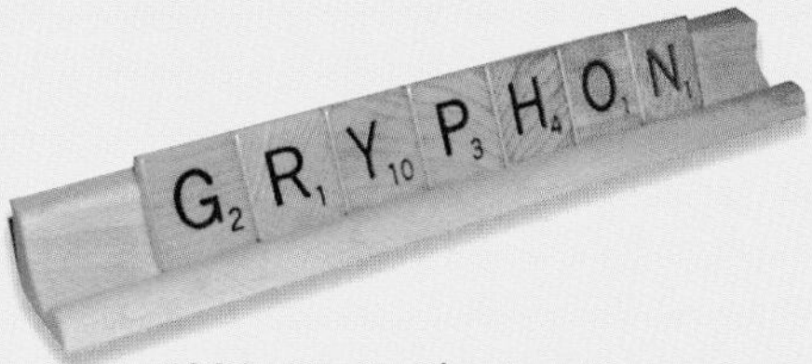

GRYPHON

In 1999, Montreal university professor Joel Wapnick won the World Scrabble Championship in Melbourne, Australia, using exotic words such as "taborets," "embogue," "rivage," and "deoxy." Joel's highest word score ever was 221 points for "gryphons"

The 3-D jigsaw

In 1975, Steve LePage of Oakville, Ont., was dumbfounded to discover that his sons, then five and seven, didn't know how many nickels were in a dime. LePage set about teaching them some financial skills using board game techniques on a game board he fashioned in the shape of a dollar sign. Recognizing the potential of his creation, he quit his job as a sales director and invested $60,000 in developing and marketing Money¢ent$, which appeared in stores in 1996.

Proud To Be Me, a conversation stimulator game co-developed by LePage and Tina Fenech of Brampton, Ont., in 1998, has become a valuable aid for parents, teachers, psychologists, and therapists.

Introduced in 1760 as educational tools for well-to-do French and English families, today jigsaw puzzles have become perenially popular without ever departing from the interlocking, snap-in flat design. In 1991, Montreal entrepreneur Paul Gallant created a three-dimensional jigsaw puzzle that stood the industry on its ear. Gallant's first creation flew off the shelves at F. A. O. Schwarz in New York and inspired a whole range of challenging and magnificent puzzles (right) ranging from world landmarks and architectural wonders to animals, classic autos, and working grandfather clocks.

Puzz 3D

Birdhous
Cabane à ois

229 PIECES

EACH BIRD'S SONG
EMET UN CHANT D'OISEAU

◆ A winter carnival warmer-upper that was hot—in England

After he emigrated to Montreal in the 1870s, Scottish nutritionist John Lawson Johnston developed a hot drink made from beef extract to warm revelers at the winter carnivals that flourished throughout Quebec in his day. "For health and strength," proclaimed the advertisements for Bovril, as the new drink was called. Merrymakers at these skating, sleighriding, snowshoeing, and tobogganing extravaganzas preferred a drop of something stronger, however, and Bovril was a flop in Quebec. His concoction, however, was marketed in England, where it became an instant hit, and still brings nostalgic memories of childhood to many.

◆ Inuit inspired Birds Eye frozen foods

While in port in Sandwich Bay, Labrador, in 1916, Clarence Birdseye got the idea for quick freezing fresh food, when he saw Inuit fishing in −46°C weather. The fish froze immediately on leaving the water, yet tasted fresh-caught when eaten months later. Capt. Birdseye parlayed the process into the "Birds Eye" frozen foods, first marketed in 1930.

◆ Bombardier changed northern life forever

The first snowmobile, a propeller-driven sled to transport one or two people, was assembled in the 1920s by J. Armand Bombardier (1908–64), a Valcourt, Que., mechanic. He called his invention the Husky, for the sled dogs that until then provided the only mode of transport in Canada's North. Commercial possibilities brightened in 1937 when Bombardier sold 50 seven-seater vehicles, mostly for winter medical transportation. A decade later, he was making 12-passenger vehicles for the military. The big breakthrough finally came in the form of a lightweight, relatively powerful engine, and by 1959 the first Ski-dogs, now called Ski-Doos, were rolling off the assembly line.

Over the next few years, the Ski-Doo changed the lives of northern communities forever, replacing sled-dog teams from one end of the Arctic to the other. In 1969, the Mounties abandoned their sled dogs for the new Bombardier innovation.

goalie mask   IMAX projector   CANDU reactor

◆ Where the reception is cold

A cold reception awaits the intrepid traveler who checks into Quebec City's Ice Hotel. But ever since it was opened in January 2001, this architectural marvel has been a seasonal hot spot for tourists. Built from 10,000 tonnes of snow and 350 tonnes of ice, the hotel features luxury suites with warm sleeping bags and deer pelts, two art galleries, a movie theatre, and an "Icecotheque."

◆ First Christmas tree in lights

In Sorel, Que., a Christmas tree sculpture stands before the Maison des Gouverneurs, a mansion built on the Richelieu River in 1781. The sculpture is a reminder of Baron Friederick von Riedesel, who lived there in the early 1780s. Von Riedesel commanded a regiment of German and Swiss mercenaries stationed in Sorel to counter a feared American invasion. At Christmas of 1781, Baron von Riedesel and his wife put up a balsam fir tree, and decorated it with lights, thus beginning a North American tradition.

◆ From chaff to snow

The snowblower (*right*) was invented by Arthur Sicard, son of a Quebec farmer, who got the idea from watching threshers at work. Old threshing machines had a stout vent through which the chaff, the grains' outer skins, was discharged and spent years developing a prototype. When he demonstrated his invention during the 1925–26 winter, the benefits were obvious, and the then City of Outremont, Que., was the first in line to buy one.

◆ The Canadian Edison

The electric streetcar, all the rage in the United States in the late 1880s, was never seriously considered for the city of Ottawa because of its winter weather. That didn't stop Thomas Ahearn (1855–1938), the man known as "The Canadian Edison."

Ahearn, who had spent his formative years learning everything he could about telegraphy, jury-rigged Ottawa's first long-distance telephone call (from Pembroke to Ottawa) in 1877 using two home-made cigar boxes, magnets and wire and existing telegraph lines. He was appointed manager of Bell Telegraphone Company's first Ottawa office.

In 1891, Ahearn helped set up the Ottawa Electric Railway, and designed streetcars that could be warmed in winter with electrically heated water running under the floors. He even invented a rotating brush cleaner to clear the tracks. These were the first electrically heated cars in North America, and were sold all across Canada until the late 1940s.

Ahearn was present at many of Canada's electrical "firsts": He was the first person in the world to cook a meal with electricity, for an 1892 dinner at Ottawa's Windsor Hotel. In 1899, Ahearn was the first person to drive an electric automobile in Ottawa.

And in 1927, Ahearn, with Prime Minister Mackenzie King and Justice Minister Ernest Lapointe, made Canada's first transatlantic telephone call to Britain.

slicklicker　Canadarm　Abdomenizer

◆ The loonie that won the gold

At the press conference following Canada's decisive triumphs in Men's and Women's Hockey at the 2002 Salt Lake City Winter Olympic Games, Team Canada Executive Director Wayne Gretzky (*see page 199*) revealed his team's secret weapon—he pulled out a dollar coin from his pocket. Unbeknownst to many of the players, the icemakers at the E Center in Salt Lake—who were Canadian—had buried the coin beneath center ice to bring Canada luck. As it turns out, the Men's Hockey team beat the United States 5-2, winning the gold medal for the first time in 50 years, just two days after the Women's team captured the gold from the Americans with a 3-2 victory. Gretzky donated the lucky loonie to the Hockey Hall of Fame.

WHITEHORSE 2000

◆ Polar pride: The Arctic Winter Games

The biennial Arctic Winter Games were first held in Yellowknife in 1970 to promote cultural and social interchange among northern people. Events include cross-country skiing, curling, figure skating, hockey and indoor soccer, shooting, snowshoeing, speedskating, triathlon, and volleyball. Traditional Arctic sports that test stamina, strength, and endurance—such as the sledge jump, knuckle hop, and high kick—are highlight events. Athletes competing in the high kick, a long established Inuit sport, leap into the air with one or both feet. The unique games attract competitors from Canada's northern territories as well as Alaska, Greenland, and on occasion Russia.

◆ Canada's greatest all-round athlete

Possibly Canada's greatest all-round athlete ever, Lionel Conacher (1902–54, *right*) had won an Ontario wrestling title and a Canadian light-heavyweight boxing title by the time he was 18. Later he would excel in football, lacrosse, baseball, and hockey. No wonder they called him "The Big Train." Conacher became a Liberal MP on his retirement from professional sport. Active to the end, he suffered a heart attack and died in 1954 while playing softball against the Parliamentary Press Corps.

◆ Joyous Jays

It was the stuff of base-ball legend: Down by one in the bottom of the ninth, a home run hit out of the park wins the game. Toronto's SkyDome went wild as Joe Carter's homer on Nov. 1, 1993, gave the Blue Jays an 8-6 win over the Philadelphia Phillies and their second consecutive World Series championship.

The thrill of

◆ Canada's first national sports star

When rower Edward "Ned" Hanlan (1855– 1908, *left*) defeated the English champion, William Elliott, by an incredible 11 lengths in 1789, he became Canada's first national sports figure, and our first athlete to gain international recognition. The son of a Toronto Island storekeeper, Hanlan grew up around boats, even rowing himself to school as a child. He won the Canadian sculling championship in 1877, and the U.S. title a year later. He became world champion in 1880 and held the title until 1884. Hanlan loved to entertain the crowds who flocked to see him race, clowning around by lying down in his boat, dropping his oars, or sculling in a circle until his competitors caught up to him, then pulling away. Hanlan's single shell, *The Cigarette*, was equipped with a revolutionary seat on rollers to increase speed. Over his racing career, he lost only six races.

victory, the agony of defeat

◆ Dubin report just says no

Established after sprinter Ben Johnson (*right*) was stripped of his 100-meter gold medal at the 1988 Seoul Olympics when he tested positive for the steroid Stanozolol, the landmark, $4 million Dubin Inquiry heard months of testimony by athletes, coaches, and specialists in sports medicine. The final report revealed widespread use of banned substances to enhance athletic performance in Canadian sport, and made 70 recommendations, most of which the government adopted. Among these were scheduled and no-notice testing of athletes, and stricter controls on the distribution of anabolic steroids.

◆ Our oldest sport

Lacrosse has its roots in the ancient game of *baggattaway* (from the Ojibwa word for ball). Originating among the Algonquin tribes of the St. Lawrence Valley, the rough-and-tumble two- to three-day melee of baggattaway played an important role in training young warriors, and is said to be the oldest organized sport in North America. French missionary Jean de Brébeuf first saw the game in 1683, and called it "la crosse" because the players' sticks reminded him of a bishop's crozier. The Oneida also played a variant of the game known as *gah-lahs* (*see page 70*).

◆ Female athlete of the half-century

Named Canadian Woman Athlete for the Half-Century by the Canadian Press in 1949, Fanny "Bobbie" Rosenfeld (1905–69) was a star in track-and-field, baseball, basketball, hockey, and tennis. The records she set in 1928 for the long jump, the standing broad jump, and the discus lasted until the 1950s. She later wrote a sports column for *The Globe and Mail*. Every year, CP still awards the Bobbie Rosenfeld trophy to Canada's Female Athlete of the Year.

◆ Hockey's first face-off

Woven into the fabric of our national heritage as surely as author Roch Carrier's famous 1979 children's story *The Hockey Sweater* is woven into our memories, ice hockey is our national pastime and Canada's contribution to world sport.

The game had its humble beginnings in Kingston, Ont., during the 1850s, when members of the Royal Canadian Rifles used oak and ash sticks to hit tennis balls around frozen Kingston harbor, playing variations of the stick and ball games known variously as shinty and bandy in their native Britain. Eventually the game became known as hockey, a name derived from the French word *hoquet* (shepherd's crook) because of the bent sticks the players used.

It wasn't until 1875 that hockey's rules were formalized by J. G. A. Creighton. Creighton is credited with setting down the first set of rules during his student days at McGill in Montreal. Before he formalized the rules of play, as many as 60 players might have been involved in the game at any one time. Creighton reduced this to nine players per team and replaced tennis balls with flat disks, or pucks.

Canada's first hockey team, the McGill Hockey Club, was formed in 1879. Kingston had four teams by 1885, and the Amateur Hockey Association of Canada was formed the following year. The sport continued as an amateur game into the early 1900s, by which time there were over 100 hockey teams in Montreal alone. Professional teams emerged after 1917 when the Eastern Canada Hockey Association and the National Hockey Association joined forces as the National Hockey League (NHL).

In the 1920s, the NHL began to add American teams, and at one point the only Canadian teams in the league were the Montreal Canadiens and the Toronto Maple Leafs. A rival organization, the World Hockey Association (WHA), arrived on the scene with 12 new teams in 1972—among them the Edmonton Oilers—only to be absorbed by the NHL seven years later. Today, Canada is represented in the NHL by the Canadiens, the Maple Leafs, the Oilers, the Vancouver Canucks, the Calgary Flames, and the Ottawa Senators.

◆ Vintage Lemieux

Most hockey players celebrate a Stanley Cup win with champagne. For former Pittsburgh Penguins center Mario Lemieux (born 1965; *below*), nothing less than a bottle of Château Latour 1982 would do. The Montreal-born hockey star is an avid and serious wine collector, with a 5,000-bottle cellar. Among his many achievements, Lemieux led the Penguins to two Stanley Cups, earned three Hart Trophies as the NHL's most valuable player, and successfully fought Hodgkin's disease in 1992. After retiring in 1997, Lemieux later became owner of the Penguins and returned to play.

200,000 said goodbye to the "Stratford Streak"

Some 200,000 people jammed the streets of Montreal and hockey fans across North America mourned when hockey's first great superstar, Howie Morenz (1902–37), died following a freak accident. Thousands of Canadiens fans filed past their idol's bier at center ice in the Montreal Forum (the Habs' home before the Bell Centre). Morenz, known for playing his heart out in game after game, suffered a badly broken leg and a head injury during a game, and died two months later from complications. One of hockey's fastest skaters and greatest stick handlers, and the NHL's top scorer in 1928 and 1931, Ontario-born Morenz (he was called the "Stratford Streak") scored 270 goals and 467 points over a 14-year career. He had begun his professional career with the Canadiens, before going on to play with Chicago and New York teams, then rejoining the Canadiens in 1936.

Guy Lafleur's flower power

His surefire, rink-length rush for the goal, blond hair flying, was hockey star Guy Lafleur's (born 1951; *right*) trademark image. "The Flower," as he was known, retired in 1982 from the Montreal Canadiens, with whom he won five Stanley Cups. A flamboyant player who lived large off the ice, Lafleur had a powerful, accurate shot, and a deft touch with the puck.

In his time with the Habs, Lafleur was named the NHL's scoring champion three times. (From 1974–80, he never scored less than 50 goals a season.) Lafleur would later come out of retirement to play with the New York Rangers and the Quebec Nordiques. When he finally left professional sport in 1991, he had chalked up 560 goals and 1,358 points. He remains the Canadiens' leading all-time scorer.

A play-by-play that spanned 50 years

"He shoots, he scores," the trademark phrase of veteran sportscaster Foster Hewitt (1902–85), was first used in a 1923 radio broadcast of one of the first-ever hockey matches aired. Broadcasting technology was in its infancy when Hewitt first went on air, making his first commentary, not by microphone but by phone. Hewitt's spirited commentaries continued for some 50 years on radio and TV and covered a wide range of sports.

AGAIN FROM COAST TO COAST IT'S "HOCKEY NIGHT" IN CANADA

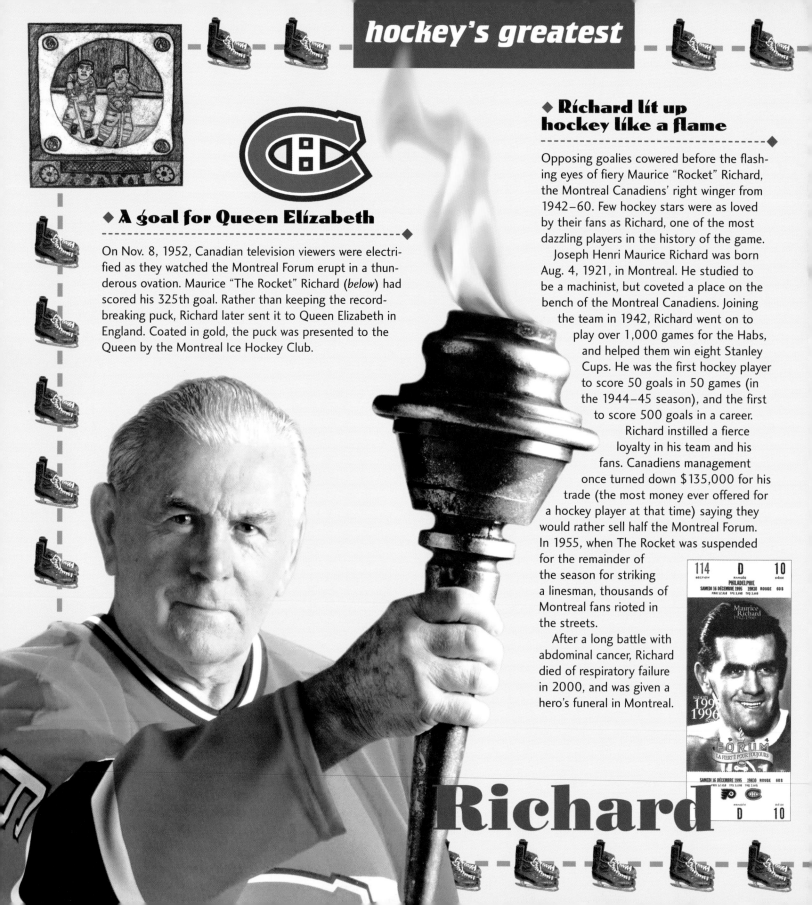

◆ A goal for Queen Elizabeth

On Nov. 8, 1952, Canadian television viewers were electrified as they watched the Montreal Forum erupt in a thunderous ovation. Maurice "The Rocket" Richard (*below*) had scored his 325th goal. Rather than keeping the record-breaking puck, Richard later sent it to Queen Elizabeth in England. Coated in gold, the puck was presented to the Queen by the Montreal Ice Hockey Club.

◆ Richard lit up hockey like a flame ◆

Opposing goalies cowered before the flashing eyes of fiery Maurice "Rocket" Richard, the Montreal Canadiens' right winger from 1942–60. Few hockey stars were as loved by their fans as Richard, one of the most dazzling players in the history of the game.

Joseph Henri Maurice Richard was born Aug. 4, 1921, in Montreal. He studied to be a machinist, but coveted a place on the bench of the Montreal Canadiens. Joining the team in 1942, Richard went on to play over 1,000 games for the Habs, and helped them win eight Stanley Cups. He was the first hockey player to score 50 goals in 50 games (in the 1944–45 season), and the first to score 500 goals in a career.

Richard instilled a fierce loyalty in his team and his fans. Canadiens management once turned down $135,000 for his trade (the most money ever offered for a hockey player at that time) saying they would rather sell half the Montreal Forum. In 1955, when The Rocket was suspended for the remainder of the season for striking a linesman, thousands of Montreal fans rioted in the streets.

After a long battle with abdominal cancer, Richard died of respiratory failure in 2000, and was given a hero's funeral in Montreal.

Richard

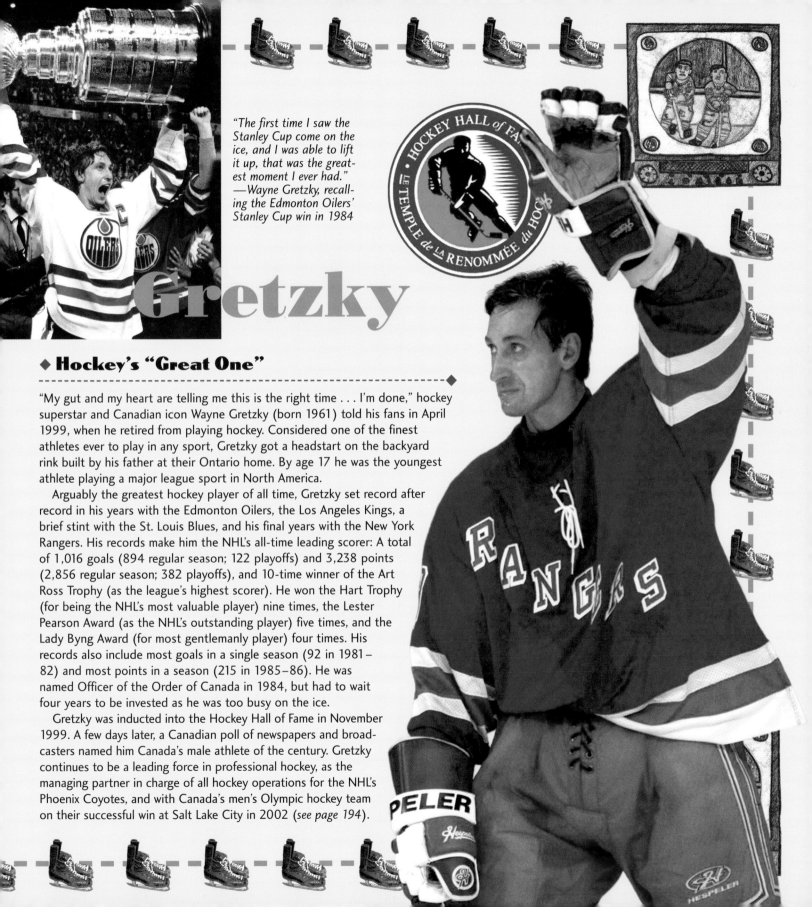

"The first time I saw the Stanley Cup come on the ice, and I was able to lift it up, that was the greatest moment I ever had."
—Wayne Gretzky, recalling the Edmonton Oilers' Stanley Cup win in 1984

HOCKEY HALL of FAME
LE TEMPLE de LA RENOMMÉE du HOCKEY

Gretzky

◆ Hockey's "Great One"

"My gut and my heart are telling me this is the right time . . . I'm done," hockey superstar and Canadian icon Wayne Gretzky (born 1961) told his fans in April 1999, when he retired from playing hockey. Considered one of the finest athletes ever to play in any sport, Gretzky got a headstart on the backyard rink built by his father at their Ontario home. By age 17 he was the youngest athlete playing a major league sport in North America.

Arguably the greatest hockey player of all time, Gretzky set record after record in his years with the Edmonton Oilers, the Los Angeles Kings, a brief stint with the St. Louis Blues, and his final years with the New York Rangers. His records make him the NHL's all-time leading scorer: A total of 1,016 goals (894 regular season; 122 playoffs) and 3,238 points (2,856 regular season; 382 playoffs), and 10-time winner of the Art Ross Trophy (as the league's highest scorer). He won the Hart Trophy (for being the NHL's most valuable player) nine times, the Lester Pearson Award (as the NHL's outstanding player) five times, and the Lady Byng Award (for most gentlemanly player) four times. His records also include most goals in a single season (92 in 1981–82) and most points in a season (215 in 1985–86). He was named Officer of the Order of Canada in 1984, but had to wait four years to be invested as he was too busy on the ice.

Gretzky was inducted into the Hockey Hall of Fame in November 1999. A few days later, a Canadian poll of newspapers and broadcasters named him Canada's male athlete of the century. Gretzky continues to be a leading force in professional hockey, as the managing partner in charge of all hockey operations for the NHL's Phoenix Coyotes, and with Canada's men's Olympic hockey team on their successful win at Salt Lake City in 2002 (*see page 194*).

◆ Howe joined the 500 club

Over five decades, Gordie Howe (born 1928), a native of Floral, Sask., became one of hockey's all-time greats, playing 32 years of professional hockey. He joined the Detroit Red Wings at 18 and played with them for 25 years, establishing more NHL records than any other player until Wayne Gretzky took over in the 1980s. Howe became the second player in NHL history after Maurice Richard (*see page 198*) to join hockey's 500 Club, scoring his 500th goal in a game against the New York Rangers in 1962. His strong offensive technique prompted legendary hockey coach and commentator Don Cherry to coin the term "Gordie Howe hat trick," bestowed on any player who scores a goal, assists in another and gets into a fight in the same game.

On March 14, 1962, Gordie Howe (left) became the second player in NHL history to score 500 goals

Boston Bruins defenseman Bobby Orr (right) won the James Norris Trophy from 1968 to 1975

◆ Hockey's most famous goal

Perhaps hockey's most famous goal hit the net in Moscow on Sept. 28, 1972. Three out of four Canadians were watching on TV or glued to their radios as the first Team Canada played the eighth and final game of what was dubbed the Summit Series against the Soviet Union. With 34 seconds remaining, the teams were tied 5-5 when Paul Henderson whipped a rebounding ball past the Soviet goalie, and Canadians coast to coast whooped and hollered with pride.

◆ Teams that hung up their jerseys

Ottawa Senators	1901–34	Philadelphia Quakers	1930–31
Renfrew Millionaires	1908–11	St. Louis Eagles	1934–35
Montreal Wanderers	1917–18	Brooklyn Americans	1941–42
Quebec Bulldogs	1919–20	Oakland Seals	1967–76
Hamilton Tigers	1920–25	Cleveland Barons	1976–78

◆ The cyclone that skated backwards

Ontario-born hockey player Fred "Cyclone" Taylor (1883–1979) earned his nickname when he was a young defenseman with the Ottawa Senators of his day. Governor-General Earl Grey was said to have remarked that Taylor was "a cyclone if ever I saw one." In 1910, Taylor joined the National Hockey Association's Renfrew Millionaires, and this became a major factor in the rivalry that developed between the two teams. While with the Renfrew team, Cyclone once made good on a boast—that he could skate backwards through the Senators' defense and score a goal against them.

◆ The man in the mask

Mandatory gear for today's hockey player, the goalie's face mask didn't exist until the 1950s. As a result, goaltenders of old frequently endured concussions and facial lacerations from speeding pucks. Jacques Plante (born 1929; *below right*), Montreal Canadiens goaltender from 1952–63, was already a veteran of some 200 stitches for facial repairs when he suffered a particularly bad gash in a game against the New York Rangers at New York's Madison Square Garden on Nov. 1, 1959.

With seven stitches closing the wound that ran from nose to mouth, Plante refused to return to the ice without the homemade mask he ordinarily used in practice. Coach Toe Blake relented, and Plante and the Canadiens went on to win the first in an 11-game winning streak that culminated later that season in the Stanley Cup. Gradually other goalies followed Plante's lead in wearing protective face masks.

◆ No socks for this defensive hero

One of hockey's all-time greats, Ontario-born defenseman Robert Gordon "Bobby" Orr (born 1948) had a dislike of new equipment, and didn't wear socks in his skates. Orr was not only a sharp hockey player—he won the NHL's top defenseman award, the James Norris trophy, eight years in a row—but a sharp businessman as well: He was the first NHL player to hire a lawyer to negotiate a contract. Most of his career was spent with the Boston Bruins, a team he was signed to at age 14 and for which he played from 1966 to 1975. Although a knee injury forced his retirement at age 30, Orr pursued a successful career in business and athlete management and was unstinting in his efforts for several charitable organizations.

◆ Hockey lore

1893: Montreal Amateur Athletic Association wins the first Stanley Cup.

1917: Formation of the National Hockey League.

1917: Birth of both the Toronto Maple Leafs and the Montreal Canadiens.

1923: First radio broadcast of a hockey game (*see page 197*).

1936: Longest-recorded game in the NHL (Montreal Maroons vs. Detroit Red Wings) includes 116 minutes of overtime.

1947: First official all-star game in Toronto.

1955: Montreal fans angry at the suspension of Maurice Richard go on a seven-hour rampage in the worst riot in hockey history.

1959: Jacques Plante dons the first goalie mask.

1971: The World Hockey Association forms, signing 70 NHL players to its 12 teams. The WHA would fold in 1979.

1972: Team Canada beats the Soviets in the "Series of the Century" (*see opposite page*).

1990: A game between the Edmonton Oilers and the Los Angeles Kings results in a staggering 85 penalties.

1995: Quebec Nordiques are sold to a group of Denver businessmen.

2002: Canada wins gold medals in Men's and Women's Hockey at the Salt Lake City Winter Olympics.

play ball!

◆ Fergie struck 'em out

A native of Chatham, Ont., Ferguson "Fergie" Jenkins (born 1943) is said to be one of baseball's greatest pitchers and the greatest Canadian player of professional baseball ever. During his 19 major league seasons, he struck out some 3,200 batters. From 1967 to 1972, he had 20 or more victories each season. At retirement in 1984, he had won 284 games, recorded 3,192 strikeouts, and set a major league record of 363 putouts by a pitcher. He won the Cy Young Award in 1971, and he is the only Canadian to be inducted into the Baseball Hall of Fame in Cooperstown, N.Y. Shortly before Jenkins received the nod, his wife died in a car accident, prompting him to muse to *The Toronto Star*, "Baseball is easy. Life is hard." Ferguson now raises Appaloosa horses on his Oklahoma ranch, and still competes in charity games across Canada.

"Baseball is easy. Life is hard."

◆ Baseball's first Canadian MVP

In 1997, the Baseball Writers of America named Larry Walker (born 1966) the National League's most valuable player. A native of Maple Ridge, B.C., Walker was the first Canadian so honored. A defensive rightfielder with the Colorado Rockies, Walker had led the league that year with 49 home runs.

◆ Birth of baseball— in Beachville?

According to a museum exhibit in Beachville, a small village near Stratford, Ont., North America's first baseball game took place on a local field on June 4, 1838. That was one whole year before the Cooperstown, N.Y., game that many consider launched the popular sport.

The museum's evidence is an 1886 letter to Philadelphia's *Sporting Life* magazine by physician and sports enthusiast Dr. Adam E. Ford. In his letter, the doctor gave a detailed description of events surrounding the game played at Beachville, and listed the names of players who had taken part. According to Dr. Ford, the playing field was divided into four "byes" plus a home bye. Runners who were "plugged" (hit by the ball) were out. Runners were allowed to detour into the field to avoid being plugged. Batters were called "knockers," and home plate was the "knocker's stone."

Canada's first professional baseball league was formed in 1876, with teams from Kingston, Guelph, Toronto, Hamilton, and London. Toronto and Montreal continued to host Triple-A professional teams. The first major-league franchise outside the U.S. was awarded in 1969 when the Montreal Expos joined the National League. The Toronto Blue Jays started in 1977 playing for the American League.

◆ Collectible Claxton

Before Jackie Robinson of the Montreal Royals broke organized baseball's color barrier in 1946, many black players disguised their identity as Indian or Spanish Cuban to play the game. One such player was Jimmy Claxton, born in 1892 in Wellington, B.C., of mixed Irish, English, black, French, and Indian blood. Claxton grew up in Tacoma, Wash., playing with the Oakland Oaks of the Pacific Coast League. In 1916, Claxton became the first black player to appear on a baseball card when Zee-Nut Cards immortalized him on one.

◆ McGill vs. Harvard game kicks off football

Canadian football began as a home-grown version of English rugby played by students at Montreal's McGill University. Invited to a tournament in 1874 at Harvard University in Cambridge, Mass., the Canadians arrived to find the Americans playing not the rugby-style sports they expected but an American variation of soccer. The teams resolved the matter by playing two games, one according to Harvard rules, the other according to McGill's. The Harvard men liked the McGill game, which they adopted as their own and introduced it to other U.S. university teams. American football was born, and from it Canadian football evolved.

◆ The Rifle from Montreal

A native of New Mexico, Sam Etcheverry (born 1930; *left*) came to Montreal in 1952 to quarterback the Montreal Alouettes. Etcheverry played with the Als for nine seasons, three of which they made to the Grey Cup, but lost. "The Rifle," as he was known, broke several records in his time. One for the longest completed pass—109 yards—is still an all-time CFL record. In 1961, Montreal traded Etcheverry creating an uproar. He played briefly in the National Football League with St. Louis and San Francisco, but an arm he had hurt in Montreal continued to give him problems. He retired after 1963. Seven years later, Etcheverry was hired as head coach of the Alouettes, and led them to their first Grey Cup win since 1949.

◆ The Grey Cup on ice?

The Grey Cup, the symbol of Canadian football supremacy, was originally intended as a hockey award! But Sir H. Montague Allan beat Earl Grey to the punch and offered the Allan Cup in 1908 as the trophy for amateur hockey competition. Undaunted, Governor General Earl Grey (1851–1917) donated the Grey Cup in 1909 to Canada's rugby football championship instead.

◆ Canada's greatest QB

Many sportsmen consider Sports Hall of Famer Russ Jackson (born 1936) football's greatest Canadian quarterback. After his graduation from McMaster University in Hamilton, Ont., Jackson joined the Ottawa Rough Riders, whom he led to victory in the Grey Cup in 1969. In his 12 years with the Rough Riders, he was renowned as a superb passer, runner, and leader. Jackson was honored with the Schenley Award and the Lou Marsh trophy.

◆ Ross Rebagliati's rad ride

Whistler, B.C., native Ross Rebagliati (born 1972) made history at the 1998 Winter Olympics in Nagano, Japan, by winning the first-ever gold medal for snowboarding. Almost immediately he was engulfed in controversy when he was found to have high levels of marijuana in his system. Rebagliati, who said he had not "inhaled" for well over a year, claimed he was subjected to second-hand pot smoke at a party. Fueling the debate was the curious fact that marijuana is not on the Olympics prohibited drugs' list. Following review by an IOC established Court of Arbitration (COA), Rebagliati—and Canada—retained the gold. "It has been quite a ride," said Rebagliati, who showed little inclination to follow a COA spokesperson's suggestion that he avoid an environment where he is exposed to marijuana users. "I'm not going to change my friends," he said, "though I might have to wear a gas mask."

◆ Quadruple feat

In 1988 Kurt Browning (born 1966) became the first figure skater to successfully complete a quadruple jump (a jump of four or more revolutions) in competition. The following year, Browning won the first of three successive World Figure Skating Championships.

◆ Canada's cross-country pioneer

The man who pioneered cross-country skiing in North America, Norwegian-born Herman Smith "Jackrabbit" Johannsen had established himself as a skiing expert in his native country long before coming to Montreal, Que., as an engineering equipment salesman in 1928. He devoted his free time to cutting alpine and cross-country trails in the nearby Laurentian Mountains. There he coached participants in skiing events he organized well into his nineties. Johanssen was made an honorary chief by the Cree, who gave him his nickname. He died in 1987 at the age of 111.

◆ Cranston's artistry flowed on the ice, at the easel

Figure skater Toller Cranston (born 1949; *left*) is renowned for his dramatic, ballet-like style, but his first public performance was far less restrained. It was an impromptu Cossack-style presentation at a Kirkland Lake, Ont., carnival when Cranston was all of eight years old. By the time he gave up competitive skating in the late 1970s, he was world famous, and had won bronze medals at the 1974 World Figure Skating Championships and the 1976 Olympics. A talented painter since high school, Cranston devoted the second phase of his career to the easel, applying his unique twist to his other love, painting (*right*).

◆ Podborski butts out

In 1983, Toronto-born skier Steve Podborski became one of the first athletes to protest the tobacco industry's sponsorship of sport by refusing to accept his award in the Export "A" Cup, the name given to Canada's national skiing championships. Before his retirement in 1984, Podborski was a downhill giant, with eight World Cup records to his name. Podborski also led the men's ski team, nicknamed the "Crazy Canucks," to capture the bronze in the downhill competition at the Lake Placid Winter Olympic Games in 1980.

◆ Elvis Stojko: Courage on ice

Owing, like many of his generation, a huge debt to Toller Cranston's free, expressive style (*see opposite page*), Elvis Stojko (born 1972) has become one of figure skating's biggest stars, building a career out of flamboyant displays of precision on ice.

The Richmond Hill, Ont., native landed his first trademark quadruple-triple combination jump ever in competition when he won his third world championship in Switzerland in 1997. But a badly pulled groin muscle in his right leg kept him from gold, when he competed in the Olympic men's free skate in Nagano, Japan, the following year. Despite his injuries and excruciating pain, he landed eight triple jumps to win silver and a nation's admiration. "If there was a medal for bravery, he'd win it hands down," said his coach. Stojko retired in March 2002.

In 1998, Elvis Stojko was awarded the Governor General's Meritorious Service Cross for his "high level of professionalism" at Nagano

◆ Salé & Pelletier: The Russian affair

On Feb. 11, 2002, after Canadian figure skaters Jamie Salé and David Pelletier finished their near-flawless pairs free program to a standing ovation at the Salt Lake City Winter Olympics, they were stunned when the gold medals went to Yelena Berezhnaya and Anton Sikharulidze and they were awarded silver. Many were outraged, as the Russian team had made several technical errors. Accusations flew that the French judge had been pressured by the French Federation to vote for the Russian pair. Five days later, the International Olympic Committee overturned the judges' decision and awarded Salé and Pelletier a second set of gold medals.

◆ Harness-racing hero

Born in 1940 into a harness-racing family in Angers, Que., Hervé Filion drove his first race at age 12, and was a leading driver at Ottawa's raceway when he was only 17. For decades, he dominated harness racing in North America, leading all drivers in purse earnings. In 1968, he broke the world record for most wins in a year, posting a total of 407 to beat the 386 record of the day held by a West German racer. Two years later, at Brandywine Racetrack in Delaware, he again made harness-racing history by driving five winners, each winner running the race in less than two minutes.

◆ North America's oldest race

The Queen's Plate, North America's oldest continuously held horse race, was inaugurated on June 27, 1860, at the Carleton Track in Toronto. The first winner was Don Juan, a horse owned by James White of Bronte, Ont. The prize was 50 guineas.

◆ The world's leading sire

The racehorse Northern Dancer, bred at self-made millionaire E. P. Taylor's famous stud farm outside Toronto, was the first Canadian horse to win the Kentucky Derby on May 2, 1964, finishing the two-kilometer course in a record two minutes. Two weeks later, the Canadian bay colt went on to win the Preakness by more than two lengths. However, hopes that he would become the first Canadian horse to win the coveted Triple Crown were dashed shortly afterward when the thoroughbred came third in the Belmont Stakes.

Back in Canada soon after to compete in the Queen's Plate at Woodbine Racetrack, Northern Dancer swept past the winning post seven lengths ahead of his nearest rival. It was the great horse's 14th and last win, for a bowed tendon later that season ended his racing career. Retired to stud, he sired Epsom Derby winners Nijinsky and The Minstrel. Elected to Canada's Sports Hall of Fame in 1965, Northern Dancer was declared the world's leading sire five years later because of the winnings claimed by his offspring.

◆ Rode 515 winners in one season

After 30 years in the saddle, 49-year-old jockey Sandy Hawley called it quits on Canada Day 1998 at Toronto's Woodbine Race Track. By then, he had accumulated purses exceeding $88 million, and ridden to victory 6,449 times (in 31,455 races). Four of his wins were Queen's Plates. Such racetrack accomplishments earned the Oshawa, Ont., man membership of both the U.S. and the Canadian Hall of Fame. The biggest thrill of his racing career, he told a reporter, was becoming the first North American rider to win 500 races in one season. Hawley pulled it off in 1973, when he was first past the finish post 515 times. Hawley now works for the Ontario Jockey Club as a public relations ambassador.

◆ Villeneuve & Son, Racers

Legendary Quebec-born race car driver Gilles Villeneuve (1950–82; *eyes far right*), Canada's top high speed racer of his day, died following a collision during a qualifying race for the Belgian Grand Prix. Five years earlier he had driven his first Grand Prix race, and by the time he died he had driven in 67 Grand Prix, six of which he had won. Cars and speed had fascinated Gilles Villeneuve from his youth, but it was as a snowmobile racer that he first won fame in one international and two Canadian championships.

Gilles' son Jacques (born in 1971; *eyes near right*) grew up to carry the torch, becoming the first Canadian ever to win the Formula One World Drivers' Championship in 1997 and the first driver of any nationality to claim the top three international motor car racing championship crowns (in different years)—Formula One, CART IndyCar, and the Indianapolis 500. Although he now lives in Monte Carlo, Quebecers claim him as their own, loyally sticking by him through his recent losing streaks of 2001 and 2002, said by many to be the result of his team's breakdown-prone racing cars.

Fueling the need for speed

◆ A filmmaker on the fast track

Toronto-based director David Cronenberg (born 1943) is acclaimed for his gruesome films that explore the nether zone between humans and technology, including *Dead Ringers*, *The Fly*, and *Crash*. He also has an obsession with the full-throttle world of auto racing, which dates back to the 1960s, when he was briefly a race car driver. Cronenberg still enjoys tooling around in vintage cars and going to races—after premiering *Crash* (a controversial work that documented the lives of people aroused by auto accidents) at the Cannes Film Festival in 1996, he flew to Monaco to cheer Jacques Villeneuve in the Formula One. Cronenberg's dream project is a film based on the life of Ferrari race car driver Phil Hill.

Guy Lombardo

◆ Swinging speedboat king

Most of us associate him with New Year's Eve and *Auld Lang Syne*, but bandleader Guy Lombardo (1902–94) was also Canada's first speedboat champion. Lombardo started racing in 1939, when he bought a hydroplane at the age of 38. He went on to win 21 of the 22 races he entered in 1942. In 1946, with his 450-hp *Tempo VI*, Lombardo won the Red Bank Sweepstakes and the Gold Cup, two of speedboat racing's prestigious Triple Crown races. Lombardo even set a world record for single-engine straightaway in 1948, when he brought *Tempo VI* to a top speed of 192.6 kph at Salton Sea, California.

◆ Formula 1 first

Peter Ryan (1940–62) was the first Canadian to compete in a Formula 1 Grand Prix on Oct. 8, 1961. (He finished ninth.) The Philadelphia-born racer grew up in Mont Tremblant, Que., and first made a splash by winning the 1961 Canadian Grand Prix. The following year, Ryan was killed in a race at Reims, France. He was 22.

◆ Canada's fastest men

In 1996, Donovan Bailey (born 1967; *left*) sprinted the 100-meter race at the Olympic Games in Atlanta in 9.84 seconds, winning the gold medal and the title of fastest man in the world. The Jamaican-born sprinter later aggressively defended his title against American runner Michael Johnson in 1995 (Johnson suffered a quadriceps injury and bowed out) and fellow Canadian Bruny Surin, who matched Bailey's record in 1999 before American Maurice Green beat it with a time of 9.79 seconds.

Bailey, however, wasn't the first Canadian to be called "fastest man in the world." At the 1928 Olympics, Vancouver-born Percy Williams (1908–82) claimed that honor, with gold medals in the 100- and 200-meter sprints. His triumphs were all the more sensational in that he ran with a damaged heart, a legacy of childhood rheumatic fever.

◆ She conquered Lake Ontario

Sixteen-year-old Marilyn Bell was too numbed with cold and exhaustion to hear the cheering throngs that greeted her when she stumbled out of icy Lake Ontario onto the Canadian National Exhibition grounds in Toronto on Sept. 9, 1954. The Toronto teenager had entered the lake at Youngstown, N.Y., the previous midnight and spent the next 21 hours battling icy water, gigantic waves, and the greatest terror of all, school after school of lamprey eels. But Bell refused to give up and succeeded where many before her had failed. She became the first person to swim Lake Ontario. The next year, Bell became the youngest person to swim the English Channel, and a year later, she conquered the Juan de Fuca Strait on the Pacific Coast. At the height of her fame, she gave up marathon swimming, got married, and went to live in the United States.

◆ Spectacular finishes were his trademark

An Onondaga from the Six Nations Reserve, near Brantford, Ont., Tom Longboat (1887–1949; *right*) was considered the best long-distance runner of his day and was known for his spectacular finishing sprints. He broke many records on his way to victories that included the Boston Marathon of 1907 and the

COO-WA-GEE
LONGBOAT

World's Professional Marathon Championship of 1909. After winning a marathon in Hamilton in 1906, Longboat entered a 19-kilometer race against a horse and won. In World War I, he enlisted in the Canadian Expeditionary Force and served with distinction as a dispatch runner in France.

◆ Hoop dreams

In December of 1891, Ontario-born James Naismith (1869–1931), a gym teacher at the Springfield, Mass., YMCA, was asked to devise indoor activities to keep the students fit between football and baseball seasons. Naismith came up with 13 rules that incorporated elements of a childhood game popular in his Almonte hometown, and an off season rugby exercise he had learned while studying divinity at McGill University in Montreal.

At first, teams of nine each tried to put a soccer ball into peach baskets Naismith had borrowed from the janitor and nailed to balconies at either end of the gymnasium. When the janitor and players got tired of climbing up and down ladders to retrieve the ball, Naismith cut the bottom from the baskets. He called his new game basketball.

Naismith was later invited as a guest of honor to the 1936 Olympic Games in Berlin, where 33 nations competed in the game he had created. Today it remains one of the world's most popular sports.

◆ Chuvalo: Down but not out

Toronto-born heavyweight boxer George Chuvalo (born 1937; *pictured below*) fought the best—Muhammad Ali, George Foreman, and other great heavyweight boxers—but was never knocked down in a fight. He won the Canadian amateur heavyweight title in 1955, and the Canadian professional title three years later. He lost the title in 1960 but later regained it and defended it successfully from 1968 to his retirement in 1979.

Chuvalo's personal life since was haunted by tragedy. Three of his sons became heroin addicts; George Lee and Steven died from overdoses and Jesse shot himself. The strain proved too much for his first wife, Lynn, who committed suicide. Yet the old fighter fought back, turning his grief into a knockout punch he used to reach young people and warn them against drug abuse. Thousands of high-school students and teens have been moved by Chuvalo's powerful presentations.

◆ Burns traded the ring for the pulpit

Canada's only world heavyweight boxing champion, Tommy Burns (1881–1955), lost only four of his 60 fights and, in one three-year period, defended his world crown 11 times before losing to American champion Jack Johnson in Sydney, Australia, on Christmas Day, 1908. The $30,000 Burns got for fighting Johnson was the first "big money" for boxers.

Born Noah Brusso in Hanover, Ont., Burns adopted his name when he began boxing; his deeply religious Methodist parents did not want the family name associated with the sport. After nearly dying from an illness in 1935, Burns turned to religion, and was ordained a minister at his home city of Coalinga, California, in 1948. He traveled throughout the northwestern U.S. and Canada as an evangelist until his death.

canada's olympians

◆ Canada's first gold medal

Canada won its first Olympic gold medal in one of our most traditional sports—lacrosse (*see page 195*). The Winnipeg Shamrocks took the gold at the 1904 games in St. Louis, handily defeating the St. Louis Amateur Athletic Association.

◆ Our most famous swimmer

Swimmer Alex Baumann (*top left*) was only 20 when he won two gold medals in the 200- and 400-meter individual medleys—establishing world records in both—at the 1984 Los Angeles games. Hailing from Sudbury, Ont., Baumann is our most famous swimmer, having won the Canadian National Championship 34 times. Baumann now lives in Australia, where he works for Queensland's tourism, sport, and racing department.

◆ Fastest woman on ice

In 2002, Calgary speedskater Catriona LeMay Doan (*born 1970; middle left*) won the World Sprint, World Cup, and Olympic gold speed skating championship titles in the 500-meter category, setting a world record with a time of 37.22 at the World Cup race in Calgary. In her spare time, the fastest woman on ice is a highly regarded motivational speaker.

◆ "Canada's Sweetheart"

One of Canada's best-loved athletes, Ottawa-born figure skater Barbara-Ann Scott (*born 1929; bottom left*) made early headlines when she won the Canadian junior figure-skating championship at the age of 11. Scott was North America's ice-skating champion from 1945–48, as well as European and world champion from 1947–48. She became a national celebrity in 1948 when she won Olympic gold in St. Moritz, Switzerland. Dubbed "Canada's Sweetheart" by the media, she was followed by adoring crowds for years.

◆ Saskatoon Lily

The 1928 Amsterdam summer games marked the first time women's track and field events were held, and Canadian women made a strong showing, led by Ethel Catherwood (born 1909). Catherwood, dubbed the "Saskatoon Lily" for her poise, beauty, and Prairie roots, won the gold medal for the women's high jump, leaping 1.6 meters.

In 1983, Canadian speedskater Gaétan Boucher (born 1958; center) shattered his ankle, seemingly dashing his hopes of ever winning Olympic gold. Yet one year later, at the winter games in Sarajevo, Boucher became a national hero by winning gold in both the 1,000- and 1,500-meter races, and bronze in the 500-meter race.

◆ The Intellectual Sled

Canada's brainiest gold medal goes to the four-man bobsled team of Victor Emery (a Montreal aircraft engineer), his brother John (a plastic surgeon), teacher Douglas Anakin, and geologist

Peter Kirby, who won the gold medal at Innsbruck in 1964. Nicknamed "The Intellectual Sled," the Canadian team pulled a spectacular upset, beating the hometown Austrians and the favored Italians.

◆ "Mighty Mouse"

Vancouver-born swimmer Elaine Tanner was a mere 15 years old at the 1966 Commonwealth Games when she broke two world records, won four gold

and three silver medals, and earned the nickname "Mighty Mouse." That year Tanner became the youngest athlete ever to win the Lou Marsh trophy, awarded annually to the outstanding athlete of the year. Elaine's last public competition was at the 1968 Olympic Games, where she won three medals, two silver and one bronze.

◆ Tiger, Tiger, burning bright

Women's skiing in the late 1960s was dominated by B.C. alpine skier Nancy Greene (born 1943; *upper right*). Selected for Canada's 1960 Olympic team at age 17, she earned her nickname "Tiger" when she captured the World Cup ski champion in 1967 and 1968. In 1968 Greene also claimed Olympic gold in the giant slalom and silver in the slalom, and Vancouver celebrated by painting its streets green for her victory parade. In November 1999, Canada's newspaper editors and broadcasters voted Greene top female athlete of the century.

◆ Morris' golden paddle

In 1977, Montreal-born canoeist Alwyn Morris (born 1957) was awarded the Tom Longboat Award (*see page 208*) for top North American native athlete. In Los Angeles, seven years later, he won Olympic gold (in the K-2 1,000 meter), and bronze (in the K-2 500 meter).

◆ Waldo swam into history

At the 1988 summer games in Seoul, Korea, swimmer Carolyn Waldo (born 1964; *middle right*) became the first Canadian woman to win two gold medals at the same Olympics. She won in the solo synchronized swimming event and in the pairs competition, where her gold-sharing partner was Michelle Cameron. Waldo is currently a sports broadcaster in Ottawa.

◆ Bédard's biathlon triumph

Quebecer Myriam Bédard (born 1969; *bottom right*) first trained in the biathlon as an army cadet. At the Lillehammer winter games in 1994, Bédard won two gold medals for the women's 7.5- and 15-kilometer events, becoming the first North American athlete ever to win Olympic biathlon gold.

CanLit,
CanCon,
and Canadian
culture

THE MEDIUM IS
THE MESSAGE

the canadian canvas

◆ Zouave stint inspired Hébert

At age 19, Louis-Philippe Hébert (1850–1917) left the family farm in Quebec to join the Zouaves, the French pontifical army. The art wealth he discovered in Rome overwhelmed him and, on returning home, he apprenticed in the studio of Napoléon Bourassa, where he learned the sculptor's craft. Hébert became Quebec's leading sculptor of his time, and Canada's first native-born commemorative sculptor, with works including Queen Victoria, Maisonneuve, and Jeanne Mance.

◆ Canada's landscape school

In 1920, Franklin Carmichael, Lawren Harris, A. Y. Jackson, Frank Johnston, Arthur Lismer, J. E. H. Macdonald, and F. H. Varley became founding members of the Group of Seven, an organization intended to support and promote their interest in modern art. All except independently wealthy Harris (*see right*) were commercial artists, and many of them worked in the same shop.

Many of them also knew Tom Thomson (*see page 132*) who inspired them to explore northern Ontario and capture its rugged grandeur on canvas. However, it was only after their first exhibition at the Art Gallery of Ontario that the Group began to describe themselves as a landscape school.

The art establishment was not overwhelmed by the Group's works or its self-promotion, but neither was it hostile, as has sometimes been claimed. In fact, the Group of Seven exerted considerable influence in the art world in 1926, when Frank Johnston resigned and A. J. Casson (*see opposite page*) became a member. By 1930, anxious to be considered a national school of painters, the Toronto Group extended membership to Edwin Holgate of Montreal and L. L. Fitzgerald of Winnipeg. When the Group disbanded in 1933, however, it had become almost as conservative as the art establishment it overthrew 13 years earlier.

Louis-Philippe Hébert's
Sigh of the Lake, *plaster with wood, 1903*

◆ Harris abandoned landscapes for abstracts

Son of the prosperous Massey-Harris farm machinery family (*see page 102*), Lawren Harris (1885–1970) was born in Brantford, Ont., and had already studied art in Germany when, in 1911, he met J. E. H. MacDonald. Together they developed a new style of realistic landscape painting that attracted like-minded artists with whom they presented the first Group of Seven exhibition in 1920. In his later years, Harris abandoned his early style for an abstract form of art.

Lawren Harris' Abstraction, *oil on canvas, 1939*

◆ A struggling artist to the end

Ontario-born David Milne (1882–1953) was a struggling artist to the end of his life, by which time his watercolors—in his own words "adventures in shape, color, texture and space"—were widely recognized. His work as a war artist in England and France in 1919 attracted the attention of critics in London, but when he mounted an exhibition in Montreal five years later, he didn't sell a single painting. Vincent Massey bought several of his works in the 1930s and eventually the Massey family acquired 300 of his paintings, many for as little as $5 a canvas.

◆ Lismer's Canada glowed

Looking for work as a commercial illustrator, British-born Arthur Lismer (1885–1969) came to Toronto in 1911, where he met members of the Group of Seven (*see opposite page*). In England for his wedding the following year, he painted such glowing pictures of Canada's natural beauty that F. H. Varley also decided to immigrate here. Lismer's canvases captured Canada's rugged landscapes with a distinguished use of color and coarse brushwork, most famously Georgian Bay, Ont., the Maritimes, and Long Beach, B.C. Lismer also devoted much of his life to teaching art to children.

◆ Casson's expertise aided police

When Torontonian Alfred Joseph Casson (1898–1992) got his first job in a Toronto commercial art house, he was apprenticed to Group of Seven founder Franklin Carmichael. Carmichael introduced him to other members of the exclusive group and took him on sketching trips. Casson went on explorations of his own to the Ontario villages and small towns he immortalized in his art. In 1926, Casson replaced Frank Johnston, whose work had figured in the Group's inaugural exhibition six years before. In later years, police officers investigating Group of Seven and other art forgeries often called on Casson's expertise.

◆ Kurelek captured Depression-era Prairies

Painter, writer, and evangelist William Kurelek (1927–77) grew up on the Prairies, where his Ukrainian parents homesteaded. His Bosch-like work recreates his vision of the Prairies at the height of the Great Depression. Vast wheat fields and small human figures dwarfed against vast skies speak of loneliness, isolation, and desperation. Kurelek's impoverished

youth was made even more painful by depression and hospitalization in a mental institution. Later in life, he converted to Catholicism and found great comfort in his faith.

◆ "Klee Wyck" went unnoticed for years

Emily Carr (1871–1945) worked unnoticed for years sketching native villages, totem poles, and the primeval forests of her native British Columbia. Discouraged by the lack of interest in her work, she supported herself for 22 years by keeping a boarding house, raising bobtail sheepdogs, and firing pottery for sale to tourists. She stopped painting altogether for 15 years. Today her paintings are represented in all Canadian collections of note and acclaimed as a record of a vanishing Northwest Coast native life. The Indians called her "Klee Wyck," the strange one, and in 1941, her book of that name won the Governor General's award for non-fiction.

◆ Kane's canvases opened up the West

The most famous of Canada's artist-explorers, Paul Kane (1810–71) came to Canada from Ireland with his family when he was about 12. A furniture decorator in York (present-day Toronto), he visited Italy in the early 1800s to copy old masters, and while passing through London was enthralled by an exhibition of George Catlin's American Indian paintings. In 1845 Kane set out to paint a similar series and arranged with Sir George Simpson of the Hudson's Bay Company to accompany fur canoes to the West. Three years later he returned to Toronto with 700 sketches of western scenery, the buffalo hunt, and native people from some 80 tribes, sketches that were the basis for hundreds of striking paintings he later produced.

◆ Michael Snow cried foul—and won

To painter, sculptor, photographer, filmmaker, and jazz musician Michael Snow (born 1929), art should be a part of life. Snow spent much of the 1960s realizing his wish by creating *Walking Woman Works*. Based on a walking woman's silhouette, she appeared in Snow's pictures and films, as well as on T-shirts, wallpaper, and signboards, always with the same outline, but in different sizes, colors, and materials (*below*).

Just how much a part of life art should be was put to the test in 1982. The Toronto Eaton Centre, owners of *Flightstop*, Snow's sculpture of 60 geese in mid-flight, decorated the sculpture with ribbons while gussying up the shopping mall for the Christmas season. Snow cried foul: To festoon his work in such a manner was a distortion of his sculpture and an infringement of his moral rights, akin to hanging earrings from the Venus de Milo. Snow petitioned the courts, and the judge hearing the case sought the opinion of other members of the art community. They all agreed with Mr. Snow, and the decorative bows were ordered removed.

Snow's Clothed Woman (In Memory of My Father), *oil and Lucite on canvas, 1963*

◆ To make ends meet, Krieghoff painted houses

Cornelius Krieghoff (1815–72) came to Canada from his native Holland via the United States, where he married a French-Canadian. The couple settled in Quebec, where Krieghoff produced the portraits of rural life and village scenes that would eventually sell for princely sums. But in 1840s Montreal, Krieghoff couldn't make a living peddling his work door to door and often had to support himself and his family painting houses. Things improved in the 1850s, when his talent was widely recognized and his work, including his portraits, was much in demand.

Krieghoff's Winter Landscape, *oil on canvas, 1849*

◆ From Waterloo to Windsor Castle

Ontario-born landscape artist Homer Watson (1855–1936) quickly achieved recognition at home and abroad with the purchase in 1878 of one of his works, *The Pioneer Mill*, for Queen Victoria. It, and another one of his works also purchased for Victoria, hang in Windsor Castle. His paintings are also found in many public galleries, including the National Gallery in Ottawa, and Toronto's Art Gallery of Ontario, as well as in many private collections. Largely self-taught, Watson grew up in the Kitchener-Waterloo region of Ontario, an area depicted in many of his canvases. His rural landscapes with fields of grain, grazing animals, and old buildings, led to comparisons with European masters such as John Constable. Lord Strathcona and Oscar Wilde were among Watson's prominent and affluent patrons.

◆ Joe Fafard's grazing bronzes

Saskatchewan son Joseph Fafard (born 1942) is known for his ceramic folk art sculptures depicting droll figures and cows. His *Pasture*, a dairy herd consisting of seven bronze animals with varying patinas, graces Toronto's Dominion Centre.

Fafard's Royal Sweet Diamond, *patinated bronze, 2000*

◆ Mary Pratt's kitchen-sink still life

To painter Mary Pratt of Saint John's, Nfld., fine art can contain everything *and* the kitchen sink. Pratt's luminous still lifes capture the whimsical, mysterious nature of everyday household objects: rising bread, gutted fish, cracked eggs, a simple bowl of apples. Born in Fredericton, N.B., in 1935, Pratt was studying fine arts at Mount Allison University in Sackville, N.B., when she met and fell in love with Newfoundlander Christopher Pratt. They settled down in Salmonier, a Newfoundland outport where Mary raised four children, and her artist husband earned an international reputation for his work. Mary continued painting during this time, and her career later took off. In 1998, the Canada Council awarded the $50,000 Molson Prize in the Arts to Pratt, recognizing a lifetime cultural achievement of one of Canada's most beloved painters.

◆ Colville's magic realism

After painting mass graves at the Bergen-Belsen concentration camp as a war artist during World War II, Toronto native Alex Colville (born 1920) taught art at his alma mater, Mount Allison University in New Brunswick. In 1963, he gave up teaching to paint full time. Colville's canvases (*see below*) are marked by an almost photographic realism, and are filled with his immediate surroundings—Maritime landscapes, his family, his animals. Critics describe Colville's work as depicting a world that is at once joyful and beautiful, dark and dangerous.

Pratt's Little Apples Waiting for Spice, *oil on canvas, 2001*

Town's Stages #24, *acrylic on NPH rag board, 1987*

Colville's Couple on Beach, *Casein tempera on hardboard, 1957*

◆ Town helped introduce Canadian abstract art

A master of diverse artistic talents, Toronto-born Harold Town (1924–90) illustrated books, painted murals and portraits, and produced collages, paintings, lithographs, sculptures, posters, and illustrations. For several decades Canada's best-known artist, Town was outspoken and controversial, once stating, "Bad art is not the enemy, mediocre art is the enemy." In the 1950s, Town was a member of Painters Eleven, a small group of artists dedicated to non-objective art—in essence, painting without subject matter. Some of his Single Automatic Prints, monochrome prints first done in the 1950s and later reworked with other colors and techniques, hang in New York's Guggenheim and Museum of Modern Art. While Town is famous for his abstract art, his work (*above center*) shows the influence of numerous artistic styles, from Pop Art to Asian painting.

◆ Suzor-Coté: A blessed talent

Success came early to Marc-Aurèle de Foy Suzor-Coté (1869–1937), renowned Quebec painter of winter and rural scenes and famous historical events. His early work was in church decoration. Later he studied abroad and traveled constantly, earning an international reputation as his pastels and oils were increasingly acclaimed at international exhibitions. In the early 1900s, he turned to sculpting, at which he also excelled. He abandoned art in 1927 after becoming paralyzed.

◆ Embracing the automatic muse

Paul-Émile Borduas (1905–60) was the first great post-war hero of Quebec culture whose 1948 manifesto *Refus Global* (total rejection), is said to have launched modern French Canada. Like Marc-Aurèle Suzor-Côté (*see page 217*), the St. Hilaire, Que.-born teacher and artist trained as a church decorator. Studies abroad in Paris introduced Borduas to surrealism and helped open his awareness of the power of color and the act of painting itself, which led to not only a questioning of traditional artistic rules but a rejection of traditional Quebec values as well.

Later Borduas would meet like-minded thinkers such as poet Claude Gauvreau, psychoanalyst Bruno Cormier, dancer-painter Françoise Sullivan, sculptor Jean-Paul Riopelle (*see below*), and painter Fernand Leduc. Under the umbrella name Le Mouvement Automatiste they had showings in makeshift galleries in Montreal in 1946–47. The Automatistes believed that every artist had unconscious forces that should be freed onto the canvas

Borduas' Self-portrait, *oil on canvas, c.1953*

in a dreamlike state, avoiding deliberate design as "the harmful weapon of reason." The movement was more an attitude than a style. Members embraced the right to freedom of expression, decried any suffocation of ideas, and were especially critical of the influence of the Catholic Church.

Shortly after *Refus Global* was published, Borduas was dismissed from his teaching post in a Montreal art college. He suffered considerable financial hardship over the next decade, when he also produced some of his best work. He went to live in New York, and later moved to Paris, but although he was often homesick, he never returned home. European critics acclaimed his work, but Borduas' health was beginning to fail. When he died from a heart attack at age 55, the last canvas on his easel was covered in black patches.

In January 1998, the Montreal Museum of Fine Arts marked the 50th anniversary of the publication of *Refus Global* by dedicating a permanent gallery to the author's work.

Deliberate design is the harmful weapon of reason

◆ First Canadian artist to fetch $1 mil

A student of Paul-Émile Borduas and a signatory of *Refus Global* (*see above*), Jean-Paul Riopelle (1923–2002) was renowned for his leviathan, vividly colored, abstract paintings (his triptych, *Hommage à Rosa Luxembourg*, measures 40 meters). In 1989, Riopelle became the first Canadian to sell a painting for more than $1 million, when an untitled work fetched $1.6 million at Sotheby's in New York. Riopelle was given the UNESCO Award for cumulative achievement in 1962.

Riopelle's Pavone, *oil on canvas, 1954*

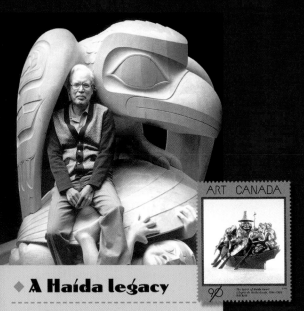

◆ A Haida legacy

In his introduction to a 1974 retrospective exhibition at the Vancouver Art Gallery, noted French anthropologist Claude Lévi-Strauss has said, "We are indebted to Bill Reid (*above*) . . . Thanks to him the art of the Indians of the Pacific coast makes its entry upon the great stage of the world; it begins to converse with the whole of mankind."

Above: *Reid with his sculpture* Raven and the First Men, *1980.* Near right: *Ivory totem pole, 9.6 cm high.* Upper right: *Gold brooch, 4 cm, 1959.* Far right: *Carved cedar bear, 2.4 m long, 1966.* Below: *Gold box, 10 cm high, 1967*

◆ In silver, cedar, and abalone, Bill Reid captured the Haida spirit

Internationally renowned British Columbia-born Haida artist Bill Reid (1920–98) was in his late teens before he discovered his mother was a Haida native. Since then the Victoria-born artist became perhaps the single most important figure in the renaissance of Haida culture, as well as an outspoken advocate for Aboriginal peoples' political and cultural rights.

Reid's works range from awesome, massive cedar carvings to delicate pieces of jewelry in abalone and gold, but he is best known for the sculpture *The Black Canoe— Spirit of Haida Gwaii* at the Canadian Embassy in Washington (Haida Gwaii is the ancient name for the Queen Charlotte Islands, traditional home of the Haida people; *see page 51*).

As a student at Toronto's Ryerson Polytechnic Institute, Reid earned his living as a broadcaster while studying European techniques for jewelry making. He also learned jewelry making from his grandfather, a silversmith schooled in the Haida tradition. At the time of his death, he was regarded by many as the greatest Aboriginal artist ever, and his accomplishments had been instrumental in reviving the Pacific Northwest Indian culture and traditions. In a most unusual honor, Reid's ashes were taken to Gwaii Haanas National Park Reserve in the Queen Charlottes, and interred at one of the ancient village sites, under the protection of Haida Watchmen.

◆ Doukhobor houses built to last

In 1932, a community of Doukhobors (*see page 105*) at Yorkton, Sask., set about building rental property for the community. The houses (*above*), with walls three bricks thick, used bricks manufactured by the local Doukhobor Brickyard Society. Doukhobor construction workers worked 12-hour days, six days a week, for which their daily wage was 10 cents. On completion, the houses were rented to non-Doukhobor families for $25 a month. Three of the houses still stand on Yorkton's Myrtle Avenue.

◆ Soddies: Prairie prefab homes

Many Prairie settlers built their first homes out of the only material available: "Prairie shingles." These slabs of sod were cut from slough bottoms, and were held together by fibrous wheatgrass roots. Piled grass side down, the sods formed the outer walls of what came to be known as soddies, simple 3.6 x 2.4-meter structures, although more elaborate ones might be as big as 6 x 7 meters. Boards were stretched from wall to wall to form a roof, and this was kept in place by more sod. Despite all these precautions, soddies were not necessarily rainproof. Violet McNaughton (1879–1968), a Saskatchewan editor of various publications dedicated to improving the lives of Prairie farm women, once described how she and her husband went to bed under an umbrella in the sod shack that was her bridal home in 1910.

Nevertheless, most soddies were cool in summer and warm in winter, the latter largely because of the cast-iron stove that was a fixture in each home. Interior walls were lined with planks or covered in white cotton, and many soddies were elaborately furnished. Hooked rugs covered the earthen floors and cloth partitions gave a sense of privacy.

◆ Life in a snow cone

Firm, compact snow cut into blocks and trimmed to slope inward helped form the traditional Inuit domed snowhouses known as igloos. Some Inuit once used igloos only when traveling; others used them as winter dwellings, with an entrance tunnel and a window—a piece of freshwater ice. Because snow acts as an insulator, the temperature inside an igloo could actually rise above the freezing point. Often a series of igloos would be connected by tunnels to house up to 20 people.

◆ Tilts sheltered Newfoundland fishermen

For years before Newfoundland's tiny Fogo Island was settled, fishermen who spent their summers there settled down in the fall at Birchy Bay on the mainland. There they cut firewood and got together materials for the next year's fishing. The fishermen lived in makeshift winter shelters known as "tilts." The Fogo Island community of Tilting (pop. 300), actually derives its name from the structures; it was once called "Tilt Town" because of its poorly constructed tilts. A replica of a tilt has been constructed on the grounds of Over the Top, a Birchy Bay museum.

◆ Architectural monkey business

Monkey heads cast in mortar—a disgruntled contractor's comment on the county council with which he quarreled over fees—are said to be concealed among the ornate capitals, the top part of the red marble columns, at entrances to the old courthouse in Woodstock, Ont. The massive sandstone courthouse, built in 1892 in a Romanesque design, is thought to have another monkey head hidden at the peak of its roof line.

◆ McQuat's curious castle

Boaters on White Otter Lake, deep in northern Ontario's heartland, are often startled when a three-story, pine log castle with an adjoining four-story tower comes into view. The curiosity is the handiwork of Scottish gold prospector and trapper Jimmy McQuat (1878–1918), a native of Ontario's Ottawa Valley, who settled beside the lake in 1903.

The middle-aged trapper was penniless at the time, having lost everything prospecting for gold. For 11 years he labored on his castle, transporting supplies— including 24 windows—from the nearest town, a 48-kilometer, 15-portage canoe trip away, cutting the logs, and winching them into place. Each log was chinked with a mixture of lime and beach sand.

Some say the castle was inspired by a lost love, others say it was a vow sworn in his youth to prove a neighbor wrong: "Jimmy, ye'll do no good," the man used to taunt. "Ye'll die in a shack." Ironically, Jimmy didn't die in his castle. In October 1918, he drowned in the lake while fishing for trout. Fire rangers found his body the following spring and buried it beside the castle.

For more than 65 years, McQuat's Castle lay crumbling in the forest. Then in the 1980s, the municipalities of Ignace and Atikokan began restoring it. Today it is part of the Turtle River-White Otter Lakeway Provincial Park.

◆ Grand Hotel

Located in the heart of Old Quebec City, Château Frontenac is the type of elegant hotel William Cornelius Van Horne (*see page 158*) needed along his newly completed Canadian Pacific Railway over a century ago. "If we can't export the scenery," he famously said, "we'll import the tourists." Van Horne selected the most stunning vantage points along the CPR railway to build lavish resorts to rival the chateaux in France's Loire Valley. He welcomed guests to the Banff Springs Hotel in 1888, Chateau Lake Louise in 1890, and Château Frontenac in 1893.

For the exquisite Château Frontenac, Van Horne commissioned New York architect Bruce Price (1845–1903, father of Emily Post), who had already completed designing Windsor Station in Montreal. In its steep copper roofs, dormers and turrets, Price drew on the architectural styles of both the Middle Ages and the Renaissance to construct what he envisoned to be a resplendent monument to the two great powers that contributed to the rich history of Quebec City. Named after the dashing French governor Louis de Buade, Count of Frontenac (*see page 126*), the hotel features a 300-year-old stone bearing the Cross of Malta in the lobby.

◆ Art Deco architect

The Supreme Court of Canada in Ottawa and the Université de Montréal are among masterworks of Ernest Cormier (1885– 1980), the dominant figure in 20th-century Quebec architecture. Montreal-born Cormier first discovered the ornamental Art Deco style he favored while studying at the École des Beaux-Arts in Paris. Cormier's Art Deco house on Pine Avenue in Montreal was the home of former Prime Minister Pierre Elliott Trudeau.

◆ Canadian Centre for Architecture

Some 195,000 volumes ranging from 15th-century editions of Vitruvius to a major collection on Frank Lloyd Wright, 50,000 photographs, 65,000 prints and drawings, as well as architectural toys and games are just some of the items that can be found at the Canadian Centre for Architecture in Montreal. Often described as one of the great architectural collections in the world, the center is the creation of Phyllis Lambert (born 1927), a trained architect who has worked with such architectural giants as Ludwig Mies van der Rohe (*see opposite page*).

A member of the wealthy Bronfman family, Lambert used her personal fortune to create this center of research for scholars and working pro-fessionals. She chose as her site Shaughnessy Park, a once fashionable enclave in downtown Montreal. With co-designer Peter Rose, she built the architecture center around the grey-stone Victorian Shaughnessy House, which visitors reach via a garden of flowering shrubs, fruit trees, and sculptures of miniature chimney stacks, grain elevators, mill tow-ers, and church steeples—architectural elements reflective of Montreal's indus-trial and working class districts. The center's exhibitions—ranging from modern architectural culture to theme parks and the North American passion for lawns—draw over 60,000 visitors annually.

Left: Phyllis Lambert. This page: Inside the Canadian Centre for Architecture

A building wraps around its function like a sea shell

◆ Cardinal's curves soar like an eagle

Architect Douglas Cardinal (born 1934) believes "a building should wrap around its function like a sea shell around a sea urchin." It is not surprising, then, that curving designs mark Cardinal masterpieces such as the Canadian Museum of Civilization in Gatineau, Que. (*above*), and St. Mary's Roman Catholic Church in Red Deer, Alta. Of Blackfoot and Métis descent, Cardinal's architectural studies began at the University of British Columbia in 1953. Two years into his course, the university asked him to withdraw; it considered his designs too radical. Cardinal spent the next two years working and traveling in Mexico after which he resumed his architectural studies at the University of Texas, from which he graduated with honors in 1956. Today, Cardinal is principal architect for the Smithsonian Institution's National Museum of the American Indian, to open in Washington D.C., in 2004.

◆ Mies van der Rohe's Bauhaus gas station

Head of the Bauhaus School of Design in his native Germany, world renowned architect Ludwig Mies van der Rohe designed some of the most elegant buildings of his day, notably Toronto's Dominion Centre, Montreal's Westmount Square, and New York's Seagram Building.

Van der Rohe's creations featured only the finest quality materials and were designed to exceedingly exacting mathematical specifications. Often associated with the famous axiom "Less is more," van der Rohe believed in simplicity. One of his most minimal designs is an Esso gas station built in 1967 on Nuns' Island, an island of condos and high-rises a few minutes drive from downtown Montreal.

◆ Erickson's portals reach out in welcome

Great buildings should move the spirit, according to internationally renowned Vancouver architect Arthur Erickson (born 1924). The Canadian Embassy in Washington, Simon Fraser University (*below*), the University of British Columbia's Museum of Anthropology, Ottawa's Bank of Canada, and Toronto's Roy Thomson Hall are all Erickson designs that ennoble and inspire. A welcoming and sheltering portal—a design motif of many West Coast native tribes—and muted colors are Erickson hallmarks.

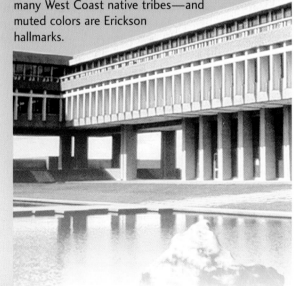

from igloos to skyscrapers

◆ Safdie's habitats balance town and country

For his student thesis at McGill University, Montreal, Moshe Safdie (born 1938) designed an informal, cellular grouping of diverse units, somewhat reminiscent of North African and Middle Eastern cities. A few years later he turned his thesis into Habitat (*above*)—a revolutionary style of housing complex—for Montreal's Expo 67. Born in Haifa, Israel, Safdie has a reputation for skillfully fitting buildings into their surroundings, and balancing the opposing desires for open space and urban convenience. He has written extensively about architecture, and has taught at McGill, Yale, and Ben Gurion Universities. His signature buildings worldwide include such Canadian masterpieces as the National Gallery in Ottawa (*far left*),

Library Square in Vancouver, the Musée de la Civilisation in Quebec City, and a major expansion to the Montreal Museum of Fine Arts (*near left*). He is currently designing the new headquarters of U.S. Institute for Peace, scheduled to open in Washington, D.C., in 2007.

◆ Towering records

In addition to being the world's tallest free-standing structure at 553 m, Toronto's CN Tower also has the world's highest public observation gallery (the Space Deck, at 447 m); the world's highest revolving restaurant (360, at 351 m); the world's longest metal staircase (2,579 steps); and the world's highest wine cellar (351 m).

◆ Frank Gehry's melody in titanium

"Frank has written a melody," Moshe Safdie (*see opposite*) said of Spain's $210 million Guggenheim Museum Bilbao, designed by Toronto-born, Los Angeles-based architect Frank Gehry (born 1929). Opened in 1997, Bilbao's soaring, gleaming titanium edifice encompasses 24,000 square meters of interconnected buildings topped by a metal roof and a giant metallic flower. Gehry is internationally renowned for his free-form curvaceous designs, and has designed bold buildings in the shape of

Buildings that reflect life's chaos

binoculars and the fluid shape of dancers Fred Astaire and Ginger Rogers. "Life is chaotic, dangerous, and surprising," he once wrote. "Buildings should reflect it."

While the Bilbao Guggenheim (*below and right*) is among the crowning jewels in a spectacularly successful career, Gehry has yet to make a splash in Canada. This could change when his first-ever Canadian commission, the Le Clos Jordan estate winery on the Niagara Peninsula, opens in 2004. "I wait until work hits me on the head," he told the *National Post*, and until the winery offer none from Canada had hit their mark.

Gehry, who was known as Goldberg in Canada, left Toronto with his family when he was 17. He changed his name at his wife's behest, she preferred the sound of Gehry, a name she plucked from a phone book.

◆ Canada's first official photographer

Though he was born in Ireland and died in Los Angeles, photographer, publisher, and watchmaker Sam McLaughlin (1826–1914) issued Canada's first photographic publication, *The Photographic Portfolio*, a series he had taken in 1858–60 in and around Quebec City, where he was a watch and chronometer maker. In 1861, he was named official photographer for the Province of Canada, and his record includes the initial construction of the Parliament Buildings in Ottawa and several public works projects.

◆ Churchill portrait crowned Karsh's career

Success became a constant of Armenian-born portrait photographer Yousuf Karsh (1908-2002) from the time he opened a studio in Ottawa in 1932. Indeed being "Karshed" was itself a measure of achievement. His career began in Boston, where he apprenticed with photographer John H. Garo, from whom he learned the dramatic use of lighting that characterizes his work. Karsh photographed famous political, literary, theatrical, and scientific personalities on every continent, but none of his portraits attracted as much attention as his 1941 portrayal of Winston Churchill. It has become one of the most widely reproduced portraits in the history of photography. Karsh's work hangs in major galleries in Europe and North America.

◆ *Canadian Illustrated News* founder pioneered news photography

In 1864, Quebec-born Georges-Édouard Desbarats (1838–93) succeeded his father as Queen's Printer in Ottawa, a position held by the Desbarats family since 1799. Five years later, he resigned his prestigious position to found the *Canadian Illustrated News*, the world's first publication to carry half-tone photographs. (Until then, illustrations in published works were from engravings prepared by artists.)

The half-tone process was a creation of Desbarats and his engraver, William Leggo. In 1873, Desbarats and Leggo went to New York to found the *Daily Graphic*, the first daily paper to use photographic illustrations.

The *Canadian Illustrated News* continued to appear weekly until 1883, providing Canada-wide coverage of political and social events, illustrated with line drawings and photographic reproductions.

◇ The photographer and the prospector

One of Canada's first and most original photographers, Hannah Maynard (1834–1918) came to Canada in the 1850s with her husband Richard, who tried to find his fortune at a number of gold rush sites. While her husband was off prospecting, Hannah studied photography and opened a photographic studio in Victoria, B.C., in 1862. On his return, Richard opened a shoe store alongside the studio that his wife would run for 50 years. Hannah experimented with photographic techniques that were new and unconventional, such as multiple exposures, camera movement, and composite images. One of her most unusual works was a montage of 22,000 faces of children (*left*).

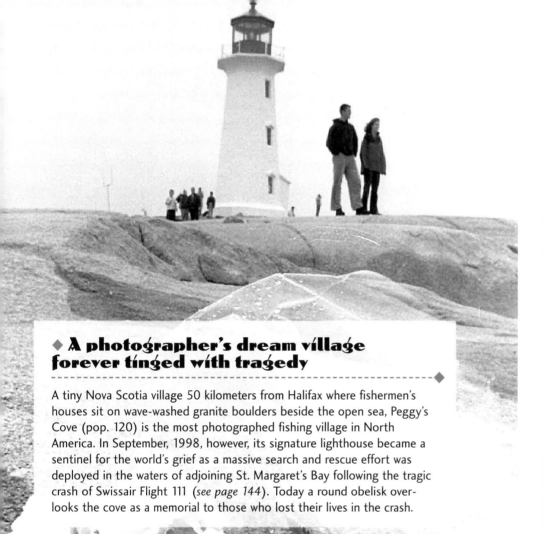

◆ Pas de paparazzi, s.v.p.

Quebec's privacy laws are more stringent than those of other parts of Canada, as the tabloid *Photo Police* and the now defunct magazine *Vice Versa* painfully discovered. In 1991, a Quebec judge ordered *Vice Versa* and one of its photographers to pay Pascale Claude Aubry $2,000 for taking and printing a photograph of her sitting on her front steps without her knowledge or permission. On appeal, the judgment was upheld by the Supreme Court of Canada. Six years later, a Quebec judge ordered *Photo Police* to pay Denise Thomas $24,000 in damages for invading her privacy. Two years earlier, the tabloid ran a photo of Thomas taken alongside her boyfriend outside a Longueuil courthouse, where the latter was facing charges of disturbing the peace.

◆ A photographer's dream village forever tinged with tragedy

A tiny Nova Scotia village 50 kilometers from Halifax where fishermen's houses sit on wave-washed granite boulders beside the open sea, Peggy's Cove (pop. 120) is the most photographed fishing village in North America. In September, 1998, however, its signature lighthouse became a sentinel for the world's grief as a massive search and rescue effort was deployed in the waters of adjoining St. Margaret's Bay following the tragic crash of Swissair Flight 111 (*see page 144*). Today a round obelisk overlooks the cove as a memorial to those who lost their lives in the crash.

◆ A watercolor wunderkind at 15

Renowned photographer Roloff Beny (1924–84; *right*) was born Wilfred Roy at Medicine Hat, Alta. He took up photography and painting as a child and held his first watercolor show at age 15. In 1950, he held his first photography show in London. Other exhibitions and several lavishly illustrated  books followed, including *To Everything There Is a Season*, a Centennial portrait of Canada published in 1967. Beny won the gold medal at the Leipzig International Book Fair the following year. He lived in Rome for several years prior to his death.

In Loving Memory OF Yolanda Navarro

◆ Patterson's Photography 101

Combining a keen photographic eye with a love for teaching, Freeman Patterson (born near Shamper's Bluff, N.B.) is one of Canada's most distinctive and respected photographers. His work ranges from documentary to impressionistic to serene minimalist compositions that focus on texture, patterns, and color. His photographs are seen in numerous publications, and he has authored books and CD-ROMs on photographic technique. Patterson obtained a Master's of Divinity degree at Columbia University, N.Y. (his thesis was "Still Photography as a Medium of Religious Expression"), before picking up a camera in the mid-1960s. After logging several years for the National Film Board, Patterson moved back to New Brunswick in 1973 to found a studio and teach workshops that continue to this day. He was made Companion of the Order of Canada in 1985.

The News Boy
1866

Fanny
c. 1858
Half plate ambrotype, tinted

C.P.R. docks, Vancouver, B.C.
1889
Silver salts and
transparent ink on glass

Right: Building after a fire,
St. James Street, Montreal
c. 1887

◆ William Notman: Canada's archivist

Upon his arrival in Canada in 1856, Scottish-born William Notman (1826–91) went to work in a wholesale dry-goods store in Montreal. In his spare time, he set up a photographic studio to put to use the daguerreotype process (producing photographs on silver plates) he had learned in Scotland. In short order, his superb portraits attracted a huge clientele from all classes of society. In 1858, the Grand Trunk Railway commissioned him to photograph construction of Montreal's Victoria Bridge.

By the 1870s, his staff of 57 included many apprentice photographers working in 14 studios in Canada and the United States. Notman photographers went across Canada to record the construction of the CPR, the settlement of the West, the life of the Plains and coastal native peoples, the lumber trade, and East Coast fishing.

Notman was also renowned for his composite photographs, mostly of snowshoe and curling clubs in and around Montreal. These large creations consisted of 300 or more individual photographs cut and pasted onto a painted background. Three of his seven children became photographers.

Today, researchers from all over the world consult the Notman Photographic Archives at the McCord Museum in Montreal, Que. Through its thousands of images—landscapes, portraits, places, events, and activities—Notman's photographs provide a window on Canada's past.

◆ O. W. Toad is no angel

"Women are human beings, and human beings are a very mixed lot," Margaret Atwood (born 1939; *right*) told *Mother Jones* magazine in 1997. "I've always been against the idea that women were Victorian angels, that they could do no wrong." Canada's best-known contemporary writer, Margaret Atwood has had continuous critical success creating complex female characters since the 1960s.

Over 50 published books include works of fiction, poetry, criticism, social history, and children's literature. Her novels include *The Edible Woman* (1969), *Lady Oracle* (1976), and *Cat's Eye* (1989). Among her accolades are two Governor General's Awards (for 1996's *Circle Game* and 1985's *The Handmaid's Tale*); the Giller Prize, Canada's most prestigious literary award, for *Alias Grace* (1996); and the Booker Prize for *The Blind Assassin* (2000).

Atwood credits a halcyon childhood—with summers often spent in the bush with her entomologist father, winters in Ottawa, Sault Ste. Marie, and Toronto, Ont.—with nurturing her gift. Her wicked sense of humor is legend and even extends to the copyright pages of her books and the name of her website: The mysterious "O. W. Toad" is actually an anagram of "Atwood."

◆ Capturing the luminosity of everyday life

Chicago-born Carol Shields (born 1936; *below*) began writing "the kind of book I wanted to read but couldn't find." And readers seeking a stimulating and exciting page-turner will not be disappointed.

Canada has been her home since 1957, when she immigrated here with her Manitoba-born husband. A long-time teacher of English and creative writing, and a Chancellor of the University of Winnipeg, Shields was propelled to fame in 1993 with *The Stone Diaries*. The novel, which won her both the Governor General's literary award and the Pulitzer Prize, traces the arc of a woman's life, following one Daisy Goodwill Flett through much of the 20th century.

Five years later Shields switched perspectives and told the tale of Larry Weller, whose hapless life is a string of missed opportunities, in *Larry's Party*.

Shields was diagnosed with breast cancer in 1998. Her novel *Unless* was published in 2002.

WINNER OF THE BOOKER PRIZE

The BLIND ASSASSIN

a novel

MARGARET ATWOOD

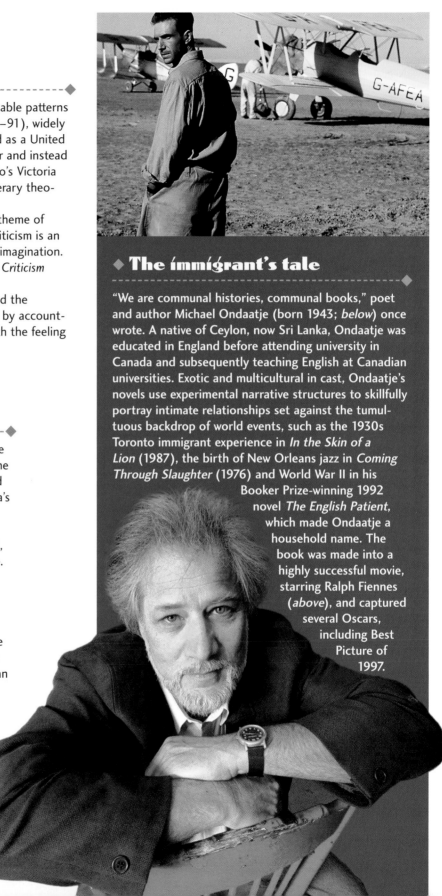

◆ Canada's greatest thinker

Literature is an integrated universe signposted in recognizable patterns of myths and symbols, according to Northrop Frye (1912–91), widely regarded as Canada's leading thinker and writer. Ordained as a United Church minister, Frye traded the pulpit for the ivory tower and instead became a professor of English at the University of Toronto's Victoria College, and an internationally renowned authority on literary theories, the work of William Blake, and biblical symbolism.

The Bible as the wellspring of western literature is the theme of his work *The Great Code* (1982). Frye held that literary criticism is an authoritative discipline that outlines the shape of human imagination. Making this point in his best-known work, *The Anatomy of Criticism* (1990), he systematically related all literary works.

What did Canada's greatest thinker think of Canada and the Canadian identity? Canada, in his view, is a country ruled by accountants, and as for the Canadian identity, "it is bound up with the feeling that the end of the rainbow never falls on Canada."

◆ Small-town folk people her stories

Many consider Alice Munro (born 1931; *left*) to be Canada's finest short story writer. Three of her nine short story collections have been awarded the Governor General's Award, Canada's highest literary honor. She has received the PEN-Malamud Award for excellence in short fiction, and, in 1998, the $25,000 Giller Prize.

Most of Munro's work is set in Ontario's Huron County, and revolves around the dilemmas of small-town characters—adolescent girls, elderly women, and women alone in the world. To critics who charged that some of her fiction was more autobiographical than fiction, Munro responded that it was "autobiographical in form but not in fact."

Born to a Wingham, Ont., fox farmer and his wife, Munro claims she has had a compulsion to write since she was 13 years old. Despite widespread acclaim, Munro has always been tentative about her work. When her publisher sent her complimentary copies of *Dance of the Happy Shades* (1968), her first work and winner of her first Governor General's Award, she hid them in a closet.

◆ The immigrant's tale

"We are communal histories, communal books," poet and author Michael Ondaatje (born 1943; *below*) once wrote. A native of Ceylon, now Sri Lanka, Ondaatje was educated in England before attending university in Canada and subsequently teaching English at Canadian universities. Exotic and multicultural in cast, Ondaatje's novels use experimental narrative structures to skillfully portray intimate relationships set against the tumultuous backdrop of world events, such as the 1930s Toronto immigrant experience in *In the Skin of a Lion* (1987), the birth of New Orleans jazz in *Coming Through Slaughter* (1976) and World War II in his Booker Prize-winning 1992 novel *The English Patient*, which made Ondaatje a household name. The book was made into a highly successful movie, starring Ralph Fiennes (*above*), and captured several Oscars, including Best Picture of 1997.

Findley

◆ Outspoken champion of Canadian history

Son of a Klondike gold-seeker, Pierre Berton (born 1920) spent his early years in the Yukon, and worked as a journalist in Vancouver and Toronto before becoming one of Canada's best-known writers and television personalities through *The Pierre Berton Show* and *Front Page Challenge* (see page 246). Berton is credited with singlehandedly popularizing Canadian history with books such as *Klondike* (1958), *The Last Spike* (1971), and *The Dionne Years* (1977). As a journalist and writer Berton is passionate and outspoken— he broke journalistic convention by writing a poem that was a scathing indictment of the death sentence when Steven Truscott was sentenced to hang in 1959 (see page 141) and he got into hot water four years later with the readers of *Maclean's* magazine by speaking out in favor of pre-marital sex.

◆ MacLennan broke Canadian ground

When Nova Scotia-born novelist Hugh MacLennan (1907–90) failed to find a publisher for his first works, both about overseas travels, he focused on Canadian themes. The result was *Barometer Rising* (1941), a book about the Halifax explosion; *Two Solitudes* (1945), a seminal novel about English-French tensions in Quebec, and *Each Man's Son* (1951) about mining in Cape Breton, making him the first major English-speaking writer to tackle Canada's national character in fiction. Although MacLennan was primarily a novelist, his erudite essays—which embrace a panoply of subjects with humanity and intuition—have also won him accolades.

Laurence

MacLennan

◆ Shakespearean scribe

Writing was the second career of popular writer Timothy Findley (1930–2002), author of *The Butterfly Plague*, *The Wars*, *Famous Last Words*, *Dust to Dust* and *Pilgrim*. A charter member of the Stratford Shakespearean Festival, he had a successful acting career before publishing his first novel (*The Last of the Crazy People*) in 1967. But once an actor, always an actor. When promoting his best-selling *The Piano Man's Daughter* in 1997, Findley attracted thousands of fans to dramatized readings that included polished performances.

Findley believed that acting is the best apprenticeship for a writer since it built a sense of "structure, dialogue, rhythm, cadence, language, and the interplay between action and words." Because of his obsession with rhythm, Findlay had his day's handwritten notes read aloud to him each night by his longtime companion, Bill Whitehead.

Findley didn't entirely forsake the footlights. His 2000 play *Elizabeth Rex*—which boldly brings together William Shakespeare and the Virgin Queen, Elizabeth I—won a Governor General's Award that year. Until his death Findley spent part of the year in Provence, France; part in Stratford, Ont., where his working areas were painted in brilliant red.

◆ The alchemist

Canada's most distinguished essayist, Robertson Davies (1913–95) has also had successful careers as a novelist, actor, journalist, editor, publisher, playwright, and teacher. As an essayist Davies wove his esoteric interests—Jung, Oscar Wilde, Barbara Cartland— into sharp, witty "table talk" which recalls the pleasure of enlightened conversation. His eclectic novels presented Canada to the world as a cultivated, contemporary culture. One of his most celebrated works, *The Deptford Trilogy*, tells the same sprawling saga of myth and magic from different points of view.

Callaghan

Davies

◆ Manitoba's stone angel of literature

Orphaned as a small child, Margaret Laurence (1926–87) spent much of her childhood under the thumb of a tyrannical grandfather. Her writing was her salvation. Although she wrote stories from the age of seven and worked as a journalist, Margaret only published her first book, *A Tree for Poverty* (her translation of Somali folktales and poetry), in 1944.

Margaret had gone to Africa with her engineer husband, John Laurence, and out of her African years came other books. When her writing became all consuming, her marriage broke down. She lived in England for a time in the 1960s and 70s, and there produced the Manawaka books—*The Stone Angel*, *A Jest of God*, *The Fire Dwellers*, *A Bird in the House*, and *The Diviners*. The fictional Manawaka was based on her Manitoba hometown of Neepawa.

After *The Diviners*, Margaret Laurence told an interviewer she would write no more novels, that she had nothing more to say. On her return to Canada, she became a writer-in-residence at various Ontario universities. In her later years in Lakefield, Ont., after suffering from cancer for some time, she died as the result of a deliberate drug overdose; meticulously recording the details in her journal. Her ashes were interred in Riverside Cemetery in Neepawa, not far from the Davidson family stone angel memorial she had immortalized.

Berton

◆ "Our own experiences"

Born on the Prairies, three-time Governor General's Award winner Gabrielle Roy (1909–83) taught school in Manitoba and studied drama in Paris before settling in Montreal in 1939. She had begun writing overseas, and in Montreal she continued to work as a freelance journalist, writing for various periodicals. She achieved international acclaim in 1945 with the publication of *Bonheur d'occasion*, translated into English as *The Tin Flute*, a novel of the war years set in Montreal's working class St. Henri, a district down track from wealthy Westmount. "We are getting down to our own truth and to our own experiences," Madame Roy said of this book, which was followed by three others. Said Brian Moore: "St. Henri had become a site in Canadian literary history." Along with literary fame, Roy's first novel won the Literary Guild of America Award and France awarded her the prestigious Prix Femina, making her the first Canadian so honored.

◆ Papa encouraged him to write

While working at *The Toronto Daily Star*, Morley Callaghan (1903–90) met Ernest Hemingway, who not only encouraged the young short story writer to write, but helped him publish his first stories in Paris in 1926. Callaghan's stories would later appear regularly in *Atlantic Monthly*, *Harper's Bazaar*, and *The New Yorker*. His first novel, *Strange Fugitive*, was published in 1928. Callaghan's work, which often championed "the little man," explores themes of spiritual versus worldly values, of sanctity versus human weakness, particularly in his masterpiece, *The Loved and the Lost* (1951), which won the Governor General's Award for that year.

Roy

◆ Literature was Lucy Maud's escape

Over her lifetime, Prince Edward Island writer Lucy Maud Montgomery (1874–1942) published scores of novels and hundreds of poems and short stories. But her fame, and a fair chunk of P.E.I.'s present-day tourism, was forged by her first novel, *Anne of Green Gables* (1908). Its red-headed orphan heroine, the delightful folk of Avonlea, and the pastoral island landscape captured the hearts of people around the world, a love affair that continues to this day. (The farmhouse featured in the Anne stories is P.E.I.'s best-known landmark.)

Growing up with strict, religious grandparents after her father remarried (her mother died when she was two), the fantasy world of writing provided an escape for Lucy Maud, who actually spent much of her life away from the island she loved. In 1911, she married Rev. Ewan MacDonald and lived the rest of her life in Ontario. Her work included seven more Anne books, the autobiographical *Emily* trilogy, 450 poems, and some 5,000 pages of unpublished personal diaries.

◆ Inventor of cyberpunk

In his 1984 novel *Neuromancer*, Vancouver, B.C.-based science fiction writer William Gibson (born 1948) wrote about "Cyberspace," the electronic netherworld inside a worldwide network of computers which his characters "jacked" into neurally. With *Neuromancer*, Gibson is credited with coining the popular term, which has come to embrace the Internet, as well as launching a new, dystopian subgenre of science fiction called cyberpunk.

◆ W. P. Kinsella's home run

The undisputed master of baseball fiction, Alberta-born William Patrick ("W. P.") Kinsella (born 1935) hit a grand-slam home run with his 1982 picaresque, *Shoeless Joe*. It's the tale of an Iowa corn farmer who hears a voice telling him "If you build it, he will come." "It" is a baseball diamond and "he" is Shoeless Joe Jackson of the 1919 Chicago White Sox. (The story became the 1989 hit movie *Field of Dreams*.)

Kinsella, who has also written extensively about native life and experience, became the subject of wide publicity in 1998, because of a libel action he launched against Evelyn Lau, his former lover and best-selling author (*Runaway: Diary of a Street Kid*). Kinsella claimed a 1997 *Vancouver* magazine article, "Me and W.P.," written by the much-younger Lau, publicly aired the dirty laundry of their relationship and contained "disparaging, demeaning, humiliating, and embarrassing references." Lau settled in 1999.

From Green Gables to cyberspace

◆ The mensch from Montreal

One of the foremost novelists of his generation, Montreal-born Mordecai Richler (1931–2001) used the Jewish working-class area where he grew up as a backdrop for his early novels. His books are crammed with a sense of Montreal's ethnic neighborhoods of the forties and fifties, of afternoons spent playing hooky from Baron Byng High School and whiling away the hours at Wilensky's Light Lunch. Many consider *The Apprenticeship of Duddy Kravitz* (1959), his acclaimed novel about a brash young man's determination to succeed (the basis of a 1974 film of the same name), a classic of modern Canadian literature. His numerous awards include the 1998 Giller Prize for his 10th novel, *Barney's Version*.

By the 1990s, Richler was almost as well known for his skewering of Quebec separatism as for his impressive body of work. An explosive 1991 screed in the *New Yorker* in particular drew the ire of separatists.

◆ Evangeline author never saw Grand Pré

Because of Henry Wadsworth Longfellow's haunting poem *Evangeline*, some 100,000 tourists annually make the trek to Grand Pré, N.S. (pop. 300), and millions worldwide know the tragic story of Evangeline's long search for her beloved Gabriel. The epic, published in 1847, and eventually translated into 130 languages, tells of two young lovers put on different ships when the Acadians were deported to British colonies in 1755–63 for refusing to swear allegiance to England. In the poem, when they are reunited after many years, Evangeline is a nun, and Gabriel is dying of smallpox.

Longfellow had no Acadian roots and never visited Grand Pré, but relied on published accounts of the expulsions for background. He is said to have first decided to name his heroine Gabrielle, then Celestine, but Evangeline won out by the time the poem was published in 1847.

◆ Stories my mother told me

Anne Hébert (1916–2000; *left*) juggled two complex plots in her acclaimed psychological gothic romance *Kamouraska*, a dramatic portrait of 19th-century Quebec based on stories her mother told her. The Quebec-born poet, playwright, and novelist won the French Prix des Libraires for the 1970 work.

A WINNER!
4 CANADIAN FILM AWARDS
SPECIAL JURY PRIZE
"ALL ROUND EXCELLENCE"
Geneviève Bujold
BEST ACTRESS GENEVIÈVE BUJOLD
BEST SUPPORTING ACTRESS
BEST ART DIRECTION
CLAUDE JUTRA'S
KAMOURASKA
Every nation has a love story that becomes a Classic!
Adapted from Anne Hébert's prize winning Canadian novel with RICHARD JORDAN PHILIPPE LEOTARD Photography Michel Brault

◆ No Grand Central Station for Canada

In 1930, writer Lawrence Durrell introduced Ontario-born novelist and poet Elizabeth Smart (1913–86) to the British poet George Barker, with whom she would later have four children. Smart worked at the British Embassy in Washington in the early 1940s, then moved to England in 1943. Because she recounted her liaison with Barker, a married man, in the devastating *By Grand Central Station I Sat Down and Wept* (1945), her mother made sure no copies circulated in Canada. However, the work was hailed as a masterpiece and republished abroad in the 1960s, and in Canada in 1982. Smart, who produced no new work until 1977, supported herself and her children by writing advertising copy and working as an editor at *Vogue* and *House and Gardens*.

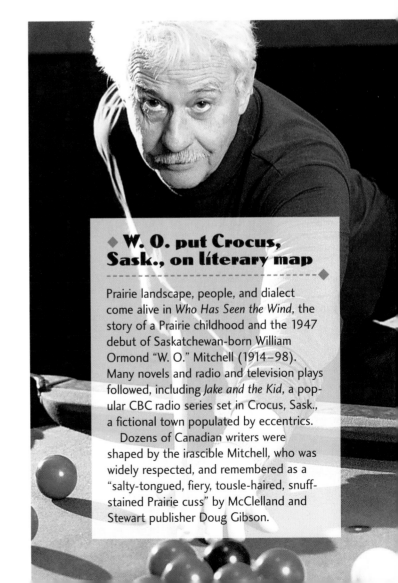

◆ W. O. put Crocus, Sask., on literary map

Prairie landscape, people, and dialect come alive in *Who Has Seen the Wind*, the story of a Prairie childhood and the 1947 debut of Saskatchewan-born William Ormond "W. O." Mitchell (1914–98). Many novels and radio and television plays followed, including *Jake and the Kid*, a popular CBC radio series set in Crocus, Sask., a fictional town populated by eccentrics.

Dozens of Canadian writers were shaped by the irascible Mitchell, who was widely respected, and remembered as a "salty-tongued, fiery, tousle-haired, snuff-stained Prairie cuss" by McClelland and Stewart publisher Doug Gibson.

The author who cried wolf

Farley Mowat (born 1921; *right*) has been described as "a natural storyteller" and his books, many of them autobiographical, have been published in over 40 countries. "Subjective nonfiction" is Mowat's own term for his books about the North and Canada's Aboriginal peoples.

He became an instant celebrity with *People of the Deer* (1952), which was highly critical of Canada's treatment of the Inuit. Controversy was rekindled again in 1996, when *Saturday Night* published an article alleging that Mowat had spent considerably less time in the North and among the Inuit than he claimed.

In 1999, Mowat provoked further controversy, with *The Farfarers: Before the Norse*, in which he suggests that Scots, known as Albans, had colonized the Arctic and subarctic long before the Norse (*see page 50*).

King of Canadiana

Poet, writer, bibliophile, and broadcaster, John Robert Colombo (born 1936) has probably more Canadiana tidbits at his fingertips than anyone else in the country. A tireless researcher of Canadian facts, jokes, folklore, and mystery, Colombo has authored nearly 80 books, including *Colombo's Canadian Quotations* and his annual *Canadian Global Almanac*.

Jack of all trades and writer of none

It was Sam Slick, a Yankee clock vendor, who first said: "The early bird catches the worm," "Jack of all trades and master of none," "barking up the wrong tree," "as quick as a wink," "raining cats and dogs," and countless other sayings that are now part of our vernacular. Only Sam Slick didn't exist. He was the creation of Sir Thomas Chandler Haliburton (1796–1865), who, beginning with *The Clockmaker* in 1836 wrote 11 Sam Slick books. Haliburton went on to became a Nova Scotia Supreme Court judge.

"I am Sam Slick, says I"

Canada's first novel

The first novel written in Canada was *The History of Emily Montague*. It was written by Frances Brooke, wife of the chaplain of the garrison at Quebec between 1763 and 1768, who wrote about life in Quebec at that time.

Canajun, eh?

The *Oxford Guide to Canadian English Usage* defines a Canadianism as "a word or expression that is used only in Canada or a sense of a word that is almost exclusively restricted to Canada." The 2001 edition of *The Canadian Oxford Dictionary* lists over 2,000 Canadianisms, some of which are printed around the margins of these pages.

The ABCs of copyright

On Dec. 1, 1841, *A Canadian Spelling Book* by Alexander Davidson (1794–1856) was the first work for which a Canadian copyright was issued.

The great Canadian novelist

Danielle Steele and Dick Francis have nothing on Canada's Daniel Ross—when it comes to prolific output, the Saint John-born novelist has them both beat. William Edward Daniel Ross (1912–95) didn't start writing until he was 51, but managed to publish 358 novels (two of them posthumously) and over 600 short stories under 21 different pseudonyms, including Tex Steel, Dana Ross, and Ruth Dorset, making him the world's most prolific author as well. Ross once wrote a 75,000-word novel in a week. His novels have sold more than 40 million copies worldwide.

◆ Woodcock stood above the heads of the crowd

In the introduction to his 1980 book, *100 Great Canadians*, Winnipeg-born poet, biographer, essayist, and author George Woodcock (1912–95) explained why the men and women he had profiled stood "above the heads of the crowd." He had chosen them, he explained, "for a willingness to live within a community, to grow with it, and, often at the expense of some degree of individuality, to serve it."

Fast forward to 1998 and the special July 1 issue of *Maclean's*, which profiled "The 100 Most Important Canadians in History." Woodcock was among the 100 chosen from reader nominations and expert panels as having made a lasting contribution to Canada. Woodcock had founded the quarterly *Canadian Literature*, the first scholarly publication on that subject, while at the University of British Columbia in 1959.

◆ The political scientist from Mariposa

A professor of political science at McGill University, Montreal, Stephen Leacock (1869–1944; *right*) was something of a campus character, often clad in an overcoat with missing buttons and a faded hat. Although he authored some 60 serious books, such as *Elements of Political Science*, Leacock is best remembered for his *Nonsense Novels*, *Sunshine Sketches of a Little Town*, and other humorous works.

His summer home was at Orillia, Ont., an industrial and resort town on Lake Simcoe that was the model for the Mariposa of his novels. Although Leacock protested Mariposa was about 70 or 80 small towns, Orillians were not fooled. In Leacock's characters they recognized their own foibles. At first, the townsfolk's disapproval was fierce, but this softened over time, then blossomed into an even fiercer pride. In 1957, the Town of Orillia purchased Leacock's home, which is now a national and provincial historic site.

◆ Pioneer DIY expert

In 1832, botanist Catharine Parr Traill (1802–99; *left*) and her husband emigrated from England to settle on a Peterborough, Ont., farm next door to brother-in-law and sister, Susannah Moodie, a prolific writer about her discontent at a settler's life. Catharine, however, adapted cheerfully to life in the backwoods. At age 16 she had published a book for children in England, and three years after arriving in Canada, she published *The Backwoods of Canada*, a factual and scientific account of pioneer life. She also wrote children's fiction, *The Female Emigrant's Guide*, *Canadian Wildflowers* and *Studies of Plant Life in Canada*, and *The Canadian Settler's Guide*. Her "guides" are full of practical advice, and generally upbeat information, and tell new arrivals how to do everything from growing corn to making soap.

◆ Champion of women's issues

A lifelong concern for women's rights marked the career of Dorothy Livesay (1909–96), prolific Winnipeg journalist, translator, writer of short fiction, and winner of two Governor General's awards for her poetry. Livesay wrote passionately about poverty and the exploitation of workers. Although she published her first poem at age 13, earning $2 from *The Vancouver Province,* she expressed concern that she could never become a writer, because "it was a man's world." Nevertheless, she published her first book, *Green Pitcher,* when she was 18 years old.

In the 1930s, Livesay was a social worker and a Communist Party organizer in Canada and the United States. After World War II, she was a journalist in Europe. In the early 1960s. she worked as a UNESCO teacher in Zambia. At home, she became a major force in developing women's voices in Canadian writing.

◆ Birney's visual verse

An outstanding poet, novelist, and playwright, Calgary-born Alfred Earle Birney (1904–96) was one of the first Canadian poets to incorporate the rhythms of speech in his poetry. He also experimented with visual poetry in his "shape poems," and performed his poetry in front of a percussion ensemble.

◆ Bard of the Yukon

Robert Service (1874–1958; *left*), "the bard of the Yukon," gave the Klondike spirit a voice in books of poems such as *Songs of a Sourdough* (1907) and *Ballads of a Cheechako* (1909). His Dawson cabin is now a national historic site, where tourists listen to his "ghost," or one of his poetic characters such as Sam McGee, recite his ballads.

Service was a Dawson bank teller when he lived and wrote in the cabin between 1908 and 1912. He had emigrated from Scotland in 1894 hoping to become a cowboy, but ended up in the banking business. He described many episodes of his action-packed life in *Ploughman of the Moon.*

Unlike the characters he wrote about, Service was a teetotaler and physical fitness buff. He covered the Balkan war as a reporter and was an ambulance driver and intelligence officer for the Canadian army during World War II. Service spent much of his life in France.

◆ Leonard Cohen: "The Silent One"

His hypnotic voice and epic-length songs about our cultural malaise and loss of soul are part of the mystique of poet, novelist, and singer-songwriter Leonard Cohen (born 1934). Cohen's poetry readings in the 1960s and 70s had the same drawing power as rock concerts. Judy Collins' recording of his haunting, melancholy song *Suzanne,* written in 1966 and now a folk classic, established him as one of Canada's best-known songwriters. In 1967, Expo year in Montreal, Cohen delighted audiences with a series of candlelight concerts. His writing in this period brought fame and a slew of awards, but Cohen began to concentrate more and more on the musical career for which he is now famous. Cohen added 11 record albums, including the acclaimed *I'm Your Man* (1988), to his eight volumes of poetry and two novels. His work, frequently autobiographical, is a blend of romance and brooding despair.

Among honors bestowed on him are the Order of Canada, several honorary doctorates and induction into the Juno Hall of Fame. Cohen withdrew from public life in the 1990s to study Zen Buddhism, living for extended periods in Greece and California. In 1996, Cohen became an ordained Zen monk. His dharma name is, appropriately, "Jikan," or "the silent one."

◆ Confederation Poets

The Confederation Poets—so called because they were born within a decade of Confederation—were a diverse group of Ottawa poets who introduced Canadian English poetry to the world. Among their ranks were journalist and editor Bliss Carman, postal clerk Archibald Lampman, civil servant Duncan Campbell Scott, and animal-story writer Charles G. D. Roberts. Their joint column written in *The Toronto Globe* from 1892–93, called "At the Mermaid Inn," also gave birth to Canadian literary criticism.

Confederation poet Bliss Carman (center), at Windermere Valley, B.C., 1922

◆ Street-fighting spirit

Humor, anger, and a street-fighting spirit pervade Ontario-born Alfred Wellington Purdy's over 40 volumes of poetry. There is no magic to writing, he told an interviewer in 1997. "Just long, careful searching for words." Born in Wooler, Ont., Purdy (1918–2000; *right*) had to earn his early living through manual occupations. His working class poetry often spoke out for the underdog and his readings in the 1960s attracted large audiences. An intrepid traveler and "versifying journalist," he wrote about his travels to the High Arctic across Canada in *North of Summer* (1967), and *Hiroshima Poems* (1972) on a trip to Japan.

◆ Maritime life central to Pratt's poetry

Considered the foremost Canadian poet of the early 20th century, Edwin John Pratt (1882–1964) grew up in various Newfoundland outports, where his father ministered to Methodist congregations. Not surprisingly, Maritime life is central to his poetry, which espouses qualities such as courage, loyalty, and self-sacrifice. Historical themes such as the Jesuits in Huronia and building the Canadian Pacific Railway figure in his later works. Ordained a minister in 1913, Pratt never served as such. Instead he taught in the English department of the University of Toronto's Victoria College for more than 30 years.

◆ The Irish *habitant*

A cairn beside Cobalt, Ont.'s library honors poet, doctor, and mine owner Dr. William Henry Drummond (1854–1907). Born in Mohill, County Leitrim, Ireland, Drummond came to Canada with his parents when he was 10 years old, studied medicine at Bishop's University, Sherbrooke, Que., and later practiced in Montreal and the Eastern Townships. Attracted to the folkways of rural Quebec, Dr. Drummond wrote narrative verse in the English idiom of the French Canadian farmer. *The Habitant*, his first book of poetry published in 1897, proved extremely popular and made him widely known as a writer of dialect verse. The library houses a large collection of memorabilia as well as works of Dr. Drummond.

◆ Canada's Father Goose

Jazz and blues fanatic, cryptic crossword addict, and poet Dennis Lee (born 1939) has been steadily feeding Canadian kids *Alligator Pie* since 1974, when his delightfully perverse book of poetry first appeared. (It has gone on to sell more than half a million copies in Canada alone.) Combining Canadian motifs with an irreverent attitude and a knockabout rhythmic sense, Lee has been dubbed Canada's "Father Goose."

Manitoba Free Press

35¢ VOL. 1 NO. 1

A MAN OF CONVICTION

One of Canada's greatest newspapermen, John Wesley Dafoe (1866–1944) was editor of the *Manitoba* (later *Winnipeg*) *Free Press* from 1901 until his death. By then his paper was one of the most influential in North America, for Dafoe was a man of conviction who stood up for his beliefs in print. He condemned the leaders of the Winnipeg General Strike (*see page 166*) and was instrumental in Canada's joining The League of Nations.

LE DEVOIR'S HENRI BOURASSA

The dynamic grandson of 1837 Patriote leader Louis-Joseph Papineau, Henri Bourassa (1868–1952) was an equally dedicated French Canadian nationalist. Journalist, politician, and flamboyant orator, Bourassa came to prominence in 1899 when he opposed Canada's participation in the South African Boer War. During World War I, he also championed resistance to compulsory armed service primarily because Robert Borden's Conservative government announced Canada's entry into the war without consulting Parliament. Bourassa feared such action was tantamount to saying all British wars would automatically be Canadian wars.

In 1910, he founded Montreal's *Le Devoir*, still an influential newspaper, and was its editor until 1932. He strongly advocated the Anglo-French nature of Canada, worried about the Americanization of the country, and warned of the inroads being made by big industry.

EYE-OPENER BOB EDWARDS

"Some men spoil a good story by sticking to the facts."

The Eye Opener was said to be the best five-cent read in the West, thanks to the barbed wit of its maverick editor and publisher, Scotsman Robert Chambers "Bob" Edwards (1864–1922). Readers were treated to such philosophic musings as: "Too many people salt away money in the brine of other people's tears," or "The woman with the ideal husband very likely wishes she had some other kind." But it was his lampooning of the establishment, the clergy, the Senate, and especially the Canadian Pacific Railway that made him something of a western legend.

Humor was his weapon in his war on corruption and snobbery. From its founding in Calgary in 1902, *The Eye Opener* appeared every Saturday, more or less, for 20 years. When it missed an issue or two, Edwards would announce in the next issue that his old enemy drink was to blame.

According to Bob Edwards, "Some men spoil a good story by sticking to the facts." Not him. If it was a slow news week, he was not above inventing a little something. He invented people, too, and kept his readers guessing about what was fact and what was fancy by placing the fictional folk at real events.

Edwards was 53 when he met his wife, a 20-year-old Scottish immigrant named Kate Penman. When he died five years later, she placed a copy of the last issue of *The Eye Opener* and a silver flask of his favorite whisky in his coffin.

MACLEAN'S STARTED LIFE AS THE BUSY MAN'S MAGAZINE

The newsmagazine *Maclean's* began life in 1905 as *The Busy Man's Magazine* and underwent several name changes up to 1911. It was the creation of John Bayne Maclean (1862–1950) who, in partnership with his brother, was already publishing the highly successful magazine *Canadian Grocer*. The contents for the August 1911 issue of *Maclean's* included "Did Laurier Betray Us?," "The Place of Verandahs in Modern Architecture," "Our Bad Manners and Who Is to Blame," and O. Henry's "A Night in New Arabia."

FAMOUS CROP FORECASTER WAS WEST'S FIRST TYPIST

Early in life Toronto-born Ella Cora Hind (1861–1942) set her sights on a journalistic career, but no newspaper would hire her because she was a woman. Shortly after leaving school, she settled in Winnipeg, where she became the first typist in the West. But her freelance articles on farming proved so popular with *Winnipeg Free Press* readers that John Wesley Dafoe hired her as agricultural editor in 1901.

Hind then spent the next 40 years writing about Canadian farmers and championing their causes. Each summer, she toured the Prairie wheat-fields, then wrote her uncannily accurate crop forecasts for which she became world famous. One westerner said of her: "Miss E. Cora Hind was rather terrifying. She was more positive about everything than most people are about anything."

FREEDOM-OF-THE-PRESS CHAMPION WAS ONE OF THE FIRST SEPARATISTS

"Poetry is the maiden I loved," red-headed, straight-talking journalist and orator Joseph Howe (1804–73) once said, "but politics is the harridan I married." A printshop apprentice at age 13, he acquired *The Novascotian* 10 years later and wandered the province writing about its country and fisherfolk. In 1835, when he was sued for libel, he won a landmark judgment establishing freedom of the press (*see page 138*).

In 1840, the feisty editor was challenged to a duel by the son of a chief justice whose honesty he had questioned. The son shot first and missed. Howe shot his pistol into the air and walked away. He refused all further challenges, claiming "A live editor is more useful than a dead hero."

Elected to the Nova Scotia House of Assembly on his 32nd birthday, Howe criticized the executive council transacting public business in secret and spent the next 12 years fighting for responsible government. Largely through his efforts, Nova Scotia did so in 1848.

A fierce opponent of Confederation—"the botheration scheme," he called it—Howe nevertheless helped negotiate better terms for his home province. He joined the federal cabinet in 1869 and was lieutenant-governor of Nova Scotia at the time of his death.

OUTSTANDING POLITICAL CARTOONIST

Toronto-born Duncan Macpherson (1924–93), political cartoonist for *The Toronto Star*, was one of the first newspaper cartoonists to take an opposing stand to his editorial board. In his illustrious career he ruthlessly caricatured the major politicians of the day, including John Diefenbaker and Lester B. Pearson (*above*).

FULFORD GAVE *SATURDAY NIGHT* SOME OF ITS FINEST ISSUES

Ottawa-born writer, essayist, editor, and critic Robert Fulford (born 1932) began his journalistic career in 1949, as a copy-boy at *The Globe and Mail*. He worked at various magazines, including *Maclean's*, and was an influential critic of books, art, and music at *The Toronto Star*. In 1968 he took over the editorship of *Saturday Night*, a post he held with distinction for more than 20 years.

Under his leadership, the magazine became known for insightful political reporting and coverage of the arts. Some of its finest film reviews were by Fulford himself, writing under the nom de plume Marshall Delaney. By introducing short stories and poems to its pages, Fulford also introduced Canadians to talented up-and-coming writers such as Margaret Atwood (*see page 230*).

◆ POW! **Canuck comics!**

In the 1940s, the War Exchange Conservation Act forbade the import of "non-essential" items into Canada—including comic books. Into the breach stepped Cy Bell, a Toronto street sign designer. Bell bought a second-hand offset printing press and hired an artist, Edmund Legault. In the summer of 1941, they published *Wow N°1*, a 64-page, full-color comic that sold for 15 cents. All 52,000 copies sold out. By the end of the war, Bell published more than 20 million copies of titles featuring Canadian comic book heroes such as *Johnny Canuck* and *Dixon of the Mounted*.

◆ **Was Superman's hometown Toronto?**

Toronto-born Joe Shuster (1914–92; *left*) was 17 in 1938 when he teamed up with writer Jerry Siegel to create the first Superman comic strip. Even though Shuster (cousin of Frank Shuster of Wayne & Shuster fame; *see page 247*) and his family were living in Cleveland, Ohio, at the time, Shuster based his Metropolis cityscape on the city where he had grown up and *The Daily Planet*, employer of Superman's alter ego Clark Kent, on *The Toronto Daily Star*.

Four years later the duo persuaded D.C. Comics to buy their creation for $150, and the first Superman appeared on the cover of *Action Comics* that year. It was an instant success. In 1947, the creative duo sued to regain control of their crusader from Krypton, but they lost their suit and were immediately fired. Warner Communications later bought the rights to Superman for their series of blockbuster movies. In the late 1970s, the Warner company awarded the comic strip creators an annual $20,000 stipend.

◆ **"Ma" kept readers chuckling weekly**

With husband George, Kansas-born Margaret "Ma" Murray (1888–1982; *right*) founded various weekly newspapers in northern British Columbia, including *Cariboo News*, *Chinook*, and *The Alaska-Highway News*. Readers of the *Bridge River-Lillooet News* (founded 1934, and edited by the down-to-earth Murray for several decades) were "guaranteed a chuckle every week and a belly laugh once a month or your money back."

"Ma" had fairly strong views about most things and swear words found their way into her editorials from time to time. Punctuation was not her forte, but she deflected criticism by regularly running a page of punctuation signs and telling readers to help themselves. Ma's deprecating humor, homespun wisdom, and mild invective (she was fond of words like "damshure," "craparoni," and "snafoo") struck just the right note with her frontier readership. When one community began to grow rapidly without orderly planning, she wrote: "Maybe it is ugly, but by God it's progressive ugliness." In 1970, she was awarded the Order of Canada medal for publishing editorials "with lots of salt in 'em."

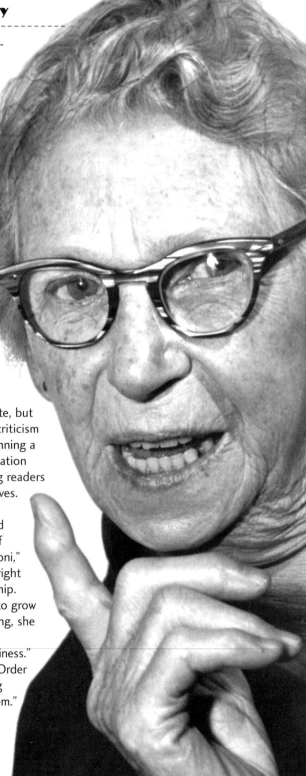

◆ A war correspondent who battled corsets on the homefront

Feisty Kathleen Blake "Kit" Coleman (1864–1915) was the first Canadian woman to have a regular newspaper job, and the world's first female war correspondent. Born in County Galway, Ireland, and educated in France, she was married at 16 and widowed at 20. Penniless, she immigrated to Canada, where she settled in Toronto, and married Edward Watkins. But within a few years, Kit found herself widowed and penniless a second time, this time with two children to support.

When *Saturday Night* published some of her articles, her writing caught the eye of Christopher Bunting, owner of *The Mail*, *The Globe and Mail*'s predecessor. Despite the fact that women columnists or editors did not exist in Canadian journalism at that time, Bunting offered her a job as weekly columnist, and Kit's "Woman's Kingdom"—a mix of features, book reviews, poems, and advice—appeared in *The Mail*'s pages in 1889. Some readers were outraged, but the column eventually became the paper's most popular feature. In 1892, Kit spent time in England writing about places associated with Charles Dickens. In 1893, she covered the Chicago World's Fair.

During her coverage of Queen Victoria's 1896 Jubilee, she accompanied Sir Wilfrid and Lady Laurier to a party at Buckingham Palace. In 1898, she was the lone woman among 135 male war correspondents in Cuba reporting on the Spanish-American War. Aghast to see a woman confronting war's brutality, an army officer ordered her aboard a hospital ship heading home. Her accounts of open-deck surgeries and the wounded and dying carnage she witnessed enroute electrified her readers.

Another of Coleman's crusades was closer to home. Women's corsets were an abomination as far as she was concerned, and she was not shy about expressing her views. When she wrote a series of articles denouncing these garments, Toronto's lingerie merchants tried to get the paper to censor its outspoken columnist. It didn't.

Kit's longtime association with *The Mail* ended unhappily nonetheless. She resigned in anger when asked to write an additional front page column with no increase in the weekly $35 she had been paid for more than 20 years. She then syndicated "Kit's Column" to several papers at $5 a piece.

The unbeatable journalist died suddenly in 1915 at her home in Hamilton, Ont., where she had lived following her marriage to her third husband, Dr. Theobald Coleman. Today, the Hamilton branch of the Canadian Women's Press Club (an organization Kit and 13 other women journalists had founded upon returning from the St. Louis Exposition in 1904) awards an annual scholarship in her honor.

◆ Canada's most cherished voice

A native of Galt (now Cambridge), Ont., Peter Gzowski (1934–2002; *below*) cut his journalistic teeth on newspapers in Timmins and Chatham, Ont., and Moose Jaw, Sask., before being hired by *Maclean's*, becoming managing editor of the news magazine at the unprecedented age of 28. Joining CBC Radio in the 1970s, he hosted the eclectic *This Country in the Morning*, which he left to host *90 Minutes Live*, a late-night TV talk show that failed after a few seasons. In 1982, Gzowski returned to radio as host of *Morningside*, a show he once described as "a sort of village bulletin board for the nation."

In over 30,000 interviews as well as in real life, Gzowski had a laid-back, disheveled charm, and an uncanny ability to relate to people from all walks of life. "Peter binds the country together. He illumines it from within," former UN ambassador Stephen Lewis wrote in 1988.

For Peter's listeners the light went out in 1997, when he declined to renew his contract and his last show aired. In New York later that year, Gzowski received the prestigious Peabody award for excellence in broadcasting; the first Canadian ever to receive the honor. He also founded the Peter Gzowski Invitational Golf tournament, raising $7 million for literacy projects in Canada. In 2002 Gzowski lost his long battle with emphysema, and a nation mourned the loss of one of its most cherished voices.

◆ CHUM's nostrums

The mighty CHUM 1050AM in Toronto was first licensed in 1945 to promote patent medicines. CHUM's license holder, Jack Q'Part, was a fast-talking entrepreneur who manufactured and marketed such palliative concoctions as Mason's 49 (*"Wheeze and sneeze and even freeze/ You'll soon be feeling fine/Call your drugstore an'/Be sure to ask for Mason's 49"*). While the patent business flourished, CHUM's ratings didn't. Q'Part's partner eventually agreed to buy the station and quickly established music and variety programming.

◆ As it happened

When she died of leukemia, few knew of her 15-year battle with the illness that killed Barbara Frum (1937–92; *right*), one of Canada's most respected journalists. Best known as the unflappable host of CBC Radio's influential current-affairs program *As It Happens* throughout the 1970s, Frum brought her incisive interviewing technique to the medium of television, where she grilled world leaders and national politicians on the CBC's acclaimed nightly public affairs program *The Journal*. Frum never shied from putting her interview subjects on the spot. One of her most famous radio interviews, with hockey mogul Harold Ballard, ended abruptly when he suggested women didn't belong in broadcasting but on their backs instead. Who hung up first is still a matter of debate.

Below: CBC Radio sound room staff, circa 1938. Radio sound effects required a highly imaginative and slightly deranged mind to repurpose everyday objects for aural effect: A swiftly closed door and a heavy knife striking a cabbage became a guillotine; shaking thin sheets of hammered steel produced thunder, a twisted celery stalk became a snapped neck; and a rubber-bladed electric fan stood in for aviation dogfights.

on the air

Canada's funny corps—Air Farce, left to right: Ferguson, Goy, and Abbott

◆ Soaring satire

The Royal Canadian Air Farce made its first broadcast on Dec. 9, 1973, gleefully skewering politicians and sending up the issues of the day. The bombardiers of this comedic troupe were former radio programmer Roger Abbott, marine engineer Dave Broadfoot, theater actress Luba Goy, photographer Don Ferguson, and Welsh pub-owner John Morgan. Ferguson deftly mimicked PMs, while Broadfoot introduced such memorable characters as Big Bobby Clobber and Sergeant Renfrew. After a 24-year mission on radio, the Air Farce was promoted to TV, where it continues to spoof Canadian politics and culture.

"Greetings out there in vacuumland!"

◆ Radio's merry pranksters

In the golden age of CBC Radio's history, Max Ferguson and Allan McFee loom large. Both were inveterate pranksters, never passing up an opportunity to pull a good practical joke. In the 1950s, Ferguson (born 1924; *see page 38*) used to warm his lunch on the vacuum tubes of CBC's Halifax transmitter, and created the popular broadcasting persona of Rawhide, a hayseed country music DJ and social critic, with just 20 minutes' notice. Ferguson's sidekick was the irrepressible McFee (1913–2000), host of the immensely popular *Eclectic Circus* for 17 years. McFee regularly drove CBC brass crazy by having conversations with a mouse in his pocket on air and reading forecasts for the imaginary Dribble Lake. He is famous for his greeting "to all those out there in vacuumland."

◆ Broadcast milestones

1919: Canada's (and North America's) first licensed radio station, XWA Montreal, goes on the air

1923: CKCK Regina broadcasts first professional hockey play-by-play

1923: CN starts radio service to trains

1924: Dominion Observatory time signals first carried

1924: First broadcast of Stanley Cup playoff games

1927: First national broadcast, on July 1: Diamond Jubilee of Confederation

1933: First daily news bulletins by Canadian Press

1936: Live coverage of trapped miners in Nova Scotia carried by 58 stations across the country

1941: Broadcasts of CBC National News Service begin

1968: The Canadian Radio-Television Commission (CRTC) is established as Canada's broadcast regulator

1971: CRTC introduces 30% Canadian content regulations for AM radio

◆ I'll take Canadian game show hosts for $500

Up to 20 million viewers per evening tune in to *Jeopardy!*, the game show hosted by Sudbury native Alex Trebek (born 1940). Mr. Trebek learned the ropes as game show host on *Reach for the Top*, a CBC quiz program featuring high school teams from across the country which began in the early 1960s and ran for two decades. Trebek originally moved to California to host *The Wizard of Odds*, a game show developed by fellow Canadian Alan Thicke. He has coauthored *The Jeopardy! Book: The Answers, the Questions, the Facts and the Stories of the Greatest Game Show in History*.

Canada begins its broadcast day

◆ Do not adjust your set

Born on the stage of Toronto's Second City comedy club, *SCTV* was Canada's answer to England's Monty Python and America's *Saturday Night Live*, a manic, stream-of-consciousness, skit-based series set in a fictitious television station in the equally fictitious town of Melonville. Dave Thomas, John Candy, Eugene Levy, Catherine O'Hara, Andrea Martin, Joe Flaherty, Rick Moranis, and Martin Short first introduced the eccentric denizens of Melonville on the Global network in 1976. Colorful characters like "hosers" Bob and Doug MacKenzie (Thomas and Moranis), spastic Ed Grimley (Short), scary movie host Count Floyd (Flaherty), polka kings the Schmenge Brothers (Candy and Levy) and station manager Edith Prickley (Martin) became fixtures in Canadian popular culture. *SCTV* ran for seven years, winning two Emmy Awards for writing, and providing the launching pad for its immensely talented pool of comedic talent: Candy (*see page 251*) became the biggest star, while Moranis became a director, and O'Hara, Levy, Flaherty, Martin, and Short went on to be successful character actors.

◆ Viewer discretion was advised

It seems hard to believe, in a day and age when sex, violence, and coarse language have become staples of prime-time programming, that many opposed CBC Television when inaugural telecasts took place in Montreal and Toronto in September of 1952. (Ottawa and Vancouver went on the air the following year.) The resistance to the new service could have had something to do with the fare the 150,000 Canadians who already had TV sets were watching on American stations.

Television "gives the children bad eyes, makes them unable to sleep, and unable to study," a Toronto school trustee complained. A teachers' organization worried: "Surely crouching in a chair or stretching out on the floor for hours in a stuffy overheated living room cannot be good for any child. What effect will it have on their posture and eyesight?" This was nothing compared to the moral indignation when *Hilda Morgan*, a play about an unwed mother, was aired in November 1952. "Filth of that kind" must not be permitted on Canada's airwaves, Opposition Leader George Drew told Parliament.

◆ Look up—look waaay up

For 26 years between 1959 and 1985, Canadian preschool children looked forward to a kind giant lowering the drawbridge, gathering some tiny furniture (including a rocking chair for those who liked to rock), and inviting them to "look up—look waaay up," to enjoy 15 minutes of music, reading and fun. Said by many to be the inspiration for *Mr. Roger's Neighborhood*, *The Friendly Giant* was Canada's most beloved children's program. The show, as well as its puppets—the harp-playing rooster Rusty and loquacious giraffe Jerome—were the brainchild of Wisconsin-born Bob Homme (1919–2000), who wanted to create a safe, familiar place where kids could be exposed to books and music. Homme was an accomplished musician; he played the clarinet when he was given the Order of Canada in 1990.

◆ Canadian TV trivia

1. What was the name of the trunk in which Mr. Dressup kept all his costumes?
2. What was the name of Nick Adonidas' (Bruno Gerussi's) boat on *The Beachcombers* (1972–89)?
3. What was the name of the first Canadian science-fiction series?
4. Which writer of *The King of Kensington* (1975–1980) went on to produce a humorous mystery series about a reporter who became a psychic?
5. What do Canadian illusionist T. A. Kreskin's initials stand for?
6. What were the school colors of Degrassi Jr. High (1986–89)?
7. Where did the first television station in Canada broadcast from?
8. Who played both the voice of Spiderman on TV and the "lawbreaker" who illustrated strange and arcane laws in *This Is the Law* (1971–81)?
9. Which 1990s TV crime drama pilot would have been illegal to film in Canada with the proper costumes?
10. What late-60s CBC series starred John Vernon as a tough-as-nails coroner and was based on the life of Toronto coroner Mort Shulman?
11. When were color television signals transmitted by Canadian stations for the first time?
12. Which Newfoundland-based comedy troupe featured many of the stars of *This Hour Has 22 Minutes*?

◆ Shatner went where no man had gone before

Montreal-born William Shatner (born 1931; *left*) has many roles to his credit but seems destined to be remembered for his role as James T. Kirk, captain of the USS *Enterprise* on the seminal 1960s series *Star Trek*. Shatner's acting career began in Montreal, where he graduated from McGill University. The Stratford Festival was in its infancy when Shatner was cast as understudy to Christopher Plummer (*see page 249*) in *Henry V*. When Plummer became ill, Shatner appeared in his stead and caught the critics' attention. High profile roles on stage, in television, and on Broadway followed, eventually leading to the role that took him "where no man had gone before." Shatner has also dabbled in singing (his rendition of *Lucy in the Sky With Diamonds* is regarded by many as an awful classic), and a more successful line of sci-fi novels.

◆ Intellectual slapstick

Revues at their Toronto high school first paired Frank Shuster (1916–2002) with Johnny Wayne (1918–1990), Canada's most popular comedic duo. The two reunited during World War II, when they wrote and performed for *The Army Show*, which many regard as the font of all Canadian comedy. After the war, they had their own radio show before Ed Sullivan invited them on his legendary stage in 1950 for the first of 67 appearances. Their witty puns and gags betrayed a keen intelligence; indeed their routine was once called "intellectual slapstick." One acclaimed routine recast Julius Caesar's assassination as a 1940s hardboiled detective mystery; another featured a Shakespearean baseball team. *The Wayne and Shuster Hour* was a staple of Canadian television in the 1980s.

◆ Answers

1. The tickle trunk
2. The Persephone
3. *The Starlost* (1973–74)
4. Louis Del Grande, *Seeing Things* (1981–87)
5. "The Amazing"
6. Blue and purple
7. Montreal. Station VE9EC, jointly owned by radio station CKAC and La Presse, started transmitting music and a test card Oct. 9, 1931.
8. Paul Soles
9. *Due South* (1994–97). It is illegal to impersonate a Mountie in Canada; so the producers had to alter Paul Gross' costume slightly. The Mounties eventually came around and donated a costume.
10. *Wojeck* (1966–68)
11. 1966
12. CODCO

Fay Wray

Norma Shearer

Raymond Burr

a cast of canadians

◆ Stage-struck engineer

Toronto-born Walter Huston (1884–1950) gave up engineering to join a road show and was reasonably successful on stage and in vaudeville by the time his son was born in 1906. His new family responsibilities prompted a return to engineering, but after a few years he was drawn back to the stage and, in the mid-1940s, to film, where he became successful as a character actor. One of his acclaimed performances was in the title role of D. W. Griffith's *Abraham Lincoln* (1930). His son grew up to become director, screenwriter, and actor John Huston, who helmed such classics as *The African Queen* (1951) and *Treasure of the Sierra Madre* (1948), which starred Walter in a supporting role and for which father and son both won Oscars. Huston's advice to his son has become legend in the industry: "Son, give 'em a good show—and always travel first class."

◆ America's Sweetheart

One of the first actresses to conquer the silver screen was Toronto-born Gladys Smith. As the innocent-eyed, silent movie heroine Mary Pickford (1892–1979), she became "America's sweetheart," the first modern celebrity. At her mother's behest, Smith had moved to the United States as a teenager. There she established a reputation as a Broadway actress before going on to Hollywood, winning the hearts of movie-goers worldwide for some two decades, and becoming the most photographed woman of her time. In the 1920s, she and husband Douglas Fairbanks were known as "Hollywood's Royal Family." Pickford gave up her acting career after she and Fairbanks divorced in 1935. She received an honorary Oscar in 1976.

◆ Fay Wray's leading man went ape for her

"They told me I was going to have the tallest, darkest leading man in Hollywood," Fay Wray (1907–97) said in 1933. The Medicine Hat, Alta., native was already a Hollywood veteran by then, having shot to fame in Erich von Stroheim's *The Wedding March* (1928). Yet Wray's mysterious leading man was not Gary Cooper, Fredric March, or William Powell (all men she would star with later in her career), but King Kong, who took her to the top of the Empire State Building—and into the pages of movie history.

◆ Her eyes were too blue

"Go back to Canada, and forget the stage," producer Florenz Ziegfeld advised Montreal-born Norma Shearer (1908–83). Director D. W. Griffith was even more to the point: "You'll never make it in movies; your eyes are too blue." She ignored the advice of both men and went on to an enormously successful career that included five Academy Award nominations. Shearer's husband, renowned MGM producer Irving Thalberg, played a critical role in guiding her career. After his death in 1936, Shearer made several poor career choices, including turning down starring roles in *Mrs. Miniver* (1942) and *Gone With the Wind* (1939). She retired in 1942.

◆ Movie villain, TV hero

A native of New Westminster, B.C., heavy set, sad-eyed Raymond Burr (1917–93) had worked on stage and in radio before he began the film career where he was frequently cast as the villain in movies such as *The Blue Gardenia* (1953) and *Rear Window* (1954). In 1957, he switched from film to TV and from villain to hero, playing starring roles first as the crusading

Leslie Nielsen

Gordon Pinsent

Donald Sutherland

lawyer *Perry Mason* (1957–66) then as the wheel-chair-bound detective *Ironside* (1967–75).

◆ Lone Ranger's sidekick

Forever associated with his role as Tonto in the Lone Ranger movies, Jay Silverheels (1919–80) was born Harold Jay Smith on the Six Nations Reserve in Ontario. Even as a youth, he achieved fame for his boxing and lacrosse-playing prowess, but it was his speed as a runner that attracted the most attention, prompting his Mohawk chief grandfather to formally rename him Jay Silverheels. When his lacrosse team played in Hollywood during a North American tour, Silverheels attracted the attention of comedian Joe E. Brown, who helped get the young Ontario man started in movies.

◆ Second banana no more

"My life is a kind of vacation," Regina-born Leslie Nielsen (born 1926) has said of his successful screen career. Early on, the Mountie's son who had served in the RCAF and worked as a DJ in Calgary had turned down roles as *Gunsmoke*'s Marshal Dillon and as one of the Cartwright sons in *Bonanza*. Instead, he played dozens of supporting roles, including a powerful performance as the ocean liner captain in *The Poseidon Adventure* (1972) before he found his greatest fame and financial rewards with the slapstick movie spoofs *Airplane!* (1980) and *The Naked Gun* (1988).

◆ Baron Von Klingon?

Indelibly associated with Baron Von Trapp in *The Sound of Music* (1965), Toronto-born actor, writer, and director Christopher Plummer (born 1927) has triumphed in several roles before and since. He has starred in some 60 major motion picture roles and won many major stage and screen awards. Great-grandson of Prime Minister John Abbott (*see page 282*), Plummer's acting career began on the Canadian stage, from which he went to Broadway in the early 1950s. One of his early triumphs was in a three-hour British television presentation of *Hamlet*. An actor of extraordinary range, Plummer's memorable roles include Field Marshal Rommel in *Night of the Generals* (1967), the psychopathic bank robber in *The Silent Partner* (1978), Klingon General Chang in *Star Trek VI—The Undiscovered Country* (1991) and *60 Minutes'* Mike Wallace in *The Insider* (1999).

◆ The Rowdyman

Actor and author Gordon Pinsent (born 1930) got his early acting experience with repertory companies in his native Newfoundland and Theatre 77 in Winnipeg. He has since appeared in plays in Winnipeg, Toronto, and the Stratford Festival, as well as on radio and television. Pinsent has written plays, screenplays, and novels, and he wrote and starred in both the screen and musical versions of his book about a womanizing, alcoholic rogue, *The Rowdyman* (1972). Pinsent played the ghost of Mountie Benton Fraser's father in the hit TV series *Due South* (1994–97), and is currently enjoying his small role as chronic liar Hap Shaughnessy on the cult hit *The Red Green Show*.

◆ The laconic superstar

Saint John, N.B., is the hometown of tall, laconic Donald Sutherland (born 1934), whose prodigious filmography has made him Canada's best-known actor. A disc jockey at a Nova Scotia radio station in his teens, Sutherland began acting during his college days at the University of Toronto. After studying at the London Academy of Music and Dramatic Art, Sutherland had many appearances on the London stage before he shot to stardom in 1970 with his role

Jim Carrey Geneviève Bujold Margot Kidder

as the irreverent Hawkeye Pierce in *M*A*S*H*. His most acclaimed roles include *The Dirty Dozen* (1967), *Klute* (1971), *Don't Look Now* (1973), *Ordinary People* (1980), and *Bethune* (1982). Sutherland is the first to admit that his long, expressive face can give directors pause. As guest of honor at a 1998 tribute by the American Film Institute, he described how one filmmaker had responded when he auditioned for the role of a next-door neighbor. Sutherland's reading was the best the auditioning filmmakers had ever seen, but they hesitated to give him the part, saying he didn't look like he'd ever lived next door to anyone.

a cast of canadians

◆ Man of 1,000 voices

The gift for mimicry that would earn the epithet "man of a thousand voices" for Rich Little (born 1938), became evident during his Ottawa school days. His ability to convulse a classroom prompted one teacher to tell him he should make a living imitating people. Little took the advice to heart and soon he was presenting his take-offs of politicians and other public figures to sell-out audiences across the country. Eventually he moved to the United States where he was immensely popular on television and in one-man shows that toured the world.

◆ Canada's class clown

Dubbed "elastic-faced" and "rubber-limbed" by reviewers, Newmarket, Ont., native Jim Carrey (born 1962) has been described by *Time* magazine as "the first star who is a live-action toon." From being the class clown at school, Carrey was forced to do factory work at 13, when his father lost his job. To hide his anger, Carrey began developing a sense of humor

and at age 15 he began presenting his kamikaze-style comedy that eventually made him an international sensation. From Toronto comedy clubs he moved on to Los Angeles. Film success followed, including roles as diverse as the gonzo pet detective *Ace Ventura* (1994), *The Cable Guy* (1996; the first time an actor earned $20 million for a movie), the Grinch (in the 2000 live-action reworking of *The Grinch Who Stole Christmas*) and gonzo performance artist/comic Andy Kaufman in *Man on the Moon* (1999). Carrey won the 1999 Golden Globe Award for his dramatic portrayal of a man being watched by the world in *The Truman Show*.

◆ Usherette job financed Bujold's studies

A job as a cinema usherette helped Montreal-born Geneviève Bujold (born 1942) work her way through drama school. She was visiting France when she was chosen to appear opposite Yves Montand in *La Guerre est finie* (1965). Later she appeared in both Canadian and French productions before winning international renown as Anne Boleyn in *Anne of a Thousand Days* (1969). Directors as disparate as Clint Eastwood, Louis Malle, and David Cronenberg (*see page 257*) were drawn to Bujold's versatile talents, and she went on to star in *King of Hearts* (1967), *Kamouraska* (1974), *Coma* (1978), and *Dead Ringers* (1988).

◆ Actor and activist

The daughter of an explosives expert in Yellowknife, N.W.T., husky-voiced Margot Kidder (born 1948) is most often associated with the role of Lois Lane, played opposite Christopher Reeves, in *Superman* (1978). Educated at the University of British Columbia, Kidder has always been outspoken about

John Candy
Dan Aykroyd
Michael J. Fox

her beliefs, her politics and her personal life (which included a brief affaire with Prime Minister Pierre Trudeau). In 1996 Kidder was found wandering, disoriented in Los Angeles. She was diagnosed manic depressive. After recovering her health, Kidder now campaigns for understanding of mental illness.

◆ Big-hearted John

John Candy (1950–94), a big man who fought a life-long battle with his weight, dealt with the inevitable cruel jokes about his girth the best way he knew how: by making people laugh. A native of Toronto, Ont., Candy's comic capacity first got wide exposure with Toronto's highly talented Second City troupe (*see page 246*). At an *SCTV* party in Los Angeles, Candy met Steven Spielberg, who offered him a part in *1941*, a 1979 war farce, and from there Candy went on to play scores of crass but lovable comic characters in films like *Splash* (1984), *Planes, Trains and Automobiles* (1987), and *Uncle Buck* (1989). Film critic Pauline Kael described Candy as "a mountainous lollipop of a man, and preposterously lovable." In 1994, at age 43, this much beloved actor died suddenly of a heart attack in Mexico, filming a western entitled *Wagons East*.

◆ Blues Brother Dan

One of a host of Canadians who found success in Hollywood, Dan Aykroyd (born 1952) began developing his comedic standup routines while attending Carleton University in his Ottawa hometown. His big break came in 1975 on the irreverent *Saturday Night Live*. One of the characters he portrayed was Elwood, half of the infamous Blues Brothers with John Belushi. Aykroyd and Belushi recorded two records as the ersatz blues duo and took their act to the big screen in *The Blues Brothers* (1980). Aykroyd proved his mettle as an actor in many hit films like *Trading Places*

(1983), *Ghostbusters* (1984), *Driving Miss Daisy* (1989), *Sneakers* (1992), and the 1997 TV miniseries *The Arrow*. Aykroyd takes his blues seriously—in 1994 he co-founded House of Blues, a U.S. chain of restaurants and nightclubs featuring live blues music.

◆ Charms with comic flare

Edmonton native Michael J. Fox (born 1961) came to prominence playing the neo-conservative yuppie Alex P. Keaton in *Family Ties* (1982–89). Switching to the screen, he starred in the successful *Back to the Future* series of movies as the time-traveling Marty McFly. While Fox made numerous movies after that, he made a celebrated return to television in the comedy *Spin City* (1996–2002), and won an Emmy for his role as Deputy Mayor Mike Flaherty. In 1998, Fox stunned viewers and fans by admitting he had been battling Parkinson's disease for several years. After leaving *Spin City* in 2000, Fox wrote a memoir, *Lucky Man*, and established the Michael J. Fox Foundation for Parkinson's Research.

◆ Mike Myers finds his groove

Wayne Campbell, the character he played for six years on TV's *Saturday Night Live* and later in two *Wayne's World* movies, made Mike Myers one of the hottest comics of the 1990s. Myers (born 1964) grew up in Scarborough, Ont. (the suburban inspiration for much of *Wayne's World*), and got his show-business start with Toronto's Second City Comedy Troupe. Myers went on to create the groovy, gormless Austin Powers in a popular string of movie spoofs sending up the swinging '60s. A long-time hockey fan, Myers has named his three dogs 99 (after Wayne Gretzky), Gilmour (after Doug Gilmour, who captained Toronto's Maple Leafs), and Borchevsky (after the Leafs' Nikolai Borchevsky).

EDISON'S GREATEST MARVEL

THE VITASCOPE

"Wonderful is The Vitascope. Pictures life size and full of color. Makes a thrilling show."
NEW YORK HERALD, April 24, '96.

◆ Ottawa saw Canada's first movies

Canada's first publicly screened movies were shown in Ottawa on July 21, 1896, three months after Thomas Edison had given the first commercial showing of his newly invented projector, the vitascope (*left*), in New York. Ottawa businessmen Andrew and George Holland promptly purchased several vitascopes, which they sold to showmen in Toronto, Ottawa, and Montreal. In 1896 also, Montrealers got a demonstration of Parisian brothers Louis and Auguste Lumière's cinématographe, the projection system from which the word "cinema" is derived.

Canada's first permanent cinemas were the Edison Electric Theatre of Vancouver, which opened in 1902, and the Ouimetoscope of Montreal and Theatorium of Toronto, both of which opened in 1906.

Movies cost a quarter in 1906

◆ First affordable family outings

When the first cinemas opened in the early 1900s, some proclaimed going to the movies was akin to going to hell in a handbasket. The idea of men and women sitting together in darkened rooms shocked some morally upright souls. Even so, audiences flocked to the cinemas sprouting across the country. At five to 25 cents admission, movies gave the poor their first-ever affordable family outings. In Montreal, a seven-piece orchestra entertained during intermissions at the 1,000-seat Grand Ouimetoscope, which offered twice-daily, $2^{1}/_{2}$-hour shows, as well as advance ticket sales, reserved seats and stalls, and featured a splendid marble and ceramic lobby and cloakroom, facilities unsurpassed in North America at that time. After the Ouimetoscope underwent a $50,000 expansion in 1907, admission was increased to 35 cents. Owner Leo-Ernest Ouimet (1877–1972) also acquired camera equipment and began making "actuality" films of family gatherings, election campaigns, and bridge construction. These were shown in cinemas he established throughout Quebec and the Maritimes.

◆ Short cuts

Yorkton, Sask., is home to North America's oldest continuously running short film festival. Since 1947, filmmakers and film buffs converge on the city each May for screenings of short films and videos that culminate in presentation of the Golden Sheaf awards.

◆ Mounties, bears were early film stars

An Acadian Elopement (1907), a saccharine love story about a Quaker maiden living in Nova Scotia, was the first U.S. film about Canada. It was followed by dozens of movies about Mounties, bears, hunters, and pioneers. All were filmed by Hollywood companies that regularly sent camera crews to Vancouver and northern British Columbia to film outdoor melodramas.

Keystone Kops chief

Born in Danville, Que., to working-class Irish immigrants, actor, writer, director, and self-made mogul Mack Sennett (1880–1960; *above*) dreamed of becoming an opera singer even during his early years as a laborer in New England. A chance encounter with Marie Dressler in 1902 convinced him to try his luck on the New York stage, where he worked in burlesque and musicals.

After a time, Sennett found work in Manhattan's Biograph Studios, performing in shorts directed by master director of the day D. W. Griffith. There Sennett learned the filming, editing, and directing techniques he employed when he and two others founded Keystone Pictures in 1912. Under Sennett's direction, Keystone went on to become a leader in slapstick comedy productions, such as the Keystone Kops. Charlie Chaplin was one of several stars who began their careers at Keystone, and starred in some 35 Keystone comedies.

When he gave up the Keystone trademark, Sennett founded Mack Sennett Comedies. His slapstick did not transfer well to sound, although Sennett himself adjusted well to the new medium. He worked as a producer and director at other studios, producing musical shorts starring Bing Crosby and comedy shorts starring W. C. Fields.

First Canadian newsreels and shorts

Canada's first private film company, Associated Screen News, was founded by the Canadian Pacific Railway in 1920. Over the next 38 years, it produced newsreels and two widely released series of short variety films, Kinograms in the 1920s and Canadian Cameos in 1932–54. The latter were produced, directed, and with one exception, written by one of the era's most talented filmmakers, Gordon Sparling (1900–93).

27 died making Canada's first talkie

Twenty-seven people died making *The Viking*, Canada's first talking movie. A cinematographic triumph, the film is the story of romance set against Newfoundland's once-thriving sealing industry. Filmed in 1930 by 28-year-old American explorer and filmmaker Varick Frizzell, its cast included sealers as well as actors.

Dissatisfied with some of the test screenings, Frizzell and 27 others set out in March 1931 to reshoot scenes. Six days out to sea, the ship exploded. Of those on board, only one crew member survived. The original film was later released.

New Brunswick junk dealer's son founded MGM

Certain Canadian expatriates in the United States were among the legendary entrepreneurs who got in on the ground floor of the Hollywood film business. Louis B. Mayer (1885–1957), son of a junk dealer from Saint John, N.B., had already acquired and renovated several New England movie theaters, when, in 1917, he formed the production company that eventually became Metro-Goldwyn-Mayer. Film distribution was the entry point of London, Ont., native Jack L. Warner (1892–1978), and his brothers, founders of the prestigious Hollywood studio Warner Bros.

◆ Evangeline was first Canadian feature film

Evangeline, the first Canadian feature-length dramatic film, was made in Nova Scotia's Annapolis Valley in 1913. It was filmed by the Canadian Bioscope Company, a division of the Charles Urban Trading Company of London, which had been hired by the CPR to make films about Canada. A critical and financial success, the 50-minute production was based on Longfellow's poem about the Canadian expulsions. In 1914, *Variety* called it "a work of art." No prints have survived.

◆ The realist who founded the NFB

In 1939, Canada invited Scottish-born documentary master John Grierson (1898–1972) to report on Canadian filmmaking. Grierson's report led to the foundation of the National Film Board (NFB), where Grierson trained and developed a generation of brilliant filmmakers whose work reflected Canada and Canadians to the world. The NFB became famed for feature-length documentaries and animated films. Grierson's kitchen-sink attitude toward realism had a deep, long-term influence on Canadian film. "Art is not a mirror," he said, "but a hammer. It is a weapon in our hands to see and say what is good and right and beautiful."

John Grierson (right)

Nanook of the North

Donald Brittain (left)

◆ Early docs were travelogues

Canada's documentary filmmaking tradition began during the 1920s with short films about forests, wheat fields, fauna, and fish. Films such as *Battling with Muskies*, an exciting 1927 documentary about fishing in Hudson, Ont., were widely distributed at home and abroad largely through the efforts of Raymond Peck (1886–1927) and the government-sponsored Motion Picture Bureau, which was formed in 1923 to "publicize Canada and Canadian products" and to "encourage tourism."

◆ Nanook was first documentary

American filmmaker Robert Flaherty (1884–1981) first experimented with film while working as a surveyor for Sir William MacKenzie in Baffin Island and the Ungava Peninsula in the early 1900s. His 21,000 meters of film documenting the life of native people in the Arctic went up in smoke when his cigarette ignited his negative. Undaunted, Flaherty returned to Hudson's Bay in 1922 to film *Nanook of the North*, which captured the daily life of an Inuit hunter. *Nanook* is cited by film historians as the first feature-length documentary. Flaherty's pupil and friend John Grierson (*see above*) coined the term "documentary" to describe the dramatization of the lives of ordinary people in a 1926 review of one of Flaherty's films.

◆ Donald Brittain documented Canada

After graduating from Queen's University in Kingston, Ont., Donald Brittain (1928–89) was a police reporter for the Ottawa *Journal* in the early 1950s, before he worked as a foreign correspondent in Europe, Mexico, and Africa. He joined the NFB in 1955 as a screenwriter, where he showed a flair for humanizing public figures and events in some of Canada's most important documentaries: *Fields of Sacrifice* (1963), about the countless lives given by Canadians in war, *Never a Backward Step* (1966), about press tycoon Roy Thomson (*see page 103*)

and *Ladies and Gentleman, Mr. Leonard Cohen* (1965). In the 1980s, Brittain championed a new form of documentary, the docu-drama, in *Sweetheart: The Saga of Hal C. Banks* (1985; *see page 153*). Brittain's work is marked by a remarkable humanism and a passion for the truth; he once famously said, "Since they went to the trouble of inventing the talkies, I figured I might as well make some noise."

John Street

◆ Zale Dalen's cutting edge

Canadian director Zale Dalen (born 1947), director of the cult hits *Skip Tracer* (1977) and *The Hounds of Notre Dame* (1980), was directing episodic television when he got bitten by the digital video bug. Inspired by the European filmmaking collective Dogme 95—which eschews production values and fancy camera work for a more direct, improvisational approach to filmmaking—Dalen helped found the Volksmovie Group, an Internet-based group of young, self-financed independent filmmakers shooting on digital video. A Volksmovie could be defined as a motion picture made by "the people," not the movie industry. "The only aesthetic rule is that there are no rules," they declare on their Web site. "Success is measured by the impact on the intended audience."

◆ Canadian cinema's golden age

A new generation of Canadian filmmakers emerged in the 1960s, partly inspired by the documentary work of the NFB (*see opposite page*), where most had been trained. Their distinctly Canadian dramas included Larry Kent's controversial *Bitter Ash* (1963), David Sector's 1965 *Winter Kept Us Warm* (the first Canadian film selected for the Cannes film festival), Don Shebib's 1970 breakthrough *Goin' Down the Road* (*see page 257*), and Zale Dalen's *The Hounds of Notre Dame* (1980). Many talented directors, such as Daniel Petrie, Arthur Hiller, Ted Kotcheff, and Norman Jewison (*page 257*) distinguished themselves behind the camera abroad. This golden age was followed by a Hollywood invasion in the 1980s where a slate of forgettable movies was shot in Canada to take advantage of tax shelter provisions. The next generation of Canadian filmmakers, whose ranks include David Cronenberg, Phillip Borsos, Atom Egoyan, Patricia Rozema, Denys Arcand, and Anne Wheeler (*pages 257–58*) have trained their cameras back on Canada and returned Canadian cinema to the world stage.

◆ Guy Maddin's reality check

"Some movies feel they have an obligation to be realistic," says Winnipeg native Guy Maddin (born 1956). "I'm not interested in that. I want the viewer to check all pretense of reality at the door." Maddin did just that with his 1988 debut *Tales of the Gimli Hospital*, an eerie black-and-white fever dream about a smallpox epidemic in 1920s Manitoba. Maddin's subsequent idiosyncratic works, *Archangel* (1990) and *Twilight of the Ice Nymphs* (1997), rival the films of David Lynch for their technical mastery and bizarre visuals, and have gained him a cult audience worldwide.

◆ Postcards from Quebec

Warmth and gentle irony are the hallmarks of films by Claude Jutra (1930–86), one of Canada's most talented filmmakers. The son of a Montreal physician, Jutra had directed several short films for the National Film Board before making *Mon Oncle Antoine* (1971; *above*). The movie, set in Thetford Mines, Que., on Christmas Eve, is one of the most popular Canadian-made films of all time, was widely acclaimed by both English and French critics, and enjoyed a successful New York run. Jutra's next film, *Kamouraska* (1973), based on the Anne Hébert novel (*see page 235*) and starring Montreal-born Geneviève Bujold (*page 250*), did not fare as well commercially or critically; some Francophone critics charged it was escapist and lacked the nationalist subtleties of *Mon Oncle Antoine*. In November of 1986, Jutra, who was diagnosed with Alzheimer's disease, disappeared from his Montreal home. Six months later his body was found in the St. Lawrence River.

Lights, camera . . .

◆ Draftsman of the soul

Presented with the Grand Prix du Jury at the Cannes Film Festival in 1997 for *The Sweet Hereafter*, filmmaker Atom Egoyan (born 1960; *left*) accepted his award "in the name of my country, Canada." The self-taught director explained he had done so because in Canada "I have the freedom to make my films in a way that I don't think I would anywhere else." Egoyan, who was born in Cairo to Armenian parents, explores the connections between memory, relationships, and loss with a draftsman's precision in films such as *The Adjuster* (1991) and *Exotica* (1994). After its success at Cannes, *The Sweet Hereafter* went on to pick up eight Genie Awards later that year, including best actor and best director. Egoyan explored his Armenian heritage in his last film, *Ararat* (2002).

◆ Lured by the siren of cinema

Movies were a forbidden pleasure in the strict religious Ontario household where Patricia Rozema grew up. Film, however, became her passion, and she learned her craft as an assistant director on the set of David Cronenberg's films (*see opposite page*). Rozema went on to write and direct several films featuring strong roles for women, including the critically acclaimed *I've Heard the Mermaids Singing* (1987), voted one of the top 10 Canadian films of the century by *Maclean's*. In 1999 Rozema adapted Jane Austen's *Mansfield Park*.

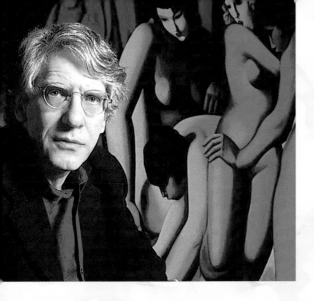

◆ The auteur of fear

A filmmaker of international status, David Cronenberg (born 1943; *left*) began making short films while studying literature at the University of Toronto. *Shivers* (1976), a film where sexually transmitted parasites run amok in an apartment block, launched his career. While his work dabbles in decidedly morbid subject matter—murderous telepaths, people aroused by car crashes, virtual reality games which inhabit and control people's nervous systems—Cronenberg excels in creating intelligent, thought-provoking films within a narrow, frequently ridiculed genre. He has also adapted what many thought were unfilmable novels by William S. Burroughs (*Naked Lunch*, 1991) and J. G. Ballard (*Crash*, 1996), the latter of which upset Time Warner's Ted Turner so much he threatened to have it pulled from distribution in the U.S. In his spare time, Cronenberg is also a race car buff (*see page 207*).

◆ Will it play in Petrograd?

The first Canadian-made feature film ever seen by Russian audiences was Don Shebib's *Goin' Down the Road*. The 1970 story of Pete and Joey, two Maritimers who set out to make it rich in the big city, brought worldwide acclaim to Toronto-born Shebib (born 1938). Sometimes called Canada's *Easy Rider*, it singlehandedly launched the Canadian film industry in the 1970s. A restored print was screened at the Toronto Film Festival in 1998.

action!

◆ He caught Bill Miner—on film

A protégé of director Francis Ford Coppola, Vancouver director and actor Phillip Borsos (1953–95) made documentaries about logging and barrelmaking before he surprised the industry with his 1983 debut feature film *The Grey Fox*. The lyrical film chronicled the life of Bill Miner, the gentleman bandit (*see page 131*), played by veteran character actor Richard Farnsworth. Borsos tried his hand at different genres afterwards—family films (*One Magic Christmas*, 1984), thrillers (*The Mean Season*, 1985), and epic biography (*Bethune: The Making of a Hero*, 1990)—before he lost a battle with leukemia.

◆ Cinema's conscience

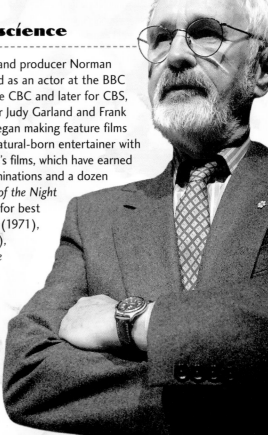

Toronto-born film director and producer Norman Jewison (born 1926) trained as an actor at the BBC before going to work for the CBC and later for CBS, where he directed shows for Judy Garland and Frank Sinatra. In the 1960s, he began making feature films that revealed him to be a natural-born entertainer with a social conscience. Jewison's films, which have earned him 45 Academy Award nominations and a dozen Oscars, include *In the Heat of the Night* (winner of the 1967 Oscar for best picture), *Fiddler on the Roof* (1971), *Jesus Christ Superstar* (1973), *Moonstruck* (1986), and *The Hurricane* (2000). In 1986, Jewison established the Canadian Film Centre in Toronto as a place where members of Canada's film and television community could advance their artistic, technical, and business skills.

◆ Canadian box office champ

The all-time highest grossing, Canadian film remains *Porky's* (1981), a low-budget sophomoric comedy about juvenile hijinks in a 1950s high school. The film took in over $12 million in its initial release. Synonymous with bad taste cinema, director Bob Clarke (born 1941) was also responsible for Sylvester Stallone singing country music in *Rhinestone* (1984).

◆ Is Snow White a Winnipegger?

In the early 1930s, Charlie Thorson, a photoengraver for Eaton's mail-order catalog, spent his lonely winter nights at Winnipeg's Wevel Café, doodling caricatures of the waitresses and patrons. He was infatuated by one waitress in particular, a raven-haired beauty, to whom he wanted to propose, but could never work up the courage.

In 1934 Thorson moved to sunny California to work for the fledgling Walt Disney Studios. He was drafted as a character designer on an ambitious project called *Snow White and the Seven Dwarfs*. While his initial sketches of Snow White were eventually redone by the famous Disney artist Grim Natwick, Thorson can claim to have had a hand in one of the greatest animated characters of all time.

◆ The man who planted hope

Conservation and ecology are the twin inspirations of internationally acclaimed animator Frédéric Back (born 1924). In 1948, Back emigrated from his native France and a few years later went to work for the French-language division of the CBC in Montreal. For decades, he designed graphics for TV shows, then in 1970 he began to concentrate on animated short films for children. In 1982, he won 20 international awards, among them an Academy Award for *Crac*, a look at Quebec history through the eyes of an old rocking chair. Six years later, he claimed another Oscar for *The Man Who Planted Trees* (*above*), the story of a European shepherd who, acorn by acorn, turns a desolate hillside into a forested paradise during a lifetime that spans two world wars. Back has been named an Officer of the Order of Canada, a Knight of the Order of Quebec, and an Officer of l'Ordre des Arts et Lettres de la France.

◆ Mr. Sandman

A sandman sculpts creatures out of sand. They build a castle and celebrate the completion of their new home, only to be interrupted by an uninvited guest. The wind blows, and the castle crumbles. Deceptively simple, Co Hoedeman's *The Sand Castle* (1977; pictured this page) went on to win over 20 awards, including the Oscar for best animated short.

A native of Amsterdam, Jacobus-Willem "Co" Hoedeman (born 1940) emigrated to Canada in 1965. He worked closely with artists from Iqaluit on his early work for the NFB, a series of animated films that used sealskin figures, soapstone carvings and drawings to illustrate Inuit legends. Traditional Inuit characters also figure in Hoedeman's most recent work, 1992's *The Sniffing Bear*, where the Bear, the Seal, and the Owl enact a cautionary tale to raise young people's awareness about substance abuse.

Norman McLaren: Canada's Walt Disney

nfluential animator Norman McLaren (1914–87) was once described as the "poet of animation" and "Canada's Walt Disney." A gentle Scotsman whose groundbreaking work experimented with color, form, humor, music, and unorthodox technique (he even drew onto and scratched the celluloid itself), McLaren joined the NFB in 1941 (*see page 255*) and went on to win more than 147 awards for the 59 short films he made over his career. *Neighbours* (which won the Oscar for short film in 1952) featured warring homeowners in a stop-motion parable about nuclear war. The graceful double exposures of *Pas de Deux* (1968) revealed McLaren's lifelong fascination with rhythm and movement.

◆ Captain of the *Yellow Submarine*

George Dunning (1920–79) was a journeyman animator from Toronto who traded a career with the NFB for commercial cartoon work in England his thirties. The success of his 1965 TV series on The Beatles led The Fab Fo then in full metaphysical flower, to tap Dunning to direct their first animated ture, 1967's *Yellow Submarine*. The film tackled unusual themes for a cartoo alienation, transcendent symbolism, Jungian archetypes and universal unity— its psychedelic visuals are still being copied today. In 1967 Dunning also produced the only triple-screen cartoon, "Canada Is My Piano." Dunning was ill during much of *Yellow Submarine*'s 11-month creation, and spent most of the 1970s in failing health, and was working on Shakespeare's *The Tempest* when he died.

Below: *Norman McLaren in his studio, 1947;* Upper left: *Pas de Deux;* lower left: *Neighbours;* near left: *La Poulette Grise*

First big top in Canada

British ringmaster Francis Ricketts brought the first circus to tour Canada from London in 1798, arriving in Quebec City for their first performance. Clowns and wild animals were included in the acts.

North America's first play

Poet, playwright, and Parisian lawyer Marc Lescarbot (1570–1642) came to Acadia in 1606 with one of his clients, colonizer Jean de Biencourt de Poutrincourt, and remained for about a year. On November 14 of that year, at Port Royal—in what is now Nova Scotia—Lescarbot staged *Le Théâtre de Neptune en Nouvelle-France*, a masque in honor of de Poutrincourt's return to new France. It is thought to be the first play written and staged in North America.

Bard of joual

Quebec City-born but Montreal-bred playwright and novelist Michel Tremblay (born 1942) transformed Quebec theater with his 1968 play *Les Belles-Sœurs*, set in the working-class neighborhood of Montreal's Plateau district. For the first time Quebec audiences saw themselves on stage, speaking dialogue peppered with *joual*, a salty Québécois vernacular dialect. Over 20 plays later, Tremblay has become Canada's most-produced playwright, and his poetic, kitchen sink realism has been translated into 22 languages, including Yiddish, Scots-English (*Les Belles-Sœurs* became *The Guid Sisters*), Haitian, Hindi, and Creole. Tremblay's prizes and distinctions include Officer of the Order of Arts and Letters of France, Chevalier de l'Ordre National du Québec, and the 1994 Molson Prize for Lifetime Achievement in the Arts.

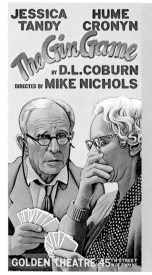

Theater's Everyman

Skilled character actor, writer, and director Hume Cronyn (1911–94) was best known for stage work with his wife, Jessica Tandy. They performed the Pulitzer Prize-winning *The Gin Game* together at Stratford, Ont., in 1978, then toured the U.S.S.R. with the play the following year. Cronyn, a native of London, Ont., made his stage debut with the Montreal Repertory Company during his student days at McGill University. Cronyn was particularly skilled at portraying ordinary people, on stage or on the silver screen. His writings include the play *Foxfire* (1980) and screenplays for the Hitchcock movies *Rope* (1948) and *Under Capricorn* (1949).

Canada's Marks Brothers

For half a century, the Marks Brothers of Christie Lake, Ont. (*left*), was one of the best known theatrical companies in Canada. From the 1870s through 1922, the firm—run by brothers Robert, George, Tom, Joe, Ernie, and Alex Marks—had several companies criss-crossing the country and the border states presenting *East Lynne*, *Uncle Tom's Cabin*, and other popular plays of the time to enthusiastic small-town audiences. Whenever a Marks Brothers production arrived in town, marching bands announced the event. The arrival of movies put the company out of business.

Theater of the air

Upton, Que., is the setting for one of the most unusual theaters in Canada. Aerial acrobatics, fireworks, elaborate life-size puppet festivals, and other large-scale spectacles are presented in the Queen of Hearts Theatre (Théâtre de la Dame-de-Cœur). Built in 1975, the open-air theater features swivel seats fitted with heating straps to keep audience members warm while they take in the action all around.

all the world's a stage

◆ Canadian theater's Big Mama

London-born Kate Reid (1939–93) was only a few months old when her parents immigrated to Canada, and settled in Oakville, Ont. Reid was studying drama at the University of Toronto, when she began her professional career with two Ontario summer stock companies: Muskoka's Straw Hat Players and Peterborough's Summer Theatre. Over a spectacular career she played thousands of roles ranging from light comedy to high drama, mostly on stage but also on radio, television, and in films. Great dramatists such as Tennessee Williams, Arthur Miller, and Edward Albee wrote roles specially for her. Williams said her portrayal of Big Mama in *Cat on a Hot Tin Roof* was the best he'd ever seen.

◆ They didn't let the sunshine in

Hair, a rock musical scored by Montrealer Galt McDermott, made its Canadian debut in Toronto's Royal Alexandra Theatre in December of 1969. The racy musical dealt with social issues of the day, such as drugs, free love and hippie culture, and its message came as a shock to Toronto audiences used to tamer fare. Some audience members were so appalled by the language of some songs they left the theater, followed later by others who were horrified when cast members began removing their clothes behind a modesty curtain.

◆ Harron's hayseeds

An exceptionally witty use of language is the hallmark of Toronto actor, writer, and broadcaster Don Harron (born 1924; *left*). Harron was a regular with the annual Spring Thaw revue in 1952 when he first introduced the character with which he is most synonymous: Charlie Farquharson, an outspoken northern Ontario hayseed farmer who went on to "write" 11 books (including the 1974 classic *Jogfree of Canada*) and become a fixture on the TV variety show *Hee Haw* for 18 years. Harron has also played major roles at Stratford and wrote the libretto for the 1956 musical *Anne of Green Gables*, Canada's longest-running musical.

◆ Solar power

Formed in 1984 by fire-breathing, stilt-walking accordionist Guy Laliberté (born 1959), Quebec's Cirque du Soleil has gone from a group of street buskers performing under a big top that seated 400 people to one of the globe's biggest cultural attractions, with rotating circuses on four continents and permanent shows in Las Vegas.

More than 20 million people have seen a Cirque show, a stunning mix of traditional big top spectacle with post-modern ideas and street attitude—and no circus animals. Each show has a specific theme and top-notch designers and performers are recruited from around the world. Their successes have included *Alegria* (1994), where clowns stage a surreal exploration of power and history; and *O* (1998), a dazzling, waterborne history of the theater.

foot notes

◆ Founded National Ballet of Canada

Celia Franca was the stage name of London-born Celia Franks (born 1921), dancer, choreographer, teacher, and founder (in 1951) of the National Ballet of Canada. Under her direction, the National Ballet presented critically acclaimed versions of *The Nutcracker, Swan Lake, Giselle*, and some 30 Canadian ballets; produced stars such as Veronica Tennant, Karen Kain, and Frank Augustyn (*see opposite*); and became one of the world's major classical ballet companies. Ms. Franca held the artistic director's post up to 1974, and continued to dance leading roles herself until 1959. She was named a Companion of the Order of Canada in 1985.

◆ Prima ballerina

Karen Kain (born 1951; *right*) was eight when she wrote, "When I grow up I am going to be a ballerina. I will be in *Giselle*." Not only would young Karen go on to conquer *Giselle*, she would grow up to become a Canadian icon and one of the world's leading dancers.

The Hamilton, Ont., native took her first ballet lesson at age six, and graduated from Toronto's National Ballet School at age 18. Her big break came two years later in Tempe, Ariz., when then-principal dancer Veronica Tennant was injured and Kain was plucked from the corps to play the lead in *Swan Lake*.

For the next two decades, her artistry delighted audiences at home and around the world. She and partner Frank Augustyn, another National Ballet School graduate, starred in numerous classical and contemporary performances worldwide, winning the best *pas de deux* at Moscow's International Ballet competition in 1973. Partnered with Rudolf Nureyev, she gained international stardom and critical acclaim for her role as Aurora in *Sleeping Beauty*. She performed with legends such as Margot Fonteyn and illustrious companies such as the Bolshoi Ballet.

In 1997, after 28 years on stage, Kain embarked on a seven-city farewell tour before retiring at the age of 46. That year, she received a Governor General's Award. Her autobiography, *Movement Never Lies*, was published in 1994.

◆ Halifax's *Show Girl*

An accomplished dancer before she was 10, Halifax-born actor, singer, and dancer Ruby Keeler (1909–93; *left*) was the headliner in various New York musicals by her late twenties. She married Al Jolson in 1928 and left her starring Broadway role in *Show Girl* to join her husband in Hollywood. There she landed leads in a string of Warner Brothers musicals, frequently costarring with Dick Powell, and they golfed at the famous Hillcrest Club (Ruby was an excellent golfer). She and Jolson divorced in 1940, and the following year she remarried and retired, except for the occasional TV spot down the years. In 1970 Ruby came out of retirement for a nostalgic and triumphant return to Broadway for a revival of the musical *No, No Nanette*.

◆ Grande dame of Canadian dance

Internationally renowned, London-born educa-
tor Betty Oliphant (born 1918; *right*) founded
the Canadian Dance Teachers Association
shortly after immigrating to Canada in 1947.
Four years later, she became ballet mistress of
the National Ballet of Canada. In 1959 she
cofounded the National Ballet School. As principal, Oliphant taught such future dance visionaries as choreographers James Kudelka and John
Alleyne. Oliphant has been honored with the
Diplôme d'honneur of the Canadian
Conference of the Arts, and the Governor
General's Award for the performing arts (1997).

◆ Real men *do* dance

The son of a Hamilton, Ont., steelworker, Frank Augustyn
(born 1953) fell in love with dance after watching the
National Ballet for the first time. The consummate skill
and elegant bearing he revealed over his illustrious career
has put to rest the old adage that men don't dance. In
the 1990s he produced the acclaimed 20-part TV series
Footnotes: The Classics of Ballet.

◆ From pirouettes to the producer's chair

A graduate of the National Ballet School and ballerina with the National
Ballet of Canada in the 1960s and 70s, Veronica Tennant (born 1946; *above*)
won international recognition when she partnered with the world's great
dancers of the day, among them Nureyev and Baryshnikov. After retiring in
1989, Tennant became a TV host and producer; her credits include films on
dancers Margie Gillis and Betty Oliphant (*top*).

◆ Full contact choreography

Maverick choreographer Edouard Lock (born 1954;
emigrated from Casablanca) and fearless dancer
Louise Lecavalier (born in Montreal in 1958;
described by one magazine as "a flame on legs")
are at the heart of the Montreal, Que.-based dance
collective La La La Human Steps. This postmodern
dance troupe's arsenal includes relentless, highly
physical, avant-garde choreography, videos projected behind the dancers, and music that has included
harpsichords, Indian ragas, and punk rock. Lock has
brought acclaimed works like *New Demons* (1987),
2 (1995), and *Salt* (2000) to Berlin, Paris, London,
Sydney, Los Angeles, and Tokyo.

canadian classics

◆ True patriot son

Composer, pianist, and music teacher, Calixa Lavallée (1842–91) of Verchères, Que., performed in concert halls in North and South America and the West Indies before becoming artistic director of New York's Grand Opera House, predecessor of the famed Metropolitan Opera. Lavallée composed the music for *O Canada* to words written by Mr. Justice (later Sir) Adolphe-Basile Routhier, at the request of the Saint-Jean-Baptiste Society of Quebec City. An English translation followed in 1908. The song was first performed publicly on the Plains of Abraham on June 24, 1880 (*see page 280*).

◆ Camelot was his kismet

Massachusetts native Robert Goulet (born 1933; *left*) was 13 years old when his family moved to Edmonton, where he began performing on radio. He had sung minor roles with the Canadian Opera Company, had performed at the Stratford Festival, and was a fixture on television, when he won international stardom as Sir Lancelot in the 1960 Broadway musical *Camelot*. After triumphant performances in Toronto and New York, Goulet was much in demand for film, concert, and nightclub roles. In the 1990s he starred in two major touring musicals, playing King Arthur in *Camelot* and Don Quixote in *Man of La Mancha*.

◆ The accidental arranger

When his concert pianist career was cut short by an accident that injured his hands, Toronto-born Percy Faith (1908–76) turned to arranging and composition. He worked as conductor-arranger of the CBC Symphony Orchestra and later with NBC, where he was musical director of "Carnation Contented Hour." From 1947 until his death he worked for Columbia Records, where he arranged hits by artists like Tony Bennett. Faith had a major hit himself with *Delicado* in 1952, but it was his version of Max Steiner's *Theme From a Summer Place* that he is best remembered for. It stayed atop the charts for 21 weeks, becoming the #1 record of 1960.

◆ From hardware to the high C's

Jonathan Vickers' singing career began in church choirs and progressed through light operettas to powerful performances in dramatic operatic roles—notably *Peter Grimes* and *Parsifal*—around the world showcasing his clarion, towering tenor voice. The road to the top for the Saskatchewan-born superstar (born 1926) hasn't been easy; he once worked as a hardware salesman to enable him to have time for his singing engagements. A three-year contract in 1956 at London's Covent Garden gave him the breakthrough he needed.

◆ Toast of Paris

Once the hub of a prosperous fishery, the Notre Dame Bay port of Twillingate, Nfld., boasted its own newspaper and championship cricket team in the 1800s. It was also the home of Newfoundland soprano Georgina Stirling (1867–1935; *left*), who, under the stage name of Marie Toulinquet (a variation on her hometown's name), became a world renowned opera singer who was the toast of the Paris Opera and La Scala, Milan. In the late 1800s, the young opera singer's voice failed. Her career over, she returned to Twillingate, where she died in 1935. Her story lives on in the Twillingate Museum, and a monument marks her grave in a local cemetery.

◆ Our foremost contralto

One of North America's most sought-after singers and Canada's foremost contralto, Montreal native Maureen Forrester (born 1930) has received a host of national and international accolades, including a Companion of the Order of Canada, membership in the Juno Hall of Fame, and some 30 honorary doctorates from Canadian universities.

MAUREEN FORRESTER

GRANDE DAME OF SONG
LA GRANDE DAME DE LA LYRIQUE

Her richly dark voice has sung the gamut from Gilbert and Sullivan to Gustav Mahler on world stages with the finest orchestras and greatest conductors. Forrester is considered one of the finest interpreters of Mahler the world has known, a fact that 8,000 spellbound Chinese discovered on her 1998 concert in Beijing. Ever a staunch promoter of Canadian artists and cultural organizations, she has discovered many young singers and premiered many Canadian composers' works.

◆ Polio couldn't silence beloved soprano

A polio victim in her youth, Lois Marshall (1924–97), Canada's most beloved soprano for decades, spent much of her first 12 years in hospital. But even then, she loved to sing and spent hours propped up in bed entertaining the hospital staff. She took voice lessons in her teens and soon was in demand on concert stages around the world. A favorite of conductors Sir Thomas Beecham and Arturo Toscanini, she was especially famed for her performances of German lieder and British folk songs. She was named an honorary fellow of the Royal Conservatory of Music in 1994.

◆ Quilico & Son, baritones

One of the leading baritones of his time, Montreal-born Louis Quilico (1925–2000) sang major roles with the best opera companies in Europe and North America, including 25 years with New York's Metropolitan Opera. At the University of Toronto, Quilico helped develop several Canadian singers, including his son Gino (*left*). In 1987, Quilico and his baritone son Gino made opera history when they became the first father-and-son team to perform at the Met.

◆ Canada's first international star

Dame Emma Albani was the stage name of Marie-Louise-Cécile-Emma Lajeunesse (1847–1930) from Chambly, Que. A renowned soprano, she was the first Canadian-born artist to distinguish herself internationally as an opera singer. Emma's mother died when she was a baby and her musician father set ambitious goals for his daughter. She was not allowed any dolls, and from a very young age had to spend four hours a day practicing her singing and piano playing. When she tried to become a nun, the convent's Mother Superior told her that God had given her a beautiful voice: "Go and use it." In Britain Dame Emma was known as the Queen of English Festivals. More than 22,000 people packed the Crystal Palace at the Handel Festival of 1877, to hear her sing the *Messiah*. At a Christmas party for newsboys sponsored by the *New York World*, one young newsboy is said to have pushed away his plate, saying: "I'd rather listen to her than eat."

◆ The Gould variations

A child prodigy who could read music at age three, wrote piano pieces when he was five, and played with the Toronto Symphony when he was 14, classical pianist Glenn Gould (1932–82; *right*) was renowned worldwide for his distinctive and eccentric tempi. In 1964, he abandoned the concert stage—he had developed an intense distaste for performing—to concentrate on studio recordings, the best known of which is Bach's *Goldberg Variations*. In the recording studio he would splice together elements of various performances to achieve his desired effect. "One of the certain effects of the electronic age," he said in a 1964 essay on Richard Strauss, "is that it will forever change the values that we attach to art."

His idiosyncratic tempo was not the only unusual thing about the Toronto pianist. Suffering from depression, he kept meticulous records of his medications and their effects. He worried obsessively about his health, wearing mufflers and gloves in the summer heat and taking his temperature every hour. He collected hotel keys, had a fascination with train travel, Canada's Arctic (*see page 159*), and '60s British pop icon Petula Clark. He became a cult figure following his death by stroke shortly after his 50th birthday.

◆ Swiss precision

The team of highly decorated Swiss Maestro Charles Dutoit (born 1943; *below*) and the Montreal Symphony Orchestra was one of the classical music world's greatest partnerships, waxing over 80 luminous, award-winning recordings since 1978, touring the globe, and putting Montreal on the map.

Some musicians charged that Dutoit, a demanding perfectionist, used fear and humiliation as motivators, and tensions were exacerbated by his increasing international commitments. An open letter in February 2002 by the Quebec Musicians Guild called Dutoit a "tyrant" who treated the musicians like "battered spouses." Unable to come to terms with the union, Dutoit stepped down from the MSO's podium that April.

◆ "78s" began in Montreal

At the turn of the century, recorded sounds were reproduced by having a pick-up needle travel over a wax cylinder. In 1900, working in his Montreal factory, German-born Emile Berliner (1851–1929) perfected the flat vulcanite discs, 17 centimeters in diameter, that turned at 78 revolutions per minute, he had invented in Washington, D.C. And thus, "78s," precursors of the vinyl LP and today's compact discs, were born. Berliner's first records featured "God Save the Queen," "The Maple Leaf Forever," and popular Canadian artists of the day.

His Master's Voice

Between 1900 and 1905, he released some 2,000 recordings that included an Iroquois chief singing ancient tribal songs, and songs such as "When Father Laid on the Carpet Floor" and "I'm Old But I'm Awfully Tough." Double-sided discs and discs of different diameters were introduced after 1905. In July of 1900, Berliner also patented "Nipper," the famous fox terrier peering into a gramophone in artist Francis Barraud's 1898 painting *His Master's Voice*. The Victor Talking Machine Company (later RCA) kept the icon for their Black Label recordings when they acquired Berliner's company in 1901.

jazz and swing

The king of New Year's Eve

Critics often disdained his musical style, but for some 50 years London, Ont.-born Guy Lombardo's Royal Canadians was the most popular band in North America. Their record sales alone exceeded 300 million, and for years the band's broadcasts were a traditional part of New Year's Eve celebrations. In addition to Guy (born Gaetano Alberto in 1902), who led the band and played violin, the members included his brothers, Carmen, saxophonist, songwriter, and singer; and Lebert, who played trumpet. Guy was almost as passionate a speedboat racer as he was a musician (*see page 207*). At his death in 1977, he had won every major U.S. speedboat race. One of his boats, as well as some of his band's colorful uniforms and his violin are among exhibits in the Guy Lombardo Music Centre, a hometown museum to his memory.

◆ The tea jingle that was an international hit

American-born jazz musician Hagood Hardy (1937–97) grew up in Ontario and was a major figure in the burgeoning Canadian recording industry. He began his career as a vibraphonist, playing jazz clubs in Toronto and New York. Later, he was much sought after as a composer of music for radio, television, and films, and as a creator of jingles. His jingle for Salada Tea, revised and recorded in 1974 as "The Homecoming," became an international hit.

◆ Moe Koffman: The swinging shepherd

Toronto-born composer and jazz musician Moe Koffman (1928–2001) chose the violin as his first instrument, but by his teens, he was performing on flute, clarinet, and saxophone, fronting his own band and various Ontario big bands of the day. He moved to New York to play, primarily as a flautist, with many of the big band greats, including Jimmy Dorsey. Upon his return to Toronto in 1958, he formed his Quartette and dashed off a jaunty instrumental called "Blues à la Canadiana," which, renamed "Swinging Shepherd Blues," became his most enduring hit.

◆ A Canadian jazz fakebook*

1929: Guy Lombardo and his Royal Canadians begin a 33-year residency playing New Year's Eve at The Roosevelt Grill in New York.

1949: Oscar Peterson debuts in *Jazz at the Philharmonic* at Carnegie Hall.

1950: Montreal trumpeter Maynard Ferguson (born 1928) draws crowds as soloist in Stan Kenton's Orchestra in New York.

1956: George's Spaghetti House, Canada's flagship nightclub for jazz, opens in Toronto. It closed in 1994.

1958: Moe Koffman Quartette releases *Swingin' Shepherd Blues*.

1964: Montreal pianist Paul Bley (born 1932) joins the October Revolution of free jazz players in New York.

1968: Trombonist Rob McConnell (born 1935) forms the 16-piece big band Boss Brass in Toronto.

1978: Joni Mitchell collaborates with jazz bassist Charles Mingus.

1980: First edition of the world-renowned Montreal Jazz Festival (*right*).

* Inexpensive alternatives to costly sheet music, fakebooks were a jazz musician's savior—mimeographed guides to the essential chord changes a player would need to fake their way through the popular hits of the day.

◆ Canada's jazz ambassador

One of the giants of jazz, Oscar Peterson (born 1925; *left*) honed his muscular, rhythmic piano style in the Montreal music scene of his teen years. Peterson's big break came in 1949, when jazz impresario Norman Granz booked him on his popular *Jazz at the Philharmonic* concert at New York's Carnegie Hall. He brought the house down. A year later, the influential jazz monthly *Downbeat* named him pianist of the year. It was an honor he would be accorded 13 more times. His pianistic speed and accuracy were legendary. When a stunned CBC announcer asked him how many hands he had, Peterson replied "Two. But I like to make 'em work hard."

In the late '50s, Peterson formed a legendary trio with bassist Ray Brown and guitarist Herb Ellis which toured the United States, Europe, and the Far East. He recorded over 200 different albums over his prodigious career, playing with luminaries such as Duke Ellington, Ella Fitzgerald, and Louis Armstrong. Some of his songs, such as "Night Train" and "One O'Clock Jump," have gone on to become classics.

◆ Nanaimo's sultry siren

Inspired by piano kings Fats Waller and Nat King Cole, Nanaimo, B.C., jazz pianist and vocalist Diana Krall (born 1964; *below*) shot to fame singing the same standards that made her heroes famous. Crossing striking ingenue looks with a sultry vocal talent, Krall won a Best Jazz Vocal Performance Grammy for *When I Look in Your Eyes* (1999).

◆ 70s disco diva

Acadian singer Patsy Gallant (born 1950) had an international hit in 1976 with *From New York to L.A.*, a disco version of Gilles Vigneault's nationalistic *Mon Pays*. The Campbellton, N.B., native joined her sisters at age 3 to sing at fairs and on radio. By the 1970s, she had become the disco diva of the day, releasing over 20 albums in English and French, and hosting a TV show. When her career at home faded, Gallant found new popularity on stages throughout Europe. In Paris, where she makes her home, she was cast in a starring role in the long-running *Starmania*.

◆ The Fab Four reunited in Toronto?

Released in the summer of 1976, Toronto pop trio Klaatu's debut album *3:47 EST* garnered little airplay or attention—until an article in the *Providence* (Rhode Island) *Journal* the following February compared the mysterious group to The Beatles and argued that the Fab Four had actually contributed to the record. The rumor that Klaatu was The Beatles shot around the world and took three years and three albums before it was debunked. Unmasked, John Woloschuk, Terry Draper, and Dee Long never did attain the status of John, Paul, George, and Ringo, although The Carpenters had a Top 40 hit with Klaatu's song *Calling Occupants of Interplanetary Craft*.

◆ Two strong winds

Ian Tyson (born 1933), a native of Victoria, B.C., and Sylvia Fricker (born 1940) from Chatham, Ont., teamed up on the Toronto coffeehouse circuit of the 1960s. As Ian  and Sylvia, the duo became one of the most popular folksinging acts of the day. Tyson had been a lumberjack, migrant farmworker, and rodeo rider, while Sylvia's early music experiences were in the hometown church choir led by her mother. Among the first to perform Gordon Lightfoot's songs (*see opposite page*), Ian and Sylvia soon became famous for their own songs (such as Ian's *Four Strong Winds*—written after Ian saw Bob Dylan write *Blowin' in the Wind* in a bar, and Sylvia's *You Were on My Mind*). They even experimented with free-form country-jazz in the 1969 band Great Speckled Bird. Eventually the couple, who had married in 1964, divorced, continuing separate, successful careers.

heart of gold

◆ Diana brought him instant fame

At age 15, Ottawa-born singer, composer, and songwriter Paul Anka (born 1941; *left*) found instant fame with *Diana*, an ode to his 18-year-old Ottawa neighbor, babysitter Diane Ayoub. At first he performed it at local functions, but it became a smash hit after he took his music and lyrics to New York. It went on to sell over 10 million copies worldwide. Anka remained a wildly popular teen idol throughout the 1950s and 60s; at one point, five of his songs were in the Top 10. While rock'n'roll and the British Invasion in the 1960s largely put an end to Anka's style of soulful crooning, he made a big comeback in 1974 with *You're Having My Baby*.

◆ From the coffeehouse to the world stage

Composer of such popular ballads as *Early Mornin' Rain*, *If You Could Read My Mind*, and *The Wreck of the Edmund Fitzgerald*, baritone balladeer-songwriter Gordon Lightfoot (born 1939; *right*) is considered by many to be Canada's finest folk artist. He first sang publicly in the church choir of his Orillia, Ont., hometown. In 1963, he was working the bars and coffeehouses of southern Ontario, singing his own songs, when Ian and Sylvia (*left*) heard him, and recorded *For Lovin' Me*, turning it into an international hit. Already a star in Canada, Lightfoot became a major international concert and recording artist in the 1970s, weaving the Canadian experience into his many timeless folk-pop hits. He has won 17 Junos and sold over 10 million of his albums worldwide. Peter, Paul and Mary, Johnny Cash, Barbra Streisand, Glen Campbell, and Elvis Presley have recorded his songs. In recognition of his contribution to Canadian culture he was inducted as an Officer of the Order of Canada in 1970 and is a charter member of Canada's Walk of Fame.

◆ P.E.I. snow buntings inspired *Snowbird*

A flock of snow buntings feeding on a Prince Edward Island beach inspired *Snowbird*, one of the biggest hit songs of the 1970s. Although songwriter/singer/guitarist Gene MacLellan found songwriting plain hard work—"I can't sit down and write any old time," he once said, "I have to be in the right frame of mind"—he wrote *Snowbird* in less than 30 minutes. A face partially disfigured by childhood polio had made MacLellan lonely and withdrawn in his early years, and he often wrote songs for himself, so he then let *Snowbird* sit around for four years before showing it to Springhill, N.S., country singer and fellow *Singalong Jubilee* star Anne Murray (born 1945; *left*). Murray's 1970 recording of the song and another MacLellan composition, *Put Your Hand in the Hand*, were international hits and launched both their careers. That year the Nashville Songwriters Association named MacLellan songwriter of the year.

Diana
PAUL ANKA
1957

Lonely Boy
PAUL ANKA
1959

Theme From "A Summer Place"
PERCY FAITH
1960

Ringo
LORNE GREENE
1964

American Woman
THE GUESS WHO
1972

Heart of Gold
NEIL YOUNG
1972

Seasons in the Sun
TERRY JACKS
1974

Sundown
GORDON LIGHTFOOT
1974

Stateside success: The first Canadian singles to hit Number One on the U.S. pop charts.

country roads

◆ The Singing Ranger

Born near Liverpool, N.S., and on his own from age 14 on, Clarence Eugene Snow (1914–99; *left*) survived by selling lobsters, insurance, Fuller's brushes, and, when all else failed, by bootlegging. He was working aboard a fishing schooner when he bought his first guitar for $5.95 from the Eaton's catalogue. In 1933, he hitchhiked to Halifax and got a spot playing guitar on a country music radio station. The show led to a two-year contract offer by RCA Victor. Snow adopted the name Hank and put together a rodeo-type show in which "The Singing Ranger" sang his songs and did trick stunts on a horse named Shawnee. Many of Snow's hits, such as *Lonesome Blue Yodel* and *I'm So Lonesome I Could Cry*, came from his own experiences, all about heartbreak, loneliness, and poverty. One of these, *I'm Movin' On*, became his theme song. Later Snow settled in Tennessee and regularly hosted and starred at the Grand Ole Opry. Over four decades he sold more than 86 million records.

◆ Queen of torch and twang

Once a rebellious cowpunk girl from Consort, Alta., singing country and polka with her band The Reclines, k. d. lang (born 1962; *right*) crossed over to become one of the finest torch singers since the great Patsy Cline on albums like *Shadowland* (1988), which swept the Canadian Country Music Awards. Her keening 1987 duet with Roy Orbison, "Crying," won her a Grammy Award. No stranger to controversy (she once claimed to be Patsy Cline reincarnated), Lang, an avowed vegetarian, ran afoul of her home province's cattle ranchers in 1990 because of her unflattering comments about beef and those who eat it.

◆ Canadian Band danced *The Last Waltz*

Originally the backup band for rockabilly king Ronnie Hawkins in the early 1960s, the group that simply called themselves The Band were guitarist Robbie Robertson, drummer Levon Helm, bassist Rick Danko, keyboardist Richard Manuel, and saxophonist Garth Hudson. After leaving Hawkins, they joined Bob Dylan, who had just gone electric, for a sensational world tour in 1965–66. When they released their 1968 debut LP *Music From Big Pink*, The Band staked out bold new territory between country, rock, and rhythm and blues. They made eight records that garnered enormous critical acclaim and a devoted audience, but no hit singles. Their farewell concert, at the Winterland in San Francisco in November of 1976, was a milestone in 1970s rock and featured performances by Hawkins, Dylan, Joni Mitchell, Eric Clapton, Van Morrison, and Neil Young, and was filmed as *The Last Waltz* by Martin Scorsese.

◆ Chatham's country rose

Olympic competition was an early goal of Chatham, Ont., native Michelle Wright (born 1962), an accomplished track and field athlete in her teens. But music became her major passion when she began playing guitar, and by 17 she had formed her own band. This smoky-voiced, Canadian country pioneer has since claimed more than 30 major music industry awards. More than a score of her songs have been Top 10 hits on Canadian country radio, including four from her best-selling 1996 album, *For Me It's You*. In 1992, with the song *Take It Like a Man*, Wright became the first Canadian-born artist to have a country music Top 10 hit in the United States. Wright won the Juno for Female Country Vocalist of the Year twice, in 1993 and 1995.

Although she now makes her home in Nashville, Tenn., Ms. Wright frequently lends her time to Canadian humanitarian projects. To acknowledge her fundraising work for hometown charities, Chatham honored its international star in 1997 by naming one of its streets the Michelle Wright Way and unveiling a specially developed floribunda hybrid, the Michelle Wright Rose.

◆ Shania's on her way

Performing since the age of eight, as a lounge act in holiday resort cabarets, and on television programs such as *The Tommy Hunter Show*, Eileen Regina "Shania" (an Ojibwa word for "I'm on my way") Twain (born 1965; *below*) led a somewhat hand-to-mouth existence as a child in northern Ontario. In her hometown of Timmins, she dreamt of security and fantasized about being a backup singer to big-name stars as she sang in local bars and helped with the reforestation program her parents operated in the Ontario bush.

Shania turned to show business in earnest in 1987 to support her sister and two brothers, when both their parents were killed in a logging truck collision. A decade later Shania had sold more albums than any female country singer in history: her 1999 CD *Come On Over* sold a staggering 36 million copies alone. Shania attributes her success to her youthful spin on a very traditional sound: "Country music is still your grandpa's music, but it's also your daughter's music," she once said. "It's getting bigger and better all the time."

◆ Chairman of the stompin' board

Now one of Canada's most popular country singers, Tom Connors grew up in Skinner's Pond, P.E.I., where he wrote his first song in 1947 at age 11. For years Connors hitchhiked around Canada, working odd jobs, and trying to interest radio stations in his songs. In 1964, the bartender at the Maple Leaf Hotel in Timmins, Ont., agreed to give Tom a beer if he would play a few songs, and regular engagements soon followed. Audiences at the Maple Leaf christened him Stompin' Tom, for his habit of forcefully keeping time with his foot. Around this time, to save the carpet, he took to using a plywood "stompin' board." Fiercely Canadian, Connors once returned his six Juno awards as a statement of protest against what he saw as the Americanization of the Canadian music industry.

The first Canadian singles certified "gold" by the Canadian Recording Industry Association, with sales of 50,000 copies

◆ Godfather of grunge

Son of journalist Scott Young, Toronto-born singer-songwriter Neil Young (born 1945; *left*) grew up in Winnipeg and began his career singing in Toronto coffee houses. Young left Toronto early on for California, where he performed with two legendary supergroups, Buffalo Springfield, who toured the U.S. in a hearse, and Crosby Stills Nash and Young. From the dark underside of the 1970s, Young and his band Crazy Horse had the million-selling hit songs "Heart of Gold," "Southern Man," and "Cinnamon Girl." The raw power of Crazy Horse would later inspire Nirvana's Kurt Cobain in the early 1990s, launching the style of "grunge" rock, typified by flannel shirts and loud, crunching guitars. Today Young appeals to both boomers and young grunge rockers alike.

In the 1980s, Young confounded his fans as he changed styles at an alarming rate, passionately testing rock's boundaries. There was the synthesizer rock of *Trans* (1982), rockabilly on *Everybody's Rockin'* (1983), traditional country on *Old Ways* (1985), and biting blues—and a swipe at the music industry—on *This Note's for You* (1988). In explaining his musical haberdashery, Young has said that the synthesizer album was an attempt of breaking through to his two sons, both of whom have cerebral palsy, and the others were a result of a general desire not to repeat himself. "I just hate being labeled," he told *Musician* magazine in 1985. "I just don't want to be anything for very long."

◆ Diamonds are forever for Bryan Adams

Melodic rock'n'roll is the stock-in-trade of Kingston, Ont.-born, Vancouver-based Bryan Adams (born 1959; *right*). Since he began waking up the neighbors and topping the charts in the 1980s, he has made more than two dozen hit singles and has had worldwide album sales exceeding 50 million. Throughout his career, Adams has lent his voice to many worthy causes, performing at scores of benefit concerts, and helping organize such extravaganzas as the 1985 "Tears Are Not Enough" Canadian all-star event for famine aid to Ethiopia. His hits include "Cuts Like a Knife" (1984), "(Everything I Do) I Do It for You" (1991), and "Have You Ever Really Loved a Woman?" (1995). His 1984 album *Reckless* was the first by a Canadian artist to be certified diamond for sales of over a million copies. Adams was made a companion of the Order of Canada in 1998.

◆ Canada's first lady of the guitar

Classical guitarist Liona Boyd (born 1950; *right*) is noted for her impeccable, clean guitar technique. She studied with both Eli Kassner and Alexandre Lagoya, and has a rare ability to play using both masters' methods of fingering. In 1976, she introduced classical guitar to North America opening for Gordon Lightfoot on tour. In her autobiography, *In My Own Key: My Life in Love and Music* (1998), Boyd described her 1970s eight-year affair with then prime minister Pierre Trudeau.

◆ She brightened pop's palette

Born Roberta Joan Anderson at Fort MacLeod, Alta., popular singer-songwriter Joni Mitchell (born 1943) was a well-known folksinger in Canada before, like Neil Young (*see opposite page*), she moved to Los Angeles in the late 1960s. There she stood out among performers because of the personal tone of her songs, their unusual melodies, and her flute-like voice. She brightened the palette of pop with a whole new set of colors on LPs like *Court and Spark* (1974) and *Heijira* (1976), and influenced a generation of singer-songwriters. "Chelsea Morning" and "Big Yellow Taxi" are among several timeless hits.

"I write in my own blood."

Among numerous awards and honors the pop legend had received down the years is the 1996 Polar Music Prize awarded by the Royal Swedish Academy of Music—the first time the prize has gone to a woman. A four-time Grammy winner, she has also received the Order of Canada and *Billboard*'s Century Award for highest creative achievement.

"I write in my own blood," Mitchell once said. "I bare intimate feelings because people should know how others feel." Perhaps nothing she wrote was as close to the bone as "Little Green," a song on her 1971 album *Blue*. In it she wrote about a daughter she gave up for adoption in 1965, when she was a 21-year-old destitute folksinger living in a Toronto rooming house. "Little Green, have a happy ending," the song said, and so it did. In 1997, Mitchell was reunited with the daughter she named Kelly (as in kelly green) Dale Anderson 32 years before.

◆ Vigneault revived the Quebec chanson

Inspired by the folksongs of his native Quebec, Gilles Vigneault (born 1928; *left*), a prospector turned librarian turned teacher, single-handedly revived the Quebec chanson, when he opened a *boîte à chanson*, delighting young café audiences with his blend of tradition and separatism. His song *Mon Pays*, which won the 1965 Sopot Song Festival in Poland, has become the anthem of Quebec nationalists.

◆ Global troubadour

After reading Jack Kerouac's *On the Road*, Ottawa folk singer-songwriter Bruce Cockburn (born 1945) began his career as a street musician in Paris. He came to national attention in the 1970s with a string of hit albums that were charged with poetic, mystical intensity. He held audiences and listeners spellbound with virtuoso guitar playing and carefully crafted lyrics. Cockburn went on to become a globetrotting troubadour and social critic, working for OXFAM and documenting the struggle for freedom and justice in songs such as "Lovers in a Dangerous Time" and "If I Had a Rocket Launcher."

The Unicorn
THE IRISH ROVERS
1978

Tu t'en vas
ALAIN BARRIÈRE
1978

Boogie Woogie Dancin' Shoes
CLAUDJA BARRY
1979

Wasn't That a Party
THE ROVERS
1981

You Needed Me
ANNE MURRAY
1984

Tears Are Not Enough
NORTHERN LIGHTS
1985

Never Surrender
COREY HART
1985

Crying Over You
PLATINUM BLONDE
1986

The first Canadian singles certified "platinum" by the Canadian Recording Industry Association, selling over 100,000 copies

◆ Sarah McLachlan's divine inspiration

Halifax native Sarah McLachlan's (born 1958; *below*) early musical development was shaped by classical training in piano, guitar, and voice, and the folk sounds of Joan Baez and Simon and Garfunkel. Renowned for her haunting voice, she was already a leading pop vocalist when she founded the all-female summer rock festival Lilith Fair in 1997.

A traveling showcase of top female acts ranging from jazz and blues to alternative rock and pop-folk, Lilith Fair went on to become the highest-grossing North American tour of the summer. Wherever it played, promising local stars were invited to perform on the festival's second and third stages, thus opening doors for scores of young female performers.

By the festival's second year, the pop songstress turned rock diva was selling albums by the million, her face had graced dozens of magazine covers, she had won her first Grammy (for best female pop vocal performance for *Building a Mystery*), and even had a private audience with Pope John Paul II in 1994 when she played at the Vatican Christmas concert.

During the final 1999 Lilith Fair, some 110 artists performed before 800,000 people in 139 concerts. Several women's charities benefited financially over the festivals, earning some $2 million from ticket sales and sponsorships.

◆ Celtic conjurer

Celtic singer-songwriter and Morden, Man., native Loreena McKennitt (born 1957; *left*) has made the leap from street busker to record executive (she runs her own record label, Quinlan Road, named for the rural road which runs past her farmhouse outside Hamilton, Ont.), along the way chalking up more than 10 million album sales worldwide.

Researching Celtic culture has taken the soprano to Venice, Italy, and the Russian steppes. On albums such as *The Visit* (1991) and *The Book of Secrets* (1997) McKennitt sees herself as a kind of musical travel writer, putting to moody music the narratives and haunting tales others express in prose.

◆ Isn't it ironic?

A child star at the age of 10 when she starred on the Nickelodeon children's series *You Can't Do That on Television*, Ottawa pop singer-songwriter Alanis Morissette (born 1974; *right*) was barely in her twenties when her 1996 sophomore LP *Jagged Little Pill* took the music world by storm, selling 33 million copies, spawning the hits "You Oughta Know" and "Ironic," and won four Grammies, including Album of the Year. In 1997, Morissette journeyed to India to escape the sudden demands of superstardom, where she found inspiration for her 1998 followup release *Supposed Former Infatuation Junkie*.

◆ Simple folk

Singer-songwriters Kate (born 1946) and Anna (born 1944) McGarrigle, children of a French and Irish musical family, began performing in Montreal coffeehouses in the 1960s. In 1975, Linda Ronstadt recorded Anna's "Heart Like a Wheel," and the sisters went on to become cult favorites for their distinctive traditional folk, Celtic, and rock stylings on albums like *Dancer with Bruised Knees* (1977). Their low-key performances echo the family singsongs that first inspired them. Music continues to run in the family—Kate's son Rufus Wainwright is a rising star in his own right, with two albums of cabaret-styled baroque pop to his name.

◆ Celine's Cinderella success story

Quebec-born Céline Dion's five-octave voice has made her one of pop's reigning divas and has sold more than 100 million albums worldwide. Born in 1968, the youngest of 14 children, she has been belting out songs since her preteens. Her first hits were in French, before she dropped the accent on her name in 1990 and began singing in English. Highlights of her career have included singing for the Pope in 1984 and the 1996 Olympic Games in Atlanta, Ga., performing the title song in the Walt Disney film *Beauty and the Beast* and raising *Titanic* to the Oscars with her song "My Heart Will Go On." Celine's Cinderella success story culminated in her fairy-tale marriage to her manager, René Angelil, in 1994. Six years later, the couple renewed their wedding vows in a lavish, eye-popping Arabian-themed ceremony—complete with camels and exotic birds—in Las Vegas.

Producer, promoter, pop star, diva

◆ Leave a song after the beep

The road to stardom was no cakewalk for Alberta-born pop singer-songwriter and six-time Juno winner Jann Arden (born 1962; *right*). She held down a variety of jobs on her way to the top, singing in lounges for rent money and battling a drinking problem, which she eventually conquered. She even tried her hand at busking in the 1970s, but got mugged for the few pieces of change in her open guitar case. Noted for the sadness of her songs as much as her self-deprecating humor, she explains that "Happiness is not something you pull out every day. It's just for special occasions." Composing for Arden is often slow and painful: the words and notes just don't come together. Other times, they come tumbling to the surface. With "Unloved," for example, the lyrics came instantly in the middle of the night—so she sang them into her telephone answering machine, in case she forgot them by morning.

Chart toppers: The best-selling Canadian singles of all time, all selling in excess of one million copies

Our body politic, from Confederation to the future

BUILDING OUR NATION

birth of a nation

◆ "Dominion from sea to sea"

Samuel Leonard Tilley (1818–96), a druggist from Gagetown, N.B., and one of the 33 Founding Fathers of Confederation, was responsible for Canada's being called a Dominion. At the London Conference of 1866, there was some discussion as to what to call Canada. Some felt it should be known as the Kingdom of Canada, but others feared this would not sit well with the United States. A strict Christian, Tilley quoted Psalm 72: "He shall have dominion also from sea to sea . . ." And so was born the Dominion of Canada and its motto: *A Mari Usque Ad Mare*.

◆ The flag that unfurled fiery passions

Canada had no flag of its own until Feb. 15, 1965, when the present maple leaf flag became our official emblem. Some 2,000 people and organizations submitted designs for the flag, which was introduced despite widespread public protests. These included a march on Ottawa, months of bitter debate in Parliament, passionate pro and con newspaper editorials and sacks of angry letters to MPs. At first the controversy swirled around discarding the Red Ensign, which was regarded as Canada's flag. When it became evident that a new flag would be introduced despite objections, the battle continued, with the new point of contention on whether the new flag should have one maple leaf or three (*right*).

◆ Constitutional work in progress

Unlike the single-document American Constitution, Canada's written Constitution—the framework by which we govern ourselves—is a collection of 25 documents (14 Acts of the British Parliament, seven Acts of the Canadian Parliament, and four British Orders-in-Council). One of its principal documents is the British North America Act, of 1867, together with all its amendments up to 1975. All these elements, along with a Canadian Charter of Rights and Freedoms, were outlined in the Constitution Act of 1982, which marked the "patriation" of the BNA Act and brought the Constitution under Canadian control.

◆ House of Commons

As Canada's elected federal legislature, the House of Commons represents the Canadian people. A formula based on representation by population determines the number of seats in the House. One candidate is elected for each of 301 electoral districts (also called ridings) in the country (*right*). Whichever party gets the most seats in an election forms the government and its leader becomes Prime Minister. The party with the second largest number of seats becomes the Official Opposition.

Ontario	103
Quebec	75
British Columbia	34
Alberta	26
Manitoba	14
Saskatchewan	14
Nova Scotia	11
New Brunswick	10
Newfoundland and Labrador	7
Prince Edward Island	4
Northwest Territories	1
Nunavut	1
Yukon	1

◆ Our anthem

O Canada was first performed on June 24, 1880, during St. Jean Baptiste Day celebrations in Quebec City. It was 20 years later before it was introduced to English Canadians. Quebec Judge Adolphe-Basile Routhier wrote the verses first sung to the music of Calixa Lavallée. An English translation, penned in 1908 by Montreal lawyer and writer Robert Stanley Weir, gained widespread popularity. With some alterations, these were adopted by Parliament as Canada's national anthem in 1967.

◆ Named after British printer

Hansard, the official, verbatim report of parliamentary debates in the House of Commons, is named for T. C. Hansard, who printed the British debates of 1812–92. When Parliament is in session, it prints by 9 a.m. daily a copy, in both official languages, of the previous day's proceedings, including members' speeches, debates, comments, and remarks. On average, one day's issue runs to 80 or 85 pages. Hansard is also accessible on the Internet by 5 a.m. daily.

◆ Senate

The Senate, Parliament's upper house, is often described as the chamber of sober second thought, since no bill can become law without its approval. Unlike the House of Commons, Senate membership is by appointment. Senators named before 1965 were appointed for life; all other Senators must retire at age 75. To be eligible for a Senate seat, a person must be a Canadian citizen, be at least 30 years of age, reside and own land in the province he or she will represent in the Senate, and have a net estate of $4,000. A Quebec Senator must either reside or own land in the division for which he or she is appointed.

The price of a Senate seat can be a hurdle. When 73-year-old Sister Mary Alice Butts of Antigonish, N.S., was appointed in 1997, the Roman Catholic nun, who had taken a vow of poverty 40 years earlier, didn't have the $4,000 in "real and personal property" required of all Senators. So, her order transferred some scrubland into her name, and Sister Mary Alice took her seat in the Red Chamber.

◆ Seal of approval

The Great Seal of Canada, of which the Governor General is the official keeper, is affixed to all formal documents issued in the name of the monarch. The Great Seal of Queen Victoria (*below right*) was Canada's first Great Seal, but its intricate engraving delayed its delivery to Canada until two years after Confederation. To the right and left of Queen Victoria on the seal are the four shields bearing the arms of the provinces that then made up Canada. A new Great Seal is created for each monarch; the Great Seal of Queen Elizabeth was the first to be made in Canada at the Royal Canadian Mint, in Ottawa.

The Great Seal of Queen Victoria. In the right and left niches are the four shields bearing the arms of the four provinces

◆ O Tuponia?

Nearly three years after delegates met in Charlottetown, P.E.I., to discuss the birth of a new nation, the provinces of Canada East, Canada West, New Brunswick, and Nova Scotia were united on July 1, 1867, as a Dominion under the name of "Canada," after the native word *kanata*, or village. Among the names the Fathers of Confederation considered but ultimately rejected for our newborn nation were:

Albertsland
Albionora
Borealia
Britannia
Cabotia
Colonia
Efisga
Hochelaga
Norland
Transatlantia
Tuponia
Victorialand

Borealia was inspired by the aurora borealis (*see page 30*); Efisga was an acronym for "England, France, Ireland, Scotland, Germany, and Aboriginal lands"; Cabotia paid homage to John Cabot; while Tuponia was an acrostic for The United Provinces of North America.

On Feb. 9, 1865, according to William B. Hamilton's *The Macmillan Book of Canadian Place Names*, Thomas D'Arcy McGee brought some much-needed humor (and sanity) to the debate: "I read in one newspaper not less than a dozen attempts to derive a new name. One individual chooses Tuponia and another Hochelaga as a suitable name for the new nationality. Now I ask any honorable member of this House how he would feel if he woke up some fine morning and found himself instead of a Canadian, a Tuponian or a Hochelagander."

◆ The cabinet maker

Canada's first Prime Minister (1867–73 and again in 1878–91) John A. Macdonald (1815–91), was a Glasgow-born lawyer, concertina player, and shrewd politician, full of charm and wit. When the Fathers of Confederation met in Charlottetown in 1864 for the meeting that made Canada a nation, Macdonald was asked to sign the guest book at Province House, where the meetings took place. He gave his occupation as "cabinet maker."

Great personal sorrow and a weakness for the bottle were twin facets of his life, and he lapsed into drinking bouts from time to time. Recovering from one of these during an election campaign, he was scheduled to speak after his Liberal opponent. When he stood up, none too steadily, he promptly threw up on stage. "Ladies and gentlemen, please forgive me," said the wily Macdonald, without missing a beat, "but that man (pointing to his opponent) makes me sick."

Macdonald had an abiding faith in Canada's future, however, and built the Canadian Pacific Railway, instituted policies of tariff protection and Western settlement, and brought British Columbia into Confederation. He accepted misfortune as part of life, once writing, "When fortune empties her chamber pot on your head, smile and say, 'We are going to have a summer shower.'"

◆ Manitoba school crisis cost him dearly

Newspaper publisher and onetime Grand Master of the Orange Order, British-born Sir Mackenzie Bowell (1823–1917) was an MP for 35 years and served as a cabinet minister in the Conservative governments of Abbott (*see below*) and Thompson (*see opposite page*). When Thompson died suddenly in 1894, Bowell became Prime Minister. But during two years in office, the staunchly anti-Catholic Bowell dithered on his cabinet's proposals to reinstate Catholic schools in Manitoba. With the Tory party steadily losing support, his cabinet finally forced his resignation. He held a seat in the Senate until his death from pneumonia at age 93.

◆ A man of high standards

Scottish-born building contractor and newspaper editor Alexander Mackenzie (1822–92), Prime Minister from 1873 to 1878, was a man of integrity, believing that success came from hard work and sober habits. His high standards shunned corruption and he had little patience for class distinctions (Mackenzie refused three knighthoods.) While his distinct lack of charisma cost him the 1878 election to John A. Macdonald (*left*), Mackenzie got the job done—the North-West Mounted Police (*see page 141*), the Supreme Court of Canada, the post of auditor general, and the secret ballot were all created during his administration.

◆ Caretaker PM

To quote himself, Senator John Joseph Caldwell Abbott (1821–93), brilliant lawyer, authority on commercial law, and former mayor of Montreal, "was not particularly obnoxious to anybody." So in 1891, at age 70, he became Canada's "caretaker" Prime Minister when Sir John A. Macdonald (*left*) died. Born in Saint-André d'Argenteuil, in what is now Quebec, Abbott was Canada's first native-born PM. He claimed to detest politics, public speeches, caucuses, and notoriety, but took delight in a game of whist or cribbage. Cleaning up a patronage scandal was only one of the tasks awaiting him as Prime Minister, but his health was not up to the task, and he resigned after a heart attack in 1892.

| Macdonald | Mackenzie | Abbott | Thompson | Bowell | Tupper | Laurier | Borden | Meighen | Mackenzie King |

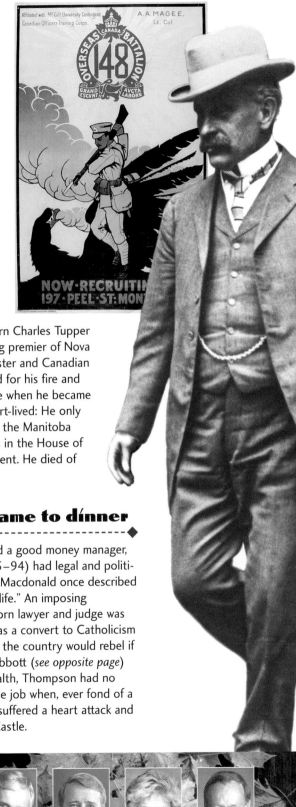

◆ The PM who cycled to work

A son of Grand Pré, N.S., Sir Robert Borden (1854–1937; *right*) is famous for leading his country into World War I, winning the 1917 election on the issue of compulsory military conscription. Yet he was also a quiet man who had a mastery of Latin and Greek, chewed tobacco, and sometimes bicycled to work. A successful lawyer when he entered politics in 1896, he became Conservative leader five years later and Prime Minister in 1911. At war's end, he won Canada's right to separate representation at the Paris Peace Conference. Because of failing health, Borden retired from politics in 1920. He was chancellor of Queen's University, Kingston, Ont., from 1924–30, a post he had held earlier at McGill University in Montreal.

◆ Renowned for oratory and charm

Prime Minister of Canada during the "Sunshine Years" of 1896 to 1911, courtly lawyer Wilfrid Laurier (1841–1919) was renowned for his charm and oratory (in French and English), his statesmanship, vision, and good looks. A native of Quebec, Laurier was a unifier and a builder, giving Canadians the confidence they needed at a crucial time in their history. During his stewardship, British troops were withdrawn from Canada and the militia came under Canadian control, the navy was founded, Canada won the right to negotiate its own trade treaties, the economy flourished, and the population grew dramatically under his government's immigration policies. Defeated in 1911 over trade reciprocity with the United States, Laurier led the Opposition in the House of Commons until his death from a stroke.

◆ Founding Father

A Father of Confederation, Amherst, N.S.-born Charles Tupper (1821–1915) was a surgeon before becoming premier of Nova Scotia. Later in life he became a federal minister and Canadian High Commissioner in London. He was noted for his fire and bluster in the House. He was 75 years of age when he became Prime Minister, but his time in office was short-lived: He only held the position for 68 days in 1896, when the Manitoba Schools bill (*see opposite page*) failed to pass in the House of Commons and forced him to dissolve Parliament. He died of heart failure in Kent, England, at age 94.

◆ The convert who came to dinner

Strong-minded, decisive, efficient, and a good money manager, John David Sparrow Thompson (1845–94) had legal and political talents so impressive that John A. Macdonald once described him as "the greatest discovery of my life." An imposing presence in the House, the Halifax-born lawyer and judge was Macdonald's obvious successor, but as a convert to Catholicism Thompson felt the Orange faction in the country would rebel if a Catholic became PM. When John Abbott (*see opposite page*) was forced to retire because of ill health, Thompson had no choice. He was barely two years in the job when, ever fond of a good table, on a visit to England he suffered a heart attack and died while having lunch at Windsor Castle.

Bennett

St. Laurent

Diefenbaker

Pearson

Trudeau

Clark

Turner

Mulroney

Campbell

Chrétien

◆ Bennett faced the Depression

The son of a shipbuilder, Richard Bedford "R. B." Bennett (1870–1947) was born in Hopewell Hill, N.B., and taught school in that province for a time before becoming a corporate lawyer in Calgary. He served in the Alberta Legislature before his election to the House of Commons in 1911. Bennett held various cabinet posts before becoming Conservative leader in 1927, then Prime Minister in 1930. The CBC, the Canadian Wheat Board, and the Bank of Canada were all created during his tenure, yet his government did little to help the vast numbers of Canadians struggling through the Depression years. In fact a whole new argot was coined by Canadians disgruntled with his leadership (*see below*). In 1935, Bennett brought his New Deal to the people: The Conservatives passed legislation on minimum wages, maximum hours, pensions, price controls, unemployment and health insurance. Despite his zealous newfound optimism, Bennett lost the 1935 election to Mackenzie King (*see opposite page*), but remained in office as leader of the Opposition for another three years. In 1939, he retired to England, where he was appointed to the British House of Lords as Viscount Bennett of Mickleham, Calgary, and Hopewell. At age 77, he suffered a heart attack and died in his bathtub.

◆ An R. B. Bennett lexicon

Bennett buggies: Horse-pulled cars on the Prairies whose owners could not afford gas
Bennett blankets: Yesterday's newspapers
Eggs Bennett: Boiled chestnuts
Bennettburghs: Towns of tar-paper shacks sheltering the unemployed and homeless

◆ A powerful orator

Leader of the Conservative Party for many years, the cold, stern Arthur Meighen (1874–1960) made some of the finest speeches ever heard in Parliament. He is famous for saying, "The only unpardonable sin in politics is lack of courage. Indecision or doubt about a course once entered upon is inevitably fatal." Meighen was Prime Minister in 1920–21, and again briefly in 1926. Before becoming a successful lawyer and entering politics, the Anderson, Ont.- native taught school and ran a small business, and in later life was involved in investment banking. At age 86, he died in Toronto of heart failure.

◆ The peacemaker

Affability was a trademark of Lester B. Pearson (1897–1972), the skillful diplomat and negotiator who fashioned Canada's peacemaking image worldwide. As Prime Minister, he steered Canada through the troubled waters of the 1960s, enduring a string of scandals (*see pages 294–95, 301*) while introducing the Canada Pension Plan, giving the country the flag (*page 280*), and focusing public attention on the Quiet Revolution in Quebec (*page 303*).

Peacekeeping is what Pearson is famous for. A native of Newtownbrook, Ont., he had served as president of the U.N. General Assembly in 1952–53, helping to defuse the Suez Crisis of the late fifties by proposing a U.N. peacekeeping force for the area. His efforts won him the 1957 Nobel Peace Prize and launched Canada's distinguished role in peacekeeping.

> ❝ ***The only unpardonable sin in politics is lack of courage.*** ❞
> —Arthur Meighen

◆ Canada boomed during the St. Laurent years

A French-Canadian nationalist, Louis St. Laurent (1882–1973) welcomed Newfoundland into Confederation during his time as Prime Minister (1948–57). Canada boomed during the St. Laurent years: The St. Lawrence Seaway, the Trans-Canada Highway, and a transcontinental natural gas pipeline were other major undertakings of this decisive Liberal PM. He also helped make the Supreme Court the final court of appeal (appeals to the Judicial Committee of the Privy Council in England were abolished). St. Laurent ran the country with such efficiency that, in the words of one of his advisers, Jack Pickersgill, Canadians thought anyone could do it and elected John Diefenbaker (*see page 293*) to succeed him. He was 91 when he died of heart failure in Quebec City.

◆ His advisers hailed from the other side ◆

Prime Minister of Canada for 22 years, Kitchener, Ont.-born William Lyon Mackenzie King (1874–1950) was generally perceived as the blandest of the bland. His diaries, however, reveal eccentric aspects of his personality. He regularly reached out to the spirit world for advice from his dead mother and even his dead dog, his beloved Irish terrier named Pat.

Politically deft, he kept the Liberals in power for almost a quarter of a century, and set Canada on the path to nationhood. A classic example of his double-talk prowess was his statement early in World War II about compulsory military service, a matter on which Canadians were bitterly divided: "Conscription if necessary, but not necessarily conscription." According to the late Jack Pickersgill, public servant, cabinet minister, and adviser of prime ministers, King lifted the phrase from a 1941 *Toronto Star* editorial. Dull and peculiar though he undoubtedly was, King had considerable political skills, took the first steps toward creating a social safety net, and was committed to the cause of unity and giving Canada an international presence.

◆ "Just watch me"

Pierre Elliott Trudeau (1919–2000), *bon vivant*, jet-set ladies man, and the only Canadian Prime Minister to have married while in office, became Prime Minister in 1968. A native Montrealer, Trudeau traveled widely before he was appointed a professor of law at the University of Montreal. Entering politics in 1965, he scandalized former PM John Diefenbaker when he turned up in the House of Commons wearing a bright yellow ascot and sandals. "Disrespectful," Dief fumed. Trudeau arrived the next day wearing a more subdued blue ascot.

When Lester B. Pearson resigned in 1968, the Liberals chose his justice minister, Trudeau, to replace him. The adulation that greeted him on the hustings became known as Trudeaumania. Women broke through police cordons to touch and kiss him. Alternately playful and stern, sophisticated and irreverent, the charismatic swinging bachelor swept into office in 1968. Three years later he married Margaret Sinclair, a woman 30 years his junior, only to go through a very public divorce in 1977.

A proud federalist, Trudeau went to extraordinary lengths to keep Canada united. "Just watch me," he famously declared before invoking the War Measures Act during the October Crisis (*see page 303*). He is noted for his defeat of René Lévesque in the first Quebec referendum, and for patriating the Constitution in 1982. Canada mourned when, afflicted with prostate cancer, Trudeau died in 2000. He lay in state on Parliament Hill before a funeral train brought him home to Montreal.

◆ The "little guy" from Shawinigan

First elected to the House of Commons in 1963, Jean Chrétien (born 1934), the self-proclaimed "little guy" from Shawinigan, Que., had served in the Pearson administration and held a variety of cabinet posts under Trudeau, but lost the Liberal leadership to John Turner (*see opposite page*) in 1984. Shortly afterward he resigned as MP and began practicing law. But he returned to politics in 1990, taking over the party leadership and leading the Liberals to a resounding victory in 1993. Chrétien has the unenviable record of being the only 20th-century francophone leader who didn't command a majority of seats in Quebec.

Prime ministerial safety became an issue during Chrétien's term in office, and was beefed up considerably after an intruder, armed with a knife, broke into 24 Sussex Drive. The man reached the Prime Minister's bedroom undetected until he came face to face with Madame Aline Chrétien, who quickly slammed and bolted the door before he could gain entry. It took several minutes before RCMP security officers answered the PM's call for assistance.

Chrétien won a second majority government in 1997, yet throughout his tenure was often under fire for failing to keep Liberal electoral promises and for reducing deficits at the cost of social programs. He was particularly criticized for mishandling the 1995 Quebec referendum (*see page 303*), and for his alleged involvement in deals surrounding a golf course and hotel in his native Shawinigan, an affair that came to be known as "Shawinigate."

◆ First woman PM

For four months in 1993, British Columbia-born political scientist Avril Phaedra "Kim" Campbell (born 1947) served as Canada's Prime Minister, the first woman to hold that post. Earlier that year, she had taken over the leadership of the Tories from Brian Mulroney (*below*), in whose Cabinet she had held various portfolios. Forced to call an election, Campbell couldn't quell the people's dissatisfaction with the GST, Free Trade, and endless constitutional debates, and the Tories were routed in one of the worst upsets in Canadian political history, winning only two seats in the House of Commons. Campbell even lost her Vancouver seat. She retired from politics and returned to teaching, where she was offered a fellowship at Harvard University.

◆ Canada's youngest leader

In May 1979, 40-year-old Charles Joseph "Joe" Clark, a native of High River, Alta., became the youngest person (and the first westerner) to become Prime Minister. The media had a field day, nicknaming him "Joe Who" and routinely sending up his seeming awkwardness. Facing a historic 14 percent inflation rate, his minority Progressive Conservative government was defeated eight months later when the Liberal Opposition called a non-confidence vote on Finance Minister John Crosbie's infamous "short-term pain for long-term gain" budget. The Liberals regained power in the general election that followed.

Clark ultimately lost the Conservative leadership to Brian Mulroney (*below*) in 1983, whom he served as External Affairs Minister and Constitutional Affairs Minister before retiring from politics in 1993. In 1998 Clarke became leader of the Conservatives again, but could not revive the fortunes of the dramatically shrunken party. He stepped down in 2002.

◆ The lifeguard who drowned

In the winter of 1965, John Napier Turner (born 1929), Minister for Consumer and Corporate Affairs in Pearson's Cabinet, was vacationing in Barbados when he saved a man from drowning who turned out to be John Diefenbaker. Turner went on to be Minister of Finance under Trudeau, but disagreed with the PM on wage and price controls, and retired in 1975. When he took over leadership of the Liberals and became Prime Minister in 1984, Turner's swimming skills failed him. The Liberals were defeated in an election that year, and again four years later. Turner continued to lead the party until 1990, when he handed the reins to Jean Chrétien.

◆ Architect of free trade

Quebec-born Martin Brian Mulroney (born 1939), a lawyer who specialized in labor negotiations, had never held public office when he became Conservative leader in 1983. Shortly afterward he won a seat in Parliament in a by-election, and in 1984, and again in 1988, he led the Conservatives to victory. During his administration, Canada signed the controversial free trade agreement with the United States and his government introduced the much-loathed Goods and Services Tax (GST).

Unable to have either the Meech Lake or Charlottetown accords ratified, initiatives aimed at making the repatriated Constitution acceptable to Quebec (*see page 302*), Mulroney retired from office in 1993. Three years later, he learned that letters to a Swiss bank said he was suspected of accepting kickbacks (*see* The $2 million seat sale, *page 295*), and sued for libel. Hours before the trial was to begin, Canada issued an apology to the former prime minister, who then dropped his suit. In 1998, with the same Liberal government still in office, Mulroney was named a companion of the Order of Canada. Today Mulroney enjoys a reputation as a skilled global business consultant and negotiator.

◆ Rideau Hall: 175 RM, $25 MIL

--◆

The official residence of the Governor General of Canada, Rideau Hall is a 175-room palatial mansion with elegantly manicured grounds, a sterling collection of fine art and antique furniture, and is situated across the road from the Prime Minister's residence.

Built in 1838 by a Scottish stonemason for Thomas MacKay, a prominent mill owner, Rideau Hall began as an 11-room limestone mansion known as MacKay's Castle. The government leased it in 1865, as a temporary residence for Viscount Monck, Canada's first Governor General, and purchased it three years later. By that time Monck had enlarged it to four times its original size. Since Confederation, all Governors General have lived at Rideau Hall, where they undertake their constitutional, diplomatic, and ceremonial duties. The 32-hectare estate has an annual operating budget of $1.5 million and a market value of $25 million.

◆ Canada's seven prestige addresses

◆ **Sussex Place**, the Prime Minister's grey limestone official residence, at 24 Sussex Drive on the Ottawa River, was originally named Gorffwysfa (Welsh for "place of peace"). It was built in 1866 by lumber baron Joseph Currier as a wedding gift for his wife. In the 1940s, the government bought the property, which briefly served as the Australian embassy. It became the Prime Minister's official residence in 1951, when Louis Saint-Laurent was in office. The 1.6-hectare property is currently valued at $4.9 million.

◆ Rustic **Harrington Lake** (*left*) at Kingsmere in Gatineau Park, north of Ottawa, was built in 1925 by Ottawa lumber tycoon Lt.-Col. Cameron Edwards. When Prime Minister John Diefenbaker's supporters suggested establishing an official country retreat near the capital in 1959, Dief wasn't convinced, but agreed to take a tour of Harrington Lake. Legend has it the property's caretaker was ordered to ensure the PM bagged some trout in the lake. He did, and since then, Canadian Prime Ministers have used it as their second official residence.

◆ The Governor General resides at **Rideau Hall** (*see opposite page*). The Governor General's summer home is the only official residence outside the Nation's Capital Region: **La Citadelle**, a massive fortress set on the heights of Cap-aux-Diamants overlooking the St. Lawrence River in Quebec City.

◆ **Stornoway**, a 2½-story stucco house in Ottawa's Rockcliffe Village built by local grocer Asconio Joseph in 1914, is the residence of the leader of the Official Opposition in the House of Commons. Princess Juliana of the Netherlands occupied the house, then a private home, during World War II. Preston Manning made headlines when he refused the keys to Stornoway after the Reform Party became the Official Opposition in 1997, saying it was a waste of the taxpayer's money. (He eventually moved in.)

◆ In 1927, Prime Minister Mackenzie King bought a rambling farmstead in Gatineau Park so he could escape from the pressures of public life. In 1935, he renovated the property as a year-round retreat. Now part of the Mackenzie King estate in Kingsmere, **The Farm** (*right*) is the residence set aside for Canada's Speaker of the House.

◆ At the east end of Ottawa's Confederation Boulevard, distinguished visitors to Canada stay at **7 Rideau Gate**, situated near Rideau Hall and 24 Sussex Drive. Built in 1861–62 by Ottawa mill-owner Henry Osgoode Burritt, the property was bought by the government in 1966 and refurbished as a pied-à-terre for foreign dignitaries headed to Canada for Centennial celebrations in 1967.

The grounds at Rideau Hall feature ornamental gardens, wooded walking paths, totem poles, a cricket pitch, and 80 trees planted by foreign leaders

◆ Canada's honor system

Canada's top honors recognize extraordinary Canadians and their achievements. They are worn by Canadians as diverse as actor Donald Sutherland, General John de Chastelain (ret.), jazz pianist Oscar Peterson, and wheelchair athlete Rick Hansen. Neither brings any special privileges or financial rewards, yet they remain Canada's top honors—the Order of Canada and the Order of Military Merit.

Established in 1967, the Order of Canada recognizes outstanding merit or achievement of the highest degree, especially for service to Canada or humanity at large. The corresponding badge is a stylized snowflake bearing a crown, a maple leaf, and the motto *Desiderantes Meliorem Patriam* (they desire a better country). Companions of the Order of Canada are limited to 150 living members. New appointments, never more than 15 a year, are made only when vacancies occur. There are no limits on the total number of officers and members, although no more than 46 officers and 92 members can be appointed in any one year.

For members of the armed forces, a blue enameled cross (*below*) is the insignia of the Order of Military Merit. Annual appointments to all grades of the Order must not exceed one-tenth of one percent of the armed forces' strength.

There are three grades of membership for both Orders: Companion (CC), Officer (OC), or Member (CM) of the Order of Canada, and a Commander (CMM), Officer (OMM), or Member (MMM) of the Order of Military Merit. In total, the Orders have been presented to more than 4,000 people. Recipients may wear their respective badges of honor on appropriate occasions and may add the above letters to their names.

◆ Gifts from the Governors General

In their role as the Queen's representative in Canada, many of our Governors General came bearing gifts—or bequeathed them to us while in office. A small sample of cultural milestones that we owe to them:

◆ A great promoter of physical fitness, Governor General Roland Michener (1900–91) was 82 in 1982, when he scaled the last 300 meters of the Alberta mountain that bears his name. Michener introduced the Order of Canada (*left*), the first exclusively Canadian system of honors for exemplary merit and achievement.

◆ The Governor General's Award, Canada's preeminent literary prize for single works, is the legacy of Scottish-born John Buchan, the first Baron Tweedsmuir (1875–1940), Governor General from 1935 until his death in 1940. In addition to his administrative duties, Buchan was a prodigious writer of poetry, historical biography, and fast-paced thrillers such as *The Thirty Nine Steps*.

◆ Sir Frederick Arthur Stanley, Baron Stanley of Preston (1841–1908), was Governor General from 1888–93. His term in Canada was marked by his strong support for culture and sports, and most especially for instituting hockey's hallowed Stanley Cup.

Patrons of sport and culture

◆ Gilbert George Elliott, the fourth Earl of Minto and Governor General from 1898 to 1904, strongly supported a national parks system and persuaded Ottawa to build the Public Archives. Located in Ottawa, the Public Archives of Canada houses millions of rare books, maps, atlases, early French and British records, medals, photographs, correspondence and papers of individuals and private societies, films, TV programs, sound recordings, and computer-generated materials. The archives also house files from all federal departments and agencies.

◆ As Governor General (1904–11), Albert Henry George Grey (1851–1917), the fourth Earl Grey, led efforts to have the Plains of Abraham in Quebec declared a national park and welcomed Saskatchewan and Alberta into the Dominion. He also helped establish the Department of External Affairs and donated the Grey Cup to Canadian football (*see page 203*).

◆ Teacher, politician, diplomat, patron of the arts, Vincent Massey (1887–1967) was Canada's first native-born Governor General, from 1952–59. In 1951, he headed the Royal Commission on National Development in Arts, Letters, and Sciences that recommended the formation of the Canada Council. Massey was the first Canadian diplomat to represent Canada in a foreign land.

honors and gifts

Legend has it that a year-old Edward Broadbent (right) was carried on the picket line during Oshawa, Ont.'s bitter 1937 strike against General Motors. Born to an auto-working family in that auto-manu-facturing town, he devoted much of his life to public service, and was leader of the New Democratic Party (NDP) from 1975 to 1989

◆ They wove the original social safety net

Forerunner of today's NDP, the Cooperative Commonwealth Federation was founded in 1932 in Regina, bringing together socialist, farm, and labor groups who wanted to reform society. The CCF was the first to call for social services such as pensions, medicare, family allowances, and unemployment insurance. In 1943 it became the Official Opposition in Ontario, and in 1944 it formed the government of Saskatchewan under Premier T. C. (Tommy) Douglas (*see page 292*).

The CCF gave a start to some of Canada's best-known social visionaries, such as Thérèse Casgrain (1896–1981), whose efforts for Quebec women's suffrage finally bore fruit in 1940, when they won the right to vote in provin-cial elections, and Polish-born David Lewis (1909–81), who gave up his Ottawa law practice to devote his life to social reform.

Thérèse Casgrain and David Lewis (center) at a CCF National Convention in 1958

◆ First member of visible minority

When 60-year-old Adrienne Clarkson became Canada's 26th Governor-General in 1999, she was the first member of a visible minority and the second woman after Jeanne Sauvé (*see page 293*) to hold the post. The former broadcaster and diplomat grew up in Ottawa, where her family had fled in 1942 following the Japanese invasion of Hong Kong. Ms. Clarkson was a familiar face to Canadians who had seen her in such CBC shows as *Take 30* and *The Fifth Estate*. From 1982–87, she served as Ontario's agent-general in Paris. On her return, she served briefly as president of McClelland and Stewart's publishing house.

◆ Father of medicare

Premier of Saskatchewan for 17 years and federal New Democratic Party leader for 10 years, T. C. "Tommy" Douglas (1904–86) formed North America's first socialist government in 1944, when he led the Cooperative Commonwealth Federation (CCF) to victory in Saskatchewan. Politics was the second career of this powerful orator who served as a Baptist minister before running for public office. The medical insurance plan he put into effect while premier was North America's first comprehensive government-sponsored medicare.

◆ "Minister of everything"

An engineer by trade, American-born Clarence "C. D." Howe (1886–1960) had made a fortune building grain elevators in what is now Thunder Bay, Ont., before he won his first seat in Parliament. Between 1935 and 1957, he held a series of cabinet posts in Liberal governments, earning the nickname Minister of Everything, and a reputation for getting things done. Howe set up the airline now known as Air Canada, and during the Second World War was the force that organized hundreds of small private firms into producers of arms and military supplies. Howe was defeated in the 1957 federal election.

◆ Quebec's Everyman

René Lévesque (1922–87; *above center*), an influential television journalist, was among the young dynamic personalities Jean Lesage attracted to the Quebec Liberal party in the early 1960s. The charismatic Lévesque persuaded Lesage to nationalize the province's utilities, becoming a key figure in Quebec's Quiet Revolution, which transformed the province into a modern society.

In 1967, dissatisfied with his party's relationship with Ottawa, Lévesque founded the organization that a year later became the Parti Québécois (PQ). After the PQ swept to power in 1976, it passed Bill 101, establishing French as the preeminent language of the province. In 1980 Canada found itself on tenterhooks, glued to TVs and radios as the PQ held and lost a province-wide referendum on sovereignty-association (see page 302).

Lévesque's mythic appeal in Quebec lies in his beleaguered, Everyman image—many Quebecers saw themselves in the chain-smoking, rumpled night owl with the outspoken and candid personality. When the Quebec legislature decided to erect a statue in his memory, his family made it clear that it should be no taller than he was in life; no giant monuments for René.

◆ Joe the Barrelman

"We are a medium-sized municipality . . . left far behind the march of time." With oratory such as this, journalist-turned-politician Joseph "Joey" Smallwood (1900–92; *right*) persuaded his fellow Newfoundlanders to join Confederation. From 1949 to 1972 he remained premier of the province he had made part of Canada.

During his earlier newspaper years, Smallwood had covered the 1919 transatlantic flights. Later he became a union organizer, and, under the *nom de plume* of Joe the Barrelman, hosted radio talk shows. During World War II, he ran a piggery at the Gander air base.

When Smallwood retired from politics in 1977, he set to work on the *Encyclopedia of Newfoundland and Labrador*, two volumes of which were published before his death.

political giants

◆ First woman Speaker

Jeanne-Mathilde Sauvé (1922–89) was 12 years old when her father showed her a bust of Agnes Macphail (*see page 97*) in the House of Commons, and told her that she too could become an MP. Sauvé went on to a distinguished career as a journalist and broadcaster before seeking a parliamentary seat and, on election, she held various cabinet posts in the Liberal government. In 1980, she became the first woman Speaker of the House of Commons. During her term she implemented wide-ranging reforms of the administration of the Commons. In 1984, Madame Sauvé became Governor General, the first woman ever to hold this office.

◆ Fiery rebel sought solace in the Bible

Journalist, leader of the 1837 Rebellion, and first mayor of Toronto, the fiery William Lyon Mackenzie (1795–1861) was a key figure in pre-Confederation life. Born in Scotland, he had read close to 1,000 books by his early twenties, had worked at merchandising and accounting, kept a general store, fathered a son out of wedlock, and run up sizable gambling debts. In 1820, he came to Canada, where he founded a store at Dundas, Ont., and later at Queenston, Ont. There in 1824, he founded *The Colonial Advocate*, which he used to rail at the ruling cliques.

Mackenzie's vision of government by the people moved others and won him the admiration and loyalty of many. His campaigns earned him beatings, threatened lynchings, destruction of his printing press, but he persevered until responsible government became a fact. Elected to the assembly, he held his seat for seven years. But true to form, he didn't much like the government he had fought for and won. Rebel to the end, he still wanted to reform everything. Wrote one observer: "He couldn't have been content under the government of an angel." The old reformer spent his last years as a semi-recluse, seeking solace in his Bible.

◆ Prairie populist gave Canada Bill of Rights

"Polls are for dogs," sniffed John George Diefenbaker (1895–1979), when a Gallup poll saw him trailing miserably in the 1957 election campaign. Ten days later he became the first Tory Prime Minister in 22 years, a post he held until 1963. Born in Neustadt, Ont., but raised in rural Saskatchewan, Diefenbaker gave Canada the 1960 Canadian Bill of Rights, and he played a leading role in forcing South Africa out of the Commonwealth because of its apartheid policies at that time. A skilled campaigner and thunderous orator, Diefenbaker had won his 13th election as an MP and was still in office when he died from heart failure at age 83.

John G. Diefenbaker (*acrylic on canvas, 1979*), *by Canadian abstract painter William Ronald (1926–98)*

Even in death, the Prairie populist exercised his penchant for being larger than life with a state funeral in Ottawa, followed by a train journey across Canada for interment beside the Diefenbaker Centre at the University of Saskatchewan in Saskatoon—all prearranged by himself.

◆ The urbane demagogue

A demagogue in public, urbane and witty in private, Maurice Duplessis (1890–1959) was a tough-as-nails lawyer and premier of Quebec in 1936–39 and 1944–59. He gained power by promising social reforms but once in office allied himself with the bosses rather than the workers. While he introduced Canada's most generous minimum wage and home ownership assistance acts; built highways, hospitals, schools, and universities; brought electricity to most of Quebec, and adopted the Quebec flag, Duplessis also dealt harshly with unions, presided over vast patronage schemes, and showed scant respect for civil rights. One of his greatest balancing acts was his relationship with the Roman Catholic Church: He managed to support its power, while asserting the state's authority over it. This relationship gave rise to the legacy of the Duplessis Orphans—orphans and children of unmarried parents and of poor families—who were declared mentally ill and deprived of education, so that their caregivers, mostly religious communities, would qualify for federal funding.

scandals and filibusters

◆ 23 years before the courts

The Labrador Boundary Dispute is one of the most celebrated legal cases in British colonial history. It began in 1902 when Labrador issued a timber license on the Churchill River and Quebec questioned Labrador's right to do so. In 1904, at Quebec's request, Ottawa asked the Privy Council to resolve the matter. The dispute dragged on unresolved until 1922, when five Privy Council judges were asked to decide on the boundary between Canada and Newfoundland. Their judgment had to be based on existing orders in council, statutes, and proclamations: they could not suggest a new boundary or a compromise. Much of the case revolved around the meaning of the word "coast." In March 1927, the judges set Labrador's boundary in its present location. The boundary was confirmed in 1949, when Newfoundland joined Confederation.

Politics that defied gravity

◆ Rhinos took humor to the hustings

In 1963, Dr. Jacques Ferron and fellow humorists in Montreal founded the Rhinoceros Party. Taking their cue from the election of a hippopotamus in São Paulo, Brazil, in the 1950s by disenfranchised voters, the Rhinos' intent was to poke fun at politics, politicians, and campaigns. By 1979, the party was sufficiently well known across the country that it came in fifth in a federal election. Over the years the pranksters promised a series of outrageous platforms. One time they announced plans to repeal the law of gravity. Another time they vowed to make bubble gum Canada's official currency. Even the Bay of Fundy was not safe—the Rhinos wanted to pave it over for parking. The party was disbanded in 1993, when changes to the electoral laws required any party wanting official status to run a minimum of 50 candidates, each of whom had to pay a $1,000 deposit to run.

◆ Lucky Lucien's fast skating

"Lucky" Lucien Rivard was a Quebec gangster whose name was, as they say, "known to the police." In 1964, after a U.S. federal grand jury indicted him on international drug trafficking charges, he was apprehended in Quebec and incarcerated at Bordeaux jail while an extradition hearing was pending. A Montreal lawyer, Pierre Lamontagne, who represented the U.S. Department of Justice, was offered a bribe of $20,000 if he wouldn't oppose Rivard's application for bail. The man accused of offering the bribe was one Raymond Denis, an executive assistant to the federal Minister of Immigration but formerly an assistant to the then Justice Minister, Guy Favreau. Additional information later revealed the involvement of Guy Rouleau, Prime Minister Lester B. Pearson's own parliamentary secretary, in this effort to thwart the course of justice.

A judicial inquiry into the Rivard affair, headed by Chief Justice Dorion, uncovered some appalling inadequacies within the RCMP, which had been asked to investigate Lamontagne's allegations. For instance, the RCMP lawyer hired for the purposes of the Dorion inquiry couldn't speak a word of French, when most of those involved were francophone. It was also revealed that two Mounties listened in on a phone call, instigated by the RCMP, wherein Lamontagne spoke to Denis hoping that he would repeat the original bribe offer. (Denis didn't oblige.) During the inquiry, the officers were asked if they had taken any notes during this phone call. "No," said one of the officers, note taking was impossible. He had needed one hand to hold the phone and the other hand to cover the receiver so Denis couldn't hear him breathing. The entire scandal took on the attributes of a farce. The Opposition used the affair to hound the Liberals in the House of Commons endlessly and eventually forced Guy Favreau to resign as Justice Minister.

Rivard meanwhile escaped from Bordeaux Jail in March of 1965, and provided Canada with some much needed comic relief. Rivard had received permission from prison authorities to flood the prison's outdoor skating rink despite the fact that it was six degrees Celsius outside. Instead he threw the hose over the prison wall and climbed out. He then "borrowed" a car from a passing motorist (to whom he gave money for taxi fare), and made good his escape.

◆ The furniture sale scandal

While the Rivard scandal (*see opposite page*) was dominating the news and received daily play by play in the House of Commons, Federal Minister of Immigration René Tremblay was having his own problems staving off scandal. Tremblay, in need of furniture for his Ottawa home, had gone shopping in Montreal, buying a house full of furniture at a store called Futurama, owned by Max and Adolph Sefkind. Before Tremblay could pay the bill, however, Futurama went bust.

The bankruptcy came under investigation by a Quebec governmental inquiry into fraudulent bankruptcies. Tremblay claimed that he was only an innocent bystander, but the so-called "furniture scandal" unearthed some interesting facts, for example: When Tremblay was a deputy minister in the Quebec government, his department loaned another business owned by the Sefkinds $1.2 million.

The inquiry also found that Maurice Lamontagne, Canada's Secretary of State, was also a beneficiary of the Sefkind brothers' kindness. After a fire at his home destroyed most of his furniture, he checked his insurance policies, only to find that they had lapsed and that his insurance agent had dropped dead. He went shopping for new furniture at Futurama. Lamontagne claimed that Max and Adolph sympathized with his loss and told him to take what he needed, not to worry about the cost, and only pay them when possible; alas, Futurama went bankrupt before he could.

In the end, neither minister received a bill for the furniture until after the bankruptcy, and neither was accused of doing anything illegal. Yet the accusations of wrongdoing tainted their careers, and on Dec. 17, 1965, both offered their resignation. Pearson wrote that "they had been so undermined as politicians that their usefulness had been practically destroyed."

◆ The $2 million seat sale

In their investigation of Air Canada's 1988 decision to buy 34 Airbus A-320 passenger jets (*below*) from European consortium Airbus Industrie, for $1.8 billion, the RCMP cast their line for some pretty big fish—only the government wasn't prepared for the fish to bite back. In a letter to Swiss authorities, Canada's justice department inquired about secret Swiss bank accounts that were alleged to hold the proceeds of multimillion dollar kickbacks related to the purchase. Named in the letter was former Progressive Conservative Prime Minister Brian Mulroney. When the letter was leaked to the press in November 1995, Mulroney promptly launched a $50 million libel suit against Ottawa and the RCMP. Two months later, on the eve of the court hearings, then Liberal Justice Minister Allan Rock apologized to Mulroney, admitting Canada had no evidence whatsoever for its allegations. Rock also agreed that the RCMP would cover Mulroney's legal and PR bills—to the tune of $2 million. In return, Mulroney dropped his suit.

◆ Que sera sera . . .

When Alliance Party leader Stockwell Day floated the idea of calling national referendums on such divisive

issues as abortion if a mere three percent of the electorate wanted one, Newfoundland humorist Rick Mercer decided to show just how easy (and dangerous) such a policy could be. On the Nov. 13, 2000, broadcast of the CBC satire *This Hour Has 22 Minutes*, Mercer announced an Internet-based petition to get Day to change his first name to Doris. To the surprise and delight of many, Mercer got the majority he needed to call a referendum—over one million Canadians signed the petition online. The story even made the front page of *The Wall Street Journal*. Day eventually lost control of his party and was voted out at a leadership convention in 2002.

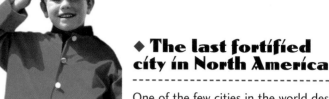

◆ Saving McCrae's medals

The verses of *In Flanders Fields* are probably the best known of any war poem. Yet 44-year-old Toronto garment manufacturer Arthur Lee, who emigrated to Canada at age 12, had never read them until one morning in October 1997, minutes before the military medals of their author, Lt.-Col. John McCrae (1872–1918; *below*), went on sale at a Toronto auction house. The medals, which McCrae's family believed were lost

at sea, turned up in a Winnipeg coin shop. Lee was aware of the controversy surrounding the medals' sale and the widespread concern that part of Canada's national heritage might be lost forever. Bidding for the medals was brisk, and when the hammer came down at $400,000, Lee's was the final bid. Saying, "We should give back what we get out of the country: it is up to individuals to do these things," he promptly turned the heirlooms over to the McCrae House Museum, John McCrae's Guelph, Ont., birthplace.

McCrae had written a number of medical texts and contributed poetry to various magazines before contributing his most enduring poem to *Punch* in 1915. The previous year, he had enlisted as a medical officer in Canada's expeditionary force. The slaughter he witnessed following the 1915 battle of Ypres—in which Canadians withstood the world's first major gas attack—inspired the poem. McCrae died of pneumonia at Boulogne, France, in January 1918.

◆ The last fortified city in North America

One of the few cities in the world designated a World Heritage Site (1985) by UNESCO (*see page 45*), Quebec City, Que., is the only walled city in North America. The old town's ramparts, gates, and defensive works are preserved in the Fortifications of Quebec National Historic Site, erected under both the French and English regimes between the 17th and 19th centuries to safeguard the city against any future land invasion by the Americans. Its famous Citadel was built atop Cap-Diamant by the British army in the 1820s, when Quebec was Canada's leading seaport. Also included in Quebec's crown of historical sites is Fort No. 1, perched atop the heights of Pointe de Lévy. The last of three forts built under the supervision of the British between 1865 and 1872, the pentagonal fort was built using innovative construction techniques for its time, including the first use of surveyor's theodolites in Canada. Today, children can dress up as soldiers (*above*), and explore the casemates, ditches, and tunnels.

A reenactment by costumed soldiers at Fort Wellington National Historic Site in Prescott, Ont. The fort provided key strategic support during the 1866 Fenian raids

◆ Boatmen were first Canadians to serve in overseas war

In 1884, 383 Canadian boatmen—French, English, Indian, and Métis—ages 18 to 64, who were recruited by the British, boarded the *Algoma* at Port Arthur (present-day Thunder Bay) bound for Egypt. Their task: to row and pole English-built boats carrying an expeditionary force through the 1,385 kilometers of rapids and cataracts on the Nile above Aswan. Their destination: Khartoum in the Sudan, where a British force under Gen. Charles Gordon was surrounded by Muslim rebels. Gordon's rescue was in the hands

of Viscount Garnet Wolseley, who, 14 years earlier, had put down the Red River Rebellion.

On Jan. 26, 1885, the rescuers were still two days' journey from Khartoum when the city fell to the attackers and Gordon was killed. Many of the Canadians had already died enroute. On the return downstream journey many more fell victim to the treacherous cataracts. Ten boats were smashed on the rocks. Members of the contingent were the first Canadians to serve in an overseas war.

◆ Les Patriotes stirred 1837 Lower Canada rebellion

An early 1800s organization of professional and businessmen, including lawyer Louis-Joseph Papineau (1786–1871), Les Patriotes were a radical reform party widely supported by Lower Canada's (largely francophone) farmers, craftsmen, and laborers. Though the Patriotes dominated the Lower House of Assembly, the aristocracy, colonial administration, and merchant bourgeoisie held all the power. When Patriote calls for reform continued to be ignored, their unresolved grievances found an outlet first in violent skirmishes throughout the countryside and eventually, in 1837–38, in armed rebellion. Hundreds died in several bloody battles. After the rebellions were put down, many were executed, and hundreds more were imprisoned and exiled to British penal colonies.

◆ World War I detention camp

Built in 1828–56, the star-shaped masonry fort at Halifax Citadel National Historic Site in Halifax, N.S. (*above*), is one of the best surviving examples of 19th-century fortifications. A key naval installation of the British Empire, the Citadel was used as a detention camp for prisoners during World War I and as a signal post and command center for Halifax's anti-aircraft defenses during World War II. The Citadel is now an army museum.

◆ Nothing else to do? Invade Canada!

Immediately following the Civil War in the United States in 1865, pre-Confederation Canada was anxious about the possibility of annexation by the victorious Northern states. The last thing they expected was to be invaded by Irishmen. The Fenian Brotherhood, an American secret society of more than 150,000 members dedicated to freeing Ireland from English rule, got it in their heads to occupy British North America. "And we'll go and capture Canada, for we've nothing else to do," went the refrain of their marching song. In June of 1866, some 1,000 Fenians crossed the Niagara River and clashed with militiamen in Ridgway, Ont. The Fenians occupied nearby Fort Erie briefly before being repulsed. Following the Fenian attack, the Canadian government launched a massive call for militia. By early summer the troop strength at Fort Wellington in Prescott, Ont., numbered some 1,200 militia and 182 regulars. Four years later, the Fenians failed at two further raids in Quebec. While the bumbling attacks did nothing for the Fenian cause, they did give the struggling Confederation movement a shot in the arm.

◆ Halifax trashed in VE-day riots

During World War II, the resources of Halifax, N.S., were taxed to the limit by the 25,000 service personnel, mostly naval, that were billeted there. Ill will seethed for years between the host Haligonians and service men and women forced to live along-side them. Both groups were exhausted by the constant threat of war, rationing, and overcrowding. The mutual animosity erupted on the night of May 7, 1945, during victory celebrations. Celebrants went on a rampage, and downtown Halifax and Dartmouth were trashed, causing an estimated $5 million in damages. Storefront windows were smashed, streetcars were overturned and set ablaze, and looting took place before rioters were brought under control.

◆ The Diefenbunker

Just west of Ottawa, below a farmer's field on the outskirts of the small Ontario farming community of Carp, Canada's Cold War secret quietly began operation in 1961. The Central Emergency Government for Canada, or the "Diefenbunker," as it was nicknamed, was built to house Canadian government leaders, civil servants, and military personnel (but not their families) in the event of a nuclear attack. An underground four-story concrete structure with a total area of 9,300 square meters, the Diefenbunker cost over $20 million, and was designed to house over 500 people with supplies for 30 days after a nuclear strike. In addition to facilities for the Governor General, the Prime Minister and his cabinet, there was a military federal warning center, a CBC emergency broadcasting studio, hospital, morgue, and a Bank of Canada vault (with separate tunnel access). Thankfully, the Diefenbunker never had to be used. Federal government budget cuts led to its being decommissioned in 1994. Part of the station's original 32 hectares have been converted into a baseball diamond. It is now a national historic site.

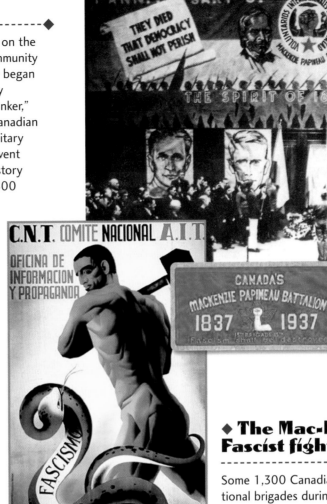

Above: A 1937 rally in Toronto sponsored by the friends of the Mackenzie-Papineau Battalion. Left: An anti-fascist poster from the Spanish Civil War

◆ Canada keeps the peace

In 1956, at the height of the Suez Canal Crisis between Israel and Egypt, a lone voice on the international stage had an idea of how to resolve the bitter conflict. Canada's Secretary of State for External Affairs, Lester B. Pearson (*see page 284*), argued that a force made up of soldiers from non-combatant countries and sponsored by the UN could separate the warring armies and supervise a cease-fire. Everyone agreed, and Canadian General E. M. L. Burns was named commander of a UN force of 6,000 men from 10 countries. Since then Canada has been on the front line of peacekeeping operations around the world. Nearly 125,000 Canadians in their blue berets (*right*) have played roles in the resolution of conflicts including Cypress, the Middle East, Haiti, Bosnia, Somalia, Cambodia, El Salvador and Angola.

◆ The Mac-Paps: Fascist fighters

Some 1,300 Canadian volunteers served in international brigades during the Spanish Civil War (July 1936–March 1939; *left*), fighting on the side of the Communist-backed Republican government against Franco's men. The Mackenzie-Papineau Battalion—named for the leaders of the 1837 Rebellion (*see page 297*) and often referred to as the Mac-Paps—became part of the English-speaking International Brigade formed in Albacete, Spain, on July 1, 1937. Other Canadians joined medical and transportation detachments, the British Battalion, and the Abraham Lincoln Battalion. Dr. Norman Bethune (*page 176*) created and led a blood transfusion service.

The Mac-Paps fought in five major campaigns. They were led by Toronto labor journalist Edward Cecil-Smith and Saul Wellman, a New York union organizer. Only half the volunteers survived. In 1937, Canada passed the Foreign Enlistment Act, outlawing participation by Canadians in foreign wars.

◆ A man called Intrepid ◆

Sir William Stephenson (1896–1989) served as a fighter pilot in World War I in which he shot down 20 enemy aircraft before being taken prisoner. Interested in wireless, the Winnipeg-born inventor developed a means of sending photographs by wireless after the war. The first photo sent officially by this method, a shot of two skiers, was printed in London's *Daily Mail* on Dec. 27, 1922. Back in service during World War II, Stephenson, under the code name "Intrepid," headed England's 1940s intelligence network in the Western Hemisphere. He was knighted in 1945.

◆ The whistle-blower ◆

A cipher clerk in the Soviet Embassy in Ottawa, Igor Gouzenko (1919–82) defected in September 1945, taking with him a mass of documents proving the existence in Canada of several spy rings run by Colonel Nikolai Zabotin, a military attaché at the Soviet Embassy. Other officials in the United States and Britain were also identified as Soviet agents. In the furor that followed (the Canadian government arrested 39 suspects during 1946 in the infamous Cold War spy trials), Gouzenko and his family were given new identities and Gouzenko spent the rest of his life in hiding. In the few times that he appeared in public he wore a hood over his head to hide his identity (*above*).

◆ Parliament's lone Communist MP ◆

In the 1930s, Fred Rose (1907–83) was active in Young Communist League activities in Montreal, where he organized unemployed and unskilled workers into unions. Convicted of sedition in 1931, he was sentenced to a year in jail. In 1943 and again in 1945, he was elected to Parliament, the only MP in Canadian history to win election on a Communist platform. In 1946, Rose, one of the earliest defendants in the Cold War spy trials, was sentenced to six years' imprisonment for communicating official secrets to a foreign power.

◆ What exactly is an "official secret"? ◆

Canada has had "official secrets" legislation of one kind or another since 1890. The Official Secrets Act of 1939 has been described as "an unwieldy statute couched in very broad and ambiguous language." Many considered its major shortcoming to be the fact there is no comprehensive definition of "official secrets." In the wake of the terrorist attacks on New York's World Trade Center in September of 2001, Canada enacted new anti-terrorism legislation which replaced the Official Secrets Act with the considerably more precise Security of Information Act.

◆ Graveyard shift ◆

Recruited by the KGB in 1956, Vancouver, B.C., postal clerk Victor George Spencer allegedly helped provide false identities to Russian operatives in Canada by snapping photos of the tombstones of dead children, clipping their obituary notices from the paper, and forwarding the notices to his superiors. Under suspicion, he was dismissed from his job in 1966, and was placed under RCMP surveillance.

In an ironic twist, Spencer admitted to being a Soviet spy, but was ultimately not charged with any offence, as the RCMP couldn't prove he had sold anything to the Russians but copies of classified ads and obituary notices—not quite the hot stuff spy scandals are made of.

◆ Bull's Babylon gun ◆

Canadian rocket scientist Gerald Bull (*far left*) was first contacted by the Iraqi government in 1981. The Iraqis were shopping for a long-range super gun for their war against Iran. The world-renowned artillery expert, then based in Europe after a falling-out with the Canadian and U.S. governments, designed the Babylon gun—a gun with a one-meter bore, a 156-meter barrel, and a recoil force of 27,000 tonnes, sufficient to knock out satellites. The gun was being built covertly in England when Bull was assassinated by the Mossad (the Israeli secret police) in Brussels in 1990, months before Iraq invaded Kuwait. The Babylon gun was subsequently destroyed by the UN.

cloak and dagger

"
There was a young woman from Munich
Whose bosom distended her tunic.
Her main undertaking
Was cabinet making
In fashions bilingue et unique.
"

◆ The strange case of Gerda Munsinger

England had Philby, Burgess, and McLean selling secrets to the Soviets from the highest echelons of British intelligence. America had Richard Ames betraying the CIA and his country. Canada never had a high-profile spy scandal—until the strange case of Gerda Munsinger.

Lucien Cardin, Justice Minister under Prime Minister Lester B. Pearson, was tired of being buttonholed by Leader of the Opposition John Diefenbaker in the House of Commons on the string of scandals that dogged Pearson throughout his term in office. Fed up with the Spencer affair (*see opposite page*), on March 4, 1966, he exhorted Diefenbaker to "tell the House about his participation in the 'Monseigneur' case when he was Prime Minister of this country." Cardin had an impenetrably thick French accent, and unfortunately mispronounced the name. Journalists scrambled to decipher what he was referring to, and wild rumors circulated—one concerned a Roman Catholic prelate and narcotics—so the Prime Minister's Office released an "oral correction" later that day: Cardin had actually said "Munsinger."

Cardin called a press conference to declare that the Munsinger affair was worse than the Profumo affair (an infamous 1950s British sex scandal), and alluded to the fact that more than one Conservative ex-minister might be involved. He also confirmed the reported fact that "Olga" Munsinger was dead. The press went wild. For the first time in its history, Canada had a bona fide spy scandal with a blonde, buxom (albeit dead) German spy. A resourceful *Toronto Daily Star* reporter, however, tracked down a "Gerda" Munsinger who was very much alive. She was living in Germany and working as a "hostess" in a Munich bar. When the *Star* reporter approached her, her initial response to his inquiry was "I suppose you want to ask me about Sévigny."

Sévigny turned out to be Pierre Sévigny, the Associate Minister of Defence in Diefenbaker's cabinet, and Munsinger was his mistress. But she was also the mistress of a Major in the Soviet Intelligence Service. Moreover, Gerda had admitted to being an espionage agent in Germany prior to coming to Canada and she also had a criminal record with convictions for prostitution, theft, and smuggling. The RCMP reported her to be a security risk in 1961, and she left the country.

Despite a Royal Commission created to inquire into the Munsinger affair, no evidence of any wrongdoing or espionage was ever uncovered. The Munsinger affair was much ado about very little—a foreign girl with a shady past whose affairs with Canadian politicians won her an early place in the pantheon of parliamentary scandal. In 1966, Stephen Ford of Toronto, won a *Maclean's* magazine contest for best Gerda Munsinger limerick, and his winning entry wittily captures her bizarre story (*see upper-left for limerick*).

◆ The feather that was mightier than the pen

On June 22, 1990, Elijah Harper (born 1949) held up an eagle feather in the back row of the Manitoba legislative assembly and said just one word: "No."

The Meech Lake Accord (*see below*), which had been negotiated and passed in secret three years earlier by all 10 provincial premiers—including Robert Bourassa of Quebec—needed the ratification by all provincial legislatures in order to be passed into law. Harper, a member of the Cree First Nation and Manitoba MLA for Rupertsland, had stalled debate on the accord in the Manitoba legislature for the previous two weeks because it failed to recognize the unique status of the Aboriginal peoples of Canada, despite promises from a parliamentary committee and Manitoba political leaders. Newfoundland Premier Clyde Wells also withdrew his support. As the deadline for ratification passed, the feather proved

mightier than the government's pen. Meech Lake was officially dead.

Elijah Harper was born on the northern Manitoba Red Sucker Lake reserve, where he grew up to be Band Chief from 1978 to 1981. The first Treaty Indian to be elected as a provincial politician, Harper served as an MLA in the Manitoba legislature from 1981 to 1992, holding the portfolios for Northern and Native Affairs. In 1993, he was elected as MP for Churchill, Man., to the House of Commons in Ottawa, where he was also a member of the Parliamentary Standing Committee of Aboriginal Affairs.

After Meech Lake, Harper called for a "Sacred Assembly" to promote Aboriginal justice and healing between native and non-native peoples. Held in Hull, Que., in 1995, that gathering was successful in bringing together many people from across Canada, and represented the elders,

women, youth, political and spiritual leaders of all faiths.

Harper received the Stanley Knowles Humanitarian Award in 1991 and a National Aboriginal Achievement Award in 1996. He was appointed Commissioner of the Indian Claims Commission on January 21, 1999. He is currently lobbying for a seat in the Senate.

◆ Chronicle of a country in search of a constitution

◆ 1931: British Parliament passes the Statute of Westminster, finally giving independence to Canada.

◆ 1969: Canada passes the Official Languages Act, making English and French official languages of the country.

◆ 1980: Quebec voters go to the polls in a referendum on sovereignty association, voting overwhelmingly to remain within Canada.

◆ 1982: Canada repatriates the Constitution, giving Canada full jurisdiction over the British North America Act. A Canadian Charter of Rights and Freedoms was also made part of the Constitution Act, which in future could be amended only with the agreement of any seven provinces representing 50 percent of the population. Patriation takes place without Quebec's approval; the resulting resentment and anger fuels the separatists.

◆ 1987: The Meech Lake Accord attempts to right the wrongs of the Constitution Act, recognizing Quebec as a distinct society, giving the province a veto over future constitutional amendments, and input into immigration policies and Supreme Court appointments. The accord needs to be ratified by all provinces by June 1990 to

become law; it dies when Manitoba and Newfoundland fail to give their approval.

◆ 1992: The Charlottetown Accord extends the veto over constitutional amendments to all provinces, offers self-government for Aboriginal Canadians, an elected Senate, and allocates 25 percent of House of Commons seats to Quebecers. The accord is defeated in a national referendum.

◆ 1995: Quebecers head for the polls in record numbers (a 94 percent turnout) for a second referendum on sovereignty. The "No" side wins, but only by 54,288 votes, a margin of 1.2 percent. Accusations of improperly rejected ballots are never investigated.

◆ 1996: The federal government asks the Supreme Court if Quebec has the right under the Constitution to secede unilaterally; if it has the right to do this under international law; and if domestic and international law conflict, which takes precedence. Two years later, the justices rule that Quebec cannot declare independence unilaterally, but can negotiate a split if a "clear majority" of Quebecers vote for secession in a referendum that poses a "clear question."

◆ 2000: The Clarity Act stipulates terms for any secession negotiations. The House of Commons will determine what constitutes a clear question and a clear majority.

◆ How the West was won

Born in Winnipeg in 1987 from a groundswell of discontent with the federal government, the Reform Party of Canada grew from a coalition of interest groups interested in a voice for western concerns at the national level.

Following in the footsteps of his father, former Alberta Social Credit premier E. C. Manning, Reform's leader, Preston Manning (born 1942), promoted fiscal responsibility, provincial equality (with no special status for Quebec) and parliamentary reform (including an elected Senate). In the wake of Meech Lake's failure, Manning channeled western resentment into a stunning upset: Voters gave Reform 52 seats in the House of Commons, ousting the Progressive Conservative Party and electing a majority of Reform candidates in Alberta and British Columbia. Four years later, Reform became the Official Opposition. In 2000, keen to shed their perceived image as an intolerant, right-wing regional party, Reform changed its name to the Canadian Alliance.

Three days before the Oct. 31, 1995, Quebec referendum, tens of thousands of federalist supporters came from across the country and packed Montreal's Place du Canada (left) in a massive "No" rally

◆ The October Crisis

In October of 1970, British Trade Commissioner James Cross and Quebec Minister of Labor and Immigration Pierre Laporte were kidnapped in Montreal, Que., by members of the Front de Libération du Québec (FLQ), whose manifesto called for an independent, socialist Quebec. Laporte was murdered, setting in motion one of the most extraordinary events in Canadian history— the October Crisis. Prime Minister Trudeau proclaimed the War Measures Act on Oct. 16, suspending civil liberties in the province and permitting the arrest and detention of citizens without charge. In early December, the police negotiated for Cross' release in return for safe conduct to Cuba for his captors. All of the kidnappers were eventually tried and convicted.

Breaking up is hard to do

looking ahead

◆ **Western memories** ◆

A monument in Regina, Sask., contains one of Canada's earliest time capsules. Dedicated to the surveyors of Saskatchewan who mapped and explored our great nation, the monument has a cairn containing a time capsule that was sealed in 1967.

The capsule contains government reports, photographs, a 1967 license plate and telephone book, flags of Saskatchewan and Canada, and samples of wheat varieties, minerals, and oil. Newspapers are also enclosed, including one article headlining the Saskatchewan Roughriders' Grey Cup win in 1966. The time capsule will be opened on Canada's 200th anniversary in the year 2067, 100 years after it was sealed.

◆ Do not open until 2020

In 1998, William Belsey, an award-winning teacher living in Rankin Inlet, N.W.T., and the person responsible for connecting much of Canada's North to the Internet under Canada's Community Access Program, was wiring Rankin Inlet's Leo Ussak School online when he had a brainstorm. Thinking of the impending millennium and its attendant celebrations, Belsey imagined a time capsule that would record Canada circa 2000 for posterity. Yet instead of creating a time capsule filled with physical objects, as many other nations and cities were busy doing, Belsey hit upon a novel idea—why not fill one with what Canadians *think* should go in a time capsule?

Time Capsule 2000 was launched with much fanfare in 1999, encouraging Canadians of all ages to record their stories, memories, and souvenirs of their time via the Internet. Electronic versions of stories, photos, and items of special significance—war medals, stock certificates, newspapers—were collected on a Web site, stored digitally, then placed in a time capsule on January 1, 2000, under an *inukshuk* at the National Archives of Canada. An inukshuk, "likeness of a person" in Inuktitut, is a cairn of stones used by the Inuit throughout the Arctic to show directions to travelers, or mark a place of respect.

The time capsule was to have been unearthed and opened by the Prime Minister of the day on July 1, 2020, but sadly the project was never brought to completion. Many municipalities across the country, however, such as Hamilton, Ont., and Dartmouth, N.S., borrowed the idea and buried time capsules of their own to preserve Canada's heritage for future generations.

◆ Time in a bottle

In 1999, the *National Post* asked leading Canadian politicians and officials what they thought should go in a time capsule to be opened in the year 3000. Their answers ranged from the predictable to the truly offbeat:

◆ Prime Minister Jean Chrétien chose a video of the July 1, 1999, reopening of Pier 21 in Halifax, N.S. It was through the gates of Pier 21 between 1928 and 1971 that over one million immigrants from around the world got a first look at their new home.

◆ Governor General Adrienne Clarkson would include a copy of Leonard Cohen's collected poems, calling him "the Bard of the 20th Century."

◆ NDP leader Alexa McDonough opted for a grab bag: a loonie, a flag, a hockey stick, a dream catcher, and a video cassette of *This Hour Has 22 Minutes*.

◆ Major General Lewis MacKenzie (ret.) would include a bayonet and blue beret as a reminder of the sacrifice of all those Canadians who fought in wars.

◆ Then-Reform leader Preston Manning would put in an Edmonton Oilers jersey with the number 99 on it, and a cup of his favorite, Tim Hortons' coffee.

In the future, we must walk in the footsteps of the past

◆ Nunavut premier Paul Okalik would include a pair of kamiks, Inuit sealskin boots, to encourage people of the future to "walk in the footsteps of the past."

historical highlights

◆ **c. 40,000 BC:** Hunter-gatherers cross into what is now Canada via land bridge from Siberia.

◆ **c. 1000:** Vikings establish a settlement in Newfoundland. (*see page 50*)

◆ **1497:** John Cabot makes landfall on the east coast of what is

**1534–41
JACQUES
CARTIER**

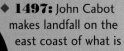

**1560
BASQUE
WHALERS**

now Canada, and claims the land for England. He revisits North America the following year. (*page 50*)

◆ **1534:** Jacques Cartier charts the Gulf of St. Lawrence, puts ashore at Gaspé, Que., and claims the territory for France. The following year, he sails up the St. Lawrence, visiting Indian villages where Quebec and Montreal now stand. (*page 51*)

◆ **1541:** Cartier and Sieur de Roberval found Charlesbourg-Royal, Que., France's first colony in the New World.

◆ **1558:** First settlers arrive at Trinity, Nfld., aboard the brig *Hawke*.

◆ **c. 1560:** Basque whalers set up operations in Newfoundland. (*page 75*)

◆ **1576–78:** Martin Frobisher of England attempts to find the Northwest Passage to the Pacific. (*page 56*)

◆ **1583:** Sir Humphrey Gilbert lays claim to Newfoundland for England. (*page 58*)

◆ **1603–08:** Samuel de Champlain explores the St. Lawrence River, meeting

many native tribes. On July 3, 1608, he founds Quebec City.

◆ **1605:** At Port Royal, N.S., Pierre de Monts founds Canada's first successful colony. (*page 60*)

◆ **1611:** The first Jesuits arrive in New France, at Port Royal in Nova Scotia.

◆ **1625:** Jesuits arrive in Quebec to begin missionary work among the native peoples.

◆ **1639:** The Jesuits found Sainte-Marie among the Hurons near present-day Midland, Ont.

**1603–08
SAMUEL
DE CHAMPLAIN**

◆ **1642:** Ville Marie (Montreal) is founded by Paul de Chomedey, Sieur de Maisonneuve. (*page 53*)

**1668–70
HUDSON'S BAY
COMPANY**

◆ **1649:** The Jesuits abandon Sainte-Marie among the Hurons, burning it to the ground to prevent its falling into Iroquois hands.

◆ **1663:** Quebec becomes a royal province.

◆ **1668–70:** French entrepreneur and fur-traders Médard Chouart des Groseilliers and Pierre-Esprit Radisson explore the Hudson Bay region for London businessmen. In 1670, the businessmen receive a royal charter giving them trading rights "forever" in Rupert's Land, forming the Hudson's Bay Company. (*pages 52, 54*)

◆ **1682:** René-Robert Cavelier de La Salle claims the entire Mississippi Valley, which he names Louisiana, for France.

◆ **1701:** The Iroquois sign the Montreal Peace Treaty, with New France.

◆ **1713:** Under the Treaty of Utrecht, England gets possession of Hudson Bay, Newfoundland, and Acadia, with the exception of Cape Breton. France begins construction of Fortress Louisbourg.

◆ **1749:** Halifax is founded.

◆ **1754:** The French and Indian War begins. It will end in the Treaty of Paris in 1763.

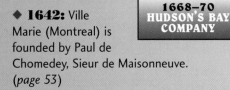

**1682
CAVELIER
DE LA SALLE**

**1759
JAMES
WOLFE**

◆ **1755:** British officials proclaim the expulsion of the Acadians, who are promptly herded onto ships and scattered throughout the British colonies.

◆ **1759:** On Sept. 13, British troops under Gen. James Wolfe defeat the French led by the Marquis de Montcalm in a 12-minute battle on the Plains of Abraham in Quebec City. Wolfe dies in battle; Montcalm, fatally wounded, succumbs the following day.

◆ **1763:** Under terms of the Treaty of Paris, France cedes Louisiana to Spain and its other New World possessions to Britain, sealing the end of New France

◆ **1774:** The Quebec Act goes into effect, setting British criminal law in force, restoring French civil law, and guaranteeing French Canadians linguistic and religious rights.

◆ **1775–76:** American rebels capture Montreal and besiege Quebec for five months. The arrival of a British fleet in early May saves the city from capture.

◆ **1778:** Capt. James Cook anchors at Nootka Sound, Vancouver.

◆ **1779:** The North West Company is born in Montreal when nine rival trading companies temporarily unite to reduce competition among themselves and to better resist advances by the Hudson's Bay Company.

◆ **1783:** The first United Empire Loyalists arrive at Saint John, N.B.

◆ **1784:** The Province of New Brunswick is created. The North West

1759
MARQUIS DE MONTCALM

1816
ROBERT SEMPLE

Company becomes a permanent formal multiple partnership controlled mainly by the Frobisher Brothers and Simon McTavish.

◆ **1791:** The Constitutional Act divides Quebec into Lower Canada (Quebec) and Upper Canada (Ontario).

◆ **1793:** York, present-day Toronto, is founded.

◆ **1794:** Jay's Treaty establishes a system of settling boundary disputes between the United States and the British colonies of Canada, and guarantees Indians free movement across the border.

◆ **1812–14:** A U.S. declaration of war on Britain marks the start of the War of 1812. Americans invade Canada, winning some battles, losing others. Canadian losses include the death of Sir Isaac Brock and the burning of York (Toronto) in 1812 and the death of the great Indian leader Tecumseh in 1813. Captured territory is returned to the Americans by the Treaty of Ghent, which brings an end to hostilities.

◆ **1816:** At the Battle of Seven Oaks in present-day Manitoba, Métis kill Robert Semple, governor of Lord Selkirk's Red River settlement, and 20 settlers. One Métis dies in the battle.

◆ **1818:** The 49th parallel becomes Canada's border from the Lake of the

1812–14
INDIAN LEADER TECUMSEH

1835
WILLIAM LYON MACKENZIE

Woods in Ontario to the Rocky Mountains.

◆ **1821:** The Hudson's Bay Company (HBC) and the North West Company amalgamate under the HBC name.

◆ **1835:** William Lyon Mackenzie becomes Toronto's first mayor.

◆ **1837:** Unsuccessful rebellions are led by William Lyon Mackenzie in Upper

Canada and by Louis-Joseph Papineau in Lower Canada. Some of the participants are executed, others are exiled. (*page 297*)

◆ **1841–44:** The Act of Union unites Upper and Lower Canada. Upper Canada becomes Canada West, Lower Canada becomes Canada East. Kingston becomes the capital, later moved to Montreal in 1844.

◆ **1846:** The Oregon Treaty sets the 49th parallel as the Western Canada-United States boundary. Three years later, the 49th parallel becomes the boundary all the way to the Pacific Ocean.

◆ **1855:** The Militia Act marks the beginnings of today's Canadian Armed Forces.

◆ **1857:** Queen Victoria names Ottawa capital of Canada.

◆ **1864:** The Charlottetown

1837
LOUIS-JOSEPH PAPINEAU

1867
JOHN A. MACDONALD

Conference takes the first steps toward Confederation.

◆ **1867:** Confederation Year. The British Parliament passes the British North America Act, and on July 1, Nova Scotia, New Brunswick, Ontario, and Quebec form the Dominion of Canada. Sir John A. Macdonald is sworn in as Prime Minister.

◆ **1869:** Canada purchases Rupert's Land and the Northwest Territories for $300,000. Métis leader Louis Riel seizes Fort Garry and proclaims a provisional government.

historical highlights

◆ **1870:** After the execution of a prisoner, Ontario Orangeman Thomas Scott, Louis Riel flees to the United States to escape arrest. Rebel demands seem to be met with the Manitoba Act of 1870, which creates the province of Manitoba and guarantees the Métis land (1,400,000 acres in settlement of their "Indian title"), language, and separate school rights.

◆ **1871:** British Columbia joins Confederation.

◆ **1873:** The massacre of Assiniboine Indians by American wolf hunters in Saskatchewan's Cypress Hills leads to the formation of the North West Mounted Police. Prince Edward Island joins Confederation.

◆ **1875:** The Supreme Court of Canada is established.

1876
SITTING
BULL

1876
NORTH WEST
MOUNTED

◆ **1876:** Canada's Indian Act (1876) gives First Nations individuals the right to seek Canadian citizenship by renouncing their Indian rights. Following the Battle of the Little Bighorn in the United States, Chief Sitting Bull and his followers seek refuge in Canada. (*page 72*)

◆ **1878:** Secret balloting is used for the first time ever in a federal general election. The Canada Temperance Act gave local governments the right to prohibit by vote the retail sale of alcohol.

◆ **1880:** Construction begins on the Canadian Pacific Railway (CPR).

◆ **1881:** Sitting Bull and his followers recross the border into the United States.

◆ **1882:** The CPR brings more and more settlers to the West. By 1882, over 60,000 settlers are already making their home on the Prairie. (*pages 78–79*)

◆ **1885:** After the Northwest Rebellion's last and decisive battle at Batoche, Louis Riel is convicted of treason and hanged in

1885
LOUIS
RIEL

Regina. (*page 60*) On Nov. 7, 1885, Donald Smith hammers home the last spike in the transcontinental railway at Craigellachie, B.C. (*page 159*)

◆ **1893:** Hockey's Stanley Cup is awarded for the first time. Winner of the 1892–93 season is the Montreal Amateur Athletic Association. (*page 201*)

◆ **1896:** Motion pictures are shown for the first time in Canada. (*page 252*)

◆ **1897:** Gold is discovered in the Yukon, sparking the Klondike gold rush. (*page 81*)

◆ **1898:** Yukon separates from the Northwest Territories.

◆ **1899:** Dispute arises over the Alaska boundary. Canadian troops are sent overseas for the first time, to the Boer War.

1893
STANLEY
CUP

◆ **1901:** Marconi receives the first transatlantic wireless message at Signal Hill, Newfoundland. Canadians mourn the death of Queen Victoria; May 24 is named Victoria Day in her honor. Fifty-year-old Annie Taylor goes over Niagara Falls in a barrel and survives.

◆ **1904:** Toronto pharmacist John J. McLaughlin creates Canada "Pale Ginger Ale," later renamed Canada Dry Ginger Ale.

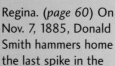

1897
KLONDIKE
GOLD RUSH

1908
LUCY MAUD
MONTGOMERY

◆ **1905:** Alberta and Saskatchewan become provinces.

◆ **1908:** After being rejected by five other publishers, *Anne of Green Gables*, by Lucy Maud Montgomery, is published by L. C. Page Co. of Boston. (*page 234*)

◆ **1909:** The first manned flight in the British Empire takes place in Nova Scotia where J. A. D. McCurdy pilots the Silver Dart. (*page 103*) University of Toronto wins the first Grey Cup, defeating the Toronto Parkdale Canoe Club.

◆ **1912:** A cyclone rips through Regina, killing 28 and leaving 2,500 homeless. (*page 142*) Stephen Leacock publishes *Sunshine Sketches of a Little Town*. (*page 237*)

◆ **1914:** Canada automatically enters World War I when Britain declares war on Germany. Parliament passes the War

Measures Act, allowing suspension of civil rights during emergencies. At least 950 perish at sea as the *Empress of Ireland* goes down in the St. Lawrence River. (*page 145*)

◆ **1915:** The Alberta legislature bows to petitions made by suffragist Nellie McClung and gives women the right to vote in municipal elections. (*page 98*) John McCrae publishes *In Flanders Fields*. (*page 296*)

◆ **1916:** Parliament Buildings are destroyed by fire. Prairie women are the first women in Canada to win the right to vote in provincial elections.

◆ **1917:** Income tax is introduced nationally. Some 2,000 die, 4,000 more are

**1915
NELLIE
McCLUNG**

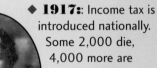

**1915
JOHN
McCRAE**

injured in the Halifax Explosion. Passing of the Military Service Bill leads to a conscription crisis between French and English Canada. The National Hockey league is formed.

◆ **1918:** World War I ends. Women vote for the first time in a federal election.

◆ **1919:** The Winnipeg General Strike paralyzes Manitoba's capital. (*page 166*)

◆ **1920:** First exhibition by the Group of Seven opens at the Art Gallery of Ontario. (*page 214*)

◆ **1922:** Frederick Banting and George Best discover insulin at the University of

Toronto. (*page 177*) Foster Hewitt makes his first hockey broadcast. (*page 197*)

◆ **1927:** Britain's Privy Council awards Labrador to Newfoundland.

◆ **1929:** The Great Depression begins. Montreal and Toronto stock markets suffer the worst crash in history.

◆ **1932:** The Cooperative Commonwealth Federation (CCF) political party is formed in Calgary. (*page 291*)

◆ **1933:** Canadian actress Fay Wray stars in *King Kong*. (*page 248*)

◆ **1934:** Parliament creates the Bank of Canada. Birth of the Dionne Quintuplets. (*page 124*)

◆ **1936:** The Canadian Broadcasting Corporation is formed. King Edward VIII abdicates the throne so that he can marry Wallis Simpson. (*page 111*)

**1922
FREDERICK
BANTING**

◆ **1937:** Trans Canada Airlines (now Air Canada) is formed and begins its first regular flights.

**1933
FAY
WRAY**

◆ **1938:** Drawn by *Toronto Star* artist Joe Shuster, Superman makes his debut in *Action Comics No. 1*. (*page 242*)

◆ **1939:** Canada enters World War II. The National Film Board is established. (*page 254*)

◆ **1941:** Unemployment Insurance is introduced.

◆ **1942:** Hundreds of Canadians are captured or killed in the Dieppe raid. Canadians of Japanese descent are declared "security risks," have their property confiscated, and are interned in remote camps.

◆ **1944:** Canadian troops make the D-Day landing in Europe.

◆ **1945:** World War II comes to an end. Canada helps found the United Nations. Igor Gouzenko defects from the Soviet embassy in Ottawa, revealing an extensive Soviet spy network in Canada. (*page 300*) Family allowances are introduced.

◆ **1947:** The Canadian Citizenship Act is enacted. Oil is discovered at Leduc, Alta.

◆ **1948:** Skater Barbara Ann Scott wins Canada's first Olympic gold medal for figure skating. (*page 210*)

◆ **1949:** Canada joins NATO. Newfoundland joins Confederation.

**1934
DIONNE
QUINTUPLETS**

**1948
BARBARA ANN
SCOTT**

◆ **1950:** The Korean War begins and Canadian troops embark for Korea as part of a United Nations force. The Red River overflows its banks in Winnipeg causing over $100 million in damage. (*page 142*)

historical highlights

◆ **1951:** Parliament introduces Old Age Security.

◆ **1952:** Canadians tune in to the CBC's new national television service. *(page 245)*

◆ **1953:** The Korean War ends. Stratford, Ont., holds its first Shakespearean Festival. The National Library is established in Ottawa.

◆ **1954:** Canada's first subway opens in Toronto. Sixteen-year-old Marilyn Bell from Toronto becomes the first person to swim across Lake Ontario. *(page 208)*

◆ **1957:** The Canada Council is created. At Oslo, Norway, Lester B. Pearson is awarded the Nobel Peace Prize for helping resolve the Suez crisis. *(page 284)*

◆ **1958:** A rock surge in a coal mine at Springhill, N.S., claims 75 lives. Ninety men were rescued. *(page 148)*

◆ **1959:** The St. Lawrence Seaway opens. The Diefenbaker government cancels the Avro Arrow project, at a cost of 14,000 jobs. *(pages 162–63)*

◆ **1960:** Quebec's Quiet Revolution begins. Parliament passes the Canadian Bill of Rights.

**1954
MARILYN
BELL**

**1957
LESTER B.
PEARSON**

◆ **1962:** The Trans-Canada Highway opens. *(page 88)* Two hangings at Toronto's Don Jail are Canada's last executions.

◆ **1964:** Canadians get social insurance numbers. Northern Dancer wins the Kentucky Derby, the first Canadian horse to do so. *(page 206)*

◆ **1965:** Canada adopts a maple leaf flag. *(page 280)* Failure of an Ontario Hydro relay device plunges eastern North America into darkness.

◆ **1966:** Canada introduces medicare and the Canada Pension Plan.

◆ **1967:** Canadians across the country celebrate Centennial Year. René Lévesque founds the Parti Québécois. Montreal hosts the Expo 67 World's Fair. Charles de Gaulle gives his famous "Vive le Québec Libre" speech in Montreal.

◆ **1968:** Canada's army, navy and air force are unified as Canada's Armed Forces. Trudeaumania sweeps the nation. *(page 286)*

◆ **1969:** Parliament passes the Official Languages Act. *(page 302)*

◆ **1970:** The country is gripped by the

**1967
RENÉ
LÉVESQUE**

**1968
PIERRE ELLIOTT
TRUDEAU**

October Crisis. James Cross was abducted by the Liberation cell and Pierre Laporte was kidnapped by the Chenier cell of the FLQ organization; Laporte is killed by his captors. Prime Minister Pierre Trudeau invokes the War Measures Act. *(page 302)* Metrification is introduced.

◆ **1972:** Paul Henderson scores the winning goal in the Team Canada-Soviet hockey series. *(page 200)*

◆ **1974:** Soviet ballet dancer Mikhail Baryshnikov defects from the Soviet troupe in Montreal.

◆ **1975:** The CN Tower, the world's tallest free-standing structure, is completed. *(page 224)*

◆ **1976:** Montreal hosts the XXI Summer Olympics. Canada abolishes capital punishment.

◆ **1977:** Quebec introduces its controversial Bill 101 to protect the French language. *(page 302)* Highway signs across Canada, except in Quebec

**1975
CN
TOWER**

**1970
JAMES
CROSS**

and Nova Scotia, are metricated.

◆ **1980:** Ken Taylor, Canada's ambassador to Iran, arranges the escape of six American embassy staff. Some 15 years later, it will be learned that the rescue was orchestrated by the CIA. Terry Fox is forced to cut short his coast-to-coast Marathon of Hope in Thunder Bay. *(page 94)*

◆ **1981:** The Canadarm waves to earth for the first time from space aboard space shuttle Columbia. *(page 179)*

◆ **1982:** By enacting the Constitution

Act, Canada moves constitutional power from England to Canada, and a Canadian Charter of Rights and Freedoms is entrenched in the new charter. (*page 302*)

◆ **1984:** Pope John Paul VI visits Canada. Marc Garneau becomes

1980 TERRY FOX

1984 MARC GARNEAU

the first Canadian in space. (*page 164*)

◆ **1986:** Vancouver hosts the Expo 86 World's Fair. Canadian John Polanyi shares the Nobel Prize for chemistry. (*page 178*)

◆ **1988:** Canada signs a Free Trade Agreement with the United States. (*page 287*) Calgary hosts the XV Winter Olympics. At the Summer Olympics in Seoul, Canadian sprinter Ben Johnson sets a world record, but loses his gold medal when he tests positive for steroids. (*page 195*) Quebec's French-only sign law is struck down by the Supreme Court, but reinstated by the province using the "notwithstanding" provision of the Charter of Rights and Freedoms. (*page 302*)

◆ **1989:** Fourteen women are killed and 13 wounded when gunman Marc Lépine opens fire on engineering students at the École Polytechnique, Montreal.

◆ **1990:** The Meech Lake Accord dies when both Newfoundland and Manitoba fail to ratify it. (*page 302*) For 78 days, the Oka Crisis transfixes the country. (*page 70*) When Iraq invades Kuwait, Canada sends

warships to support U.N. forces fighting Iraq in the Persian Gulf.

1993 KIM CAMPBELL

1997 BRIAN MULRONEY

◆ **1991:** Canada introduces the Goods and Services Tax (GST).

◆ **1992:** The Charlottetown Accord is rejected. The Toronto Blue Jays defeat the Atlanta Braves, winning the World Series. (*page 194*) In an effort to save the declining fishery, the Atlantic cod fishery is shut down for two years.

◆ **1993:** Kim Campbell becomes Canada's first woman Prime Minister. In the election she calls shortly after taking office, the Liberals win a decisive victory and the once-powerful Progressive Conservatives are reduced to two Commons seats. (*page 287*) The cod moratorium of 1992 is extended and not foreseen to end before the year 2000. Canadian Dr. Michael Smith was named cowinner of the Nobel Prize for chemistry for his pioneering research into genetic codes.

◆ **1995:** A Quebec referendum on separation is defeated by a mere 1.2 percent—49.4 percent of the votes in favor of separation, 50.6 percent against. (*page 302*)

◆ **1996:** Ten people die and several communities are destroyed when flash flooding knocks out dams and reservoirs in the Saguenay district of Quebec. (*page 147*)

◆ **1997:** Confederation Bridge, linking Prince Edward Island to the mainland, opens. (*page 89*) The federal government

2000 NUNAVUT

2002 WAYNE GRETZKY

makes an out-of-court settlement with former Prime Minister Brian Mulroney, who was seeking $50 million damages for libel. (*page 295*)

◆ **1998:** A severe winter ice storm puts much of Quebec in freezing darkness for 13 days. (*page 143*) All 229 passengers and crew die when Swissair Flight 111 plunges into the Atlantic Ocean off Peggy's Cove, N.S. (*page 144*)

◆ **1999:** Canada's third territory, Nunavut, is created. (*page 87*) Wayne Gretzky retires. (*page 199*)

◆ **2000:** The Canadian Alliance is formed out of the ashes of the Reform Party. (*page 303*) Water tainted with *E. coli* bacteria causes 11 deaths in Walkerton, Ont., launching a judicial inquiry. Pierre Trudeau dies. (*page 286*)

◆ **2001:** After terrorists attack the U.S., Canada accepts 224 diverted planes and provides emergency accommodation for more than 33,000 passengers and crew.

◆ **2002:** Canada sends troops to Afghanistan in the U.S.-led war on terrorism. Canadian athletes win two gold medals in men's and women's hockey at the Salt Lake City Winter Olympics with Wayne Gretzky leading the men's team to victory.

Credits are from left to right, top to bottom
Abbreviations used: RD-Reader's Digest Collection; RD GID-Reader's Digest Global Image Database; CP-Canadian Press; l-left; r-right; b-bottom; t-top; c-center

1 CP; **2** New Brunswick Museum; **3** Eric Wynne/CP; Gramophone/871 Musée des ondes Emile Berliner; Museum of Visual Science, University of Waterloo; **5** Terry Elliott/Ivy Images; **6** Gunter Marx; New York Historical Society; R.C.M.P. Archives; courtesy Museum of Games; Travel Manitoba; **7** courtesy Elizabeth Arden; Museum of Anthropology, University of British Columbia; courtesy Hockey Hall of Fame; CP.

I OUR HOME AND NATIVE LAND

10 Allan Harvey; **11** Barrett & MacKay; CP; **12** Barrett & MacKay (inset); PhotoDisc; **13** PhotoDisc; RD; Barrett & MacKay; Anaïs Mallet; **14** Gunter Marx; **15** Winston Fraser; RD (2c); Barrett & MacKay (2b); **16** Winston Fraser; **16–17** Tourism Victoria; **17** RD; Sherman Hines; **18** Gunter Marx (3); **19** Mauritius/Megapress; courtesy Vegreville Chamber of Commerce (2); Jacques Pharand/Megapress (bl); **20** Peterborough Centennial Museum and Archives, Balsillie Collection; Gunter Marx; **21** Winston Fraser; Paul G. Adam/Publiphoto (inset); **22** Jon Turk; Ponopresse (tr); **22–23** Gregory Horne; **23** Gregory Horne; Winston Fraser (r); Mike Beedell; **24** Gerri Mulley; RD (2); **25** courtesy Garden for the Blind; courtesy *Perth Courier*; Gerri Mulley; **26** Gunter Marx; Don Johnston/Ivy Images; **27** courtesy Hydro Quebec (2); Gunter Marx; **28** Gunter Marx; Commonwealth, Maritime Museum of the Atlantic (c); Zoe Lucas; **29** Barrett & MacKay; **30–31** Terry Elliott/Ivy Images; **31** Winston Fraser; **32** John de Visser; **33** PhotoDisc; illustration from *A Field Guide to Insects of America North of Mexico* © 1970 Donald J. Borro & Richard E. White, reprinted by permission Houghton Mifflin Co.; RD GID; National Portrait Gallery, Smithsonian, Art Resource, N.Y.; **34** Jim Tinios; **35** Gunter Marx; Norman Lightfoot/Ivy Images; PhotoDisc; **36** Bill Ivy/Ivy Images (t); Ivy Images; **36–37** Bill Ivy/Ivy Images; **37** RD; Ivy Images (r); Barrett & MacKay; **38** CBC Broadcast Material, Halifax; **39** PhotoDisc; Ivy Images (c); Eric Wynne/CP (b); **40** White River Museum (2); J. Leanne Dumont/*The Advance Gazette*; RD (br); **41** courtesy Charles Vandenouden for Beautiful Joe Heritage Society (3); Olena Kassian; **42** Barrett & MacKay; Glenbow's Cultural History Collection; **42–43** PhotoDisc; **43** Parks Canada; **44** Barrett & MacKay; **44–45** PhotoDisc; **45** Publiphoto; Parks Canada; **46** Seton Museum; **46–47** Y. Derome/Publiphoto; **47** Monik Durivage, Dimension DPR.

II HEWERS OF WOOD, DRAWERS OF WATER

50 Jim Bruce; Barrett & MacKay; **51** British Museum; PhotoDisc; Gunter Marx; RD; **52** Buffalo Bill Historical Center; National Archives C013986; **53** Glenbow Museum; National Archives; **54** John Cadiz; **54–55** from *Wilderness Kingdom* by Nicholas Point; **55** Radio Canada; Barrett & MacKay; **56** Metro Toronto Library Board; National Archives C5912; **56–57** Jon Turk; National Archives C30267 (c); **57** National Archives C6674; National Portrait Gallery, London (2); National Archives C09686; **58** McCord Museum; Hudson's Bay Co. Archives; from Symbols of Canada, Dept. of Canadian Heritage; **59** Brown Collection, Provincial Museum and Archives of Alberta; Glenbow Museum (2); Hudson's Bay Co. Archives (r); **60** Manitoba Archives; Barrett & MacKay; **60–61** National Archives C041455; **61** M. Gagné/Megapress; **62** Musée des arts décoratifs, Paris; Ministère des Affaires Culturelles du Québec; National Archives C1410; **62–63** PhotoDisc; **63** National Portrait Gallery, London; National Maritime Museum; from *Arctic Breakthrough* by Paul Nantor; **64** American Museum of Natural History; Royal Ontario Museum; **64–65** RD; **65** *The Gazette*; **66** Montreal Museum of Fine Arts; **66–67** RD; **67** Brant County Museum; Montreal Museum of Fine Arts; **68** Glenbow Museum; from *America's Fascinating Heritage*; **68–69** RD; **69** Glenbow Museum; Canadian Museum of Civilization; **70** Tom Hanson/CP; **70–71** RD; **71** B.C. Provincial Archives H-03977; **72** Paul von Baich; Buffalo Nation's Luxton Museum; **72–73** RD; **73** © Glenbow, courtesy Buffalo Nation's Luxton Museum; **74** Barrett & MacKay; from *Frank Leslie's Illustrated Newspaper* Sept. 23, 1871, New York Historical Society; R.C.M.P. Archives; **75** Lazare & Parker courtesy NFB; Parks Canada; **76** National Archives NMC40461; **76–77** Kevin Redmond/Parks Canada; **77** B.C. Archives I-51551; **78** Symbols of Canada; Canadian Pacific Archives; **79** Barrett & MacKay (2); **80** National Archives C-81812; Getty HH2375/Magma; B.C. Archives A-00347; **81** NFB, City of Gold 81028; National Archives PA 13444; **82** B.C. Archives G00817; Symbols of Canada, **82–83** Ontario Archives S5639; **83** RD; **84** Symbols of Canada (crests); Parks

Canada; **84–85** Barrett & MacKay; **85** National Postal Archives e000009305; **86** Winston Fraser (t); Science Photo Library/Publiphoto; **87** Sheila Naimon/ Megapress; Eric Hayes; Symbols of Canada; **88–89** Barrett & MacKay; **90** Marie Payette-Hébert (t); Solange Laberge; **90–91** PhotoDisc; **91** RD.

III THE GLOBAL VILLAGE

94 Gail Harvey/Terry Fox Association; National Archives C-85881 (t); courtesy Free the Children; **95** National Postal Archives 1158; PhotoDisc; Maureen & Glen Lee (b); **96** RD; Stockbyte (c); Sun Media Corp.; **97** National Archives C21557; Morgan Creek/Warner Bros./MPTV; Notman Photographic Archives/McCord Museum; **98–99** Symbols of Canada; B.C. Archives 3986; **99** Glenbow NC-6-1746; National Archives PA 30212; **100** National Archives C-22876 (r); Kevin Redmond/Parks Canada (c); Ponopresse (bl); from *Adrift on an Ice-Pan* by Sir Wilfred Grenfell (bc); **101** National Archives C-85284; Doctors Without Borders; University Health Network; **102** Canada Science & Technology Museum; courtesy CBC; **103** Canada Science and Technology Museum; Karsh/Comstock; Sun Media Corp.; **104** Mark Fram/Sharon Temple; National Archives pa203443; **104–105** PhotoDisc; E. Dugas/Ponopresse; **105** Hulton/Getty; **106** Carl Hiebert; **106–107** PhotoDisc; E. Dugas/Ponopresse; **107** Les photographes KEDL; **108** Megapress; Dale Wilson (c); **109** RD; L. A. Romanet Fonds, University of Alberta; Nancy Millar (b); **110** RD; **111** Symbols of Canada; *The Record* (t); David Bebee; Hulton/Getty; **112** courtesy Parkwood Estate; courtesy Casa Loma; **113** Castle Kilbride; Craigdarroch Castle; Barrett & MacKay; **114–115** courtesy Ontario Heritage Foundation/Fulford Place; **116** B.C. Archives C02443 **116–117** B.C. Archives 04699; **117** Canadian Postal Archives 3637; CN Archives; **118** Museum of Visual Science, University of Waterloo; courtesy Bata Museum; **118–119** PhotoDisc; **119** Canadian Children's Museum; courtesy Royal Ontario Museum; **120** courtesy Museum of Games, University of Waterloo; courtesy Canadian Clock Museum, Deep River, Ont.; **120–121** PhotoDisc; **121** Barrett & MacKay; Canadian War Museum; **122** Danny & Judy Boyer; **123** Canadian Museum of Civilization; courtesy CBC; **124** courtesy North Bay Chamber of Commerce (3); Fred Davis/*Toronto Star* (r); **124–125** Ontario Tourism; **125** Toronto Public Library; **126** Charles Humber Collection; Canadian Museum of Civilization; **127** Janus-faced "Solar Grove" © Campbell/Divay 1996, used with permission of University of Manitoba Archives & Special Collections; from *Pirates* by David Mitchell with permission of Thames & Hudson Ltd.; Canadian Currency Museum; Scala, Art Resources; **128** McCord Museum; www.picturehistory.com (cl); Bridgeport Public Library; Musée Pointe à Callière, Montreal; **128–129** Joe Stryk/Richmond Internet Services; **130** Glenbow Museum; Winston Fraser; from *Pirates* by David Mitchell with permission of Thames & Hudson Ltd.; **131** Glenbow NA-1258, NA-1258-119, NA-654-5; **132** from *Tom Thomson* © 1937; Museum of Northern History at the Sir Harry Oaks Chateau; **133** courtesy The Grand Theatre; *London Free Press*; Sullivan Entertainment; **134** Barrett & MacKay; **135** Charles Vinh; **136** Leslie Kahl/Graphistock (b); from *Atlas of the Mysterious in North America* © 1995 Rosemary Ellen Guiley, reprinted by permission of Facts on File; Canadian Postal Archives 1242; **137** Superstock; **138** Corbis/Magma; B.C. Archives; **139** Paulo Pereira; Sun Media Corp.; **140** CP; RD; **141** CP; RCMP Photo; **142** Metro Toronto Reference Library; RD; **143** Sun Media Corp. (2); Martin Chamberland/*La Presse*; **144** Bettmann/Corbis/Magma; CP; **145** Musée de la mer de Pointe au Père; Marc Ellefson; National Archives C53924; **146–147** National Archives PA109498; *The Gazette*; Jeannot Lévesque, *Le quotidien du Saguenay Lac Saint-Jean*, courtesy Emergency Preparedness Canada; Alberta Fire Training School; **148–149** National Archives.

IV MOVERS AND SHAKERS

152 New Brunswick Museum (2); **153** Barrett & MacKay; *The Gazette*; Symbols of Canada; Canadian Postal Archives 0195; **154** Corbis/Magma (2); **155** Barrett & MacKay; National Archives C26668; **156** CN; **157** PhotoDisc; Todd Korol; **158** Provincial Archives of Newfoundland and Labrador; O'Neill/Megapress; CP Archives; **158–159** Gunter Marx; **159** National Library; Dudley Witney; CBC; **160** RD; Western Canada Airways Museum (2); from *Canada's Fighting Airmen* © 1931 by George Drew; **160–161** "Fox in Henhouse" by Rich Thistle; **161** from *Canada's Fighting Airmen* © 1931 by George Drew; Provincial Museum of Alberta, Denny May Collection; **162** National Archives C61731; Avro Alliance; **163** Avroland.ca; **164** Canadian Space Agency; **164–165** PhotoDisc; **165** Canadian

Space Agency; **166** McCord Museum; National Archives PA093846; **167** Canadian Postal Museum (2); PhotoDisc; **168** Phil Hossack/CP; HO/CP; Eaton Archives; Hulton; Pugwash Park Commission Archives; **169** Richard Lautens/CP; Joe Hourigan/CP; **170** courtesy Elizabeth Arden; **170–71** Canadian Currency Museum; **171** RD (t); Vintage Photo & Frame Ltd. (r); Digital Stock; **172** Canadian Currency Museum; Bank of Montreal Archives; **173** courtesy Desjardins; Société historique Alphonse Desjardins; RD; **174** Bridgeport Public Library; RD; Ingersoll Cheese Museum; **175** Travel Manitoba; **176** National Archives PA114788; **176–177** PhotoDisc; **177** University Health Network; National Archives C001350; **178** Osler Archives, McGill; **178–179** PhotoDisc; **179** Canadian Space Agency; PhotoDisc; **180** Notman Archives, McCord Museum; **181** Corbis/Magma; University Health Network; Superstock; **182** *San Francisco Chronicle*; Maurice Green/UW Graphics, University of Waterloo; **182–183** PhotoDisc; **183** Corbis/Magma; **184** courtesy Ganong Bros. Ltd.; courtesy Fuller Brush Co.; George Eastman House; Canada Leg Inc.; New Brunswick Museum; **185** RD; Cadbury Beverages Canada Inc.; Stockbyte; University of Toronto Archives; **186** François Crozat/Kodansha-Europa verlag (t); Getty; University Health Network; **187** Bell Telephone Historical Collection; Collection of Saskatchewan Western Development Museum; **188** courtesy Robertson; University of Toronto Museum of Scientific Instruments; Cape Breton Miners' Museum; **189** courtesy SNO; **190** Marie Payette-Hébert (border); courtesy Hasbro (t); courtesy Kid Games Ltd (2); **191** Marie Payette-Hébert; courtesy Wrebbit Inc. (3); **192** private collection (t); courtesy Bombardier; **192–193** Winston Fraser; **193** E. Clusiau/Publiphoto; Olena Kassian, from *One Special Tree*, © 2000 Les éditions Scholastic; *The Gazette*; **194** RD; courtesy Arctic Winter Games (2); CP; **195** National Archives C-025324; McCord Museum; Hans Deryk/CP; McCord Museum; **196** CP; **196–197** Pierre St Jacques/Imagination; **197** CP (t); CBC (bl); National Archives PA-98735; **198** Pierre-Marc Lajeunesse, courtesy *La Presse*; courtesy Montreal Canadiens; **198–199** courtesy Hockey Hall of Fame; **199** Mike Ridewood/CP; CP; Pierre-Marc Lajeunesse, courtesy *La Presse*; Paul Chiasson/CP; **200** Sun Media Corp.; **201** Hockey Hall of Fame (2); **202** Bettmann/Corbis/Magma; Paul Chiasson/CP; Canadian Baseball Hall of Fame; MLB Photos; **203** Canadian Football Hall of Fame (2); Montreal Alouettes; **204** Jacques Boissinot/CP; Skate Canada Hall of Fame; Toller Cranston Gallery; **205** CP (all); **206** Harness Racing Museum and Hall of Fame, Goshen, N.Y.; Michael Burns Photography; **207** CP (3); courtesy Hydroplane and Raceboat Museum; **208** CP (2); Canada's Sports Hall of Fame (bc); **209** CP; **210** CP (2); M. Ziebert/Method (c); **210–211** PhotoDisc; T. O'Lett/CP; **211** CP; Fred Chartrand/CP; CP.

V *THE MEDIUM IS THE MESSAGE*

214 National Gallery of Canada (2); **215** National Gallery of Canada; Edmonton Art Gallery; **216** National Gallery of Canada (2); Fafard Sculpture Inc.; **217** Mary Pratt; Gallery One, Toronto; National Gallery of Canada; **218** National Gallery of Canada (c); Kinéimage; **219** Museum of Anthropology, University of British Columbia (5); Canadian Postal Museum 1530; **220** Glenbow Archives; RD; Saskatchewan Western Development Museum; **221** Y. Tessier/Publiphoto; Ivy Images; **222** George Zimbel/Publiphoto; *The Gazette*; **223** Pierre St Jacques/Imagination; Arthur Erickson Architectural Corp.; **224** Megapress; Pierre St Jacques/Imagination; P. G. Adam/Publiphoto; **225** Lara Swimmer/Esto; GreatBuildings.com photo © Artifice Images; **226** from *Cartes-de-Visite* by Ellisson & Co. © 1863; Karsh/Comstock; B.C. Archives I-51988; **227** Jonathan Hayward/CP; Roloff Beny Collection, National Archives of Canada, photographer unknown; **228** Freeman Patterson (2); **229** Notman Archives/McCord Museum; **230** Adrian Dennis/CP (bl); Peter Bregg/Macleans/Magma; RD; **231** John Reeves; Phil Bray MPTV (tr); Kevin Frayer/CP; **232** Harper Collins; Sun Media Corp; **233** www.canadianheritage.org; Peter Bregg/CP; Sun Media Corp; **234** Barrett & MacKay; P.E.I. Public Archives; Ryan Remiorz/CP; **235** NFB; RD; Hulton/Getty; Sun Media Corp; **236** Sun Media Corp.; from *Sam Slick*, Thomas Chandler Haliburton; **237** Trent University Archives; *McGill Daily*; **238** Yukon Archives; Marcel Hartmann/Ponopresse; **238–239** RD; **239** Glenbow Archives NA-11-35-2; Frank O'Connor/CP; **240** *Manitoba Free Press*; Glenbow Museum NA-450-1; National Archives 27360; **241** *The Toronto Star*; National Archives C220002; **242** courtesy *Comic Book Confidential*; from *The Newspapering Murrays*; *Vancouver Sun*/CP; **243** Hulton Getty; National Archives PA-164916; Musée de la civilisation C1987-02065-000-000; **244** Adrian Ross-Allard/CP; CBC (2); **244–245** Classic Photographic Image Objects Library; **245** CBC; **246** Pablo Kosmick/CP; CBC; **246–247** CBC; **247** CBC; MPTV;

248 Gamma/Ponopresse; Ponopresse; Shooting Star/Ponopresse; **248–249** Pedro Rodriguez, from *Montreal Movie Palaces*, © Dane Lanken, Penumbra Press; **249** Rex/Ponopresse; Sun Media Corp.; Camerapress/Ponopresse; **250** Retna/Ponopresse; Shooting Star/Ponopresse; Gamma/Ponopresse; **250–251** Pedro Rodriguez from *Montreal Movie Palaces*, © Dane Lanken, Penumbra Press; **251** Liaison/Ponopresse; Kahyi/Ponopresse; Shooting Star/Ponopresse; **252** Corbis/Magma; anonymous, Cinémathèque Québécoise; **253** Hulton/Getty; National Archives, Varick Frisell Collection; MGM; **254** National Archives PA200145; from *My Eskimo Friends*; National Archives PA184071; **255** NFB; National Archives PA169536; **256** NFB; John Lehmann/CP; **256–257** www.comstock.com; **257** Phill Snel/CP; Aaron Harris/CP; **258** NFB; Radio Canada; **259** NFB (3); **260** from *100 Years of Circus Posters*; RD; from "A Stage in Our Past," Toronto Public Library; **261** Sun Media Corp; courtesy Cirque du Soleil; **262** Corbis/Magma; Anthony Crickman/National Ballet of Canada Archives; **263** National Ballet of Canada Archives; David Street; Edouard Lock/La La La Human Steps (r); **264** MPTV; **265** Twillingate Museum; CBC; Visual Science Museum, University of Waterloo; Stage Image; **266** CP; **267** Frédéric Huybregts/Corbis/Magma (c); Gramophone/871 Musée des ondes Emile Berliner; **268** Academy of Motion Pictures; C. Riopel/Megapress Images; Y. Beaulieu/Publiphoto; **269** Sun Media Corp; Phill Snel/CP; **270** Terrasson/Ponopresse; CBC; **271** Globe Photos; CBC; Ponomareff/Ponopresse; **272** Andrew Vaughan/CP; Massey Paul/Spooner/Ponopresse; **272–273** PhotoDisc; **273** Ron Danos/Ponopresse; London Features/Ponopresse; **274** Luc Vidal/Ponopresse; Brian Rasic/Rex/Ponopresse; Tizziana Orzinil, courtesy Liona Boyd; **275** Aaron Chang/Ponopresse; Sébastien Raymond/Ponopresse; **276** © Quinlan Road Ltd./photo Ann Rutting; Kevin Mazur/London Features/Ponopresse; Michael Schreiber/Retna/Ponopresse; **277** Stéphane Richard/Omedias/Ponopresse (r); Mark O'Neill/Sun Media Corp.

VI *BUILDING A NATION*

280 CP; **280–281** Symbols of Canada; **281** National Archives C006792; **282** Will Davies; RD; Glenbow NA 293-2; PA0026308, PA033933, 68645, a027159, a027743, C001971, 028128, 026987, 027645; **283** National Archives C00687, C010461, C006779, PA126393, C046600; Mia & Klaus; Al Gilbert; Karsh/Comstock; Denise Grant; Office of the Prime Minister; National Archives C109764 (t), C2003 (r); **284** PhotoDisc; National Archives C94168; **285** Toronto Public Library; **286** from *Pierre, Jean, René, Claude et les autres* by Berthio © 1980 Libre Expression; Jean Demers/Les Productions La Fête (c); CP; **287** Chuck Stoody/CP; from *Pierre, Jean, René, Claude et les autres* by Berthio © 1980 Libre Expression; Ron Poling/CP; Tom Hanson/CP (br); **288** Pierre St Jacques/Imagination; **289** National Capital Commission (t); Louise Tanguay (r); Pierre St Jacques/Imagination; **290** Rideau Hall; **291** Tom Hanson/CP; Jean François Bérubé (r); National Archives C000567; **292** National Archives C79007; CP; **293** Fred Chartrand/CP; Barry Callaghan; **294** www.comstock.com; CP; RD; **295** RD; Bettmann/Corbis/Magma; CP; **296** Parks Canada (t); National Archives C046284; **297** Ivy Images (b); Parks Canada; **298** *Halifax Herald*; **299** from *The MacKenzie Papineau Battalion*; Mandeville Special Collections Library; www.cam.org; United Nations Photo Library; **300** from *A Man Called Intrepid*; Bettmann/Magma; CP; **301** *The Gazette*; **302** Wayne Glowacki/CP; Ryan Ramiorz/CP; **303** Ryan Ramiorz; CP (2); **304–305** Mike Grandmaison; **306** British Museum; National Archives 6643; National Archives 40461; Hudson's Bay Company Archives; National Archives C008520; National Archives 069926; **307** National Archives C041221; National Archives C000624; Field Museum of Natural History, Chicago; Collection of the Province of Ontario; National Archives C095588; NFB; **308** RCMP Ottawa; Manitoba Archives; St. Boniface Museum; National Archives PA13444; Pierre St Jacques/Imagination; P.E.I. Public Archives; **309** National Archives PA30212; National Archives C046284; National Archives C001350; Gamma/Ponopresse; Fred Davis/*Toronto Star*; CP; **310** Canada Sports Hall of Fame; National Archives C94168; CP (3); Publiphoto; **311** Gail Harvey, Terry Fox Association; Canadian Space Agency; CP; Ron Polling/CP; Symbols of Canada; Paul Chiasson/CP.

Cover: courtesy Ontario Heritage Foundation/Fulford Place; Gunter Marx; CP; London Features/Ponopresse; Gilbert/Ponopresse; National Archives; First Light (2).

Back Cover: Ivy Images; private collection; courtesy Canadian Clock Museum, Deep River, Ont.; Hudson's Bay Co. Archives; courtesy Ganong Bros. Ltd; Ponopresse.